Free-for-All

Free-for-All

THE STRUGGLE FOR DOMINANCE
ON THE DIGITAL FRONTIER

Matthew Fraser

Stoddart

Riverside Community College
Library
4800 Magnolia Avenue
Riverside, CA 92506

...ddart Publishing Co. Limited
...ronto, Canada M3B 2T6
...0 Varick Street, 9th Floor, New York, New York 10014

Distributed in Canada by:
General Distribution Services Ltd.
325 Humber College Boulevard, Toronto, Ontario M9W 7C3
Tel. (416) 213-1919   Fax (416) 213-1917
Email customer.service@ccmailgw.genpub.com

03 02 01 00 99   1 2 3 4 5

Canadian Cataloguing in Publication Data

Fraser, Matthew
Free-for-all : the struggle for dominance on the digital frontier

Includes bibliographical references and index.
ISBN 0-7737-3165-2

1. Artificial satellites in telecommunication.
2. Earth stations (Satellite telecommunication). 3. Digital communications.
4. Telecommunications systems. I. Title.

TK5104.F74 1999   384.5'1   C98-933084-2

Cover Design: Angel Guerra
Text Design and Page Composition: Joseph Gisini/Andrew Smith Graphics Inc.

Printed and bound in Canada

The author and publishers have made every effort to contact and credit the copyright
owners of the photographs reprinted in this book. The publishers would welcome
information regarding any omissions or inaccuracies that may exist.

*We acknowledge for their financial support of our publishing program the Government
of Canada through the Book Publishing Industry Development Program (BPIDP),
the Canada Council, and the Ontario Arts Council.*

Contents

Acknowledgements

I HAVE BEEN RESEARCHING AND WRITING THIS BOOK ON AND OFF FOR THE past fifteen years. I began covering broadcasting issues for the *Globe and Mail* in the early 1980s and, at the end of the decade, joined the Montreal *Gazette* where I wrote a weekly column for five years. In late 1994 Gordon Ritchie invited me to serve as secretary to the federal government's policy review on direct-to-home satellite broadcasting. The government had called upon Ritchie and two other eminent Canadians, Robert Rabinovitch and Roger Tassé, to examine and propose a solution to a highly publicized controversy pitting Canada's broadcasting regulator and some of its powerful industry clients against the American satellite TV service, DirecTV. It was a tremendous honour to work with MM. Ritchie, Rabinovitch, and Tassé — all three former deputy ministers — from whom I learned a great deal about the delicate task of finessing policy solutions to sensitive situations.

When the satellite TV saga wound up in mid-1995, I promised myself that some day I would write a book about satellite television. In the couple of years that followed, a more ambitious project began taking shape: a book not limited to satellite TV, but a broader examination of the Digital Revolution's impact on the media and entertainment industries and on government regulations and policies. I also decided not to restrict my analysis to Canada, but to widen its scope to North America and, where appropriate, to offer some comparative analysis of trends in Europe, whose broadcasting systems I had examined in my doctoral thesis.

My professional situation allowed me to make a number of working trips to several countries during the period when I was reflecting on the salient themes in this book. In 1996 I began working as a special adviser to the Senate of Canada's standing committee on transport and communications, for which I drafted two reports — one on international telecom competitiveness, the other on the multimedia revolution. During the course of my work for the Senate, I made three separate trips on fact-finding missions. In early 1997 I joined senators on a visit to Boston to meet with policy and technology experts at Harvard University and the MIT Media Lab. In early 1998 I travelled on behalf of the Senate to Los Angeles and Silicon Valley to meet with senior executives at the Hollywood studios and high-tech companies such as Intel, Cisco Systems, and Netscape. And in the fall of 1998 I travelled with senators to Brussels and Paris to meet with senior officials at the European Commission, in the French government, and at France's public television network. In another capacity, I made a three-week trip throughout the United States in early 1997 at the invitation of the U.S. government as part of an exchange program whose theme that year was telecommunications. During that trip, I met with senior government and industry leaders in Washington, D.C., New York City, New Orleans, Denver, and Silicon Valley.

I am grateful to the many senators with whom I have had the opportunity to work, particularly the Honourable Lise Bacon, Marie-Paule Poulin, Janis Johnson, Mira Spivak, William Rompkey, and Shirley Maheu. Also, I would like to thank the Senate committee clerks, Michel Patrice and Timothy Ross Wilson, for their support and friendship. Dr. Terry Thomas, an economist in the Library of Parliament, has also been a terrific colleague and friend. I thank also another friend, Ken Katz, a senior counsel with the constitutional and administrative law section at the federal Department of Justice. I called upon Ken's encyclopaedic knowledge of policy and regulatory issues on many occasions — doubtless too often — while writing this book.

As a research professor at Ryerson Polytechnic University's School of Radio and Television Arts, I have been fortunate to find myself in a milieu that affords me the time necessary to research and write books. I am grateful to Ryerson colleagues who have encouraged and supported my research, notably the dean of my faculty, Dr. Ira Levine.

I also owe a debt of gratitude to my publishers at Stoddart. This book was born at a lunch in September 1997, shortly after I published an essay analyzing the "Information Superhighway" in the *Globe and Mail*. A few days later my agent, Bruce Westwood, invited me to meet Jack Stoddart over lunch at Toronto's Il Posto restaurant. Before the lunch was over, we had agreed to proceed with a book. I am grateful to Bruce and Jack for making it so easy. I also would like to thank Don Bastian at Stoddart for his intelligent guidance, and editor David Kilgour for his excellent work on the manuscript.

I have been writing a column on media in the *National Post* since the newspaper was launched in October 1998. I would like to thank Ken Whyte, the *National Post*'s editor-in-chief, and the newspaper's business editor, Terry Corcoran, for offering me the opportunity to formulate my thinking on "Media & Markets" in a regular column. Thanks, too, to graphics editor Jeff Wasserman for generously according me access to the newspaper's photo library.

Above all, I am deeply indebted to Allan Gotlieb for his wise counsel on the book's major themes. I cannot think of anyone more qualified to have provided advice on this book than Allan. He was Canada's first deputy minister of communications from 1968 to 1973, and from 1981 to 1989 he was Canada's ambassador to the United States. Allan was able to offer me advice based on his vast knowledge of technology, business, politics, foreign policy, and cultural issues. If there are any errors of judgement in this book, they can be attributed to my insufficient attentiveness to his counsel.

Finally, I owe everything to Allan and Sondra's beautiful daughter, Rebecca. Her support, patience, and love got me through the isolating task of writing this book over a period of nearly fifteen months.

M. W. F.

Introduction

YOU HAVE HEARD THE MEDIA HYPE ABOUT THE "500-CHANNEL UNIVERSE" — and probably wondered why you are still zapping through only fifty channels. And you have read the techno-hoopla about the "Information Super-highway" — and doubtless wondered why it hasn't been built to your door.

The vaunted Digital Revolution has been championed by battalions of pundits and prophets, most of them well armed with an impressive artillery of buzz-words and catch-phrases. Technological "convergence," which was supposed to merge the television and telephone into a single piece of high-tech consumer equipment, has been heralded for more than a decade now — and indeed was first envisaged as far back as the late 1960s. But if you are like most people, you probably still get your TV service from a local cable company and still pay monthly phone bills to a monopoly telephone giant. "Interactive TV," "video-on-demand," "multimedia" — these and myriad other technological marvels were supposed to consign the couch potato to the status of sociological museum piece. Heavy-handed regulations also seemed doomed to vanish, as states ceded their bureaucratic power to the technology-empowered "new consumer" in the digital universe. And yet governments are still the official guardians of the famed couch potato, who seems unshakeably lodged on his comfy sofa, gazing passively at a limited selection of pre-programmed, state-regulated TV channels.

So what happened? Today, few talk anymore of 500 television channels, except in an unmistakable tone of mocking irony. Many derisively refer to the "Information Super-*hypeway*." Others are asking: convergence, what convergence?

If you have asked these questions, read on. This book offers a critical analysis of the extraordinary climate of techno-optimism engendered by the Digital Revolution, and the complex set of interests and circumstances that conspired against its loudly trumpeted arrival. It is a story of how, in the free-for-all race to cash in on the communications revolution, technological promise and public expectations were frustrated by ambition, greed, paranoia, opportunism, and muddle. In short, human folly.

The lesson of the past decade has been that the Digital Revolution was thwarted — or at least delayed — by the same industry interests who claimed to be its principal advocates. Digital television and high-speed electronic highways were attractive themes for political leaders, for these visions held out the promise of technological innovation, economic growth, and job creation. Not surprisingly, politicians in the United States, Canada, and elsewhere were only too happy to embrace the high-minded discourse exploited to promote these visions. Political leaders failed to realize, however, that their chosen corporate instruments of technological and commercial dynamism — notably the cable and telephone industries — were rigid monopoly structures that were, in fact, profoundly hostile to change. They soon learned, however, that the 500-channel universe and the Information Superhighway were inspired more by marketing fiction than by technological fact.

In the end, as we shall see, it wasn't the cable barons or the telephone monopolies who put in place the digital infrastructure of the Information Age. The electronic highways of the future were being built elsewhere — on the World Wide Web. The explosion of the Web has had a profound impact on the media and entertainment industries — and the old players in the cable, telephone, movie, music, and publishing industries are now frantically racing to catch up.

There are many major themes in the pages that follow — the power of transborder technologies, the effects of commercial globalization, the ambitions of cultural nationalism, and the growing incapacity of states to impose their will in an increasingly borderless world, to name a few. But I would like to underscore at the outset three recurrent themes that can best be expressed as paradoxes. The first is the Confidence-Crisis Paradox; the second the Competition-Consolidation Paradox; and the third the Citizen-Consumer Paradox.

The **Confidence-Crisis Paradox** describes how pervasive uncertainty about the impact of technological "convergence" and commercial "globalization" led to a well-orchestrated paradox based on the illusion of industry confidence and the reality of industry crisis.

Over the past decade, most major players in the global broadcasting, telecom, entertainment, and software industries have eagerly seized on the high symbolism of the Digital Revolution in a desperate attempt to position themselves on the leading edge of the coming paradigm shift — to get "in front of the parade." The 500-channel universe and the Information Super-highway are the heroic technological visions that were fabricated to capture the public imagination — and occupy the political high ground. Yet, as we shall see, many of the mega-mergers and strategic alliances that these surpassing visions triggered have been, paradoxically, symptoms of profound crisis as the media industries face the cruel realities of an uncertain future. The line between confidence and crisis is often imperceptibly thin, further intensifying the pervasive feeling of anxiety about the coming shake-out in the Digital Revolution.

The **Competition-Consolidation Paradox** describes the inherent tension between market forces and corporate concentration — and the media industries offer a particularly graphic illustration of this contradiction.

Only a few years ago, it was commonplace to predict that the Digital Revolution would unleash an explosion of competitive market forces; instead, the media industries have undergone a tremendous consolidation in a rash of large-scale mergers and acquisitions. Giant media companies have benefitted from deregulation, which has increased their market value significantly. But the loudly proclaimed promises of robust competition, consumer choice, service innovation, lower prices, and job creation have proved much more elusive.

The accelerating trend towards industry consolidation signals the emer-gence of a new market paradigm known as "digital capitalism." The dynamic of digital capitalism is radically different from the market forces that shaped the construction of previous communications systems — telephone, motor-ways, cable TV — which were carefully regulated and guided by government objectives. Today, the consolidation of the global media industries has bene-fitted from a largely hands-off approach by governments. The Information Superhighway can thus be more accurately compared to the unregulated chaos of the railway construction in the nineteenth century, when rival "robber barons" fought for market dominance in a brutal Darwinistic struggle. It should not be surprising that software billionaire Bill Gates has been called the John D. Rockefeller of the Information Age.

The **Citizen-Consumer Paradox** describes the growing tension between citizenship loyalties and consumer reflexes, which has become particularly acute in a world where the logic of markets appears to be over-whelming the power of states.

With the emergence of the Web, conflicts between other traditionally incompatible notions can be added: states vs. markets, regulation vs. commerce, legitimacy vs. efficiency, local culture vs. global commerce, national identity vs. supranational spheres, and so on. It has been observed that civilization is returning to a chaotic, fragmented form of social organization like that of the Middle Ages — hence predictions of a "New Feudalism." As this trend accelerates, many foresee the emergence of new identity structures as commerce and culture globalize and the Internet's influence becomes increasingly pervasive as a powerful fabricator of technology-mediated communities. So far, however, there is no definite answer — at least not a reassuring one — to troubling questions such as the nature of individual loyalties, cultural identities, social organization, economic rights, and political authority in the emerging Information Age.

These three paradoxes resonate with particular relevance in a country like Canada, where technology, territory, market power, citizenship loyalties, and regional identities have been veritable obsessions since the country's birth in the nineteenth century. In the past, the Canadian response to many of these issues has been a deeply entrenched tradition of "technological nationalism," which has been elevated to the status of a cherished national mythology. According to this myth, the integrity of Canadian nationhood has been maintained, protected, and reinforced by communications systems — the railway, the telegraph system, broadcasting, and so on. One need only think of the popular image of the railway as Canada's "national dream."

This national mythology, nourished by each successive generation of Canadian artists, intellectuals, politicians, and even profit-seeking businessmen, has succeeded in withstanding a powerful contradiction: Since the birth of Canada as a nation, virtually every new communications system — from the telegraph to cable TV — has facilitated a north-south continental integration with the United States, rather than, as is commonly believed, fabricating and reinforcing an east-west feeling of Canadian national identity.

Today, Canada is a nation that, thanks to the tremendous efficiency of its infrastructure systems, communicates more with the outside world than with itself. Canada, a nation that cannot escape the dictates of geography, has always favoured hardware over software, media over messages, carriage over content. The language of cultural nationalism — notably vis-à-vis the American leviathan — has become a necessary illusion conveniently exploited to legitimize the ambitions of state-protected Canadian business interests that, in fact, are more attached to the rewards of global markets than to the ambitions of so-called Canadian "cultural sovereignty."

This book is divided into two sections. The first section deals chiefly with issues related to *carriage*, or communications infrastructures — such as satellite TV, cable systems, telephone networks, and the Internet — with particular focus on the competitive rivalry among these different distribution systems, and notably their attempts to seize the symbolic high ground by portraying themselves as the main architects of the 500-channel universe and the Information Superhighway.

The second section shifts the focus from infrastructure and distribution systems to *content* — specifically the place of mass-audience broadcasting in a fragmented television landscape, the trend towards "Me TV" niche broadcasting, the threat of American "cultural imperialism" in movies, the growth of Canada's "Hollywood North," and the emergence of the Web in the multimedia revolution.

I focus largely on the interplay — and indeed interdependencies — between corporate strategies and government policies. In the conclusion, I shall engage in some analytical speculation about the impact of the Digital Revolution on states and markets — and the possible consequences for individuals, whether as citizens or as consumers. There can be little doubt that decoding the dynamic between media globalization and international affairs can offer an important key to understanding the march of history in the Information Age.

MATTHEW FRASER
TORONTO, JANUARY 1999

PART I

Carriage

CHAPTER 1

The 500-Channel Universe

THE 500-CHANNEL UNIVERSE WAS UNDOUBTEDLY THE BOLDEST TECHNO-logical vision in the history of television. Like a magnificent fireworks display, its dazzling brilliance lit up the sky and, fleetingly, promised to open up the heavens. We all held our breath — and then nothing happened. In an industry where the line between confidence and crisis has always been strangely indiscernible, the 500-channel universe today ranks among the most spectacular — and embarrassing — technological flame-outs in history.

Darth Vader's Cable Cosa Nostra

There can be no doubt about the paternity of the 500-channel universe. It was the brainchild of John C. Malone, the most powerful player in the American cable industry — indeed, the biggest cable TV baron on the planet. Nor is there any doubt about the place and time Malone chose to announce his revolutionary technological vision. The 500-channel universe was born on December 2, 1992, in Anaheim, California, home of Disneyland, when Malone stepped up to the podium at the Western Cable Show as the industry's de facto leader and spokesman.

Malone was long accustomed to addressing his brethren of North American cable executives. In late 1992, however, his was not an enviable task. Facing a nervous audience assembled at the industry's annual convention, Malone knew the pressure was on — he had to pull off something big. His industry was on the verge of a collective nervous breakdown. After years of riding high — too high, its many critics said — the cable TV industry was in the toilet and its future looked grim.

It had been a bad year for Malone personally, too. A hard-driving, big-talking dealmaker who liked to count dollars in "gazillions," Malone was probably one of the most hated men in America. In the U.S. cable business, which was deeply resented by consumers for its history of ruthless price-gouging, rancour came with the territory. Next to John Malone, Canadian cable tycoon Ted Rogers, hardly the beneficiary of general public affection, looked like Santa Claus. Malone provoked every possible hostile metaphor and epithet in the American public imagination — from the villainous "Darth Vader" to the equally contemptible "ringleader of the Cable Cosa Nostra."

And yet, paradoxically, there was something positively all-American about John Malone. His strong build, six-foot frame, square jaw, and full head of silver hair gave him the impressive physical stature of a former all-star quarterback or Hollywood movie idol. His powerful physique seemed to express his formidable corporate muscle. Indeed, in an industry known for its big egos and rough play, Malone's authority was conferred by the colossal dimensions of his corporate holdings. His Colorado-based Tele-Communications Inc. (TCI) counted some 14 million subscribers in the United States — more than all the TV households in Canada. What's more, most of TCI's subscribers spent a good deal of their time watching channels that Malone controlled — Discovery Channel, Family Channel, Home Shopping Network, Court TV, American Movie Classics, and Black Entertainment Television, to name only a few.

Malone was different from other North American cable tycoons. From its earliest days, the cable TV business has been dominated by entrepreneurial, paternalistic, self-made men who built family businesses into powerful, territorially based, quasi-feudal empires. Not John Malone. He was a scientifically trained rationalist from New England — more a thinker than a doer. And he assiduously separated his family assets from his business fortunes.

Malone, whose mother was a world-class swimmer and whose father was a vice-president at General Electric, grew up comfortably in a large eighteenth-century house in Milford, Connecticut. At Yale, where he studied engineering, Malone was a Phi Beta Kappa man. Married, he got his start in the early 1960s as an engineer at Bell Labs, where he gained attention by writing a 300-page strategy report on how to maximize profits in a regulated company. He subsequently earned a post-graduate degree in industrial management followed by a Ph.D. in organizational theory from Johns Hopkins University. After completing a stint at the McKinsey & Company consulting firm, Malone hung out a shingle for a while at the technology giant, General Instrument. He was appointed first group vice-president and then president of a GI subsidiary called Jerrold, which manufactured cable TV equipment. Shortly afterwards, Malone shifted his career towards cable TV, a business still relatively low on the growth curve in the early 1970s.

In 1973 Malone joined TCI, a small Colorado cable TV company founded in 1956 by a gap-toothed, jug-eared cottonseed salesman and part-time rancher from Texas named Bob Magness. Magness, who had served as a rifleman under General George Patton in the Second World War before returning home and earning a business degree from Southwestern State College, had stumbled into the cable TV business by accident. One day, while buying cottonseed for the Anderson Clayton Corporation in Paducah, Texas, Magness came across some hitchhikers whose truck had broken down. He offered them a lift into town, and along the way the strangers started talking about a new-fangled technology that brought TV signals into homes via wires. Magness was intrigued. Soon after, he sold his cattle to build his first cable TV system in Memphis, Texas. A decade later, after acquiring cable systems in Montana, Nevada, Utah, and Colorado, Magness moved the company to Denver to serve small Rocky Mountain towns where the local topography made it difficult for households to receive off-air signals with conventional TV antennas.[1]

Magness's business strategy was inspired by one basic tenet: "Pay Interest, Not Taxes." In other words, the best way to build a business is to borrow heavily and report low — or no — profits, a strategy that would later be adopted by many other North American cable companies. In 1970 Magness took his company public, but it was soon overextended and on the verge of bankruptcy. So in 1973 Magness hired thirty-two-year-old John Malone to turn around his tottering cable TV company. It was a hiring decision that Magness would never regret: at the end of his life, he would own a stable of 300 Arabian horses and boast a personal fortune estimated at about $1 billion.

Malone, who left his $150,000 salary at Jerrold to earn $60,000 a year working for Magness, was perfect for the job. At a time when the capital-intensive cable industry was starting to take off and consolidate, Malone had a shrewd analytical understanding of both the industry's structure and the dynamics of dealmaking. He quickly began courting junk-bond dealers and persuading Wall Street to focus on cable's robust cash flows and soaring asset value, rather than dwell on heavy debt and slim earnings.

Malone could not neglect, however, the rough-and-tumble character of the high-growth industry onto which he had grafted his considerable ambitions. He knew that his New England roots and East Coast education would not play well in an industry driven by the mythology of rugged individualism. So Malone reinvented himself when he moved to Colorado with his wife Leslie and young children to resurrect the company that Bob Magness had founded. Soon Malone was known as "The Cowboy" — the title of a *New Yorker* magazine profile of him. His blunt, straight-shooting talk helped to reinforce this image, and his openly ultra-conservative values played well in the rough-hewn cable TV industry.

"There is a huge diversity of values in this country — between what people in Manhattan think of the values of our society and what people in Peoria think the values of our society are," said Malone. "Manhattan thinks that single parents are fine. I think it's a much more socialistic world there, where the government does everything for you." [2]

Malone's academic credentials were also deceiving. He understood, to be sure, the technical and organizational side of the cable TV business. But above all he was a canny dealmaker — and he was not afraid to think big. He was, as one observer put it, "more baron than boffin." It wasn't long before Bob Magness faded into the background, hugely rich and devoted to his Arabian horses, and Malone began running the show.

"What I really love is strategy," said Malone. "I like financial strategy, I like technical strategy. I hate running things. I hate getting subpoenas. I hate giving depositions. I hate getting called before a city council. And I hate having 35,000 employees who need to be patted on the back. Just give me a corner somewhere where I can just sit and scheme — come up with creative structural ideas, technical or financial. That's me, that's my personality." [3]

After restructuring TCI's debt, Malone started buying up cable franchises at hefty discounts. He remained unswervingly loyal to Bob Magness's axiom about interest before taxes. Instead of paying taxes on operating income, TCI paid interest costs related to its ambitious acquisitions. Malone's buying binge was an unstoppable juggernaut, starting with small bite-size purchases, then moving to large-scale takeovers of major cable companies such as United Artists Communications. At the same time, Malone was aggressively bullying his way into equity positions in major TV programming interests, which he grouped together under a subsidiary called Liberty Media.

His big break came in 1976, shortly after Time Inc. — publisher of *Time* magazine and owner of cable systems in New York City — launched the Home Box Office pay TV channel. At the time, Malone controlled 666,000 cable homes and was one of the ten largest cable operators in the United States. Time needed Malone's cable systems as an outlet for HBO, so it accorded Malone a multi-million-dollar loan on highly preferential terms to build earth stations that would pull down the HBO signal from satellites. As it turned out, HBO was the main engine driving cable penetration in the United States in the late 1970s. And John Malone had been one of the first beneficiaries, thanks to almost free financing from HBO's owners. Almost immediately, TCI's cash flow grew and Malone was soon negotiating a $70.5-million loan from a consortium of insurance companies and pension funds — the biggest loan ever in the cable industry at the time — to finance his expansion plans.

Though undeniably a shrewd operator, Malone owed much of his success to the deregulatory fervour of the 1980s. The decade began with Ronald Reagan's political victory, which ushered in the "greed is good" era of unfettered capitalism. The Reagan Revolution was a godsend for the expanding U.S. cable industry. In 1984, Congress passed an avowedly pro-cable Communications Act which, among other gifts, removed rate regulation on monthly cable bills. The cable industry showed its gratitude for this bottom-line bonanza by creating C-SPAN, the public affairs cable channel devoted to the policy pronouncements, partisan squabbling, and local tub-thumping of American politicians.

After the Communications Act was passed, cable rates shot up by more than 60 percent over the next five years, or three times the U.S. rate of inflation over the same period. During this period, Malone's TCI aggressively gobbled up more than 150 cable companies. In the fifteen years after Malone arrived at TCI, the company's share value soared 91,000 percent — from $1 to $913. In 1990, TCI was nearly three times bigger than the second-largest U.S. cable company, American Television & Communications (owned today by Time Warner).

By the early 1990s John Malone had emerged from relative obscurity to become one of the most powerful figures in the U.S. entertainment industry. It was Malone, for example, who in 1987 led the $568-million bailout of cash-strapped Ted Turner, and took a 21-percent piece of Turner's global CNN television empire — thus becoming a crucial player when media giant Time Warner made a successful takeover bid for Turner's broadcasting interests. In the early 1990s TCI had annual revenues of roughly $4 billion — more than the total gross revenues for the entire Canadian cable industry — and an annual cash flow in the $1.5-billion range.

In those days Malone was doing deals with just about everybody: a joint cable venture with global media tycoon Rupert Murdoch; a deal with Hollywood studio chief Barry Diller to buy the QVC Network and merge it with rival Home Shopping Network; a $90-million stake in movie producer Carolco, which counted the *Rambo* films among its hits. When Barry Diller needed $500 million to top up his bid against the Viacom conglomerate for Paramount Pictures, he turned to John Malone.

"You may be reading about Barry Diller and Ted Turner," said one Hollywood dealmaker. "But John Malone is the kingmaker, and neither would even be in this game without him."

Malone was admired and feared in equal measure. If he wasn't a self-made entrepreneur in the classic cable TV tradition, Malone nonetheless had a reputation as a tough bargainer who knew how to play rough. According to one legend, in his early days in cable TV Malone once physically fought an equipment supplier and beat the man to a pulp.[4]

"I play hardball," Malone admitted. "But I am very direct. And I win, frequently."

Many of Malone's early battles were waged against municipal bureaucrats, who in the United States share with state and federal authorities the power to regulate the cable TV business. When local officials in Vail, Colorado, threatened to take action against TCI after consumer complaints about poor service and high monthly rates, Malone struck back by cancelling TCI's regular programming and broadcasting non-stop the names and phone numbers of city officials. Calls from consumers frustrated by the cessation of their regular TV programming came flooding in. The city backed down.

Malone also became adept at putting the squeeze on programming interests. In 1985, for example, he encouraged the NBC network's attempt to launch an all-news channel in order to gain bargaining leverage on the rates charged to cable companies by Ted Turner's CNN. The tactic worked: CNN cut its rates. Almost immediately afterwards, Malone backed away from NBC's all-news plans. He even ended up buying a stake in CNN.

A more spectacular illustration of Malone's questionable tactics was his heavy-handed takeover of The Learning Channel. When TLC was put up for sale in 1990, a corporate triumvirate composed of Hearst Corporation, Viacom, and ABC/Capital Cities made a $39-million offer for the channel. The three companies already jointly owned the Lifetime Network, so the proposed addition of TLC was a strategic move. But Malone also had his sights set on TLC. He responded to the Hearst-led bid by threatening to remove The Learning Channel from TCI's cable systems across the United States. Hearst and its Lifetime Network partners were, needless to say, outraged by Malone's muscle-flexing. Still, faced with the prospect of owning a programming asset deprived of distribution by the biggest U.S. cable company, they withdrew their bid. Four months later, Malone moved in and scooped up TLC for the bargain price of $30 million.

To his admirers and detractors alike, Malone's Byzantine business strategy appeared to be based on two main goals: to make TCI so big that he was an unavoidable player in all important deals, and to maintain his market power by owning at least a piece of everybody — even competitors.

Malone had almost single-handedly spearheaded the rapid consolidation of the U.S. cable TV industry, a trend that critics saw as potentially dangerous and contrary to the public interest. In the early days of cable TV, the business had been considered a "natural monopoly" because of the costly capital outlay needed to build infrastructure and wire up millions of homes. For two decades, big cable companies in the United States and Canada enjoyed steady cash flows, high margins, and tremendous expansion, thanks to regulatory indulgence. By the early 1990s the North American cable industry was dominated by a small clutch of major players — the "Big Six" in the United States (Malone's TCI, Time Warner, Comcast, Continental, Cox, and Cablevision), and the "Big Three" in Canada (Rogers, Shaw, and Vidéotron).

This high degree of concentration in a monopoly business soon provoked a groundswell of public antipathy. The widespread hatred of cable companies was largely due to the high-handed manner in which they exploited their monopoly stranglehold on captive consumers, especially through the vexing combination of unreliable service and reliable monthly rate increases. The word "monopoly" was becoming anathema in the minds of consumers. In the United States, the animosity quickly fixed its scorn on the figure of John Malone.

Malone's admirers called him a "one-man military-industrial complex." But others remarked that the cable tycoon suffered from a rare psychological condition called "mega-Malonia." Malone's admission that he identified with Charles Foster Kane, Orson Welles's ruthless media tycoon (based on William Randolph Hearst) in the classic movie *Citizen Kane*, did nothing to improve his public image. The press portrayed Malone as the Jay Gould of his era — a modern-day robber baron conspiring against the public interest. The "Darth Vader" tag came from an ambitious young senator from Tennessee named Albert Gore Jr., who often locked horns with Malone during Senate oversight hearings. The future vice-president denounced Malone as the "ringleader" of the "Cable Cosa Nostra."

As media pundit George Gilder put it: "As Malone consummated his network, he and TCI were still discussed by the press chiefly in the idiom of organized crime. . . . Malone and his colleagues appeared in the pages of the *Wall Street Journal* and the *New York Times* in exposés of corporate chicanery." [5] In early 1992, a front-page *Wall Street Journal* headline read:

"How Giant TCI Uses Self-Dealing, Hardball to Dominate Market."[6] Another measure of the antipathy towards Malone was a joke that briefly circulated in the industry: "You are in a room with Saddam Hussein, Abu Nidal, and John Malone. You have a gun and two bullets. Question: Who do you shoot? Answer: John Malone — twice, to make sure he's dead."

Malone was, to a large extent, the author of his own public relations misfortunes. Over the years, TCI's tactics had provoked the hostility of numerous U.S. municipalities, which grant local cable franchises. Not all local politicians proved as timid as those in Vail, Colorado. In Morganton, North Carolina, when city officials complained to TCI that it charged subscribers too much and offered too few channels, TCI attempted to use its muscle to get the city council voted out of office. In the end, it was the Morganton council that tossed out TCI — literally — by ripping out its cables and installing a city-run cable system.

"People are tired of the way TCI has bullied its way across the country for years," said Morganton's mayor, Mel Cohen, following his victory over Malone.

By 1992 Malone's luck finally seemed to be running out. He was now under attack from all quarters. American legislators, anxious to appease public hostility towards cable monopolies, decided to take action. Congress passed the Cable Television Consumer Protection and Competition Act, which ordered the Federal Communications Commission (FCC) to use its regulatory powers to roll back monthly cable rates by as much as 17 percent. Congress's get-tough-with-cable law was a stern message to the cable industry that its monopoly market power was becoming a menace to the public interest. President George Bush, a longtime friend of the cable industry, attempted to exercise a presidential veto, but without success.

Malone was even linked in the media to the international criminal scandal involving the collapse of the shady Bank of Credit and Commerce International (BCCI), which in the late 1980s was seized by financial regulators and indicted for laundering drug profits, brokering illegal arms sales, and harbouring terrorist funds. Malone's chairman, TCI founder Bob Magness, was an original shareholder in a company called Capcom Financial Services, which was BCCI's investment arm. In 1988 Capcom had been indicted in a $32-million money-laundering and cocaine-trafficking case. In 1992 British and American investigators found that TCI executives had served as "strategic conduits" for BCCI in its attempt to enter the U.S. real estate and communications industries.[7]

The media attacks on Malone soon became personal, and he grew increasingly paranoid about physical threats to himself and his family. His wife, Leslie, was pleading with him to retire. In mid-1992 Malone decided to abandon his corporate headquarters near Denver and go into hiding with his wife and children at their summer home in Maine. He even took the extraordinary step of hiring bodyguards to protect his family.

During that summer away from the hot glare of the media spotlight, Malone came to an epiphany about his troubles. He had two major problems. First, the cable industry had an ugly public-relations black eye that had to be cleaned up. Second, TCI's biggest vulnerability was its catastrophic debt, created mainly through junk-bond financing.

Junk-bonds had indeed created tremendous debt leverage in the North American cable industry. Michael Milken, the infamous Wall Street junk-bond dealer who ended up in prison, had channelled some $10 billion in high-yield securities to several major cable giants — including TCI, Time Warner, Viacom, and Ted Rogers in Canada. Consequently, cable companies had a debt-to-equity ratio more than eight times higher than the telephone industry. But with robust cash flows drawn from cable's monopoly rents, junk-bond financing was always available from Milken's Drexel Burnham Lambert firm.

Still, debt financing through heavy dependence on cash flow was a perilous enterprise. In theory, there was little reason to worry, so long as monthly cable TV rates were deregulated and cable's monopoly franchise was insulated from competitive threats by new market entrants. But that was precisely the problem. Competition was looming on the horizon from high-powered, direct-broadcast satellites. Moreover, the first satellite TV rival that rocketed off the launch pad was a formidable competitor: DirecTV.

On the surface, the North American cable industry had no logical reason to fear satellite TV as a serious threat. Cable television had the incumbency advantages of its massively installed base of subscribers — 65-percent household penetration in the United States, and nearly 80 percent in Canada. Satellite TV, it was true, had taken off in places in the United Kingdom and elsewhere in Europe, but those countries had virtually no cable TV infrastructure at all. In Britain, it was cable TV that had difficulty gaining market entry once satellite TV was established as the dominant market incumbent. The success of satellite TV in Britain was based largely on its differentiation from conventional off-air television, which offered only a handful of channels — BBC 1 and 2, ITV, and Channel 4.

Satellite TV in Europe was not digital, but it didn't have to be. Competing with a handful of channels was easy without digital video compression (DVC), a technology that could squeeze ten or more television channels into the space previously occupied by a single channel. A non-digital channel lineup of only twenty or thirty channels was sufficient to convince bored British or German couch potatoes to toss away their rooftop antennas. In North America, however, cable TV systems were already offering about fifty channels in major cities. So any satellite TV service that hoped to compete with cable TV would have to offer many more channels — and, moreover, at a reasonable price. DirecTV could do that. Thanks to digital technology, DirecTV was offering 150 to 200 channels at competitive rates.

The cable industry could not afford to underestimate the DirecTV threat. Controlled by Hughes Electronics, a wholly owned subsidiary of the giant automaker General Motors, DirecTV had deep pockets and plenty of time to launch an assault on cable's core market. In 1985 GM had paid $2.7 billion for Hughes, a world leader in defence products such as missile and radar systems. The company's profits, however, were declining as the Cold War wound down in the late 1980s. Hughes therefore decided to shift its focus from the waning defence industry to the high-growth consumer electronics business. Its new satellite TV business could be piggybacked on the huge satellite-system costs the company had already sunk into research and development (R&D) and infrastructure.

When Hughes first examined the possibility of entering the satellite TV market in the mid-1980s, it immediately realized that U.S. cable companies would do everything in their power to sandbag any competitive threat from broadcast satellites. For example, when Hughes executives attempted to sign tentative program-supply deals with Turner Broadcasting, ESPN, Home Box Office, Playboy Entertainment, and the Disney Channel, the big cable companies threatened to pull these channels from their lineups. Hughes acquiesced and agreed to soften its satellite TV strategy in order to obtain programming rights. It promised to offer service in *non-cabled* areas only.

Anticipating an inevitable threat from the skies, the major U.S. cable companies decided that the best way to prevent market-share and cash-flow losses was to own and control satellite TV themselves. General Electric, a competitor of Hughes in satellite manufacturing (and also the owner of major broadcasting interests that depended on cable TV), offered U.S. cable companies a GE-made "bird" to launch their own satellite TV service as an alternative to the Hughes project. That offer led to the birth of PrimeStar Partners, a cable-controlled satellite TV service which, a few years later, would be used as a model in Canada by the Canadian Radio-Television and Telecommunications Commission (CRTC) when the regulator decided to impose a similarly cable-friendly regime on the Canadian marketplace.

When PrimeStar began its service in 1990, it was controlled by a cartel-like club of American cable companies: John Malone's TCI, Comcast, Time Warner Cable, Viacom, Continental Cable, Cox Cable, New Vision, and General Electric's satellite subsidiary. The anti-trust implications of this alliance were so flagrant that the federal Justice Department and the New York Attorney General quickly charged PrimeStar Partners with a series of illegal activities. Among the accusations, the Attorney General stated that PrimeStar's cable owners had engaged in a "combination or conspiracy in unreasonable restraint of trade in an effort to suppress and eliminate DBS [direct-broadcast satellite] competition in the delivery of multi-channel subscription television programming to consumers." Specifically, the New York justice officials charged that PrimeStar, through its cable owners, had prevented prospective rival DBS services from obtaining rights to TV channels under their control, such as Home Box Office, Showtime, Cinemax, and MTV. [8]

The U.S. Congress also understood that an anti-competitive conspiracy was afoot. In October 1988 Congress had already passed the Satellite Home Viewer Act, which established a compulsory licensing regime in order to ensure that satellite TV operators gained fair access to TV signals such as "superstations." In 1992 Congress passed yet another law, the Cable Regulation Act, as a direct warning to the cable industry about its skyrocketing monthly rates. In the previous fifteen years — from 1976 to 1991 — cable rates in the United States had increased by more than 2,100 percent. In the decade from 1980 to 1990 alone, the monthly "basic service" cable rate in the United States had increased by 223 percent. Against this backdrop, Congress was determined to ensure that cable giants like TCI could not thwart a competitive threat from satellite TV operators, whose market presence brought the prospect of price competition and greater choice for consumers. Accordingly, the 1992 law prevented cable companies from withholding TV channels under their control from their satellite TV rivals.

Along with support from Congress, DirecTV enjoyed the backing of the U.S. broadcast regulator, which granted Hughes neccesary orbital slots for its high-powered satellites. The FCC's green light was an explicit endorsement of satellite TV as a direct competitor to cable TV. Congress and the FCC had put the cable industry on notice.

These victories in Washington were good news for Hughes, whose satellite TV ambitions would now be less constrained by cable's monopoly tactics. Hughes was now under the leadership of the hard-driving Michael Armstrong, who took over as CEO in 1992. It was Armstrong who began shifting the company's focus away from Pentagon contracts and closer to

Hollywood and the satellite broadcasting business. The year before Armstrong arrived at Hughes, an earlier satellite TV project called SkyCable — a partnership with Rupert Murdoch, NBC, and Cablevision — had fizzled. Now free to abandon its cable-friendly strategy, Hughes invested $1 billion to launch a series of high-powered direct-broadcast satellites and build uplink facilities in Castle Rock, Colorado — right next door to John Malone's TCI headquarters.

By late 1992 Hughes Electronics was actively preparing to launch a major broadcasting assault on U.S. cable markets. In 1992 the cable TV industry still had not deployed DVC technology to increase its channel offering to subscribers. Consequently, most cable subscribers received no more than a few dozen channels. DirecTV, on the other hand, was preparing to launch by Christmas 1993 with at least 150 digital channels, including dozens of movie and sports pay-per-view offerings. Against even the biggest U.S. cable giants like TCI, there was no contest.

In November 1992 the U.S. cable industry got even more bad news. Bill Clinton was elected to the White House. The pro-cable Republicans were out, the anti-cable Democrats were in. Even worse, Clinton's vice-president, Al Gore, was the Tennessee senator who had publicly denounced Malone as "Darth Vader" and compared the cable industry to organized crime.

Only a month after the Clinton-Gore political victory, John Malone found himself at the Western Cable Show in Anaheim, California. As the industry's undisputed leader, Malone's speech at the annual December convention was without question the main event. Every year, Malone stepped up to the podium and, with his powerful presence and personal charisma, galvanized the top brass of an industry known for its stubborn conservatism. This time, however, Malone had the unenviable task of rousing an audience of cable executives whose restlessness had degenerated into despair and paranoia with each new rumour of DirecTV's imminent launch. In late 1992 the North American cable industry looked like an empire on the verge of collapse. All eyes were now on John Malone for a hopeful sign that the empire could strike back.

Malone boldly walked up to the podium, taking inspiration from a tactic that had long served him well: *when in doubt, think big — and talk bigger.* It had worked for Bill Gates when the Microsoft founder said: "A computer on every desk and in every home." Now it was Malone's turn to take the high ground, to evoke a compelling vision, to merge his industry's well-being with a lofty sense of national purpose, to transform crisis into confidence.

How many channels was DirecTV going to offer? More than 150? Well, John Malone could top that.

Malone announced that, within two years, TCI would make the investments necessary to digitize TCI's cable systems and offer not 200, not 300, not 400 — but 500 channels. Malone had found a slogan for his vision. He called it the 500-channel universe.

"We're creating a new platform for the distribution and deployment of new programming and information ideas for the industry," declared Malone. "Our ultimate goal here is to give our customers control of their TV service. That means giving them hundreds and hundreds of options, letting them control what they want to see and what they pay for it."

By early 1994, Malone said, TCI would spend $200 million to bankroll an initial rollout of one million digital boxes that would each "be the most powerful piece of electronics in anyone's home today." The set-top boxes would allow subscribers to receive scores of pay-per-view channels with round-the-clock movies, lots of free channels for interactive and computer services, multiple versions of networks such as MTV and HBO, and an endless selection of niche channels ranging from sports to gardening. There would even be channels devoted exclusively to reruns of popular shows like *60 Minutes*. This cornucopia of TV offerings would be easily accessible to viewers with an interactive program guide that could be effortlessly navigated with a remote control.

"This is just the beginning," declared Malone, adding that the days of one-size-fits-all TV were over. In the future, cable subscribers would have channels customized to their own personal tastes.

"This isn't a TCI decision — this is a North America cable industry decision," said Malone — alluding to Canadian cable barons like Ted Rogers and J. R. Shaw.

Merger Mania: The Empire Strikes Back

Malone's "500-channel universe" outburst in Anaheim provoked an immediate frenzy throughout the U.S. entertainment industry. Most were astounded, few knew what to think — but all agreed that this was big news.

The *Wall Street Journal*, which previously had been highly critical of Malone's hardball tactics, was now seduced by the sheer audacity of the TCI boss's digital dreams. The day after his announcement, the newspaper enthusiastically reported: "The move by the U.S.'s largest cable television operator could lend a major boost to digital compression, long pursued as the Holy Grail by the cable industry because it can effectively yield a ten-fold increase in the number of cable channels that can fit on a local system. The new technology could also open the gates for a vast sea of entertainment and information options for cable subscribers." [9]

During the first half of 1993 some of the biggest players in the global entertainment industry scrambled to catch up to Malone. The result was a flurry of major deals. And Wall Street, equally caught up in the excitement, was eager to finance the corporate frenzy.

The media were quick to pick up on the industry hype. In April 1993, *Time* magazine ran a cover story on the 500-channel universe subtitled: "Coming Soon to Your TV Screen." A few weeks later *Newsweek* joined the hoopla with its own cover story about how the technological revolution sweeping through the gazillion-dollar media industry would change the way we shop, learn, and distract ourselves. In the summer of 1993 the magazine *Business Week* published a cover story charting the mega-merger frenzy under the title "Media Mania." The conversational cliché on the New York–Hollywood–Silicon Valley axis was "Everybody's talking to everybody." The trade newsletter *Digital Media* reported that no fewer than 348 strategic multimedia alliances, big and small, had been struck to prepare for the brave new digital world announced by John Malone.

Even Time Warner, the giant media conglomerate, eagerly jumped on Malone's digital bandwagon. Time Warner boss Gerald Levin, who had been instrumental in the launch of HBO in the mid-1970s, attempted to harness Malone's hyperbole and brand it as a Time Warner vision.

"When I turn on my television, I'll be able to switch to anything, anywhere," said Levin, adding that his company would launch an ambitious interactive cable TV experiment in Orlando, Florida. "It's not just a Time Warner dream. It's a ubiquitous notion."

Some remained skeptical, however. *Business Week*, for example, wondered whether, in the final analysis, Malone's digital vision might turn out to be "just another way to sell more costume jewelry on cable TV." The magazine also posed the more fundamental question about the billion-dollar digital bonanza: "The trouble is, a good chunk of this money has to be spent without knowing whether consumers really want all these services. Or whether they'll be willing to pay for them. . . . Who will supply the thousands of movies and sitcoms to fill the channels? If consumers won't pay full freight, how will the industry finance itself?"

Frank Biondi, the Hollywood studio boss in charge of Paramount Pictures, understood the appeal of Malone's 500-channel vision. But Biondi remained doubtful.

"Any time you go into uncharted waters, there is a desire to latch on to someone to make things more certain," he cautioned.

Still, Malone was unstoppable. And he knew he would now have to live up to his own 500-channel hype. Following the megadeals triggered by his

Anaheim speech, Malone began plotting the biggest deal of them all. During the summer of 1993 he held secret negotiations in New York's Waldorf Astoria Hotel with Ray Smith, the CEO of the giant Bell Atlantic telephone company.

In October Malone announced a $33-billion merger with Bell Atlantic. The deal was immediately hailed as the "perfect information age marriage." Once merged, TCI and Bell Atlantic would shoot up the corporate ranking to become the sixth-largest company in the United States — after General Motors, Exxon Corp., Ford Motor Co., IBM, and General Electric. Together, TCI and Bell Atlantic had wires running into households representing more than 40 percent of the American population.

"This will bring an enormous increase in the efficiency of our society — the way we work and shop and educate," said Malone when announcing the merger. "This represents putting the consumer in total control. You will be able to watch any movie, any video at your convenience. You will be able, with high fidelity, to check in on your grandchildren, or see your children on a screen."

By the end of 1993 Malone appeared to have pulled it off. He had dragged cable TV out of the toilet, wiped off its black eye, and placed the industry front and centre of the incoming Clinton-Gore administration's objective to promote economic growth and create jobs by building the digital communications infrastructure of the twenty-first century. Malone had also saved his debt-ridden cable empire from collapse, thanks to a badly needed cash injection from Bell Atlantic.

With his fortunes now improving, Malone underwent a PR makeover to shed his negative "Darth Vader" image. He was now "Dr. John C. Malone" — his Ph.D. from Johns Hopkins had come in handy for the TCI spin doctors. No more "Cable Cosa Nostra." Even Al Gore, once Malone's tormentor during many Senate oversight hearings, remarked jovially about Malone from his White House office in late 1993: "I find myself engaging in fewer ad hominems as vice-president than I did as chairman of a Senate Subcommittee. I think he's — Luke Skywalker!"[10]

North of the border, Canadian cable tycoons — especially Ted Rogers — were equally inspired by Malone's surpassing visions. In the fallout of Malone's 500-channel speech, the Canadian cable industry came up with its own version: "Cable Vision 2000." The industry promised digital cable TV in Canada by mid-1994, a few months behind Malone's self-imposed deadline. There was bold talk of interactive TV and video-on-demand as the unclaimed territories of the Canadian broadcasting landscape.

Ted Rogers was Canada's answer to John Malone. Rogers — the most powerful cable baron in Canada, controlling shareholder of the Maclean Hunter publishing empire, major force behind the Unitel long-distance and Rogers Cantel wireless phone companies, founding member of the CTV television network, owner of a string of popular radio stations and the Rogers Video chain — was, and remains, a legendary figure in Canadian business. Rogers was also a man who embodied many powerful paradoxes. Like John Malone, Rogers cultivated the image of a self-made man, yet in fact he was a scion of Toronto's WASP Anglican establishment. He was educated at Upper Canada College, the University of Toronto's Trinity College, then Osgoode Law School, before reading law with the prestigious Bay Street firm of Tory Tory DesLauriers & Binnington (John Tory *fils* is a Rogers executive and partner at Tory's). Rogers's wife, Loretta, is the daughter of the Right Honourable Lord and Lady Martonmere of Bermuda and Nassau, and Rogers is a member of Nassau's Lyford Cay club — as well as the Royal Canadian Yacht Club, York Club, Albany Club, Granite Club, the Rideau Club in Ottawa, and other clubs in New York and California.

Phil Lind, who was Rogers's trusted right hand until suffering a stroke in mid-1998, was also an Anglican alumnus of exclusive Ontario boys' schools: Upper Canada College and Ridley College. And, like his boss, Lind was a card-carrying Progressive Conservative with memberships in the ultra-Tory Albany Club as well as the Toronto Club. Very few cable TV entrepreneurs enjoyed backgrounds of such privilege. Indeed, the status of Ted Rogers and Phil Lind as the undisputed leaders of the Canadian cable industry said just as much about Canada's socio-political elites as it did about the cable business.

Rogers nonetheless portrayed himself as a rugged entrepreneur who built his impressive communications empire out of sheer guts and determination. In truth, he owed much of his fortune to the regulated monopoly profits of his broadcasting interests. Also, Rogers was portrayed as a great Canadian patriot who believed that Canada should be protected from the steamroller of American cultural domination, yet he amassed his colossal fortune largely by importing U.S. television channels and videocassettes into Canada.

These paradoxes notwithstanding, Rogers was the first Canadian cable tycoon to emulate John Malone and transform pervasive industry anxiety into bold technological heroism. Rogers and Malone had many things in common: both were undisputed visionaries, both had tremendous egos, and above all both were heavily in debt. But whereas Malone attempted to solve his debt crisis by selling out to a major U.S. phone company, Rogers jumped on the media-merger frenzy by taking on even more debt.

In February 1994 Rogers announced a $3.1-billion hostile takeover bid on the Canadian publishing group Maclean Hunter. Rogers cleverly exploited the prevailing climate of mega-merger excitement, insisting that his own big-is-beautiful deal would provide Rogers with strategic "synergies." Rogers owned cable wires, Maclean Hunter controlled a publishing empire. It was a perfect match of carriage and content. In truth, Rogers was chiefly interested in acquiring Maclean Hunter's cable TV assets in Ontario, thus benefitting from the advantages of "clustering" cable systems in densely populated areas. The unwanted takeover would give Rogers control of 70 percent of cabled households in Canada's richest and most populous province. [11]

Rogers had studied John Malone's anti-satellite TV campaigns south of the border. The 500-channel universe slogan had been a positive, proactive marketing ploy. But the cable industry wasn't above using dirty tricks, too. With DirecTV cast as the new enemy, the Malone-led cable industry looked again to outer space for a hostile metaphor to use in its negative-publicity campaign against satellite TV. Thus, satellite television was labelled "death stars." The cable industry's marketing gurus also exploited the acronym of DirecTV's satellite technology, quickly spreading the word that "DBS" stood for "Don't Be Stupid."

Benefitting from the anti-satellite TV tactics of his American counterparts, Rogers happily exploited the "death stars" threat of DirecTV to scare the CRTC into rubber-stamping regulatory approval for his Maclean Hunter takeover bid. Appearing before a panel of CRTC commissioners in September 1994, Rogers treated the regulatory tribunal and its assembled staff to a bizarre, but brilliant, show-and-tell demonstration of DirecTV's impressive technology.

"This is what we're up against, Mr. Chairman," said the wily Rogers to CRTC chairman Keith Spicer as he walked a panel of commissioners through a guided tour of DirecTV's on-screen navigation system.

Rogers neglected to mention that Canadian television viewers felt less threatened by DirecTV than did the Canadian cable industry, whose non-digital assets would quickly depreciate and whose cash flows would dry up if a fully digital satellite TV service were brought into Canada. Nor did Rogers mention that he and his fellow cable tycoons had failed to deliver on their promise to offer digital cable TV by 1994. The CRTC nonetheless approved Rogers's takeover bid for Maclean Hunter.

Rogers was right about DirecTV's impressive technology platform. DirecTV was an instant commercial success south of the border. Within a year of its launch in June 1994 DirecTV was the most popular new consumer electronics product in history, surpassing first-year sales of video-cassette recorders, CD players, and big-screen TV sets. In its first twelve months, DirecTV counted more than a million U.S. subscribers. Moreover, the prices for the DirecTV dish antenna had plummeted from nearly $1,000 (U.S.) to only $199, making satellite TV an attractive alternative to cable TV.

Throughout 1994 DirecTV's commercial success had a devastating psychological impact on the U.S. cable industry. It could not have come at a worse time. John Malone's megadeal with Bell Atlantic had fallen apart in early 1994. Industry experts said that Malone had duped Ray Smith into paying too much for TCI's network of depreciated cable assets. Others attributed the merger's collapse to the FCC's rate rollback on U.S. cable companies. Whatever the cause, the aborted TCI–Bell Atlantic deal triggered a meltdown of the merger mania that swept the country.

Malone, the jilted party in the courtship with Bell Atlantic, reacted bitterly by hurling insults at the phone company that had almost made him an awesomely rich man. The phone industry, fleetingly his partner, was now his mortal enemy.

"The phone companies are never going to be the winners in this race," warned Malone. "They have too many layers of detritus weighing down their cost structure. You know, whale shit." [12]

Malone's bravado was a bluff, for he knew well that cable companies like TCI were facing another imminent crisis. The only way big cable operators could respond competitively to DirecTV was by spending billions to upgrade and digitize old analogue networks. But satellite TV was stealing market share and reducing cable's cash flow, adversely affecting cable's ability to raise money. Malone and other major cable companies were already heavily in debt. Worst of all, cable stocks had started to plummet. The 500-channel universe had been a mating call to seduce Wall Street, government policy makers, and potential corporate suitors like Bell Atlantic. It had worked its charms briefly, but now the cable industry was back in the doldrums. Worse, cable's crisis coincided precisely with the spectacular market launch of DirecTV.

With its continent-wide satellite "footprint," DirecTV was not limited to American households. Its signal could reach virtually the entire Canadian population. And not surprisingly, DirecTV quickly achieved the same commercial success in Canada as in the United States. Unofficial estimates put the number of DirecTV subscribers in Canada at 200,000 or more.

Ottawa was in a serious quandary. The lauded 500-channel universe was now exposed in the United States as an embarrassingly hollow promise.

But the industry hype had spilled across the border, and a great deal of political momentum had already been invested in this over-hyped vision. It was too late to regroup and learn from the lessons south of the border. To make matters even more complicated, the only market player that actually seemed to be delivering on its digital promises was DirecTV — the one company that, because of CRTC-imposed obstacles, was not operating legally in Canada.

DirecTV's controversial entry into the Canadian broadcasting market would quickly provoke one of the most wrenching policy dilemmas — and bitter lobbying wars — that Ottawa had ever known.

CHAPTER 2

Death Stars
The Satellite TV Saga

W HEN DIRECTV BEGAN SPRAYING ITS HIGH-POWERED SATELLITE SIGNALS over Canada in the summer of 1994, in many respects it was a case of technological déjà vu. Canada, a country long challenged by its vast geography, had been one of the first nations to understand the importance — and potential threat — of satellite communications.

Satellite TV and Technological Nationalism

Arthur C. Clarke, author of *2001: A Space Odyssey*, had envisaged the use of satellites in geo-synchronous orbit in 1945, when he was chairman of the British Interplanetary Society. Seventeen years later, on September 29, 1962, Canada became the third nation in space — after the Soviet Union and the United States — with the launch of the Alouette 1 satellite. The Alouette bird was a strictly scientific satellite whose mission was limited to the study of atmospheric conditions. By the mid-1960s, however, the federal government, realizing the importance of satellites for national prestige and high-technology development, began focusing on the more commercial potential of satellites.

"In those days, there was a feeling that satellites were going to change the world," recalls Allan Gotlieb, the architect of Canada's satellite policy in the late 1960s, and later the country's ambassador to the United States. "Our belief was that if we were on the leading edge with satellites, it would give us some sovereignty protection because we would be out in front." [1]

The arrival of high-powered broadcasting satellites was also troubling Ottawa's power elite for domestic political reasons. In Quebec, the nationalist Union Nationale government had seized on satellite broadcasting as a potential political weapon against Ottawa. The Quebec government had entered into discussions with France to participate in a satellite project called "Symphonie," which was designed as a cultural and technological extension of French grandeur. Ottawa naturally perceived the Symphonie project as a direct threat to its authority and legitimacy. It came, moreover, in the wake of the Québécois nationalist excitement over Charles de Gaulle's famous "Vive le Québec libre!" speech in Montreal in 1967.

Ottawa could not stand back and do nothing. Pierre Trudeau, who became prime minister in 1968, was adamant that Quebec should not be empowered to enter into international agreements such as Symphonie as if it were an autonomous state. Trudeau insisted that Ottawa speak for Canada and that, consequently, the nationalist Quebec government of Daniel Johnson had no right to sign satellite deals with foreign countries. It was against this backdrop that a national satellite project was conceived as a way of asserting Ottawa's authority over communications.

Power Corporation of Canada had already asked Ottawa for a licence to build, launch, and operate a Canadian broadcasting satellite system. Power Corp.'s partner in the project was Niagara Television Ltd., which owned the CHCH television station in Hamilton, Ontario. Their satellite company, to be called "Cansat," promised to deliver programming to a new television network baptized NTV. While a timely proposal, the Power Corp. bid immediately encountered fierce hostility from powerful quarters: Canada's major telephone companies. The phone companies joined with CNCP (later Unitel/AT&T Canada) and lobbied Ottawa to put the kibosh on the Power Corp. project. The big phone companies regarded satellites as potential "telephone poles in the sky," and consequently felt threatened by the prospect of a competing national communications infrastructure that was not under their control. The phone companies argued, predictably, that Canada already had an adequate land-based communications infrastructure — the telephone system — that could meet all present and future needs.

In 1967 the federal "Chapman Report" disagreed with the telephone consortium. Expressing concern that control over satellite space segment "might not reside in Canada," the report, named after senior Ottawa mandarin John Chapman, who headed the Defence Research and Telecommunications Establishment, called for fast action to build and launch a national satellite system. The same year, another report submitted to the government by Hughes Aircraft — a satellite-system manufacturer whose self-interest should have been obvious — likewise argued that a Canadian satellite system could be financially viable. The new Science Council of Canada also released a report, in July 1967, calling for the creation of a central space agency that would be a Crown corporation subject to a "buy Canadian" mandate. Faced with this gaining momentum in favour of a national satellite system, the phone companies decided to flip-flop on the issue and get in front of the parade. They now volunteered to build and operate the national satellite system themselves. [2]

The main issue for Ottawa was control. A national satellite infrastructure was needed, but it couldn't be left entirely to the vagaries of the marketplace. Thus, the federal government opted for the same approach it had taken with the creation of the CBC: direct government intervention.

Ottawa took two steps to ensure state control of a Canadian satellite system. First, in 1968, the government created a new ministry, the Department of Communications, as the institutional expression of Ottawa's new technological ambitions. Allan Gotlieb headed the new department as deputy minister, and Eric Kierans was its first minister. The CRTC, created in the same year, was to regulate content on radio and television, or cultural policy, while the Department of Communications was charged with high-tech and hardware policy. Second, in 1969, Ottawa created a public corporation, Telesat Canada, as the chosen instrument of Canada's technological nationalism in outer space. The government sponsored a nationwide competition to name Canada's new satellites, and a jury that included Marshall McLuhan and Leonard Cohen was given the task of selecting a name from among the thousands of proposals. The jury chose "Anik," an Inuit word for "little brother."

The creation of Telesat constituted a formal rejection of Power Corp.'s Cansat project — though, as we shall see, this would not be Power Corp.'s last foray into the satellite business. Besides Power Corp., the other loser in the federal satellite initiative was Quebec. Ottawa had decided that Telesat Canada would be a national project controlled by the federal government. At first, Ottawa had considered modelling the ownership structure of Telesat after the U.S. Comsat satellites, which were owned by the public through the sale of shares. Ottawa's original plan was to control one third of Telesat's shares, offer another third to Canadian phone companies, and sell the final third to Canadians. But in the end the government decided to keep 51-percent control and offer the minority stake to the telephone monopolies.

The historic importance of satellites for Canadian nation-building did not escape Prime Minister Trudeau, who declared: "In our second century, satellites may well prove as essential to the unity of our country as our transportation systems have been since Confederation." It was a noble vision, inspired by high purpose, patriotism, and a strong commitment to national unity. It was also a classic example of Canada's time-honoured reflex of technological nationalism. The railway had been constructed hastily in the late nineteenth century as a counterforce to American expansion. Now a national satellite system was needed to strengthen Canada's territorial integrity.

Yet Canada's technological nationalism in the skies quickly encountered less lofty realities. Telesat, while a public corporation, soon fell under the control of Bell Canada and the country's other major phone companies, which owned nearly half of Telesat's stock. Reduced to the status of a "carrier's carrier," Telesat was prevented contractually from doing anything that would bring competition to its telephone masters. All of Telesat's transponders were owned by the phone giants, though some excess capacity went to the state-owned broadcaster, the CBC. Another brief exception was made for the U.S.-based company, RCA Corp. — a sign that, even in its earliest days, Telesat acknowledged the cross-border nature of satellite communications.

Emasculated by Canada's telephone companies, Telesat languished, under-utilized, for more than a decade. In the mid-1970s, after the CRTC was given regulatory authority over telecommunications, it attempted to loosen the telephone consortium's stranglehold on Telesat by making its spectrum available to competitors. But the federal government reliably supported the interests of the country's powerful telephone cartel. Canada's technological nationalism thus was synonymous with suffocating monopoly power.

By the early 1980s the Canadian broadcasting landscape had changed considerably, and a new role for satellites was now becoming apparent. Cable TV had become the preferred means of television reception in Canada, reaching nearly 60 percent of Canadian households. Still, almost half of Canadians, many living in rural regions, had no access to cable TV and received only a few off-air channels. The CRTC, flexing its regulatory muscles, decided to remedy this technological inequality by creating a Canadian supplier of domestic television signals, via Telesat's satellites, to "under-served" regions — those without cable TV.

Following a competitive licensing process, the CRTC chose a consortium of private Canadian broadcasters, led by Philippe de Gaspé Beaubien's Télémédia, whose own TV signals naturally made up the satellite-delivered channel offering. The new company, called Cancom, had two sources of revenues: sending Canadian signals via Telesat's birds to newly created cable systems in remote areas, and selling "direct-to-home" channels to individual households beyond the reach of cable TV.

Cancom undeniably helped achieve the objectives of a legitimate public policy goal — the universality of broadcasting service. Some complained, though, that the CRTC had awarded the licence to a consortium of private broadcasters instead of a public-service enterprise. Also, local broadcasters felt threatened by the imminent invasion of distant Canadian signals via Cancom's satellite-to-cable systems. More fundamentally, the CRTC's creation of Cancom established a pro–cable TV regulatory paradigm. Cancom's chief mission was based on an "extension-of-service" objective: its signals were to be made available only to small cable companies and directly to homes *not served* by cable TV. The CRTC's message was thus unambiguous: broadcast satellites would not compete with cable television. In effect, Cancom was created as the corporate handmaiden of the cable industry.

Cancom's early days were hardly glorious. The CRTC-mandated company immediately began losing money, partly because it was offering Canadian signals only — three English channels and one French station, plus eight radio stations. The crisis was so serious that, in 1982, Cancom's founding management team was cleared out. André Bureau, a business executive from Télémédia, took charge of the struggling company.

Bureau quickly learned that many Canadians were not particularly receptive to the imposition by government fiat of satellite-to-cable systems in their regions. In remote places in western Canada, local residents accustomed to receiving U.S. television signals with big backyard dishes noisily opposed the arrival of Cancom and its technological nationalism. In Flin Flon, Manitoba, a hostile group of residents actually rolled a Cancom truck into a ditch. Hockey stars like Wayne Gretzky were brought into small towns to help market the regulatory imposition of Cancom's Canadian-only brand of cable TV.

"At first, they didn't want us because they thought we were coming from Toronto with the Canadian flag," recalls Bureau. "But that changed." [3]

In March 1983 the CRTC's cable-friendly approach was formalized by the Liberal government. Francis Fox, the communications minister, announced a new policy that officially designated cable TV as the gatekeeper of the Canadian broadcasting system. Fox also awarded a cellular telephone licence to Cantel, a consortium including cable TV tycoon Ted Rogers and Philippe de Gaspé Beaubien. Francis Fox would later become a Rogers executive and a member of the Cantel board of directors. He would also join the board of Astral Communications, whose president today is André Bureau. In late 1983 Bureau was asked to leave the struggling Cancom to become chairman of the CRTC. The man who appointed him as head of the regulator was Francis Fox.

As CRTC chairman, Bureau aggressively championed Fox's pro-cable broadcasting policy. He didn't need much encouragement, in fact, for as president of Cancom he had been running a CRTC-created company whose business was entirely dependent on the build-out of small cable systems across Canada. Bureau would prove to be a highly effective leader who was determined to shake up the lethargic regulator and galvanize it with a new sense of purpose.

A diminutive, impeccably dressed lawyer from Trois-Rivières with a vaguely Napoleonic appearance, Bureau was a man of considerable charm and undoubted intellectual powers. When he arrived at the CRTC, he immediately imposed order and discipline on a regulatory body that had been floundering rudderless under weak leadership since the mid-1970s, following the departure of Pierre Juneau. Under Juneau, the CRTC had played a central, proactive role in cultural policy by imposing Canadian-content quotas on radio and television stations. By the late 1970s the regulator was sliding into a subtle complicity with the major industry interests it regulated, notably the cable industry. In the period from 1975 to 1983, three chairmen had come and left — first, broadcaster Harry Boyle, then private television lobbyist Pierre Camu, followed by academic John Meisel. All three men were talented and well-intentioned, but none left durable fingerprints on the regulator.

André Bureau was different. Forceful and charismatic, he was a refreshing change after the dilettantish image of his immediate predecessor, John Meisel, a rumpled professor from Queen's University. Bureau quickly reasserted the centralized-management style the CRTC had known under Pierre Juneau. He also brought qualities to the job that were theretofore unknown at the regulator. Unlike his predecessors, Bureau was not a product of public service, politics, or academia. He was a businessman, and as such he was not particularly preoccupied with cultural issues.

Most telling of all, Bureau came straight from a company, Cancom, created by the CRTC to extend the reach and commercial power of the cable industry. Yet this fact seemed to trouble no one. As Hershel Hardin put it: "When Pierre Camu, the president of the Canadian Association of Broadcasters, was appointed CRTC chairman in 1978, there were denunciations approaching furore about putting the fox in charge of the chicken coop. Now, nobody bothered." [4]

The CRTC had been succumbing gradually to regulatory "capture" by the cable industry throughout the 1970s. But Bureau's leadership at the CRTC marked a decided shift towards an "industry approach."

"After I arrived there, the CRTC's decisions moved from the arts pages to the business pages of the newspapers," says Bureau candidly. "People at the CRTC saw me as the industry's guy, and there was some hostility. The belief was that there should be no contact with the industry. They were like monks. My first reaction was that they were pretty far from the real world and from what was happening in the market. I was frankly shocked by the degree to which, under the guise of independence, the people at the Commission were disconnected."

Soon after Bureau's arrival, the CRTC's extension-of-service policy favouring cable TV quickly ran into trouble. First, there weren't enough small cable systems established in remote regions to provide Cancom with a profitable market for its satellite TV signals. Consequently, the CRTC found itself hastily handing out cable licences to just about anybody, often highly dubious characters with few motives beyond getting rich quick. Second, many Canadians were shunning Cancom and subscribing to unauthorized U.S. satellite TV services that delivered American signals to large "C-band" backyard dishes. Soon roughly 500,000 Canadians had bought backyard dishes to watch banned channels like Home Box Office, Disney Channel, Showtime, Cinemax, Satellite Sports Net, Playboy Channel, and Exxxtasy. Cancom, which found it difficult to compete with the U.S. packages of sports, movies, and porn channels, counted only 30,000 subscribers for its own package of CRTC-approved channels. Its market performance was, on that front, an embarrassing public-policy failure.

Bureau, having been Cancom's president, knew that the national satellite service was a flop because its offering was limited to Canadian signals. Putting pragmatism before patriotism, Bureau reversed official CRTC policy and authorized inclusion of the "3 + 1" American signals — ABC, CBS, NBC, and PBS — as part of Cancom's satellite feed. This decision, however understandable from a strictly business point of view, made a mockery of the technological nationalism that had inspired Cancom's creation in the first place. Under Bureau's leadership, the CRTC now acknowledged that Canadians — or at least the cable companies that distributed TV signals to them — were more interested in receiving American television signals than in watching Canadian channels. The CRTC's flip-flop moreover demonstrated how technological nationalism inevitably backfires. New delivery systems — especially satellites — invariably prove to be remarkably efficient importers of foreign cultural signals.

While Cancom floundered, Telesat Canada was doing no better. In the mid-1980s Telesat had spare capacity on its Anik C satellite and was desperately seeking demand for its transponder space. Finally, Telesat fixed on the idea of creating a market for its transponders by getting into the direct-to-home — or "DTH" — broadcasting business. It seemed like a brilliant idea, though some bureaucratic obstacles would have to be overcome. For example, Telesat was obliged to obtain official government approval for the plan in the form of an Order-in-Council. After this was done, Telesat set up a satellite TV subsidiary called "Anikasting."

Telesat's DTH ambitions faced one serious opponent, however: Cancom. The CRTC's cable-friendly offspring naturally felt threatened by the prospect of competition from Telesat, particularly since Telesat's birds were the "common carrier" transmitting Cancom's own signals. If Telesat became a DTH broadcaster, Cancom argued, it would be dependent on its chief competitor for satellite transponders. There was no denying that Cancom had a point.

The matter was settled in 1987 by André Bureau, whose loyalty to Cancom and the cable industry was never in doubt. Bureau issued a CRTC notice announcing that any party seeking to enter the DTH business in Canada would first have to obtain regulatory approval in the form of a licence. There was no mistaking the CRTC's message to Telesat: don't call us, we'll call you – and if you call us, don't expect to get a licence.

The CRTC's institutionalized complicity with the cable industry was a mutually reinforcing symbiosis. Wires fixed firmly in Canadian soil are easy to regulate and control because they are, in the last resort, seizable assets. Satellites in orbit, on the other hand, are beyond the power of any national regulatory body — unless governments are prepared to blast them out of the sky. Given these basic material facts, cable's privilege as Canada's broadcasting "gatekeeper" was wholly understandable, if somewhat frustrating for potential competitors and vexing for Canadians seeking an alternative to the cable TV monopoly. For the CRTC and the cable industry, it was a tidy little arrangement. The industry needed the CRTC's regulatory protection from competitive threats, and the dominance of the regulated cable industry affirmed the CRTC's institutional legitimacy.

But this tacit pact would soon encounter a powerful threat from outer space. In the early 1990s direct-broadcast satellites promised to beam hundreds of TV signals over the entire North American continent. This time the threat was coming from U.S. satellites over which the CRTC had no control.

Regulatory Resistance to DBS: No War on Cable!

Though portrayed as an ominous new technology, DBS satellites actually brought back a familiar experience to the Canadian broadcasting industry. Satellite television reproduced the early pre-cable days of television in the 1950s. When CBC Television was created in 1952, many Canadians were already watching cross-border American channels received with bunny-ears and roof-top antennas. Forty years later, the arrival of satellite broadcasting was no different: satellite TV signals, like off-air Hertzian signals, crossed the border via the airwaves.

There was one important difference, however. In the 1940s television was an entirely new medium and TV sets were a new household consumer product. Consequently, television did not threaten existing companies in the same business — except radio stations and movie theatres, which were forced to adapt to television's powerful presence. In the 1990s the advent of satellite TV represented a powerful threat to the cable industry, which had established itself as the broadcasting industry's monopoly gatekeeper. The potential popularity of digital satellite TV threatened to attack debt-heavy cable TV's robust cash flows and, worse, provoke the rapid depreciation of cable's analogue plant of coaxial wires.

When DBS satellites first loomed on the horizon in the early 1990s, the CRTC saw the new technology as a threat not only to the commercial interests of its most powerful client — the cable industry — but also to its own institutional legitimacy. In 1991 a new Broadcasting Act had been passed, followed in 1993 by its sister statute, the Telecommunications Act. Both laws recognized the emergence of new technologies such as satellite TV and called for a "technology neutral" approach — neither policy nor regulation should favour any particular distribution system. The CRTC, however, was stuck in the old-think, pro-cable regulatory paradigm and was thus openly hostile to satellite TV.

The first satellite TV threat came from Skypix, a Seattle-based company started in 1988 by two brothers, Fred and Richard Greenberg. On the surface, Skypix looked like a potentially powerful force in broadcasting, if only because it was financially backed by Paul Allen, the software billionaire who in 1975 had founded Microsoft with Bill Gates. Also, Japanese consumer electronics giant Mitsubishi had agreed to manufacture Skypix's home receiver units, and Hollywood studios like Warner Bros. had signed on as content providers.

The CRTC regarded Skypix as a foreign intruder that could potentially destabilize Canada's broadcasting system. A flurry of studies, reports, and intelligence gathering on Skypix offered proof that the CRTC was taking the threat seriously. The regulator was enthusiastically supported in these efforts by the major Canadian industry players, who also felt threatened by Skypix.

Peter Grant, a well-connected Toronto communications lawyer, wrote an opinion for Telesat Canada claiming that the regulator could assert its jurisdiction over Skypix as soon as it began transmitting its signals for reception by Canadians. Grant recommended that the CRTC assert its authority over Skypix by taking action against its agent in Canada, Aladdin. Grant essentially called for a classic old-paradigm reflex based on territorial logic and motivated by a combination of cultural policy concerns and, less explicitly stated, a desire to protect the financial interests of certain established Canadian industry players.

Grant was saying precisely what the CRTC wanted to hear. But there were those who disagreed. Andrew Roman, a lawyer with Miller Thomson in Toronto, argued that regulators were powerless in the face of transnational satellite signals. Attempting to take action against Skypix, he said, was like building a "CRTC-constructed Berlin wall around Canada." [5]

Roman could have dismissed Grant's argument with a less imaginative effort merely by pointing out that television broadcasting in Canada started off, in the late 1940s, as cross-border off-signals just like satellite TV. At that time, the Canadian government did not issue mandatory orders, prosecute, or assert its jurisdiction over the border affiliates of NBC, CBS, and ABC. On the contrary, the U.S. network signals were not only popular with Canadians, but soon became entrenched in the notion of "basic" cable TV service in Canada. Moreover, the Canadian cable industry got rich by helping themselves to these U.S. signals and retransmitting them to their subscribers without compensating the U.S. cable companies. It was hypocritical, to say the least, for the same Canadian cable barons to ask the CRTC to protect their cash flows from U.S. signals coming into the country via satellite.

Some players in the Canadian broadcasting system were less paranoid about U.S.-based satellite services, doubtless because they had less to lose. Michael McCabe, the head of the private broadcasters' lobby, called for a "more reasoned assessment" of the negative impact of U.S. satellite TV systems. David Ellis, a broadcasting consultant, put it more bluntly:

> The issue at hand is not how many Canadian cable subscribers will actually defect or what damage Death Stars may bring about in our culture — if any. The issue is how vested interests are using this and other new technologies as weapons in their defence of the market power that has gone hand-in-hand with protectionism, quotas, subsidies, and monopolistic control of distribution. Let's stop demonizing foreign market power long enough to take stock of what's happening to market power in our own back yard.

In the end, the Skypix threat was short-lived. In April 1992 Skypix missed its launch deadline, and soon the financially troubled company collapsed and went into bankruptcy. Even before Skypix flamed out, the U.S. Securities and Exchange Commission was looking into a number of controversies involving the Greenberg brothers, including the failure of the Bank of New England and Florida real estate deals. *Wired* magazine described the Skypix venture as "more business operetta than deal-of-the-century."

If the CRTC was relieved by the Skypix fiasco, the reprieve was brief. By late 1992 the giant automaker General Motors was getting serious about its plans to launch DirecTV, an all-digital, high-powered DBS system. DirecTV posed a much greater threat to the Canadian cable industry than Skypix, especially since DirecTV's satellite "footprint" would cover most of Canada. John Malone had been the first to sound the alarm bells about DirecTV with his 500-channel-universe speech and warnings about DBS death stars.

The Canadian cable industry was no less paranoid about the potential competitive impact of DirecTV. Some industry analysts were predicting that DirecTV would have a total of 15 million subscribers in North America by the year 2000. In acknowledgement of the mounting anxiety, the Canadian Cable Television Association published a report in late 1992 on the threat of U.S.-based satellite TV systems. The report, a well-researched booklet called *The DBS Report*, was a carefully disguised rallying cry to the cable industry and the CRTC to meet the DBS threat head-on. It warned that the impact of DBS services like DirecTV could have a "devastating" impact on the cable industry.

DirecTV's lethal weapon was its sixty channels of pay-per-view movies and sports events, as well as its all-movie Home Box Office channel. In Canada, two companies held exclusive pay-per-view licences on cable systems: Viewer's Choice had a monopoly in eastern Canada, and Home Theatre had exclusive rights for the western provinces. Viewer's Choice was owned by Montreal-based Astral Communications, controlled by Montreal businessman Harold Greenberg and his family. Astral also owned The Movie Network, whose all-movie monopoly in Canada was protected by the CRTC ban on Home Box Office. André Bureau, as CRTC chairman, had presided over a number of key decisions that had helped the Greenbergs shift their business from risky movie production to regulated and risk-free specialty and pay TV channels.

By the early 1990s the president of Astral was none other than André Bureau, who had returned in 1989 to the private sector to run the Greenbergs' burgeoning, CRTC-protected broadcasting interests. The intricate web of mutually reinforcing interests was made even tighter with the ties between Astral and the Canadian cable industry. Ted Rogers owned a piece of Astral as well as a 25-percent stake in Viewer's Choice. Phil Lind, the longtime Rogers executive, sat on the Astral board. And Bureau sat on the board of Shaw Communications, the big Calgary-based cable company and owner of several specialty TV channels.

To appreciate how threatened André Bureau must have felt when the spectre of DirecTV first loomed, it is necessary to recall the optimism about the commercial success of pay-per-view in the early 1990s. Many believed that pay-per-view would put video retail stores like Blockbuster — and Rogers Video — out of business. No wonder, indeed, that Ted Rogers was so keen to invest in Viewer's Choice. He would thus be well positioned to retreat from bricks-and-mortar retail video and concentrate on electronic delivery of movies via cable. The prospect of DirecTV entering the Canadian pay TV and pay-per-view market to compete directly with Viewer's Choice must have been infuriating to André Bureau, Harold Greenberg, and Ted Rogers, who had invested so much energy and money to win CRTC licences guaranteeing them monopolies in these areas.

As the panic mounted, the Canadian cable lobby hastily imported Malone's "death stars" label into Canada to smear DirecTV. Predictably, the Canadian media gleefully seized on the concocted but compelling pejorative. Many major Canadian newspapers began casually referring to broadcast satellites as "death stars" without giving any consideration to the self-interested origins of the epithet. The nationalistic *Toronto Star* published a story under the headline "The Fight for Control of TV's 'Death Stars.'" The Montreal *Gazette*, for its part, didn't even distance itself from the Hollywood metaphor with quotation marks when it went to press with a similarly foreboding headline: "Canadian Death Star to Hit TVs by Fall '95."

The Canadian cable lobby had another powerful anti-DBS weapon that was not in John Malone's arsenal. In Canada, DirecTV could be denounced as an agent of American "cultural imperialism." This battle cry was sure to strike the right chord in certain quarters, particularly among the cultural nationalists in Toronto and, more important, at the CRTC. The CRTC, now headed by Keith Spicer, was in fact secretly orchestrating the anti-DirecTV campaign.

After Bureau stepped down from the Commission in 1989, he must have been flabbergasted when Brian Mulroney named the mercurial Keith Spicer as his successor. It was widely known that Spicer owed the appointment to a series of sycophantic pro–free trade editorials he had written as editor-in-chief of the *Ottawa Citizen*. Spicer had cut a flamboyant figure in Ottawa's power circles. He was immensely charming and had many friends and admirers, particularly among the chattering classes. Spicer was known in Ottawa as something of a grandstander with an undeniable talent for attracting headlines. As Canada's official languages commissioner, he had declared publicly that the best place to learn French was in bed. Spicer had relatively little knowledge of the broadcasting and telecom industries, however, and certainly didn't seem like an inspired choice for the CRTC chairmanship. His appointment revealed how little Brian Mulroney knew or cared about communications regulation.

When Spicer installed himself in Bureau's office at the CRTC, he was unaware that Bureau had laid his own succession plans by anointing his hand-picked CRTC lieutenant, Fernand Bélisle, as his de facto successor. Bélisle was a fascinating, enigmatic character, at once affable and intimidating. The son of a Tory senator, Bélisle had — like his boss André Bureau — worked at Télémédia before joining the CRTC. In late 1983, when Bureau arrived at the CRTC as chairman, Bélisle was labouring in a relatively junior Ottawa job at the Department of Communications. Bureau summoned Bélisle to the CRTC and, within only months, appointed him to the top bureaucratic post as CRTC secretary-general. It was an astonishing ascendancy that normally would not be possible in the federal bureaucracy. Yet Bureau made it happen.

For the entire duration of Bureau's tenure at the helm of the regulator, Bélisle was his trusted right hand — the iron in Bureau's velvet glove. When Spicer moved into Bureau's CRTC office, Bélisle was already firmly in charge of the Commission. Spicer failed to decode the internal politics of the Commission to see who his potential friends and adversaries were. Instead, he naively succumbed to the entreaties and blandishments of Bélisle's supporters, and went along with Bélisle's elevation to the rank of CRTC commissioner. And, because of his long institutional memory and effective power over the CRTC machinery, Bélisle's authority was soon unquestioned.

Only a year after arriving at the CRTC, Spicer took a "sabbatical" to chair Mulroney's Citizen's Forum on Canada's Future. In 1991, after that circus-like spectacle, which Spicer did not fail to exploit as a publicity vehicle, he returned to the CRTC with his hands less firmly on the reins of the Commission. Fern Bélisle, now installed as vice-chairman of broadcasting, was the undisputed boss of the CRTC. For the remainder of his chairmanship, Spicer worked hard on such issues as television violence, but largely performed an honorary role as the CRTC's unofficial ambassador on the Ottawa cocktail circuit — and on many junkets to U.S. and European capitals. At the CRTC, some staffers dismissed him as a flake consumed by social issues and his own media image. Spicer found the minutiae of regulation exceedingly soporific and described the task as *enculer des mouches* (sodomizing flies). Most Commission meetings were run by Fern Bélisle.

"Bélisle knew where the bodies were hidden at the Commission," recalls one longtime CRTC insider. "He had been there for a long time and effectively ran the place. When Spicer arrived, he didn't have a chance."

Not surprisingly, Spicer and Bélisle cordially despised each other. "Fern's game is power, plots, and intrigue," Spicer often whispered to his advisers. Bélisle, for his part, dismissed Spicer as a self-promoter and ranked him as the worst CRTC chairman in the regulator's history. In many respects, both had a point.

The two men were certainly very different creatures, each with his own virtues and vices. Spicer, for all his personal idiosyncrasies, was a gifted communicator who was not indifferent to the public interest. He was highly effective on particular issues and he cleverly exploited his chosen causes to build his media profile. But he tended to champion issues with relatively small financial stakes for the big players in the industry. To his credit, Spicer was no industry stooge; but neither did he attempt to put an end to the tacit complicity between powerful industry interests and the CRTC. More interested in form than in substance, he lacked the intellectual courage and political skills to put his high minded principles into practice. Bélisle, on the other hand, was a complex figure with a definite talent for the subtle art of bureaucratic politics. A financial accountant by training, he had a mind for detailed analysis — and in broadcasting regulation the "devil is in the details." As Bélisle was a CRTC veteran, his institutional memory made him a formidable presence. He was tough-minded, often intellectually intimidating, and few at the CRTC ever dared to contradict him.

Above all, Bélisle was a fierce promoter of the pro-cable regulatory paradigm and "industry approach" that had been established by his mentor, André Bureau. In his many years at the CRTC, Bélisle was the guy that powerful industry players went to see to cut backroom deals with the regulator.

When DirecTV first announced its plans to launch commercially, Spicer was focusing on television violence. When it appeared that the CRTC was orchestrating the counteroffensive against DirecTV, some saw the hand of Fern Bélisle. Under his leadership, the regulator's first manoeuvre was a series of public hearings to examine the changing structure of the Canadian broadcasting system. While a wholly legitimate exercise in principle, the so-called Structural Hearings were an elaborate quasi-judicial process whose real purpose was to bolster the cable industry against the DBS threat, mainly through monthly rate increases to pay for digital upgrades. Even the official CRTC notice announcing the hearings betrayed an obvious preoccupation with the potential impact of foreign DBS services — namely, DirecTV. The CRTC was putting DirecTV on notice: non-Canadian satellite TV services were not welcome in Canada.

Unmoved, DirecTV responded with a brash, in-your-face attitude towards Canada's regulatory resistance. Jim Ramo, a senior DirecTV executive in Los Angeles, flew to Ottawa to make an appearance at the Structural Hearings in early 1993 — only a few months after John Malone's 500-channel-universe declaration. Ramo bluntly told a panel of CRTC commissioners that DirecTV was going to launch its service in Canada within a year — and moreover there was nothing the CRTC could do about it. For one thing, he said, some 500,000 Canadian households were already pulling down U.S. television signals. DirecTV, he added, was confident that many Canadians would find its all-digital, small-dish service even more appealing.

Ramo had hired Gregory Kane, a well-connected communications lawyer with Stikeman, Elliott, who happened to be married to a CRTC commissioner, Adrian Burns. Perhaps Ramo believed that Kane's conjugal proximity to commissioner Burns would smooth his relationship with the CRTC. He was wrong. Burns was an immensely likeable woman, but she exerted little influence over CRTC decisions. The real power at the CRTC was — as any Canadian broadcasting insider knew — Fern Bélisle. And Bélisle was hell-bent on keeping DirecTV out of Canada.

Bélisle matter-of-factly informed Ramo that DirecTV was illegal in Canada because it was not at least 80-percent Canadian-controlled. Ramo persisted in his view that, as a practical matter, there was nothing the CRTC could do to stop DirecTV from soliciting subscribers in Canada. The spectacle of the two men locking horns was fascinating sport for all those present, most of them longtime industry veterans of CRTC hearings who, unlike Ramo, knew how to speak the regulatory double-talk. In the eyes of many, Ramo's performance was preposterous. When Chris Frank, a Telesat executive, followed Ramo at the CRTC hearings, he made jocular references to the American as "Mr. Rambo" — a Hollywood allusion that elicited chuckles with its evocation of American cultural imperialism.

From a public-relations point of view, Ramo's appearance before the CRTC was a disaster. When he returned to his California corporate headquarters in the spring of 1993, DirecTV had virtually no chance of entering the Canadian market with formal regulatory approval. Another solution would have to be found. The CRTC also needed to find a solution to the DBS threat. DirecTV's signals would soon be available in Canada, legally or illegally, and a concerted Canadian response was now an urgent priority.

Telesat, meanwhile, was desperately looking for a new lease on life. In the early 1990s Telesat was still a corporate eunuch suffering under the domination of Bell Canada, especially after 1991, when Ottawa dumped its Telesat shares as part of the Mulroney government's privatization policy. The Stentor phone companies had moved in to take complete control of Telesat, with a small portion of the stock going to Spar Aerospace. Under Stentor's control, Telesat underwent a painful downsizing ordeal and started posting losses of about $30 million a year. In 1993 Telesat was still clinging to the hope of a burgeoning domestic satellite TV industry that would lease its Anik transponders.

In late 1993 Telesat submitted a proposal to the CRTC urging the regulator to greenlight the launch of a national satellite TV service that would use Telesat space capacity. While Telesat was motivated primarily by bottom-line survival, its pitch to the CRTC was made in the lofty language of technological nationalism. Above all, a Canadian satellite TV service would not compete with cable TV.

For the CRTC, it was a timely pretext for the launching of a cable-friendly, made-in-Canada satellite TV service. The marriage of technological nationalism and regulatory expedience was thus happily consummated.

Power DirecTV: Political Nepotism or Regulatory Cronyism?

Joel Bell had watched from the sidelines during the head-butting match between Jim Ramo and Fern Bélisle. Bell was waiting his turn to make an oral intervention on behalf of Power Corporation, the giant conglomerate controlled by French Canadian billionaire Paul Desmarais.

Power Corp., though a formidable corporate force in Canada and globally, was not a major player in the Canadian broadcasting industry. In Europe, Power Corp. jointly controlled the Luxembourg-based broadcaster, CLT, the continent's first private trans-border broadcasting powerhouse. In Canadian broadcasting, however, Power Corp. owned only a handful of radio and TV stations in Ontario and Quebec. Consequently, it was not a member of the tight clique of major broadcasting interests that clustered around the CRTC.

Joel Bell himself was a newcomer to broadcasting. A lawyer by training, he was a longtime Liberal insider who, while still in his thirties, had served as Pierre Trudeau's senior economic adviser in the Prime Minister's Office. Towards the end of the Trudeau years, Bell had been a top executive at the state-run oil company, Petro-Canada, and was one of the chief architects of the Liberal government's controversial National Energy Program. He had also headed the Canadian government's industrial holding, the Canada Development Investment Corporation, which controlled major industrial assets, including Telesat, Teleglobe, Canadair, and de Havilland. When the Tories took power in 1984, Bell was near the top of Brian Mulroney's hit list — and was summarily fired in the first purge of top Liberal mandarins close to Pierre Trudeau. In the early 1990s Bell — like several other high-ranking Liberals from the Trudeau era — had found a corporate home at Power Corp. Unlike ex-mandarins Michael Pitfield and Gérard Veilleux, Bell was not officially a Power Corp. executive, but was rather a full-time in-house consultant. He was Power's Toronto-based antenna, occupying the company's luxurious offices atop a Bay Street tower with a spectacular view of the city's harbour.

In the spring of 1993 Bell was working on Power's long-term strategy in the North American broadcasting market. In Europe, Power Corp.'s controlling interest in CLT had given the company insights into issues related to cross-border television. CLT's television signals — beamed from Luxembourg's ASTRA satellites into neighbouring France, Germany, and the Benelux countries — had often been the source of intense irritation to governments, especially France, which resented the foreign incursion into their state-controlled broadcasting landscapes. CLT was nonetheless the most successful private broadcaster in Europe, and would later join the U.K.-based conglomerate, Pearson, to beat Canada's Izzy Asper in a bid for Britain's Channel 5 licence.

"We were very knowledgeable about the cross-border issues," recalls Bell. "We were already talking to DirecTV because we were hoping to do business with them on the programming front. It was in the course of those discussions that I suggested to Jim Ramo that, as far as DirecTV in Canada was concerned, a public sparring match with the CRTC just wasn't the way things were done in Canada. I told him that he should take a different approach. And he listened." [6]

Power Corp. had been negotiating with DirecTV to put two Canadian channels packaged by Power on its DBS bird so they would be available to DirecTV subscribers. One channel, called TRIO, was a package of Canadian dramas from both the CBC and Canada's private producers; the other was an international version of CBC's Newsworld. DirecTV agreed to carry both Canadian channels, marketed jointly by Power Corp. and the CBC under a subsidiary called Northbridge. DirecTV also consummated talks with CHUM to air its popular music-video channel, MuchMusic. These deals were a sign that, as in Europe, broadcasting landscapes were expanding beyond disparate national systems and forming continental spheres. They also demonstrated that, in Canada, television transmission did not necessarily have to be one-way from the United States.

Having established mutual trust with his Canadian interlocutors, Jim Ramo decided to take Joel Bell's advice and back off from his aggressive attitude to the CRTC. Since the major obstacle to DirecTV's entry into Canada was ownership and control, Ramo agreed to launch his service in Canada under a joint venture with Power Corp. to be called "Power DirecTV." In full compliance with Canadian ownership rules, Power DirecTV would be 80 percent controlled by Power Corp. and 20 percent owned by DirecTV. Moreover, Power DirecTV promised to abide by all Canadian rules and regulations imposed on programming, including the deletion of unauthorized U.S. channels such as MTV and Home Box Office.

The deal looked good on paper, but the politics were still complicated and potentially explosive. Bell therefore spent the first period of the Power DirecTV partnership in a damage-control exercise attempting to counter the negative "death stars" image being widely disseminated in the Canadian media. Canadian reporters were quick to point to Bell's earlier career as a staunch Trudeau nationalist, and wondered what road-to-Damascus experience had converted him to the virtues of North American continentalism.

"It's a judo play," explained Bell. "Do you try to knock the guy over by running directly into him, or do you capture his force and energy to your advantage? We think that we have to accept the inevitable and work with it. It's not a controllable world any more."

The Power DirecTV merger had undeniable appeal. The CRTC had been concerned about the imminent entry into Canada of a powerful satellite TV service that offered *only* American channels, and would therefore bypass the Canadian broadcasting system. Power Corp. was offering the CRTC an ingenious turn-key solution to the U.S. satellite TV threat. It would harness DirecTV by "Canadianizing" it and making it subject to Canada's regulatory authority. Indeed, the Power DirecTV venture fitted squarely in the long-established economic model in Canadian broadcasting based on cross-subsidizing the domestic industry through partnerships with U.S. broadcasters. Power Corp. was to DirecTV what Canada's TSN was to ESPN, what Canada's Family Channel was to the Disney Channel, and what Canada's Home and Garden Television was to its U.S. namesake.

By early 1994 Power Corp. wasn't the only Canadian company hoping to launch a satellite TV service. Bell Canada Enterprises, the telephone giant based in central Canada, was also looking closely at the possibility of moving into the video-delivery business via direct-to-home satellites. Power Corp. was not necessarily hostile to the prospect of Bell Canada as part of the Power DirecTV deal. With BCE and Power Corp. as its Canadian partners, DirecTV could enter Canada with the backing of the country's two most powerful corporations. Soon high-level meetings were arranged between the Power DirecTV camp and Bell Canada chairman Red Wilson. The meetings produced a tentative agreement.

Meanwhile, the Vancouver-based broadcaster WIC (Western International Communications) was also contemplating a foray into satellite TV. Under the leadership of Doug Holtby, WIC was known as the most anti-cable broadcaster in Canada. Besides owning a stable of radio and TV stations, WIC was already in the satellite business as the new controlling shareholder of Cancom — the CRTC creation of the early 1980s. Moreover, through its subsidiary, Allarcom, WIC owned pay TV and pay-per-view channels in western Canada. But these channels were struggling financially because cable companies couldn't provide them with a sufficient number of outlets to generate decent revenues. WIC therefore had a business interest in liberating itself from cable's stranglehold by launching its own satellite TV business to give some "lift" to its pay TV and pay-per-view channels.

WIC had one major problem, however. Cable tycoon Ted Rogers was a minority shareholder in WIC-controlled Cancom. What was more, Rogers had a seat on the Cancom board. When he heard that WIC was thinking about using satellite TV to compete head-on with cable, a stern warning was delivered to Doug Holtby: if you get involved in satellite TV, we will destroy you. Holtby, unimpressed by the bullying tactics of Rogers executives, went straight to BCE and joined the discussions between the phone company and Power Corp. WIC's defection to Bell Canada, the most feared enemy of the cable industry, sent the Rogers camp into a black rage.

Even more apoplectic was André Bureau. If Power DirecTV entered the Canadian market, its all-digital sixty-channel pay-per-view service was sure to decimate his struggling pay TV and pay-per-view channels — The Movie Network and Viewer's Choice.

Bureau also had a more personal reason to resent Power DirecTV. In the early 1970s he had been a senior executive at *La Presse*, the Montreal daily newspaper owned by Power Corp.'s Paul Desmarais. Desmarais fired Bureau, who remained bitter about the episode for years. When Bureau was CRTC chairman in the 1980s, Power Corp. made a bid for the popular Montreal television station, Télé-Métropole. Bureau blocked the deal on the grounds that Power's financial commitments to the station were weak — and, moreover, that concerns had been raised about concentration of ownership, since Power Corp. also owned *La Presse*. Télé-Métropole instead went to the big Quebec cable company, Vidéotron. The announced launch of Power DirecTV in early 1994 must have seemed to André Bureau like Paul Desmarais's sweet revenge.

Bureau had a powerful ally within the CRTC in his former second-in-command, Fern Bélisle, who was determined to keep Power DirecTV out of Canada. But the potential involvement of Bell Canada and WIC in the DirecTV deal presented a nettlesome problem for the CRTC, as DirecTV would be sponsored by two of the regulator's own industry clients — a telephone giant and a major broadcaster. Bélisle had to find the consortium's Achilles' heel.

Soon implied threats were communicated to WIC and BCE: as owners of regulated monopolies, they would have to think carefully before openly defying the regulator's wishes. If WIC persisted in its dalliance with Power DirecTV, there would be a price to pay when its Cancom subsidiary next came before the CRTC for licence renewal. If Bell Canada launched a competitive assault on cable TV from the skies, it too would be punished. The message from the CRTC was unequivocal: NO WAR ON CABLE.

Michael Neuman, a bright young executive at BCE, was Bell Canada's point man in the satellite TV talks at this stage. When Neuman first heard about the CRTC's uncompromising hostility to the Power DirecTV group, he called Fern Bélisle to ask for an appointment. The two had breakfast at the Holiday Inn adjoining the CRTC headquarters in Hull, Quebec, across the river from Parliament Hill.

"Bélisle made it very clear," recalls Neuman. "He said we had to make peace with the cable companies. He said we had to find a place for them in the deal. His message was that we wouldn't be competing with cable — that cable would be our partners." [7]

In January 1994 Bélisle made a discreet visit, with Keith Spicer in tow, to Boulder, Colorado, for a meeting with Jim Ramo. The pretext of the meeting was to inspect DirecTV's satellite uplink facility, located in Colorado to take advantage of the region's high altitude. The real purpose of the meeting, however, was to deliver a message to Ramo. Bélisle warned Ramo that DirecTV wouldn't be able to market its service in Canada unless it used *Canadian* satellites.

On the surface, this presented no serious material problem. Power DirecTV's business plan was based on a two-satellite delivery: the American channels would be beamed directly from DirecTV's Hughes bird, and all Canadian channels would use Canadian transponders on Telesat's Anik satellites. But the CRTC still had an arsenal of regulatory obstacles that could thwart Power DirecTV's commercial launch in Canada. And the regulator was actively encouraged by the Canadian cable industry to use all its powers to accomplish that goal.

When Ted Rogers announced his $3.1-billion takeover bid on the

Maclean Hunter publishing empire in early 1994, he did not neglect to invoke the DirecTV threat in a ploy to create a sense of urgency about regulatory approval for his hostile takeover attempt.

"Our cultural and information industries are at risk," said Rogers in a speech at Toronto's York University. "If we are going to keep pace with international developments, we must do so by reinforcing our existing strengths. Our cable industry is fragmented and remains highly vulnerable to competitors such as big American direct-broadcast satellites that will soon be beaming in foreign shows to Canadian homes."

Rogers and other major cable companies were now actively mobilizing to neutralize the Power DirecTV threat. The chosen strategy: launch an all-Canadian satellite TV company controlled by cable interests while sandbagging Power DirecTV with onerous regulations. This strategy germinated at the Ontario Cable Television Association's "Cable Day" in late March 1994, and was discussed in early May at the annual symposium sponsored by the Law Society of Upper Canada's communications law branch, composed mainly of well-connected lawyers with close links to the major players in the Canadian broadcasting industry. The plan was finalized in mid-May at the Canadian Cable Television Association's convention in Montreal.

As was customary at the annual CCTA event, the real action took place away from the convention floor. In a suite at the nearby InterContinental Hotel, a discreet meeting brought together some of the biggest players in Canadian broadcasting: Phil Lind and Colin Watson from Rogers Communications; Gordon Craig, president of Labatt-owned broadcasting interests such as TSN; J. R. Shaw, the founder of the Calgary-based cable empire that bore his name; Adrian Pouliot from CFCF in Montreal; Alain Gourd, president of Cancom; André Bureau, president of Astral Communications; and Bureau's longtime protegé, Lisa de Wilde, head of Astral's struggling pay TV and pay-per-view channels.

When Michael Neuman from BCE arrived, he was the lone telephone executive in the room — and, as such, was a conspicuous outsider. Neuman took a seat in the middle of the room. Immediately, he felt like a schoolboy who was about to be chastised — and he was astounded by what happened next.

"Basically, they presented me with a fait accompli," recalls Neuman. "They told me that we would all be creating a satellite TV company together, but that BCE would have only a small percentage of the company. Also, they said that the company would *not* offer service in areas passed by cable. There would be no competition with cable. I told them that it all sounded very interesting, but it wasn't the kind of deal I had in mind."

Neuman and his allies at WIC were furious. They understood, however, that this meeting had received the blessing of the CRTC — indeed that it had probably been orchestrated by the regulator. In short, the deal was a shotgun marriage that Neuman found distasteful. But the tacit threat from the CRTC gave WIC and BCE little room to manoeuvre.

On May 17 André Bureau and his cable-allied colleagues held a press conference at the CCTA convention to announce the creation of "DTH Canada," an all-Canadian satellite TV company. Bureau did not mention to the assembled reporters that DTH Canada was to be controlled by Canada's major cable companies and therefore would not offer a competitive alternative to Canadian consumers. Nor did Bureau mention that two of his partners, WIC and BCE, were so outraged by the strong-arm tactics that forced them into the deal that they were angrily boycotting the press conference.

Sitting in the front row at the press conference was none other than Fern Bélisle, smiling like a proud father. Immediately afterwards, Bélisle walked through Old Montreal to the Power Corp. offices for a scheduled meeting with Joel Bell and Power executive Peter Kruyt, who had been shocked by the sudden turn of events. The meeting was frosty. Bell and Kruyt understood that the creation of DTH Canada had been a blatant attempt to isolate Power Corp. by forcing BCE and WIC into an uncomfortable alliance with Ted Rogers, André Bureau, and their corporate friends. Bélisle had masterfully redrawn the balance of power on the battlefield. It was now Power DirecTV against an uneasy alliance of Canada's most powerful broadcasting and telephone interests.

But the war against Power DirecTV was not yet over. In late August 1994 the CRTC fired another shot, announcing that it would exempt from licensing any satellite TV company that used Canadian satellites for all its TV signals. This decision effectively fast-tracked DTH Canada's market entry, for it was planning to use Telesat transponders only. Power DirecTV, on the other hand, would not be allowed to enter the Canadian market because, while it planned to use Telesat transponders for its Canadian channels, it was obliged to use American satellites for the U.S. signals beamed down by its partner, DirecTV. If Power DirecTV wished to operate its service in Canada, it would have to face the many hurdles of a foot-dragging licensing process conducted by a regulator that was openly hostile to its presence in Canada. The CRTC's ploy was a regulatory kick in the teeth to Power DirecTV.

The CRTC's all-Canadian satellite decision might have cleverly exploited the long-cherished theme of technological nationalism, but it contradicted the government's official satellite-usage policy. There were no valid policy grounds for blocking DirecTV's market entry in Canada merely because it planned to use U.S. satellites to deliver American television signals. Official Canadian policy was unequivocal: the use of Canadian satellite facilities was mandatory only for Canadian television signals — not for American channels. Indeed, Canadian cable companies routinely used American satellites to capture the U.S. television signals they retransmitted to Canadian homes. The hypocrisy of the Canadian cable industry on this point was egregious. More shocking, however, was the behaviour of the CTRC. The regulator was either badly advised or, more likely, simply being mischievous.

The CRTC, whose longstanding policy was that "our decisions speak for themselves," remained silent on the matter. Senior executives at the favoured DTH Canada consortium displayed more candour about the intended effect of the CRTC's regulatory scheming.

"I think it's going to knock them out of the box," said Ted Boyle, DTH Canada's newly appointed president, referring to Power DirectTV. "We applaud the CRTC for showing considerable courage in making this decision."

It would soon become evident, however, that the CRTC decision had been more careless than courageous.

The "Three Wise Men": Ottawa Policy Battles

Joel Bell was incensed by the CRTC's rebuff. He was familiar with the intent of Canada's official satellite policy. He had sat on Telesat's board of directors during the Trudeau era, and he knew that the government's policy insisted on Canadian transponder usage for Canadian signals only.

Immediately after the CRTC decision, Bell headed up to Ottawa in high dudgeon to expose what he believed was an appalling abuse of regulatory power. He knocked on the door of virtually every senior government official who had authority over satellite policy. He also visited Eddie Goldenberg, the prime minister's closest adviser. Bell and Goldenberg, both Montreal lawyers and longtime Liberal insiders, had been friends for many years. When Bell arrived at Goldenberg's door, he learned that he'd actually been late to swing into action.

"Eddie said to me: 'Joel, what took you so long? The other guys have already been here,'" recalls Bell. "André Bureau and his friends had already been up there to lobby everybody."

Ironically, Bell and Bureau were well connected in the same Ottawa power circles. Both men knew the prime minister personally: Bureau had been a school chum of Jean Chrétien in Trois-Rivières, and Bell had been Pierre Trudeau's senior economic adviser when Chrétien was a minister in the Trudeau cabinet. Bell enjoyed a more contemporary connection with the prime minister: as a Power Corp. insider, he was working closely with Paul

Desmarais's son André, who was married to Chrétien's daughter, France.

The family links between Power Corp. and the prime minister made Bell's lobbying efforts extremely delicate. He compensated for this by opting for a low-key approach in Ottawa. He carried Power DirecTV's brief himself, though he was often accompanied by Peter Kruyt, president of Power Corp.'s broadcasting subsidiary, Power Broadcasting Inc. The two were an interesting study in contrasts: Bell was intense, driven, and intellectually overpowering while the younger Kruyt was cool, suave, and affable.

In contrast to Power Corp.'s discreet approach, the DTH Canada consortium adopted a blitzkrieg lobbying strategy by hiring battalions of lawyers and high-level lobbyists to cover the capital. Dubbed the "Friendly Alliance," the DTH Canada group held its strategy meetings in the boardroom of the Ottawa offices of the Canadian Cable Television Association. Worried that its members were mainly from major monopoly cable and broadcasting companies, the Friendly Alliance made an attempt to broaden its representation with the inclusion of groups defending the interests of the artists who toil at the bottom of the food chain. But the arts groups, long frustrated by the monopoly dominance of cable TV and broadcasting interests, spurned the overtures.

The satellite TV battle put the Chrétien government in a difficult position. The CRTC clearly had violated official satellite policy on the fabricated pretext that Power DirecTV planned to use U.S. satellites for its American channels. But the prime minister's family connection to Power Corp. made a quick political solution perilous, for the DTH Canada camp would almost certainly level charges of nepotism. Realizing that the only acceptable solution would require some form of impartial arbitration, the government decided to call upon an independent panel of experts to referee what was rapidly degenerating into an acrimonious feud between warring commercial interests.

In late November 1994 the government named three eminent Canadians — all of whom had served in Ottawa as deputy ministers — to conduct a review of satellite broadcasting policy and propose an appropriate course of action. The three panelists were Gordon Ritchie, Roger Tassé, and Robert Rabinovitch. The panel was chaired by Ritchie, a shrewd strategist and veteran of Ottawa's internecine bureaucratic battles. Ritchie was a trade expert who, as Canada's deputy chief trade negotiator, had played a key role in the bilateral talks that led to the 1987 Free Trade Agreement with the United States. Tassé, one of Canada's most eminent jurists, had served as deputy minister of justice during the negotiations leading to the patriation of Canada's constitution. Rabinovitch, a Liberal political aide and

brilliant policy wonk in the high-flying Trudeau years, had risen to the rank
of deputy minister of communications at the tender age of thirty-nine. Fired
in 1984 by Brian Mulroney because of his high-level Liberal connections,
Rabinovitch was now a senior executive at Charles Bronfman's holding
company, Claridge Inc., and sat on the board of Cineplex Odeon.

There could be no denying that Ritchie, Tassé, and Rabinovitch had
close connections with the prime minister. Ritchie had been a business
associate of Chrétien's political mentor, Mitchell Sharp, and both had
worked with the PM in the Ottawa law offices of Lang Michener. Likewise,
Roger Tassé had been the PM's deputy when Chrétien was minister of
justice fifteen years earlier; and he had been Chretien's law partner at Lang
along with Eddie Goldenberg. Rabinovitch was a friend of some of the
prime minister's closest advisers, including Goldenberg. Rabinovitch was
also a bureaucratic protégé of Michael Pitfield, who was Pierre Trudeau's
top civil servant before joining Power Corp. as a senior executive. None of
these facts, however, precluded Ritchie, Tassé, and Rabinovitch from
rendering an impartial judgement. Indeed, so impeccable were the triumvirate's credentials that they were immediately dubbed the "Three Wise Men."

Still, some in the DTH camp were suspicious, and promptly stepped
up their campaign of calumny with open accusations of nepotism. They
spoke to Bloc Quebecois MPs, who denounced Ritchie, Tasse, and Rabinovitch in the House of Commons, and innuendo was spread in the press
about the links between Power Corp. and the prime minister.

In truth, the DTH Canada clique was not indignant because the Three
Wise Men were, as some claimed, working for the interests of Power Corp.
Rather the source of their uneasiness was that a new and untested approach
was being taken and they did not know how it might affect them. This fresh
initiative meant that a significant public process regarding the future of
Canadian broadcasting was being conducted in total isolation from the
customary backroom blandishments and dealmaking that determined the outcome of so many CRTC decisions.

Eddie Goldenberg nonetheless found himself in the awkward position
of publicly defending the appointments.

"If anybody suggests there is any favouritism," he said, "I would like
them to make that allegation, because it is totally unsubstantiated. You can't
take people out of a Trappist monastery. People have to know something.
The question you have to ask is whether people are impartial."

The Three Wise Men's secretariat, which was supported by staff analysts
from the ministries of Canadian Heritage and Industry, operated out of
Gordon Ritchie's corporate offices in Ottawa's World Exchange building. It

was in these same offices that Mitchell Sharp, Ritchie's business associate, had vetted the prime minister's first cabinet choices in late 1993. Down the hallway, the Three Wise Men used the boardroom of the Blake Cassels law firm for their meetings and briefings by senior government officials. Ironically, the CRTC's newest commissioner, Andrée Wylie, was finishing up her last few months at Blake Cassels during the satellite TV saga before moving into her office at the Commission, and she mingled occasionally with the Three Wise Men and their staff during those hectic months. Two of the government's brightest lawyers joined the team to offer expert legal advice: Konrad von Finckenstein, assistant deputy minister of business affairs at Industry Canada (and today head of the federal Competition Bureau); and Ken Katz, a Justice department lawyer who had worked at the CRTC and Department of Communications in a number of key posts over two decades. At DOC in the mid-1970s, Katz had co-authored with his deputy minister Allan Gotlieb and policy lawyer Charles Dalfen (who later became a CRTC commissioner) a paper examining cross-border satellite systems.

The policy review received some 300 briefs in a two-stage process, including hefty submissions by virtually all the major players in the Canadian broadcasting system — TV networks, cable companies, telephone companies, specialty channels, producers, directors, actors. Some of the briefs were impressive and well-argued. Others were inflammatory and belligerent.

André Bureau's brief submitted by Astral was entitled "Now Is Not the Time to Surrender!" In a passionate plea for cultural protectionism that revealed a tenuous grasp on ancient Greek history, Astral compared Power DirecTV to a "Trojan Horse" whose arsenal of American channels and Hollywood movies threatened to undermine Canadian cultural sovereignty. Astral dismissed Power Corp. as an "agent" for DirecTV's invasion of Canada. The irony of this tirade was peculiar to say the least. A recent investment report by Richardson Greenshields had approvingly observed that Astral's profits were up, thanks to the many deals the company had signed with major Hollywood studios to distribute their products in Canada. Astral's Family Channel, moreover, was itself an "agent" in Canada for the American programs of the Disney Channel.

The satellite TV story rapidly degenerated into an ugly war between DTH Canada and Power DirecTV. As the *Globe and Mail* put it in a front-page story:

> Behind the government's decision to wade into a fight between two business groups racing to cash in on the coming generation of satellite television services is a trail of pressure and persuasion

winding through the heart of the Liberal power structure in Ottawa to the office of Prime Minister Jean Chrétien. There is a lot more involved in the battle to exploit the new entertainment jackpot than apparent favouritism for the company involving Mr. Chrétien's son-in-law. . . . It is also the rekindling of old feuds in a saga of intense lobbying, bureaucratic arm-twisting and international intrigue.

The *Globe*'s editorial board came down against the CRTC and its favoured DTH Canada clique: "It is one of the many ironies of Canadian broadcasting that the Prime Minister's family connections may be the only thing that can save us from the officially authorized cronyism of the industry regulator."

As the media scrutiny intensified, innuendo about political favours for the PM's son-in-law ceased and the press turned against the CRTC and its privileged clients. It was now obvious that if there was any collusion it was between the regulator and the Friendly Alliance. In truth, DTH Canada was a fragile alliance, and not altogether friendly. With major cable interests and Bell Canada as co-owners, the consortium was composed of very strange bedfellows. A consensus on strategic issues was impossible as long as cable and telephone interests were at the table.

While the partners in DTH Canada bickered, the Competition Bureau delivered the coup de grâce by threatening to initiate an anti-trust investigation into the consortium on the grounds that the satellite TV group, which was supposed to compete with cable, was in fact controlled by the country's two biggest cable companies, Rogers and Shaw, and other monopoly interests. The Competition Bureau's threat provoked Rogers and Shaw to withdraw hastily from the consortium. DTH Canada was renamed "ExpressVu" and — controlled jointly by BCE, WIC, and a feisty upstart hardware firm called Tee-Comm Electronics Inc. — adopted a less actively pro-cable stance.

In early 1995 the Canadian cable industry found itself under attack in yet another public controversy. After the market launch of a new package of specialty TV channels — including Showcase, The Life Network, Bravo!, and Women's Television Network — a groundswell of exasperation erupted when cable subscribers learned they had been billed automatically for the new channels without their prior consent. Most of the outrage against the cable industry's "negative-option" marketing tactics was directed against Ted Rogers, particularly in Toronto and Vancouver. The negative-option marketing fiasco was hardly a propitious backdrop for cable TV's defensive war against satellite TV. If anything, it made satellite TV seem like the only salvation from the arrogant cable monopoly.

It was in this tumultuous climate that the Three Wise Men issued their report in early April 1995. Those who had expected the report to condemn the CRTC and hand the Canadian market to Power DirecTV were disarmed by the report's main recommendations. The report did criticize the CRTC's preposterous interpretation of the government's satellite-usage policy, but it also reaffirmed the CRTC's licensing powers. The Three Wise Men advised the government to take extraordinary measures provided for in a rarely invoked clause in the Broadcasting Act, and order the CRTC to conduct fair and impartial licensing hearings for all potential satellite TV players. In short, the CRTC would be forced to put ExpressVu and Power DirecTV on an equal footing.

Facing the threat of a Cabinet directive, the CRTC squawked sanctimoniously about its status as an arm's-length "quasi-judicial" body and railed against perceived meddling by politicians. Keith Spicer foolishly allowed himself to be cajoled into playing the absurd role of Defender of the Faith, protecting the CRTC's virginity against the corrupting influence of *dirigiste* politicians. As Gordon Ritchie observed in his 1997 memoirs *Wrestling with the Elephant*, the gullible Spicer got "taken for a ride" in the satellite TV affair by his calculating vice-chairman, Fernand Bélisle.

"Bélisle was much too savvy to stand front and centre when the [CRTC] decision came under attack," recalled Ritchie. "Instead, he had apparently persuaded Spicer that the government was challenging his — the chairman's — prerogatives. Did Spicer want to go down in history as the man who had surrendered the independence of the CRTC? This certainly had engaged Spicer's attention, and he put his communications skills to work."

Spicer arranged to make two high-profile, back-to-back appearances at House of Commons and Senate committees before he left for a holiday in Europe. True to form, he made a dashing appearance on Parliament Hill with his trademark cape cascading jauntily from his shoulders and the customary retinue in his swirling wake. Seated before his parliamentary inquisitors, Spicer put on quite a show. He lashed out at the government's meddling in the CRTC's affairs, and made insinuations about the prime minister's conduct, charging him with nepotism in the satellite TV saga.

Spicer's public outburst did little to redeem the CRTC's negative public image. It succeeded, however, in jeopardizing Spicer's future on the government payroll after his term at the Commission expired. He was now persona non grata in the eyes of the ruling Liberals. When John Manley, the industry minister, was asked what he thought of Spicer's tenure at the CRTC, Manley replied, "Long." Spicer's string of patronage appointments to plum federal posts was over. If Bélisle had nudged Spicer to the edge of the precipice, the strategy worked wonderfully. Spicer, the irrepressible showman, took the leap.

Despite Spicer's insinuation that the Three Wise Men were Power Corp. puppets, Ritchie, Tassé, and Rabinovitch remained stoically confident that they had come to the right decision. Their logic was based on a need to "bring the camel into the tent" — that is, that DirecTV should be brought under the CRTC's regulatory authority as a Canadian-controlled company, Power DirecTV. The Three Wise Men had doubts, however, about the predictability of the CRTC's behaviour now that the ball was in the regulator's court. While licensing was a legitimate role for a regulator in a competitive market, it could also be used as a tool, through the imposition of onerous terms and conditions, to stall or sandbag competition. As Gordon Ritchie often confided to his colleagues: "I am convinced we are doing the right thing, but I fear we are throwing Joel Bell back into the hands of his tormentors."

That remark proved to be prescient. The CRTC was not stupid enough to deny Power DirecTV a licence. In a climate of overwhelming public support for competition to cable TV, continued regulatory resistance would have been politically damaging for the CRTC. However, the Commission could always issue a licence to Power DirecTV that made it difficult for the satellite TV company to compete effectively with cable. And that is precisely what the CRTC did in late December 1995, when it issued direct-to-home satellite TV licences to both ExpressVu and Power DirecTV. Once again, the devil was in the details.

Bell understood immediately that Power DirecTV — and ExpressVu for that matter — had been snookered by the CRTC. The licences were a poisoned chalice. The satellite TV companies would be obliged to pay the distribution costs to receive television channels at their uplink facilities, while cable TV companies could use their market power to impose these costs on the owners of the channels.

In early 1996 Joel Bell coldly announced that Power DirecTV would not go forward under the conditions imposed by the CRTC. ExpressVu, now controlled by Bell Canada, suddenly realized that cable TV was the real enemy.

"I have to admit that Power DirecTV's business plan was elegant," says ExpressVu president Michael Neuman. "In early 1996 we were still kicking the tires of our technology platform, but we knew that DirecTV had an excellent system from a technological point of view."

With Power DirecTV out of the market, the battle was now between the Canadian cable industry and Bell Canada–controlled ExpressVu. The cable industry couldn't believe its luck when, in March 1996, one of Telesat's Anik satellites suffered a major power failure in orbit. The accident wiped out transponder space allocated for direct-to-home satellite TV signals. With no Telesat transponders there would be no satellite TV in Canada — except, of course, the unauthorized "grey market" signals beamed down directly from DirecTV's U.S. satellite.

By mid-1996 some 200,000 grey-market DirecTV dishes had been sold across Canada. By contrast, the number of subscribers to ExpressVu was zero. Following the Telesat disaster, ExpressVu was ready to call it quits. After three years of squabbling, it now seemed there would never be a Canadian satellite TV industry.

Technological Nationalism vs. Continental Pragmatism

The Telesat power failure put the federal government in a vexing quandary. The crisis was an alarming demonstration of the vulnerability of the entire Canadian broadcasting system, which depended on the technical capacity of a single "national champion" satellite system. Canada clearly needed a backup satellite strategy to diminish the risks inherent in reliance on Telesat's birds.

A possible solution soon surfaced. Canada could launch its own high-powered satellites in vacant DBS orbital slots allocated under international agreements. There was one not insignificant problem, however: the Canadian domestic market was too small to support the enormous costs of launching high-powered DBS birds. Telesat's own sad fortunes as an under-utilized satellite system offered ample evidence of that market reality.

The high cost of launching DBS birds had to be amortized over a much larger market. This fact led to the inescapable conclusion that American partners would have to be found to help Canada finance its satellite rescue plan. In other words, the only way out of Canada's satellite capacity crisis was to adopt the Power DirecTV model of exploiting the cross-border potential of DBS broadcast satellites.

The irony for Power Corp. was understandably wrenching. The very same Canadian business interests that had accused Power DirecTV of selling out to American interests were now scrambling to negotiate joint U.S.-Canada satellite deals of their own. Shaw Cablesystems, for example, announced a deal with U.S. cable companies to launch a satellite TV service to be called Frontier — and later Homestar. Shaw attempted to sell the deal in Ottawa with the slogan "Serve Canada First," but could not conceal the decidedly less patriotic fact that Homestar's main purpose was to provide satellite capacity for American commercial interests.

Even Telesat, a former state-controlled corporation, announced a U.S.-Canada deal of its own. Telesat negotiated a twelve-year agreement to launch two high-powered DBS birds owned by John Malone's TCI and use them from Canadian orbital slots. According to the complicated deal, Telesat would buy the high-powered American birds for $600 million (U.S.), but TCI would pay a one-time rights fee of $300 million for use of twenty-seven of the satellite's thirty-two transponders — plus $2.5 million annually per transponder to lease capacity. In total, TCI would spend $1.6 billion over the twelve years. Canada, for its part, could use the five remaining transponders.

The Telesat-TCI deal was simply an American satellite project operating from Canadian orbital slots, with leftover transponder space going to Canada as residual gratitude. The main beneficiary was the U.S. cable industry, whose medium-powered PrimeStar satellite service was seeking to graduate to high-powered DBS birds. It was just the kind of deal that Canada's technological nationalists — Telesat first among them — were usually quick to denounce, if only because an "inequality of benefits" accrued to Canadian interests. Now those voices were silent.

In the United States, John Malone's TCI was facing a different set of political obstacles. TCI-controlled PrimeStar, seeking to migrate to DBS birds to compete head-on with DirecTV, had few supporters in Washington. MCI, the long-distance phone giant, was particularly vocal in its opposition to the sweetheart deal between TCI and Telesat. In a DBS spectrum auction, MCI and Rupert Murdoch's News Corp. had beat TCI's bid for a U.S. DBS slot with their higher $682.5-million offer. Now TCI, the loser in the auction, was seeking to park its own satellites in Canadian orbital slots on suspiciously preferential terms. MCI and News Corp. cried foul. They argued that they had paid a colossal sum to compete against the U.S. cable industry but their investment was now a write-off because cable-controlled PrimeStar would get its DBS orbital slots through a backdoor Canadian deal.

The MCI–News Corp. case against TCI was unimpeachable. Still, TCI frantically attempted to sell the Telesat deal in Washington not as a transnational arrangement, but as an "American" project. Telesat, for its part, was selling the deal in Ottawa as "Canadian." Thus, the TCI-Telesat venture became the satellite deal that dared not speak its name.

In early 1996 the U.S. government was in no mood to countenance friendly deals with Canadian commercial interests. A year earlier, the CRTC had provoked the ire of the White House by retroactively banning a U.S. channel, Country Music Television, on the pretext that a similar Canadian-owned channel called New Country Network was soon going on the air. Both the White House and Congress had denounced the CRTC decision as "cultural protectionism" and threatened retaliation against other Canadian communications companies seeking market entry in the United States — in particular, the long-distance phone company Teleglobe Inc. Meanwhile, Canada and the U.S. were engaged in another skirmish on the cultural front. The Canadian government was taking measures to ban the sale in Canada of so-called split-run editions of American magazines like *Sports Illustrated*. In Washington, political leaders were beginning to view their friendly neighbour to the north as a bilateral nuisance.

The U.S. Federal Communications Commission had the formal authority to approve, or block, the Telesat-TCI deal. On July 15, 1996, the FCC formally rejected it.

John Manley, Canada's industry minister, was put in the unenviable position of defending the CRTC's right to impose cultural regulations in Canada. Manley moreover accused the United States of using the CRTC as a red herring.

"The FCC's decision is disappointing because the business arrangement negotiated between Telesat Canada and its American partners would have benefitted consumers in both Canada and the United States," stated Manley, adding that Ottawa would find a "made-in-Canada" solution to its satellite capacity crisis.

After three years of muddling through, Canada's satellite policy was lurching from one fiasco to another, and the result was satisfactory to no one.

Made-in-Canada Satellite TV: The Aftermath

It took another full year for satellite TV to launch in Canada. Three years after DirecTV started beaming nearly 200 channels across North America, Telesat fixed its technical problems and two Canadian satellite TV operators — ExpressVu and StarChoice — finally began offering service in 1997.

In some respects, the fact that Canada finally had a domestic satellite TV industry was cause for celebration. But for consumers hoping for aggressive price competition with the cable TV industry, the frustration would continue. For one thing, both ExpressVu and StarChoice — unlike DirecTV — had limited satellite capacity and therefore could offer a selection of channels that barely matched what Canadians could already get from cable TV. Even with additional satellite transponders, neither ExpressVu nor Star-Choice could offer an attractively differentiated package from cable, because the CRTC had imposed a series of constricting rules on satellite TV in the name of a "level playing field." In Canada, satellite television was being punished by regulation for having the advantage of an all-digital delivery system, which the cable industry had loudly promised but failed to deploy.

The ownership structure of the two Canadian DTH players was all too familiar in a country long accustomed to monopoly power. ExpressVu, while no longer tamed from within by cable ownership, was owned by phone giant Bell Canada, which also controlled Telesat. StarChoice, for its part, had begun as a feisty start-up launched by a few New Brunswick businessmen who had won a DTH licence by promising the CRTC that it would launch promptly. But as soon as StarChoice's founders walked off with their licence, they cynically cashed out by selling control to the big Calgary-based cable company, Shaw.

After five years of Byzantine intrigue and bitter bureaucratic battles, the Canadian satellite TV saga had ended in a duopolistic truce. The domestic satellite TV industry was controlled by a big cable company and a monopoly telephone giant. It was a typically Canadian outcome.

Today, the Canadian satellite TV market is an embarrassment compared with the dynamic satellite-cable rivalry in the United States. In late 1998 DirecTV was juggernauting past the 4-million subscriber threshold — a bigger subscriber base than most big U.S. cable companies. DirecTV was so popular, in fact, that it could actually influence the creative process in Hollywood movie-making. For example, as part of an exclusive pay-per-view marketing deal with Warner Bros., DirecTV sponsored a contest that offered the winner a part in a *Lethal Weapon* movie. The lucky winner, Kelly McNight from Missouri, appeared in the film as a photographer chasing down the movie's star, Mel Gibson.

EchoStar, another major U.S. satellite television operator, boasted about 2 million subscribers in late 1998. EchoStar was building its subscriber base by offering ethnic and foreign-language channels that appealed to immigrant populations in the United States — a marketing strategy that DirecTV has since copied. PrimeStar, the cable-owned DTH system, also counted about 2 million subscribers, but its service was sputtering because it wasn't digital and depended on medium-power satellites. Also, about 2 million American households, mainly in remote areas, subscribed to satellite TV services using backyard C-band dishes. In total, more than 10 million American homes subscribed to satellite TV at the end of 1998.

In Canada, the story was quite different. In early 1999 DirecTV counted some 250,000 grey-market subscribers. ExpressVu and StarChoice were trailing behind with about 200,000 subscribers each. Given that about 500,000 Canadian households were still pulling down U.S. television signals with big C-band dishes, Canada's two officially authorized DTH satellite companies were small-scale upstarts compared with their U.S.

rivals. More important, ExpressVu and StarChoice had made no significant competitive dent in the dominance of Canadian cable TV companies, which counted some 8 million subscribers — most paying monthly bills to Rogers, Shaw, and Vidéotron, which together control two thirds of the Canadian market. True, Rogers lost 6,600 cable subscribers in 1998. But the main target market for ExpressVu and StarChoice was the so-called low-hanging fruit — rural households beyond cable's reach.

ExpressVu president Michael Neuman remained optimistic that his company would make rapid gains on cable, especially after the launch of Telesat's $400-million high-powered DBS bird in 1999. ExpressVu has seventeen of the DBS bird's transponders, which cost $4.8 million each plus a monthly lease charge of $150,000 per transponder.

"The Canadian satellite TV market will probably plateau at about 2 million subscribers," said Neuman. "We will have about 1.5 million of those. That's a good business."

If ownership of a satellite TV company by a big phone monopoly is hardly a triumph of public policy, at least Bell Canada has an incentive to offer competition to cable TV. It is possible, indeed likely, that Bell Canada will offer its telephone subscribers a "bundled" package of phone and satellite TV — putting ExpressVu and telephone service on the same monthly bill. The presence of Shaw in the satellite TV business, on the other hand, is frankly astonishing.

"This is a very powerful combination," said Jim Shaw Jr. when announcing his takeover of StarChoice. Brian Neill, StarChoice chairman and one of the New Brunswickers who sold out to Shaw, added: "This alliance is great news for Canadians. Our team is now stronger and able to offer the most comprehensive, high-quality DTH service available to Canadians."

In truth, the StarChoice-Shaw merger was a bad deal for Canadians. And the corporate fusion was a "powerful combination" only in that it further consolidated Shaw's market power in the Canadian broadcasting industry. Shaw, the second-biggest Canadian cable company, has been pursuing an aggressive acquisition strategy aimed at maximizing the benefits of vertical and horizontal integration. Basing its business model on John Malone's TCI cable empire, the two main prongs of the Shaw strategy are, first, buy up lots of programming interests and, second, get into the satellite business as a wholesale supplier of TV signals to small cable companies. Shaw has succeeded remarkably on both counts. In programming, Shaw has stakes in YTV, Treehouse TV, The Comedy Network, Teletoon, and Country Music Television. And in satellite distribution, not only does Shaw control StarChoice, but it has bought control of Cancom through its purchase of WIC. In short, Shaw has vertically integrated cable and content and cornered the Canadian market in TV signal distribution via satellite — thus reducing risks and minimizing competitive threats to its core cable TV business.

In business, the Shaws are known for their indifference to the Queensberry rules. They talk tough and play rough — a style that doubtless plays well in their western home base. When Michael Neuman went out to Alberta to promote ExpressVu, Jim Shaw Jr. dismissed the suave, youthful Neuman with characteristic gruffness.

"Basically, what we're dealing with, with Michael Neuman, is big hat, no cattle, and he wants to start ranching," snorted Shaw.

That scoffing putdown might have evoked a chuckle from the locals reading the remark in the Calgary newspapers — that is, if they didn't know that Jim Shaw Jr. himself was hardly a cattle rancher. Though the younger Shaw looked like a truck driver and cussed like a sailor, he was no cowboy. In fact, he came from a wealthy business family from that place so beloved in Alberta — Ontario.

It would require a highly developed capacity for self-delusion to argue that Shaw's acquisitive drive into programming and satellite TV is in the public interest. In fact, Shaw's takeover of StarChoice represents a return to the original CRTC-sanctioned design of cable-friendly satellite TV. It is difficult to believe that Shaw would ever use StarChoice as a vehicle to compete aggressively with other big cable TV companies like Rogers. If Shaw were to do so, it would almost certainly provoke an internal war within the cable industry, which is working together on many joint projects like vision.com and the @Home high-speed Internet service.

At the end of 1998 Shaw-controlled Cancom took control of StarChoice as a housekeeping measure. As it happens, Ted Rogers is a minority shareholder in Cancom. Thus, StarChoice is now jointly controlled by Canada's two biggest cable companies, Shaw and Rogers.

In the United States, the federal regulator has aggressively attempted to drive cable interests out of the satellite TV business due to their negative impact on competition. In early 1998 the FCC initiated an investigation into the role of U.S. cable interests in the satellite TV business via PrimeStar. Shortly afterwards, the U.S. Department of Justice launched an anti-trust suit against PrimeStar, which was seeking to enhance its service by buying a DBS orbital slot from MCI and News Corp. for an estimated $1.1 billion. That deal evidently was the consummation of secret talks between Rupert Murdoch and TCI's John Malone, who were eager to bury the hatchet after a number of disputes about Murdoch's programming access to Malone's cable wires. By bringing Murdoch into PrimeStar as a 30-percent non-voting partner, PrimeStar's cable owners were effectively neutralizing the competitive threat of Murdoch, who they feared might deploy his satellite slot to compete against cable TV in the United States.

When the U.S. Department of Justice got wind of the deal, its reaction was unequivocal: PrimeStar would not be allowed to go ahead unless its cable owners divested their interests in the company.

"Rather than compete, the cable companies decided to merge," declared Joel Klein, U.S. assistant attorney general for anti-trust. Klein, perhaps the most famous trustbuster in Washington, called the cable industry "one of the most durable and powerful monopolies in this country" and stated that the PrimeStar deal would lead to higher monthly cable rates for Americans. Consumer advocates praised Klein's tough stance.

"This transaction would have been catastrophic for competition," said Gene Kimmelman, director of Consumers Union's Washington office. "They would have had a stranglehold on video competition."

DirecTV and EchoStar were, needless to say, delighted that U.S. anti-trust authorities were taking action against their cable-owned satellite TV rival. "It is not in the public interest to give the single piece of real estate in space — the one that is most capable of fostering effective competition to cable — to the largest cable and content cartel in the world," said EchoStar chairman Charlie Ergen.

In late 1998 Rupert Murdoch was poised to take control of PrimeStar in a buyout of its cable owners and launch the service as an American version of his BSkyB service in Britain. But the deal fell through at the last minute. While Murdoch regrouped to plan another strategy to compete with cable as a U.S.-based satellite broadcaster, anti-trust authorities finally drove big-cable interests out of DBS satellite TV. Threats from the U.S. Department of Justice, combined with PrimeStar's inability to move to a high-powered DBS bird, finally forced the company to call it quits. In November 1998 PrimeStar was on the verge of collapse and contemplating selling off its assets to DirecTV. The only other possible course of action for PrimeStar was to continue offering a dying medium-powered service that was doomed to fail in the marketplace.

In Canada, where the broadcasting market is much more concentrated in fewer hands, not a single utterance could be heard from the CRTC on the same issue. If the U.S. example were followed, both Shaw and Rogers would be forced to divest their interests in StarChoice. Yet there has been no regulatory inquiry into Shaw's cross-ownership interests in StarChoice. The Competition Bureau, too, has been silent. Not even consumer advocacy groups have spoken up on the matter. Such bureaucratic pusillanimity can only be interpreted as the institutional expression of a deep-seated cultural deference to monopoly power. Canadians have much to learn from their American neighbours.

In the final analysis, Joel Bell was proven right about the pragmatic virtue of harnessing cross-border satellite systems. But it was too late, at least for Power DirecTV. Power Corp., a global conglomerate with little patience for the noisy, incestuous world of Canadian broadcasting regulation, had quietly walked away from its deal with DirecTV, leaving the domestic satellite TV market for the cable and phone industries to dispute.

For Joel Bell, the bitter lesson from the satellite TV saga was as old as the Bible. You are never a prophet in your own land.

CHAPTER 3

Convergence, Divergence
The Information Superhighway

WHILE NORTH AMERICAN CABLE BARONS WERE DESPERATELY FIGHTING off the "death stars" threat from satellite TV, they were also engaged in another bitter war whose weapons were similarly an arsenal of techno-hype and marketing hyperbole. In the race towards technological "convergence," however, the cable tycoons were facing an even more formidable competitor: the giant telephone companies. And if the high-stakes contest to capture the attention of couch potatoes was not for the faint of heart, building the "Information Superhighway" was an even more daunting project.

Technological convergence and the Information Superhighway are, in fact, different expressions of the same ambition. Convergence, generally speaking, describes the technological connection between commercial applications and personal behaviour — the TV set used as a telephone or personal computer, for example. In business, the frenzy of cross-sectoral mergers and acquisitions in broadcasting, telecommunications, and publishing is the corporate expression of convergence.

The Information Superhighway, on the other hand, is the infrastructure that makes possible the connection between technology and personal behaviour, just as motorways make possible travel by automobile. In that respect, the Information Superhighway derives its inspiration from broader social, economic, and political goals. It's for this reason that the Information Superhighway has tremendous appeal as a winning political issue. Indeed, in the early 1990s political leaders and policy makers were quick to seize on the Information Superhighway as a high-tech metaphor to promote their lofty designs and visions. They would quickly learn, however, that — like the 500-channel universe — the Information Superhighway was a long and tortuous road cluttered with vexing obstacles and complicated by unexpected detours.

From the White House to Your House

When John Malone made his 500-channel-universe declaration in late 1992, Bill Clinton and Al Gore had just won the U.S. presidential election but hadn't yet moved into the White House. The Clinton-Gore team had run successfully on a platform stressing competition in the marketplace. It was somewhat ironic that their Republican adversaries, usually staunch defenders of free enterprise, were notoriously tight with the entrenched monopoly interests of the American cable and telephone industries. The Democrats, consequently, did not regard big cable and local telephone lobbies as their natural allies. As Al Gore's senatorial tirades against John Malone and the "Cable Cosa Nostra" amply demonstrated, the Democrats and the cable industry were, if anything, political enemies.

The Democrats therefore sought financial support and political backing in other quarters, notably in Hollywood and Silicon Valley. Bill Clinton enjoyed strong Hollywood connections through his friend and campaign adviser, Mickey Kantor, a longtime Tinseltown lawyer who would be rewarded with a spot in the Clinton cabinet. Al Gore, for his part, had opened up a political pipeline between the White House and the software billionaires farther north along the California coast.

The arrival of the Clinton-Gore tandem on the American political scene marked a revival of U.S. federal industrial policy. The Clinton-Gore White House understood the powerful links between U.S. foreign policy and the global fortunes of Hollywood and Silicon Valley. In the early 1990s this alliance had weakened, largely because Ronald Reagan and the Republicans steadfastly rejected industrial policy as a symptom of the pervasive pessimism about America.

Throughout the 1980s foreign policy experts had talked about U.S. "declinism" to describe the prevailing gloom. The voices of declinism were articulate — from David Halberstam's *The Reckoning* to Steven Schlosstein's *The End of the American Century* — though they had their contradictors in "traditionalists" like Henry Nau, who wrote *The Myth of America's Decline* in 1990. The declinists pointed out that U.S. share of world manufacturing output had dropped from 33 percent in 1950 to only 23 percent in the 1980s. As early as the 1960s foreign competitors had hammered U.S. shipbuilding and apparel industries; in the 1970s consumer electronics, steel, and automobiles joined the list of vulnerable U.S. commercial sectors. In the 1980s foreign competitors began making aggressive forays into industries that had previously been regarded as invincible U.S. strongholds — particularly semiconductors, computers, and the media and entertainment industries.

If the declinists were right, the figure of Ronald Reagan provided a powerful irony. It was on the watch of a former Hollywood actor that a massive sell-off of the U.S. entertainment industry to foreign interests had occurred. Sony's takeover of Columbia Pictures, while a catastrophic corporate manoeuvre, was particularly controversial. If *Time* and *Newsweek* covers were an accurate reflection of the public mood, the Japanese assault on Hollywood convinced Middle America that the perpetrators of Pearl Harbor were now buying the "soul" of the country. Also, while the break-up of AT&T into one long-distance company and several regional "Baby Bells" undoubtedly helped liberalize the U.S. telecom market, it also flung open the door to overseas hardware manufacturers. Reagan left the White House just in time to avoid the economic downturn that would destroy the chances of his successor, George Bush, winning a second term in 1992. There could be no doubt that, after the collapse of the Soviet Union, the United States was the world's only superpower. Still, in the early 1990s, the hard realities of massive job losses throughout the United States had turned public opinion against the Republicans.

Bill Clinton shrewdly read the public mood in America in 1992. As the Democrats' presidential candidate, Clinton embraced a new political discourse in favour of public-private partnerships in order to promote job creation and reaffirm American pre-eminence around the world. The link between American "soft" and "hard" power was, of course, nothing new. Hollywood and the White House had long been close allies. But the explosion of information technologies gave Clinton a fresh theme to convey the same message. Communications technologies — perfect vehicles for economic growth, quality-of-life social policy, and military strategy — became one of the main planks of the Clinton-Gore electoral platform.

In early 1992 Clinton outlined his technological vision in a speech at Philadelphia's prestigious Wharton School. He did not neglect to note that Wharton counted among its alumni some of the more notorious apostles — including dealmaker Donald Trump and convicted Wall Street junk-bond dealer Michael Milken — of the greed-is-good frenzy of the 1980s. Clinton denounced the quick-buck culture and called on the new crop of Wharton graduates to share his vision of an America pursuing high-minded public goals as part of a "New Economy." The building of a national communications infrastructure — or Information Superhighway — was the centrepiece of Clinton's vision.

Declared candidate Clinton in April 1992,

> In the new economy, infrastructure means information as well as
> transportation. More than half the U.S. workforce is employed in
> information-intensive industries, yet we have no national strategy
> to create a national information network. Just as the Interstate
> Highway System in the 1950s spurred two decades of economic
> growth, we need a door-to-door fiber optics system by the year 2015
> to link every home, every lab, every classroom, and every business
> in America.

Clinton was particularly alarmed by the U.S. decline in the strategic
computer industry. He noted that the world market share of U.S. computer
companies had dropped from 81 percent in 1983 to 61 percent in 1989,
and that the U.S. computer industry was increasingly dependent on foreign
components for its products.

"For many people, the U.S. computer industry symbolizes U.S. technological pre-eminence," said Clinton. "Advances in computers and software have driven major changes in virtually every other sector of the
economy and are also critical to national defence."

Clinton's reference to U.S. national defence underscored the strategic
link between American business strength and U.S. political power. American geopolitical strategy had long been dependent on U.S. domination of
the global communications industries. The notion of "Hollywood imperialism" — profoundly resented in countries like France — illustrated this
linkage and its effects. The construction of the U.S. Interstate Highway
System in the 1950s had also been motivated largely by strategic military
considerations. While new highways undoubtedly improved the American
way of life, they were built primarily to facilitate domestic military transportation at the height of the Cold War.

Clinton's information infrastructure project traced its origins back to
the Pentagon's Cold War strategies. The Internet was a Pentagon invention
originally known as ARPANET (the first part of the acronym borrowed from
the U.S. Department of Defense's Advanced Research Projects Agency).
The Pentagon built a communications system whose decentralized design
ensured that, if one piece of the network were damaged or destroyed by
Soviet bombs, the command system could still function.

When the Cold War was defused following the collapse of the Soviet
Union in the late 1980s, the United States remained determined to assert its
role as global leader in the New World Order. But the American preoccupation with military domination shifted towards concerns about commercial

advantages, cultural influence, and corporate espionage. Thus a new lexicon of geopolitical buzz-words was coined for the Information Age — "cyberpolitik," "infosphere," "soft power," and "electronic sovereignty." [1]

Once installed in the White House, Clinton delegated responsibility for all aspects of U.S. communications policy to Al Gore. Gore was a perfect candidate for the job. His father, Senator Albert Gore Sr., had been the prime mover behind the government-financed Interstate Highway System. When Gore *fils* was elected to the Senate two decades later, he established a solid reputation for sponsoring important legislation in the communications sector, including the 1992 Information Infrastructure and Technology Act. In the White House, Gore seized on the Information Superhighway as a way of carrying forward his father's legacy as one of America's political builders of a high-minded infrastructure project.

The Information Superhighway was hardly an original idea. As far back as 1909, AT&T advertised its Bell System telephone lines as a "highway of communication." A half-century later, the upstart cable TV industry trumpeted its wiring of America as a great social project. In 1968 broadcasting pioneer Fred Friendly headed a New York City task force that identified cable TV as a tremendous opportunity for urban development in the United States. The task force recommended that New York be wired up with two-way cable systems offering a combination of video and telecommunications services. Cable TV also became associated with the emergence of a "New Rural Society" in the United States: the entire country, not just the densely populated cities, could be hooked up to the same broadcasting system, thanks to coaxial cables. In the same spirit, Ralph Lee Smith predicted in his 1972 book, *The Wired Nation,* that cable TV would unleash a "revolution in communications" by offering a "single, unified system of electronic communication."

In the early 1990s virtually nobody was against the construction of an Information Superhighway. True, some technophobes grumbled that electronic highways were bound to make life impossibly complex and inhuman. Charles Kuralt, the American broadcaster from CBS News, groused on the air: "Thanks to the Interstate Highway System, it's possible to travel across the country without seeing anything. I wonder if the Information Superhighway will offer a corollary — a dulling impact on our cerebral cortex." Still, most were tremendously excited by the prospect of an Information Superhighway. The main question was financial: who was going to foot the bill to get the thing built?

Al Gore was, as noted, sentimentally attached to the precedent of his father's Interstate Highway System, which had been government-driven and publicly financed. With that in mind, Gore questioned whether the private sector alone would make the necessary investments to ensure that all Americans enjoyed the benefits of the coming wired world. He believed that the U.S. government should play a major role in the construction of the Information Superhighway. But Gore's public-sector vision met with hostility from major industry interests even before he moved into the White House. During the final stages of the Clinton transition-team discussions in Little Rock, Arkansas, in mid-December 1992, Gore attended an economic summit meeting of powerful business leaders and top Clinton advisers. At that meeting, Robert Allen, chairman of AT&T, asserted that the Information Superhighway was too important to the economic strength of America to be left to the government. Gore argued that, on the contrary, government involvement was necessary to ensure that schools, libraries, and hospitals were not bypassed by the Information Superhighway. In the end, Allen's view prevailed.

Following this setback, Gore was obliged to tone down references to his father's Interstate Highway System when announcing the White House's "National Information Infrastructure" initiative. Gore's script instead made lofty comparisons with the private-sector thrust behind the nineteenth-century telegraph system. Thus, the Clinton-Gore industrial policy in the communications sector was effectively aborted even before the new Administration took office.

Gore was a team player, and he understood the political limitations of the vice-presidency. He swallowed his pride and concentrated on providing competent leadership for the White House's infrastructure project. The Information Superhighway policy, announced on September 15, 1993, was based on a few key principles: encouraging private investment, promoting competition, providing open communications networks, ensuring universal service so there would be no information "haves" and "have nots," and putting in place flexible legislative and regulatory regimes. To complement the work of the National Telecommunications and Information Administration (NTIA), the White House created a special Information Infrastructure Task Force, which was mandated to produce a report within two years.

Gore launched his infrastructure initiative with a speech at the National Press Club in Washington on December 21, 1993. He stuck to the official White House script for the most part, but could not resist evoking his father's legacy — though he carefully avoided the issue of public versus private financing.

"It used to be that nations were more or less successful in their competition with other nations depending upon the kind of transportation infrastructure they had," declared Gore. "Nations with deep-water ports did better than nations unable to exploit the technology of ocean transportation. After World War II, when tens of millions of American families bought automobiles, we found our network of two-lane highways completely inadequate. We built a network of interstate highways, and that contributed enormously to our economic dominance around the world. Today, commerce rolls not just on asphalt highways but along information highways. And tens of millions of American families and businesses now use computers and find that the two-lane information pathways built for telephone service are no longer adequate."

In private, Gore remained skeptical about the commitment of business interests to achieving public-interest goals such as universal service. In particular, Gore suspected that cable and telephone companies would eschew open competition and content themselves with cream-skimming only the most lucrative markets — a commercial practice called "electronic red-lining." The cable and telephone industries were concerned, for their part, that Gore might want to regulate — or worse, tax — the Information Superhighway. Gore indeed had spoken publicly about establishing "rules of the road," which led big industry interests to characterize him in the media as a "highway cop." As a pre-emptive strike against Gore's inclination towards government supervision, major industry interests — cable operators, telephone companies, computer makers, Hollywood studios — formed a lobby group called the Council of Competitiveness. In December 1993 the group published a report, *Unlocking the National Information Infrastructure*, which called on the White House to refrain from regulating the electronic highway.

"Just as the nation is poised to deliver a seamless web of communications and information products and services," the report stated, "we find ourselves stymied by a tangled web of regulations and public policies. . . . Excessive government regulation could put a roadblock on the Information Superhighway."

On January 11, 1994, Gore was in Los Angeles at UCLA's Royce Hall to attend a "Superhighway Summit" sponsored by the Academy of Television Arts and Sciences. As keynote speaker, the vice-president chose the occasion to announce the White House's legislative program for the Information Superhighway. In the audience were some of the most powerful figures in the global entertainment industries, all awaiting a positive signal from the White House. That morning, John Malone had participated in a panel debate billed as "Couch Potato 2000: The Shape of Tomorrow's TV," moderated by TV talk-show personality Dick Cavett. Other participants included America Online chairman and CEO Stephen Case, Hollywood mogul Barry Diller, Silicon Valley billionaire Larry Ellison, and Richard

Notebaert, chairman and CEO of the Chicago-based Baby Bell phone company, Ameritech. Also present were Disney CEO Michael Eisner, News Corp. boss Rupert Murdoch, Time Warner chairman Gerald Levin, and Ray Smith, chairman of Bell Atlantic.

Reminding the audience that the federal government had built the U.S. Interstate Highway System, Gore added: "Today we have a different dream for a different kind of superhighway — an Information Superhighway that can save lives, create jobs, and give every American, young and old, the chance for the best education available to anyone, anywhere." Gore challenged the audience of media moguls to connect all American classrooms, libraries, and hospitals before the end of the century.

"Our nation can and must meet this challenge," he said. "The best way to do so is by working together. Just as communications industries are moving to the unified information marketplace of the future, so must we move from the traditional adversarial relationship between business and government to a more productive relationship based on consensus. We must build a new model of public-private co-operation that, if properly pursued, can obviate many governmental mandates. But make no mistake about it — one way or another, we will meet this goal."

Gore had also come to Los Angeles to offer the big industry players assurances that he was no "highway cop."

"This Administration will not let existing regulatory structures impede or distort the evolution of the communications industry," said Gore. "In the information marketplace of the future, we will obtain our goals of investment, competition, and open access only if regulation matches the marketplace. That requires a flexible, adaptable regulatory regime that encourages the widespread provision of broadband, interactive digital services."

In February 1995 Gore was in Brussels spearheading a U.S. vision of the Global Information Infrastructure at a G-7 summit conference on the "Information Society." If job creation and universal service were key preoccupations of the Clinton-Gore infrastructure policy at home, international competitiveness was its main concern abroad. Gore believed the United States would, as an extension of its status as sole global superpower, build and control much of the global information infrastructure. In particular, the White House was determined to prevent the European Union from taking the lead in this area of strategic importance to the United States's global economic, cultural, and military power. His public statements, however, remained tactfully diplomatic.

"Just as human beings once dreamed of steamships, railroads, and superhighways, we now dream of the global information infrastructure that can lead to a global information society," declared Gore in Brussels.

A Canadian delegation was present at the Brussels summit, but the United States hardly viewed its compliant neighbour to the north with the same suspicion it reserved for the potential global rival of a united Europe. True, Canada's vital interests, especially in areas such as cultural policy, did not always correspond to those of the United States. But the White House knew that Ottawa had little stomach for aggressively pursuing a "third option" policy in the media, entertainment, and communications industries. In fact, Canada's infrastructure policy would borrow liberally from Al Gore's Information Superhighway initiative.

Canada's Information Highway: Back to the Future

In early 1994 when Jean Chrétien's newly elected Liberal government announced its Information Highway policy, themes like technological "convergence" and "electronic highways" had been kicking around Ottawa for decades.

As in satellite broadcasting, the heady days of Pierre Trudeau's first government in the late 1960s produced a great burst of forward-looking thought about the potential of new communications technologies. When Ottawa created the Department of Communications in 1968, one of the first projects initiated by the new ministry was a national communications infrastructure. DOC's first minister, Eric Kierans, declared that "communications has moved to the forefront of our national affairs" and was "the nerve system of a nation in search of itself." As a formal acknowledgement of the "information explosion," the federal government would later establish a Canadian Computer/Communications Agency to build a national computer network.

In 1971 Kierans's deputy minister, Allan Gotlieb, set up a "Telecommission" of experts to develop a national communications strategy. Its five-member executive committee comprised some of the most distinguished figures in Ottawa: Gotlieb himself, one of the Trudeau era's most brilliant minds, as the Telecommission's chairman; Pierre Juneau, the powerful chairman of the CRTC; Paul Tellier, assistant secretary to the Cabinet; de Montigny Marchand, the Telecommission's research director, and later deputy minister; and Gilles Bergeron, assistant deputy minister at DOC. Others involved in the Telecommission included Jean-Claude Delorme from Telesat Canada; Henry Hindley, a veteran civil servant who had written the 1968 Broadcasting Act; André Fortier, assistant undersecretary of state; lawyer John Hylton from the CRTC; and Richard Gwyn, the political journalist who at the time was Eric Kierans's executive assistant.

The Telecommission produced more than forty studies, but the pièce de résistance was a report called *Instant World*. Among other things, *Instant World* called for the merging of broadcasting and telecom regulation, and predicted the switch from passive one-way television to interactive TV. "More and more people," the report said, "will be able to decide for themselves what they want to watch and when they want to watch it and, still more importantly, to originate programs themselves." *Instant World*'s authors also foresaw the marriage of computers and communications, and warned that most of the strategic planning for the coming technological fusion was being undertaken in the United States. [2]

The vision articulated in *Instant World* could have been dusted off and republished, word for word, twenty years later in the early 1990s — and have won praise as a stimulating, forward-looking document. Retrospectively, *Instant World* demonstrated how little had been accomplished in the intervening two decades. Indeed, when visionary discourse about information infrastructures finally re-emerged in the early 1990s, it was old wine in new bottles. In late 1993 the incoming Liberal government asked long-time cultural mandarin Bernard Ostry to furnish advice on an Information Highway strategy for Canada. Ostry observed that the policy interest in electronic highways was in fact "a new beginning for an old idea." He produced a report titled *The Electronic Connection,* which observed that Canada's techno-optimism of the late 1960s had sadly fizzled, largely due to bureaucratic obstacles in Ottawa, while the Americans were racing ahead on the electronic highway. [3]

Jean Chrétien's electoral triumph in October 1993 — ending nearly a decade of Tory rule under Brian Mulroney — came in the wake of the Clinton-Gore victory in the United States. The Liberals therefore were able to take inspiration from the policy excitement created by Al Gore's Information Superhighway. The newly elected Liberal government used the Speech from the Throne in early 1994 as the occasion to announce Canada's "Information Highway." In a characteristically Canadian gesture, the Ottawa policy dropped the over-reaching American prefix "super."

Chrétien made an excellent choice for his industry minister responsible for Information Highway policy: John Manley, an MP from Ottawa first elected in 1988. Manley, a lawyer who was said to be hoping for the justice portfolio, quickly proved to be a solid, fair, and competent minister in charge of the massive Department of Industry. Normally he would have shared responsibility for Information Highway issues with his Cabinet colleague, Michel Dupuy, who as heritage minister was in charge of broadcasting. But Dupuy immediately stumbled and seemed incapable of making tough decisions, leaving Manley with most of the heavy lifting on major issues. In the Chrétien government, Manley was Al Gore's counterpart.

Like the U.S. policy, Canada's Information Highway project evoked the economic benefits of efficient communications infrastructure — growth, job creation, and the provision of universal service at reasonable cost to consumers. But whereas the Gore policy combined domestic job creation with U.S. industrial power, the Canadian policy placed greater emphasis on one objective that, for obvious reasons, was totally absent from the U.S. initiative: cultural sovereignty. Predictably, the language of technological nationalism found its way into the Canadian policy alongside themes like globalization and international competitiveness. Canada's Information Highway initiative thus was a conceptual grab bag, the result of the customary tradeoffs between bureaucratic fiefdoms in Ottawa and their major industry clients.

When the Information Highway policy was announced, very little progress had been made on issues related to "convergence." The CRTC, it is true, had introduced competition in the long-distance telephone market after much resistance from Bell Canada and the other regional phone monopolies. But bringing competition to the local, residential side of the business — in both telephony and cable TV — proved a much more difficult task. In September 1992 a special committee made up of big industry interests had submitted to the government a report entitled *Convergence: Competition and Co-operation*. It was, to no one's surprise, a resounding endorsement of the status quo.

In 1994 the new government seemed determined to move more expeditiously, if only to gain some political momentum with a tremendously appealing policy fashion. In April, John Manley announced the creation of an Information Highway Advisory Council — or IHAC — modelled largely on the White House's Information Infrastructure Task Force. The IHAC was split into five working groups that reflected a mixture of social and industrial objectives: access and social impacts; competition and job creation; learning and training; research and development; and Canadian content and culture.

"Together, as Canadians, we must decide how we want to develop and use the Information Highway for the economic, cultural, and social advantage of all Canadians," declared Manley.

In many respects, Canada's Information Highway initiative should have been much less complicated than the U.S. infrastructure project. Although sixty-year-old communications legislation in the United States badly needed revision, a new Broadcasting Act had been passed in Canada in

1991 and a new Telecommunications Act in 1993. Also, in the United States responsibility for communications was shared among the White House, Congress, the FCC, and state and local authorities. This bureaucratic overlap rendered political oversight and regulatory supervision horrendously complex. In Canada, by contrast, the federal government had almost exclusive jurisdiction over broadcasting and telecommunications.

The main difficulty in Canada was not legislative or inter-jurisdictional. It was rather the incessant bureaucratic rivalry and infighting within the former Department of Communications, which Kim Campbell's short-lived Tory government in 1993 had split in two — creating separate industry and heritage departments. Industry Canada, with its pro-market culture, was in charge of telecom policy; and Heritage Canada, with its entrenched biases in favour of cultural protectionism, was responsible for broadcasting and arts policy. To make matters more complicated, both ministries often resented the CRTC, which as regulator had a history of filling policy vacuums with its quasi-judicial decision-making powers. In short, the Ottawa policy system was bureaucratically fragmented and ideologically divided on many communications issues. As a result, a coherent approach was vexingly difficult to achieve.

Given this bureaucratic rivalry, the IHAC might have functioned as a valuable non-governmental brain trust. On the surface, its creation gave the impression that the government was showing openness to "consultation" with expert opinion before taking official action. But the IHAC, composed mainly of the CEOs of major industry players, contained too many conflicting commercial interests. Members of the Canadian cultural community criticized the IHAC for its overwhelming majority of big business interests. But even without culture vultures at the table, the IHAC's deliberations rapidly degenerated into a series of blue-ribbon bitching sessions. Moreover, its meetings were not held in public, and the closed-door nature of its proceedings made the IHAC appear more like an industry round table than a public consultation process.

Faced with these criticisms, the government called on the CRTC to hold public hearings on convergence and report back with its findings. The CRTC was naturally delighted by the gesture. Its hand was tremendously strengthened by the government's decision to shift the consultative process to the regulator. By producing a report on convergence, the CRTC could impose its own agenda on the government's policy framework for the coming battles between cable TV and the telephone companies. At a minimum, the CRTC could seize on the convergence issue to redeem itself following its own battles with the Liberal government over satellite TV.

Wired to Win? Cable TV vs. Telephony

When cable TV first emerged in the late 1940s, no one could have imagined that the handful of small-time entrepreneurs running coaxial wires into a few thousand North American homes were laying the foundation for the Information Superhighway of the twenty-first century.

Cable TV's original ambitions were in fact exceedingly modest: to offer local television signals to households located in mountainous areas where over-the-air antenna reception was poor or impossible. At the outset, cable was a rinky-dink business that attracted mainly small entrepreneurs, many of them owners of television stores looking for a marketing scheme to sell more TV sets. The very first U.S. cable system was installed in 1948 in Mahanoy City, Pennsylvania, a small town northwest of Philadelphia that did not have off-air television because it was surrounded by the Poconos. John Walson, a lineman for Pennsylvania Power & Light Company, built a seventy-foot antenna atop New Boston Mountain and wired up Mahanoy households willing to pay $2 a month for local signals. That same year, Ed Parsons built a cable system in Astoria, Oregon, so local residents could receive Seattle television signals that were blocked by mountains. In the early days of cable, the signals received were those of local broadcasters only — hence cable TV's first name, Community Antenna TV, or "CATV."

Cable TV didn't arrive in Canada until the early 1950s. One of the first Canadian systems was built in Montreal by Rediffusion Ltd., a British company that had constructed single-channel cable systems in the United Kingdom following the Second World War. By late 1952 Rediffusion Ltd. had run 200 miles of cable past 58,000 homes in Montreal. But the system quickly ran into problems because Montrealers could already receive free off-air signals from the CBC's French and English networks as well as American channels. Cable TV had more success in London, Ontario, where in 1951 two backyard electronics buffs, Ed Jarmain and Harry Anderson, built their first cable system following a visit to Pottsville, Pennsylvania, to inspect an upstart cable system there. By the end of the 1950s, *TV Digest* magazine reported that about 200 cable TV systems in Canada were serving some 135,000 homes — a modest beginning compared with what was to come.

In the United States, cable companies soon began using microwave technology to pick up broadcast signals from hundreds of miles away and retransmit them to their local subscribers. By the late 1950s access to these "distant signals" had changed the focus of cable's role from transmitting only local broadcast signals to providing subscribers with new programming choices. While the importation of distant signals into local markets gave cable TV a tremendous commercial boost, local television stations resented the intrusion of these signals as a competitive threat to their revenues. In response to these concerns, the FCC asserted its jurisdiction over cable TV and placed restrictions on distant signals.

In Canada, cable companies quickly realized that an easy way to attract subscribers was to pull down U.S. television signals via microwave — some called it a condoned form of theft — and offer these American television channels to Canadians who lived too far from the border to pick up clear U.S. signals with rooftop antennas. Established over-the-air broadcasters like CBC and CTV stations, who felt threatened by cable TV for the same reason as local broadcasters in the United States, promptly cast cable as a Trojan Horse menace to the entire Canadian broadcasting system. They were not altogether wrong. Cable TV's arrival in Canada was a free-for-all that paid little heed to cherished national issues like cultural sovereignty. In fact, in the early 1960s the American television network, CBS, actually owned a cable TV business in Vancouver. In those days, just about anybody could get into cable TV, including many quick-buck schemers of highly dubious entrepreneurial virtue.

"The guys who got into cable in the early days were just plain lucky," says a well-known Canadian broadcasting executive. "They were just like the guys who were lucky enough to have bought property near Highway 401. The land's value went from $10,000 to $10 million. That's what happened to the early cable guys. The only problem was that, when they suddenly got rich, they thought that they must be smart, too."

If a nuisance to Canadian cultural nationalists, the early growth of cable TV actually suffered terribly at the hands of the big telephone monopolies. Cable entrepreneurs depended on phone companies for pole and duct space to run their coaxial wires down streets and into homes, and the phone companies exploited this dependence mercilessly. Bell Canada, for example, insisted on building all cable systems on its telephone turf, charging cable companies 80 percent of the building costs while retaining ownership of the cables attached to Bell-owned poles. Moreover, Bell charged an additional monthly fee for cable companies to lease portions of their own coaxial capacity, while preventing cable from offering any services that competed with phone companies. Bell Canada was also known to cut the wires of cable systems upon expiration of their contractual agreements. In the United States, the phone companies not only used pole attachments and conduits to exercise market power over cable companies, but actually began offering "channel service," carrying programming distributed by cable companies. This provoked the FCC to impose, in

1970, a video restriction and cross-ownership ban on the telephone industry.

Despite the opportunistic behaviour of the phone monopolies, cable TV grew rapidly throughout the 1960s and 1970s. In Canada, the newly created CRTC realized that Ottawa had made a strategic error in allowing cable TV to develop largely unregulated, outside the Canadian broadcasting system. In the late 1960s the CRTC resolutely opposed the widespread implantation of cable TV and, fearing that American channels would soon overwhelm the Canadian broadcasting landscape, attempted to stop cable's practice of importing U.S. signals into the country via microwave. The CRTC described the growth of cable TV in Canada as "the most serious threat to Canadian broadcasting" since the invasion of U.S. radio in the 1920s, adding that cable TV "could disrupt the Canadian broadcasting system within a few years." [4]

"The CRTC could go only so far with that approach," recalls Phil Lind, who has been Ted Rogers's trusted lieutenant and regulatory point man in Ottawa for more than two decades. "You have to balance it against what people will tolerate. The CRTC can hold it off as much as it can. But when the dam breaks, they have to retreat." [5]

Lind was right. By the early 1970s the CRTC had been forced to back down in the face of a public outcry, mainly from angry Canadian television viewers in cities like Calgary, Edmonton, and Halifax who were too far from the U.S. border to receive American television signals directly off-air. They wanted access to American television just like the geographically fortunate folk in Toronto and Windsor, Ontario — and they demanded it as their right. Facing these pressures, the CRTC reversed its initial hostile view of cable TV and attempted to "integrate" cable into the Canadian broadcasting system. Thus, the CRTC made an extraordinary pirouette by switching its approach from resistance to cable TV to active *promotion* of the cable industry. Thus began a long, fruitful process of regulatory "capture" by Canada's major cable barons.

There was still some resistance to cable's rapid growth in Canada's provinces, however. In Saskatchewan, for example, the NDP government of Allan Blakeney announced that cable TV in the province would be run as a Crown corporation. That idea was eventually dropped, but non-profit cable TV co-operatives began sprouting up with plans to offer television service using the wires of the government-owned phone company, SaskTel. When a number of Saskatchewan cable co-operatives attempted to obtain licences from the CRTC, the cable lobby enlisted the services of lawyer Jerry Grafstein, who was not only an investor in Toronto cable systems but was also a close adviser of Prime Minister Pierre Trudeau. Grafstein, who today is a Liberal senator, argued against the co-operatives by evoking the dangers of government control. In 1976 the CRTC rejected cable licence applications associated with SaskTel, though it awarded licences to co-ops in Regina and North Battleford. The decision was considered a victory for the private cable TV industry.

The cable industry would fight — and even lose — other battles against co-operatives in the future. But in the mid-1970s the industry was taking off, and with its tremendous growth came both market power and political clout. The industry was also rapidly consolidating, especially the cable empire of Ted Rogers, who was characterized by his enemies as a "people eater." His takeover of Canadian Cablesystems, which counted 465,000 sub-scribers in the Toronto area, was a particularly acrimonious affair in which Rogers was portrayed as a scheming, villainous character. Yet the CRTC rubber-stamped Rogers's machinations, just as it would do two decades later when he made his unfriendly takeover bid for Maclean Hunter.

By 1980 cable companies were so commercially powerful that they virtually became the market. This produced an ironic reversal of fortune: no longer cable TV's public castigator, the CRTC now depended on cable to implement its broadcasting decisions.

In 1983 Francis Fox, the Liberal communications minister, announced Ottawa's new broadcasting policy designating cable as the broadcasting system's chosen gatekeeper.

"In short, cable will become a major vehicle for delivering the 'information revolution' to Canadian homes," declared Fox. "Canadian high techno-logy industries should benefit directly as cable operators retool their plants to carry these new programming and non-programming services. Cable companies will require significant amounts of new capital equipment — such as earth stations, scrambling and descrambling equipment and a vari-ety of other types of cable hardware. Canadian high technology industries manufacture much of this equipment and jobs should be created as a result."

The CRTC had, in fact, already been captured by Canada's cable tycoons. Now Ottawa's honeymoon with the cable TV industry was offi-cially consummated by the federal government's explicit policy.

In the United States, the growth of cable TV did not provoke the same concerns about cultural sovereignty that it did in Canada. The main issue in the United States was cable's financial threat to established broadcasting interests — especially after the cable network Home Box Office appeared in the early 1970s. In 1972 the FCC overhauled its cable TV rules and obliged cable systems to carry the signals of all local broadcasters — the so-called must-carry rule — which guaranteed a prominent place for local off-air broadcasters on cable TV lineups. In Canada, the CRTC imposed a similar rule, thus ensuring that the CBC, CTV, and other local television signals were included in all basic cable packages. At the same time, the CRTC guaranteed the major U.S. networks a similarly prominent place in Canadian cable packages with its "3 + 1" rule, which allowed cable companies to include ABC, NBC, CBS, and PBS as part of their basic service. Thus the American networks enjoyed a privileged place at the Canadian broadcasting system's table of honour along with the CBC and CTV.

The 1980s marked the triumph of the cable industry in North America. President Ronald Reagan appointed fellow free-market conservative Mark Fowler as head of the FCC. Fowler described the FCC as a "New Deal dinosaur," and stated publicly that he believed the regulator should be abolished. In 1984 Congress passed a Cable Act, which deregulated monthly cable rates and thus gave the American cable industry the financial power to expand and consolidate. In the period from 1980 to 1990 the number of "cable" channels increased nearly threefold, from twenty-eight to seventy-four, and by the end of the decade nearly 53 million U.S. households subscribed to cable. In Canada, some 7 million households subscribed to cable, or roughly 70 percent of television homes.

There can be little doubt that North American cable TV companies, thanks chiefly to their market dominance, were well positioned to exploit the possibilities of the Information Superhighway. Cable companies had run wires into virtually every household in both Canada and the United States — a tremendous accomplishment for two countries with huge land masses. The telephone industry could easily match this achievement, but cable companies had one major advantage over phone companies: coaxial cables. Cable's broadband coaxial wires have much more capacity than the telephone industry's "twisted pair" copper wires, and thus can pump much more video, audio, and data into homes than narrowband telephone infrastructure.

Still, the telephone companies enjoyed a strategic advantage that the cable industry lacked: two-way, interactive networks. The early cable pioneers, showing little foresight, had built out their plant along the "tree-and-branch" configuration, allowing for TV signals to be "pushed" one way towards households, much like off-air broadcast signals. It was impossible, however, for people to send back information upstream or communicate with one another via cable systems. Some major cable companies, it is true, had begun experimenting with interactive TV to test consumer demand. Warner Cable, for example, launched its QUBE service in Columbus, Ohio, in the late 1970s. Warner (later Time Warner) offered thirty channels — an embarrassment of riches at the time — with an upstream capability that allowed subscribers to request programs among ten pay TV channels. By 1979 the QUBE system was installed in 38,000 homes in Columbus. The experiment produced some interesting results, but consumers showed a remarkable lack of interest in its interactive, talk-back features. Neither did services like electronic banking and home shopping generate much enthusiasm. In the late 1980s Warner pulled the plug. A few years later, Time Warner launched a similar interactive TV experiment in Orlando, Florida, where selected households enjoyed a "full-service network," including home shopping, movies on demand, and video games. Again, the early results were mixed.

Unlike cable, the phone system was by definition designed for interactive communication — a perfect configuration for the Information Superhighway. But U.S. phone companies were barred by regulation — and by the 1984 Cable Act — from offering television service in their own franchise areas. In Canada, a cable-telephone cross-ownership ban was also in force: in 1968 the CRTC had ruled that it would not be in the public interest for telephone companies to offer television service. The same year, Parliament revised Bell Canada's charter to prohibit the phone company from applying for a cable TV licence.

The telephone companies nonetheless experimented with interactive TV trials, though these tests failed to produce more promising results than those conducted by the cable industry. In 1983, for example, AT&T teamed up with the Knight-Ridder publishing group to launch a switched, two-way service called "Viewtron," which provided mainly videotext. A market test in southern Florida produced abysmal results, and in 1986 AT&T walked away $50 million poorer.

Rochester Telephone Corporation learned the same lesson in upstate New York. In 1995 the telephone company (now called Frontier Corp.) abandoned an experimental video-on-demand (VOD) service offering one hundred digital videos to a selected cluster of homes. Despite the convenience of VOD, couch potatoes continued getting up, putting on their shoes, and going out to rent movies from local video stores. Clearly, the problem was not the chosen technology, but consumer habits.

Overall, by the early 1990s the telephone industry was better prepared for commercial competition on the Information Superhighway than the cable industry. For one thing, the telephone industry had actual exposure to the rigours of competition, at least in long-distance service. In the United States, Judge Harold Greene's famous court decision had broken up the AT&T telephone leviathan in the early 1980s, resulting in the creation of one long-distance giant and seven regional Baby Bells. Also, in the late

1980s the U.S. Baby Bells were making forays into the cable business in foreign markets, especially Europe, where little competition and promising growth prospects gave them a relatively risk-free learning experience in cable TV. At the same time, their local monopoly strongholds in the home U.S. market remained safe — to the intense frustration of long-distance companies like AT&T, MCI, and Sprint — from any competitive incursions. Most important, the U.S. telephone companies appeared more determined to compete against cable in video delivery than vice versa.

Bell Atlantic, the largest Baby Bell, was particularly determined to move into video delivery and challenged the constitutionality of the telephone-cable cross-ownership ban before a U.S. District Court in Alexandria, Virginia. The FCC, which had initiated the cross-ownership ban, meanwhile had changed its thinking on the issue. In August 1992 the FCC recommended to Congress that the 1984 Cable Act be amended to allow telephone companies to provide video programming directly to subscribers in their own service areas. The FCC argued that the risk of anti-competitive behaviour by phone companies had been attenuated by the enormous growth of the cable industry.

On August 24, 1993, the U.S. District Court struck down the section of the Cable Act barring the Baby Bells from creating, owning, and packaging programming within their own service areas. The court agreed that the cross-ownership ban violated the plaintiff's First Amendment rights of free expression. The so-called Big Bang court ruling promised to blow open rigid monopoly doors to full convergence competition between U.S. telephone and cable companies.

And, once again, Canada would find itself playing catch-up.

Mega-Merger Mania on the Information Highway

It was not Bell Atlantic, but another Baby Bell, that was first to take advantage of the Big Bang court victory. US West, the monopoly phone company throughout much of the western United States, announced in May 1993 that it would pay $2.5 billion to acquire a 25-percent piece of Time Warner Entertainment.

The deal included a 50-percent stake in Time Warner's cable TV operations and smaller holdings in the Warner Bros. movie studio and in the all-movie channel, Home Box Office. About $1 billion of the Baby Bell's investment would be dedicated to upgrading Time Warner's cable systems so they could offer subscribers a fully digital, interactive network. US West also kicked in $1.5 billion to help Time Warner shed some of its gigantic debt. The deal gave the Baby Bell access to a vast supply of content —

everything from Bugs Bunny and Batman to CNN and *Time* magazine — owned by a media conglomerate that also counted more than 7 million cable subscribers in large urban centres, including New York City.

US West's bold move in 1993 was the first sign that the previously separate worlds of cable TV and local phone monopolies were about to converge. It also threatened to break up the alliance of Baby Bells. By buying in to Time Warner's cable operations, notably in New York, US West was launching an assault on the turf of NYNEX, its sister Baby Bell. The deal also gave Time Warner access, via US West's telephone wires, to the same households in the western United States served by John Malone's TCI coaxial cables — and thus threatened to trigger a battle within the U.S. cable industry. Dark clouds of war were now hanging low over the American media landscape.

Bell Atlantic, the Big Bang victor in the courts, followed up on the US West–Time Warner deal with a promise to spend $15 billion to run fibre-optic lines to households in its home territory throughout the eastern United States. There was even speculation that Bell Atlantic planned to buy a Hollywood studio to compete with other integrated cable-content empires like Time Warner and Viacom-Paramount.

"It doesn't sound sexy," said Ray Smith, Bell Atlantic's jovial CEO, "but I concluded that our communication network had to deliver every kind of information that was ever going to exist, including video, or we'd be at a disadvantage."

By late 1993 "convergence" was the buzz-word electrifying the boardrooms of virtually every major U.S. media company. It was difficult to keep up with the frenzy of major takeovers and mergers between Baby Bells, big cable companies, and content conglomerates. To cite only a few of the major deals that year: MCI, the long-distance phone giant, announced a $4.3-billion deal giving U.K.-based British Telecom 20 percent of its stock; the giant Baby Bell, NYNEX, invested $1.2 billion in Viacom; and the Canadian telecom giant, Bell Canada Enterprises, parent of Bell Canada, paid $400 million (U.S.) for a 30-percent stake in the U.S. cable group, Jones Intercable.

Amidst this flurry of merger activity, John Malone was plotting his own megadeal. Shortly after his highly publicized 500-channel-universe speech in late 1992, Malone had announced that TCI would spend $1.9 billion over four years to build fibre-optic networks in thirty-seven states, giving more than 9 million TCI customers access to thousands — not hundreds, but *thousands* — of channels ranging from video games and pay-per-view sports to on-demand weather reports and telephone service.

At first blush, Malone's fibre-optic Information Superhighway plans seemed like a strategic foray into the $100-billion local phone market. It could not have come at a worse time for the regional Baby Bells. Following the breakup of AT&T, the Baby Bells had begun feeling heat from Wall Street to increase profits and dividends. This left little cushion for downturns or capital reinvestment — a strategic error at the very moment when the phone companies needed to install digital switches, lay fibre, and devote more energies to marketing. One way around this challenge, of course, was simply to buy a cable giant outright.

Ray Smith understood that Baby Bells had to move quickly into cable TV and content. And John Malone had both. TCI not only counted some 14 million cable households, but also controlled a vast array of programming assets through its Liberty Media subsidiary — Discovery Channel, Family Channel, Home Shopping Network, Court TV, American Movie Classics, and Black Entertainment Television, as well as a stable of regional sports channels. Malone, for his part, realized that TCI was collapsing under the weight of an enormous debt load, and that if satellite TV started taking a significant bite out of his cash flow he wouldn't be able to finance construction of his fibre-optic network.

It was in this context that Malone and Smith, realizing their mutual self-interest, started talking in the summer of 1993.

After a few months of intense courtship, Bell Atlantic and TCI announced their impending corporate marriage in New York City on October 13, 1993. According to the terms of the deal, Bell Atlantic would pay a colossal $33 billion — $10 billion to lighten TCI's debt, the rest for stock — to take control of Malone's company. Smith would become chairman; Malone would be vice-chairman. It was the second-biggest corporate takeover in U.S. history — narrowly edged out by the 1989 takeover of RJR Nabisco Inc. by Kohlberg, Kravis, Roberts & Company.

"We have three information instruments in the home — the telephone, the television, and the computer — and they are all coming together to communication on a full-service network," said Smith. "The time is not far off when you will be answering your television set and watching your telephone."

The day of their corporate nuptial announcement, Malone was fielding media questions on his cell phone as his limousine whisked him and Ray Smith through Manhattan's rush-hour traffic. As a "cable guy," Malone was still searching for a humorous way to rationalize his surrender to a Bell phone company.

"I got up this morning and looked in the mirror and I noticed that my head was taking on a vague bell shape," he quipped to a journalist.

Smith seized on the Information Superhighway metaphor by comparing the newly merged company with transportation infrastructure. "We are providing the flexibility of the automobile," he said. "You will be able to go anywhere you want, when you want."

A few weeks later, Smith announced an ambitious, five-year Information Superhighway plan. Bell Atlantic and TCI would spend $15 billion to deliver interactive services — including movies on demand and home shopping — to about 9 million American households. Smith also said Bell Atlantic, thanks to its merger with TCI, planned to get into the U.S. long-distance telephone market.

The Bell Atlantic–TCI deal immediately received the FCC's regulatory benediction. James Quello, acting FCC chairman at the time, stated: "The Bell Atlantic purchase of TCI represents the most momentous deal at this time of huge mergers, acquisitions, and joint ventures. It has the constructive potential to expedite the initiation of competitive super electronic highways with multi-channel, multi-faceted service to the public."

The media pundits joined the spontaneous outburst of enthusiasm. The *New York Times* observed: "If the synergy is real, the biggest winner to emerge from the planned acquisition of TCI by Bell Atlantic Corp. may be the American consumer." In the corporate world, too, the reaction was unquestioning. Larry Ellison, chairman of Oracle Corp., predicted: "This is going to forever change our lives and rearrange the whole computer and the communications industries."

In Canada, Ted Rogers undoubtedly was closely following the U.S. mega-media excitement. Rogers had made an incursion into the U.S. cable market in the 1980s. But having sold his U.S. cable assets to buy the Unitel long-distance phone company, Rogers was excluded from the American mega-merger action. He would now have to focus his me-too ambitions on Canada.

In early February 1994 Rogers announced his $3.1-billion hostile takeover bid on the century-old Maclean Hunter publishing empire. Maclean Hunter was a highly coveted corporate prize: it owned a vast stable of publishing assets, including *Maclean's* magazine and the *Sun* newspaper chain. The Rogers–Maclean Hunter deal was impressive by any yardstick. Applying the customary ten-to-one ratio when making U.S.-Canada comparisons, the Rogers takeover was of the same magnitude as the $33-billion (U.S.) TCI–Bell Atlantic merger — except that Ted Rogers, unlike Malone, was the happy predator, not the junior player in the deal.

The Canadian media were as uncritical of the Rogers–Maclean Hunter deal as the U.S. media had been of the Bell Atlantic–TCI merger. Ted

Rogers shrewdly exploited the pervasive big-is-beautiful climate, though he did not neglect to send the requisite cultural flag-waving message to Ottawa. In front of the CRTC, Rogers promised that the merged Rogers and Maclean Hunter would create a national media giant that would "tell Canadian stories and paint national dreams." His patriotic slogans were highly seductive: Rogers owned cable wires to people's homes, and Maclean Hunter would give the company strategic "synergies" by providing Rogers with valuable content to pump through its coaxial wires.

"If Canadians are going to maintain distinctive vehicles for the expression of their own ideas and interests, while at the same time facing enormous competition from foreign information sources," said Rogers in May 1994, "we need policies that support and develop materials unique to the Canadian market. . . . In the race to build the Information Highway of the future and to develop the services that these highways will deliver, Canada is starting well behind."

Rogers put less emphasis on the real reason for his acquisitive interest in Maclean Hunter: its cable assets in southern Ontario. By clustering Rogers and Maclean Hunter cable systems, Rogers would gain control of roughly 70 percent of cabled households in Canada's richest and most populous province. Indeed, the deal was about cable clustering, not Canadian culture.

The Rogers takeover bid nonetheless struck the right chord in Canada at a time of tremendous excitement about digital technology, media megadeals, and the coming onslaught of "globalization." The deal also fit perfectly into the policy agenda in Ottawa following the announcement of the government's Information Highway initiative. In the new climate favouring competitive advantages, concerns about corporate concentration were quietly swept aside. Canadian policy was now focused on harnessing the advantages of strategic "synergies," "critical mass," and "national champions" in the global market.

Canada's big phone companies must have been incensed by Rogers's brilliant media coup. After all, it was Stentor — the alliance of Canadian telephone companies — that had taken the lead on the Information Highway theme. In October 1993 Stentor had outlined its Information Highway vision for Canada as a "network of networks" integrating small facilities with the main infrastructure owned by the phone companies. Four months later, Stentor was not about to let Ted Rogers steal its thunder on a symbolically charged and politically appealing issue like the Information Superhighway.

On April 5, 1994 — only two months after Rogers's takeover bid — Stentor added concrete plans and dollar investments to its Information

Highway vision: the $10-billion "Beacon Initiative" aimed at upgrading and digitizing Canada's copper phone wires so that telephone companies could carry TV signals, data, and multimedia services to Canadian homes and schools. Specifically, the Beacon Initiative included five main components: first, about $8 billion towards network upgrades; second, $500 million for regional infrastructure investments; third, the creation of a new multimedia company to produce content for the Info Highway; fourth, a venture capital fund to finance the development of new services for the Info Highway; and fifth, investments to ensure that schools, hospitals, and cultural institutions benefitted from interactive and multimedia services.

With the Beacon Initiative, the Canadian phone companies recaptured the high ground on the Information Highway. The general feeling in Ottawa was that the government looked more favourably upon phone companies like Bell Canada than on mercurial cable barons like Ted Rogers. For one thing, the Bell Canada family of companies was Canada's biggest private-sector employer, thanks mainly to decades of monopoly rents extracted from Canadian consumers to finance global expansion and R&D divisions like Bell-owned Northern Telecom. Also, politically, Bell Canada had long enjoyed special access to key decision makers within the Ottawa power structure. It was often commented that the bureaucratic interests of the Department of Industry and the financial interests of Bell Canada were so intertwined that the latter had become a de facto policy adjunct of the former. The cable industry, to be sure, enjoyed tremendous clout at the CRTC and its top executives were no slouches in the lobbying game. But cable barons like Ted Rogers were well known as Tories — a decided disadvantage after the Liberals returned to power in 1993. True, Rogers and his cable confrères wasted little time in dumping or sidelining most of their Tory-friendly lobbyists in Ottawa and replacing them with Liberal-connected insiders.

Still, in the race for control of Canada's Information Highway it appeared that — like the U.S. Baby Bells — Bell Canada and the Stentor phone companies were on the inside track.

Breakdown on the Info Highway On-Ramp

Ted Rogers had the right idea when he made his takeover bid for Maclean Hunter, but it came at the wrong time. In fact, the timing could not have been worse. Only a few weeks later, the U.S. media-merger mania was in rapid meltdown.

Black Tuesday came on February 22, 1994. In Washington, the FCC ordered U.S. cable companies to roll back their monthly rates by 7 percent

— the second forced rate cut in six months. John Malone was outraged, claiming the ruling would reduce TCI's annual cash flow by $300 million (U.S.). He also feared the regulatory ruling would spoil his still unconsummated courtship with Bell Atlantic.

Malone was right. On February 23 — the day after the FCC decision — Ray Smith abruptly called off the merger. Bell Atlantic's engineers had already been warning Smith that TCI's physical plant was hopelessly antiquated. The deal-breaker, however, was the news of the rate rollback. Jilted, Malone was left alone with his crushing debt and a regulatory nightmare.

The TCI–Bell Atlantic breakup sent a chill through the U.S. media industries. Suddenly, "convergence" and "mega" were dropped from the industry lexicon. It was business as usual — back to the old game of drawing monopoly rents and defending turf. Instead of plotting strategies aimed at delivering multimedia video to households, the Baby Bells turned their efforts towards complicated legal manoeuvres to block the long-distance giants from entering their local markets. The cable companies, for their part, retreated to their television franchise where their main priority became minimizing the competitive threat from satellite TV. Soon, the "500-channel universe" and "Information Superhighway" were evoked almost as a double-barrelled hoax.

Al Gore had been right. Leaving the construction of the Information Superhighway solely to the vagaries of market forces was a risky business. Perhaps firmer guidance from government was necessary. But it was too late. The policy-making machinery was already in motion. As the media-merger madness of 1993–94 continued to melt down, U.S. legislators were putting the finishing touches on the new Telecommunications Act. In Ottawa, bureaucrats were busy drafting convergence and Information Highway policies. The policy makers were like Orpheus leaving Hades: there was no looking back without serious consequences.

In February 1996 the U.S. Telecommunications Act was passed after a frenetic lobbying circus that was excessive even by Washington standards. The general thrust of the law aimed to facilitate two types of competition. First, competition within sectors — that is, between local and long-distance telephone companies, and between cable TV and satellite broadcasting companies. Second, competition among previously distinct sectors — between telephone and cable TV companies in voice traffic and video delivery. The problem, however, was that the major U.S. media players were already on the defensive in early 1996 after the alarming spectacle of media mega-merger meltdown. Consequently, the pro-competitive law found few enthusiasts. The Telecom Act, moreover, was a legislative dog's breakfast cluttered with myriad "safeguards" that gave big industry players an arsenal of legal pretexts to block competition in the courts. The law was a classic example of legislative gridlock. Its immediate effect was not to promote competition, but to cement monopolies.

It didn't take Congress long to realize that it had goofed, especially when voters continued complaining about high cable rates. Congressmen blamed the "Washington legal-industrial complex" which, they claimed, had descended like jackals on the legislation during the drafting phase. As usual, many lawyers had gotten rich while consumers saw no benefits. The law was even dubbed the "Communications Attorneys and Consultants Full-Employment Act."

The situation in Canada was slightly more complicated, but fundamentally no different. Once his mega-merger ambitions received regulatory approval, Ted Rogers promptly reneged on his bold promise to create a Canadian multimedia giant to "tell Canadian stories and paint Canadian dreams." As Ian Morrison, head of the Friends of Canadian Broadcasting, put it: "The only story he has told is his own." It was a predictable tale of monopoly consolidation, asset stripping, and, saddest of all, the dismantling of one of Canada's proudest companies, Maclean Hunter.

Maclean Hunter admittedly had been a stodgy old company with a "widow and orphan" shareholder base, and consequently was vulnerable to the predation of cable monopolists like Ted Rogers. Within three years of the takeover, Rogers had broken up the venerable company and sold off its disparate parts to finance the purchase. Rogers held on to Maclean Hunter's coveted Canadian cable assets, of course, and he kept control of its publishing empire, notably the influential magazines *Maclean's* and *Canadian Business*. But the rest was sold. Rogers dumped Maclean Hunter's U.S. cable assets for $1.7 billion. Its Ontario and Maritimes radio stations were sold for $42.3 million. The North American and European publishing operations fetched $355 million. Maclean Hunter's Calgary CTV Television affiliate was liquidated, as ordered by the CRTC, for $84 million. The company's 63-percent controlling stake in Sun Media was sold for $259 million. The sale of its 87.3-percent interest in a U.S.-based business-forms maker, Transkrit Corp., raised $103 million, and the Davis + Henderson cheque printer went for $53.5 million. When the fire sale was completed, Rogers had dismembered Maclean Hunter and sold many of its assets for a total of about $2.9 billion.

A few years after the deal it was difficult to find anyone — aside from Rogers executives — who had anything positive to say about the Maclean Hunter dismemberment. The deal didn't even add value to parent company

Rogers Communications Inc. In the three years from the day the takeover was announced, Rogers stock plummeted from $22.50 to $9.15 per share. It seemed that everybody — including Ted Rogers himself — had been duped by the multimedia and mega-merger hype.

"Clearly, the takeover was negative," said Ron Osborne, who was president of Maclean Hunter when the CRTC approved the deal. "How could it be anything but negative for Maclean Hunter? Maclean Hunter does not exist and most of the pieces have been scattered and there's precious little left of what one would recognize as Maclean Hunter." [6]

In Ottawa, meanwhile, the government finally issued its Information Highway policy on May 23, 1996. After many months of bumbling and bickering by the IHAC, which had produced a tepid report in September 1995, the government had not advanced much beyond general principles and vague policy jargon. John Manley, the industry minister, even confessed that his Information Highway policy was a "work in progress." In a press release, Manley's department said: "The federal government put an 'At Work' sign up on the Information Highway today."

The IHAC continued to lurch forward into a second phase of protracted deliberations, but this time the council met much more discreetly — and, it was hoped, was less likely to cause political embarrassment. [7]

Ottawa's "Convergence Policy" was measurably more promising. The CRTC had dutifully conducted public hearings and, in May 1995, submitted its findings to the government in a report called *Competition and Culture on Canada's Information Highway: Managing the Realities of Transition.* In the report, the CRTC finally deferred, after years of regulatory resistance, to the government's desideratum in favour of market competition:

> In the opinion of some, the old era was characterized by limited
> spectrum, over-regulation, and concepts of public service that may
> have encouraged attitudes of paternalism on the part of legislators,
> regulators, or even broadcasters. It is now clear that any such atti-
> tudes cannot survive in an era of virtually unlimited capacity,
> where control is increasingly in the hands of consumers.

That statement was characteristic of the CRTC's general tone in the report. The regulator distanced itself from self-criticism, shared the blame for past errors with others, and indulged in predictable rhetoric about consumer empowerment. Overall, however, the report was a stimulating discussion paper. But the CRTC's general approach to key issues was decidedly cautious. The CRTC seemed to accept grudgingly the government's policy in favour of competition, but remained unmistakably suspicious of market forces. In sum, the CRTC pushed no envelopes, shifted no para-digms, kicked down no doors.

The government issued its Convergence Policy on August 6, 1996 — six months after passage of the U.S. Telecom Act. On the surface, the Convergence Policy seemed to merit more praise than the Information Highway non-policy. The Convergence Policy dealt with three broad areas: interconnection and interoperability of network facilities; competition in facilities, products, and services; and continued support for Canadian content. But when the regulatory jargon was stripped away, the policy's chief preoccupation was the setting of rules for competition between cable and telephone companies. A government statement accompanying the Convergence Policy declared: "Getting cable service from your phone company or telephone services from the local cable company moved closer to reality today."

The media and industry pundits, who had tracked the mega-merger meltdown, were rather less optimistic. The *Globe and Mail* reacted to the Convergence Policy with two headlines: "Markets yawn at telco stocks" and "Cable TV, phone links still far off." The *Globe* reported: "Canadians hoping to buy cable television from their telephone companies or phone service from their cable operator will have to wait a while — probably into the next millennium." Bill Stanley, president of Fundy Cable in New Brunswick, confirmed this view: "We have not seen a business model to lead us to be interested in the residential telephone business." Industry expert Eamon Hoey commented: "If you listen to the voice in the woods, the telephone companies are now becoming less enamoured of being in the cable busi-ness than they were four years ago, and the cable entities are now having a real close look at the telephone business and slowly concluding that it's not as simple as they thought it was. These policy statements may open up markets, but that doesn't mean there will be market entrants."

By mid-1996 the cable industry was starting to pay the price for its 500-channel-universe and Information Superhighway hype. Unlike local phone monopolies, cable companies had a consumer-friendly competitor in satel-lite TV. It didn't help matters that DirecTV had signed up 2 million U.S. subscribers and some 250,000 grey-market subscribers in Canada. Indeed, satellite TV was the most successful consumer product launch ever. Contrary to widespread predictions, the cost of a pizza-sized dish and receiver unit wasn't an obstacle to satellite TV's market ramp-up. Many Americans and Canadians were taking considerable delight in the sole act of unplugging from their local cable companies.

By the end of 1996 cable TV stocks had taken a beating. They were among the worst-performing stock categories in Standard & Poor's 500. The meltdown on Wall Street was particularly disastrous for cable tycoons suffocated by massive debt — notably John Malone and Ted Rogers. In October 1996 *Business Week* magazine published a cover story titled: "Cable TV: The Looming Crisis."

By Christmas John Malone had finally decided it was time to say uncle. TCI's stock price was trading in the basement at only $13 (U.S.) a share — a far cry from the $35 per share that Bell Atlantic had almost paid for TCI three years earlier. With $15 billion in debts, Malone was caught in a desperate financial straitjacket. His hyper-confident promises and digital visions had failed to divert attention from the profound crisis into which he and the cable industry had sunk.

On January 2, 1997, Malone made a now-famous public confession to the *Wall Street Journal* in a front-page interview under the headline "Malone says TCI push into phones, Internet isn't working for now." The newspaper said of America's most powerful cable tycoon: "His widely hailed vision for TCI's future as a multimedia powerhouse, straddling television, telephones and the Internet isn't working. It was too ambitious, over-hyped, and impossible to carry out on schedule." Malone admitted he'd been terribly wrong about the 500-channel universe and the Information Superhighway, and took full blame for his over-optimism.

"We were just chasing too many rabbits at the same time," confessed Malone. "My job now is to prick the bubble. Let's get real."[8]

Malone's public mea culpa hit the American cable industry like an atom bomb. The industry's leader had been bluffing for years. The 500-channel universe was a hoax. In the fallout, Wall Street grew even more skittish about the value of cable stocks.

In late January 1997 Ted Rogers rushed down to New York City to assure Wall Street that, despite John Malone's public self-flagellation three weeks earlier, the Canadian cable industry was different. Speaking to a group of Wall Street junk-bond dealers, Rogers insisted that satellite TV in Canada did not present the same threat to cable cash flows that it did in the United States.

"Much of the success of the American satellite TV services has been based on the fact that they offer a differentiated product from cable companies or other broadcasters — this is particularly true with sports," said Rogers, adding that satellite TV in Canada did not enjoy the same commercial advantages.

Rogers had good reason to pander to New York junk-bond dealers. Michael Milken, the junk-bond high-flyer turned convicted felon, had channelled some $10 billion (U.S.) in high-yield securities to the major U.S. cable giants. Ted Rogers also got a piece of the action: Milken once raised $300 million for Rogers Communications Inc. in only thirty minutes.

In mid-February Rogers was back on Wall Street to meet with media investment analysts. This time he announced that, by the end of 1997, he would spend $400 million to upgrade and digitize his Canadian cable systems. By the end of 1998, he said, all 2.2 million of his Canadian subscribers would have interactive, digital capability in their homes. It was an extraordinary bluff that proved Rogers had learned a thing or two from John Malone. His strategy seemed to be: when in doubt, up the ante. [9]

This time, however, Rogers's digital bravado failed to seduce Wall Street. Investment analysts knew that, like Malone, Rogers was in a desperate financial situation. His company was carrying more than $5 billion in debt — even heavier, on a per-subscriber basis, than Malone's $15-billion (U.S.) debt. Rogers moreover had taken a $67.8-million restructuring charge in late 1996, and the company was going through the nasty business of making painful layoffs in programming, customer service, and engineering — the three areas where, ironically, Rogers needed the most help. In early 1997 Rogers announced yet another monthly rate increase for his cable subscribers — a 4-percent hike, or 82 cents a month. Blinkered by short-termism, Rogers was desperately attempting to cut costs and improve revenues through job losses and customer price hikes. This result was precisely the opposite of what Ottawa had envisaged in its Information Highway policy.

Some believed the problem at Rogers Communications Inc. was Ted Rogers himself. Though only in his mid-sixties, the workaholic Rogers was not in the pink of condition. He had a reputation as an obsessive, hands-on micro-manager. Top Rogers executives were rushing for the exit doors, and former colleagues were stating publicly that Rogers "isn't in touch with reality." [10]

The media and financial markets were crying out for Rogers's early retirement — though he had no obvious successor. In early 1997 one industry player stated publicly that, if Ted Rogers died, his extinction would be "good for the stock." Rogers, for his part, insisted that he took tremendous pleasure from running the company he founded, and he wouldn't be retiring before his seventieth birthday — on May 27, 2003. Failing eyesight, a coronary aneurysm, and triple bypass surgery had not slowed him down. Rogers still had a few more fights in him. He publicly railed against the phone companies as "Soviet-style bureaucracies," and denounced ExpressVu as a Bell Canada–subsidized attack on the cable industry.

"I think the phone companies in this country are dedicated to going after us in every way they can," declared Rogers at the Canadian cable industry's annual convention in May 1997.

At that same Toronto event, American TV tycoon Ted Turner delivered a stern warning to his Canadian confrères by comparing the cable industry to Poland in 1939.

"The Germans are on the one side and the Russians are on the other," Turner told his audience of 2,000 Canadian cable executives, adding that cable TV owners should seriously think about capitulating outright if the telephone blitzkrieg proved unstoppable.

"Don't put all your eggs in cable," said Turner. "We may have to sell out to the telephone companies at some point in the future if they give us too much trouble, so we want to maintain good relations with them. So keep their number handy. Do it early rather than late. The people who were in a real bad spot were the ones who sailed the *Titanic*. The ones who toured it while it was still tied to the dock weren't the ones who went down with the ship."

Ted Rogers was hardly battle-ready for a counterattack against the phone giants. Many frankly doubted his navigational skills as the captain of his own corporate ship. Rogers certainly no longer seemed committed to convergence. He had retreated from Unitel, which was now controlled by AT&T. He had even called upon the branding powers of AT&T to help salvage his struggling Cantel cellular phone company. And in May 1998 Rogers sold off for $1 billion his telecom unit, Rogers Telecom, to Calgary-based niche player MetroNet Communications. It was a premium price paid for a small telecom unit with only $56 million in annual revenues. But for MetroNet, Rogers Telecom's 3,000 kilometres of fibre-optic wires connecting 1,200 buildings was a strategic asset for its long-term plan to skim the cream off the lucrative business market in major Canadian cities. For Rogers, who received $600 million in cash and roughly $400 million in non-voting MetroNet shares, the deal provided badly needed cash to help alleviate the company's massive debt. From a business strategy point of view, however, the sale marked Rogers's retreat from the telecom business.

"This is the beginning of a full withdrawal by Ted Rogers from the telecom market," said industry analyst Eamon Hoey. "I think Rogers got the idea when he went to New York earlier this year with the idea of raising more money for yet another telecom venture and was told by financiers, 'Not here.'"

In January 1998 the *Globe and Mail* published an in-depth analysis of the Rogers empire under the headline: "Ted Rogers' Troubled Neighbourhood." The devastating assessment portrayed Rogers as an eccentric media baron losing touch with reality, talking boldly about the future but firmly stuck in the nostalgic past. The *Globe* observed:

> There's talk on the street and inside his company that perhaps an older Mr. Rogers, a renowned visionary of future technologies, is squinting in a world dominated by Microsofts and Intels as he tries to also make his company a major Internet player. Some question the effects on staff morale and recruitment of his micro-managing — from insisting on approving cable channel line-ups across the country to phoning employees at home at all hours.

Rogers himself deflected innuendo about his own managerial idiosyncrasies and rumours about the demoralized corporate culture within the Rogers empire. "Listen," he said, "I am a hands-on operator. When things are going well, you don't see me. When things are not going well, I am very much there. I don't think that is very different from most good CEOs." [11]

His personal eccentricities aside, Rogers was not showing much enthusiasm for the 500-channel universe and the Information Superhighway. There was no sign, for example, of the digital boxes he had been promising for several years to put into the homes of his subscribers. He talked about improving revenues by selling high-speed Internet access, but he seemed to be retreating into his core business of cable TV while hanging on to prestige publishing assets like *Maclean's*. In mid-1998 *Maclean's* published a cover story listing the "100 most important Canadians in history." The honour roll included Ted Rogers's late father, radio pioneer E.S. Rogers. The *Maclean's* editors clearly understood that, as Oscar Wilde once remarked, flattery will get you — everywhere.

Some industry observers thought Rogers, burdened by debt and shunned by bond markets, was actually quite lucky. As Doug Cunningham, an analyst with Walwyn Capital, put it: "Rogers is the most leveraged of all cable companies in Canada and it is very fortunate that the satellite TV companies were two years late getting to market, because that gave it time to rebuild without impact on cash flow."

At the Rogers Communications Inc. annual shareholders' meeting in 1998, Rogers delivered a feisty speech, promising to alleviate the company's debt and pay dividends within five years. He promised that he'd step down as CEO on December 31, 2003, at age seventy, though he would continue to be paid $706,000 annually and to act as a consultant to the company for five more years. After his death, said Rogers, his family would continue to control the company through a trust. Rogers had learned, like many other corporate tycoons, that genes are highly unreliable. He had one son, Edward, and three daughters, but none seemed prepared to run the company their father had founded. They would be rich, but they would not be powerful.

"Mark my words," Rogers told a Canadian Club audience in a speech just before the 1998 annual meeting, "if the Lord allows me to finish my final five years as CEO of the Rogers companies, by then we will be investment grade and paying dividends."

This was an extraordinary commitment from a cable company that had paid only one dividend in its history — in 1979. Rogers, an unrepentant disciple of TCI's "pay interest, not taxes" philosophy, hadn't reported a profit since 1989. But those interest payments were finally catching up with the company: total debt was now $5.6 billion, and servicing it had cost $475 million in 1997.

"I know we have to get the level of debt down," Rogers told shareholders, confessing that his foray into long-distance telephone competition with Unitel was a "disaster" that had cost the company at least $500 million.

This was a very different Ted Rogers from the man who, two years earlier, had stood beside Canada's other major cable barons to announce with great fanfare the creation of vision.com, the cable industry's answer to the Stentor alliance's Beacon Initiative. At that time, Rogers and his fellow cable tycoons promised that 75 percent of Canadians would have access to high-speed cable modems by 1997, and that the entire Canadian population would be served by 1999. Now the first deadline had come and gone, and the cable industry was nowhere near 75-percent penetration in Internet access — the figure wasn't even 0.75 percent.

In 1998 Rogers seemed more concerned about the fortunes of his shareholders than about those of his customers. Indeed, Rogers's customers would have to pay the price of his strategic retreat: there would be no rollout of digital set-top boxes to his 2.2 million cable subscribers until at least the autumn of 1999. The boxes, moreover, would be sold directly to subscribers at retail prices, like VCR machines, so Rogers could move the cost off his books. In short, after nearly a decade of support from the CRTC to upgrade his plant to digital, including generous capital expenditure allowances, Rogers now was openly reneging on promises he had been making for years. The telephone companies could now relax, there would be no cable-built Information Highway — at least not in the short term.

What had gone wrong? Put simply, the major industry players never believed in the Digital Revolution they were hyping. They saw the marketing advantages in the hype, and they kept spinning the story — sometimes as scare tactics to keep their competitors guessing. But they knew it wasn't for real. The appearance of industry confidence was an illusion masking industry crisis — or the Confidence-Crisis Paradox.

The industry foot-dragging and legal stonewalling must have been vexing for the regulators, policy makers, and political leaders who had been swept up in the digital hype. Regulators had worked tirelessly on the thankless task of disentangling all the nettlesome rules on highly technical issues that only regulatory lawyers could possibly find interesting — price caps, interconnection, unbundling, co-location, rate restructuring, and number portability. In Canada, the CRTC opened up the residential market to full competition between cable and the telephone companies by early 1998. The regulator also gave the green light to both Bell Canada and the Alberta phone company, Telus, to offer their subscribers interactive multimedia services on a trial basis for two years. Bell chose two prosperous towns — London, Ontario, and Repentigny, Quebec — and 3,500 homes in each were hooked up to high-speed digital networks. Telus chose suburbs of Calgary and Edmonton for its trial. Both Bell and Telus built out a special network for their convergence trials, using high-capacity fibre-coaxial wires and digital hardware to store and deliver video and data.

While these projects were intended only as trials, the cable lobby — now in defensive turf-protecting mode — bitterly opposed their regulatory approval. Cable lobbyists claimed that Bell and Telus were not merely experimenting with a new technology, but were in fact conducting the initial stages of a full "market launch." The cable industry also argued, unsuccessfully, that the phone companies should not have a competitive headstart. The CRTC dismissed that claim, but showed more concern when Telus abandoned its all-digital market trial and began offering analogue TV channels that merely duplicated channel packages offered by the local cable company, Shaw. Shaw moreover complained that Telus workers were cutting Shaw's coaxial cables when installing new lines into homes for the Alberta phone company's market trial. The CRTC reprimanded Telus for reneging on its commitment to offer only digital multimedia services. And Shaw, no slouch itself when it came to playing hardball with its smaller competitors, won a court injunction ordering Telus to stop tampering with its cable wires. The cable pot was calling the telephone kettle black.

In late June 1998 the CRTC awarded NB Tel, the New Brunswick telephone company, a broadcast licence. It remained uncertain, however, whether major phone companies like Bell Canada, Telus, and BC Tel intended to follow through with their announced plans to upgrade their copper wires using ADSL (asymmetric digital subscriber line) technology, which gives phone wires high-speed capacity. Some believed the phone companies would attempt to deliver video into the local loop via wireless technologies. In late July 1998 Jean Monty, the CEO of Bell Canada Enterprises, seemed to confirm this when he announced that Bell was taking a $392-million write-down related to its experiments in London and Repentigny and withdrawing from its wireline broadband strategy to compete against cable TV.

"We think we are better off using satellites and ExpressVu," admitted Monty.

This was an extraordinary confession. After all the tough talk from telephone executives about spending billions to build a new fibre-coaxial infrastructure, Canada's biggest phone company was now retreating from its ground war with cable. There could be little doubt that Ted Rogers's own travails had something to do with the sudden competitive lethargy of the telephone industry. Indeed, it seemed there was an undeclared truce between the cable and telephone industries on the convergence front.

Given the lacklustre pace of competition between the two titans, perhaps the only hope for effective market competition was from "third force" delivery systems such as local off-air wireless operators. The federal government had issued three wireless licences to companies seeking to compete with cable and the phone companies as "LMCS" (Local Multipoint Communication Service) providers. Also, the CRTC had issued licences to broadcasters seeking to compete with cable TV as "MMDS" (Multipoint Multichannel Distribution System) service providers using local wireless technology. The main advantage of local wireless systems is their low start-up costs, because the infrastructure of antenna nodes on buildings is scaleable and customers pay the rest of the infrastructure costs by buying dishes to capture over-the-air signals from their homes. However, local wireless systems not only need lots of spectrum to compete with incumbents like cable and telephony with a full range of video and data services but they also depend on line-of-sight delivery and thus face physical obstacles such as buildings and trees.

After some delay, the winning wireless applicants launched their services in late 1998, but it is still too early to tell whether they will have a significant competitive impact on cable and telephony. One LMCS firm, MaxLink — headed by Joel Bell — appears to be focusing on premium telecom services like data and teleconferencing. Another company, Connexus, is owned by Vancouver-based broadcaster WIC, which was bought in 1998 by the big Calgary-based cable company, Shaw. In August 1998 both MaxLink and Connexus placed hardware equipment orders worth $850 million.

Two promising MMDS firms are SkyCable, owned by Manitoba's Craig family, and Look TV, which is backed by the deep pockets and long-term vision of telecom superstar Charles Sirois. The Craigs finally won their "wireless cable" licence in December 1995 after being turned down by the CRTC on the preposterous grounds that SkyCable actually planned to compete with cable TV. Look TV, for its part, launched in 1998 as a battle-ready rival to cable TV throughout Ontario and Quebec.

In early 1999, Look TV complained to the CRTC that Shaw, the big cable company, was blocking out infomercials promoting the Look TV service. In an astoundingly arrogant admission of anti-competitive behaviour, Shaw said it had the contractual right to block any advertising that it deemed "injurious" to its commercial relations with its subscribers. The Look TV–Shaw spat offered dismaying proof that, while the cable industry claimed to be pro-competition, it was in fact still behaving like a monopoly bully.

Look TV represents only a piece of a much larger puzzle in Sirois's global game plan. In Canada, Sirois has cleverly exploited the monopoly rents provided by Teleglobe Canada to leverage a series of bold acquisitions and ventures, including the Fido-branded digital mobile telephone and Quebec's Coscient film production studio.

Sirois is undoubtedly one of the most fascinating figures in the Canadian telecom and media industries. From the remote Quebec town of Chicoutimi, while only in his twenties, he turned a modest family paging business with 200 customers into a national operation called National Pagette. In the late 1980s the boyish-looking Sirois befriended Bell Canada executive Jean Monty, who arranged a merger with Sirois's company and Bell Cellular to form Bell Mobility, with Sirois himself, barely thirty years old, as chairman and CEO. In 1992, when Bell Canada made a move to oust the management at Teleglobe Canada, the privatized former Crown corporation in which Bell was a large shareholder, the phone giant installed Sirois as Teleglobe's new president. Labelled as a "Bell Boy," Sirois played his cards shrewdly at the helm of Teleglobe and surprised those who thought he was merely a compliant Bell proxy. By the mid-1990s Sirois owned a piece of Teleglobe himself and had a colossal paper fortune. In 1998 he masterminded a strategic merger between Teleglobe and U.S.-based Excel Communications. The two companies had nearly 5,000 employees and about $5 billion in revenues.

Sirois's frankness, intellectual energy, and affable demeanour have made him a favourite of the media, especially in Quebec, where he is treated as a local hero. He is unquestionably a brilliant visionary, and he has assembled an impressive management team. Still, Sirois has his critics. They claim that, while his spin doctors portray him as a dynamic entrepreneur, he owes everything to Teleglobe's monopoly rents. To his credit, however, Sirois realized that Teleglobe's monopoly would not last forever — it expired in October 1998 — and he shrewdly transformed the company from a "national champion" to a major global telecom player in a highly competitive international market.

"Sirois's game is not a juggling act, it's walking a tightrope," said Iain Grant of the Yankee Group telecom research firm, "and the entire system he's building could fall into the pit." [12]

So far, Sirois has performed a dazzling high-wire act. He has even become a star at the Sun Valley Conference, the annual gathering of global media movers and shakers organized by the powerful New York investment banker Herb Allen. That entrée into the media stratosphere put him into direct contact with Bill Gates, Rupert Murdoch, Michael Eisner, and Edgar Bronfman Jr. Sirois's recent foray into content production with his 20-percent stake in Coscient Group, Canada's second-biggest film producer after Alliance Atlantis, has made many wonder about his plans. Whatever he does, it would be imprudent to bet against Sirois. He could well become Canada's most powerful media mogul.

The most neglected players in the wire wars are public utilities. Some believe that hydro companies, once lazy monopoly providers of electricity, are poised to become major players in communications. They are certainly well positioned to make a strategic foray into the industry, thanks mainly to their installed network of wires running into homes, underground conduits, and rights of way.

In European countries like France, the major utilities are already active in the cable TV and broadcasting industry. The giant French water utility, Compagnie Générale des Eaux, has renamed itself Vivendi, sold off diversified assets in everything from travel agencies to funeral parlours, and has been engaged in a bold strategy of acquisitions of communications and multimedia companies. In November 1998 Vivendi bought U.S.-based software publisher, Cendent Corp., for $800 million (U.S.) through its Havas publishing division. In the United Kingdom in late 1997, a group called United Utilities launched — along with Canada's Nortel — a company called Norweb to make Internet access possible through electrical wires instead of phone or cable connections. Norweb says its "digital power line" technology is a revolutionary breakthrough because it can offer Internet access via power lines at one-third to half the cost of existing phone and cable wireline connections. Norweb appears to be targeting its service at the European market, where cable TV is a much less powerful force, except in Germany and the Benelux countries.

In North America, no hydro utility has yet made a significant foray into the cable or telephone market. In Canada, Ontario's privatization of electricity monopolies could create some market dynamism towards convergence competition, and indeed Ontario Hydro has created a telecom division under the leadership of former Maclean Hunter president Ron Osborne. If utilities manage to exploit the advantages of their infrastructure, access to homes, and billing relationships with customers, they could well prove to be the dark horse champions of the convergence battles.

In the meantime, despite alternative attempts to bring new-entrant market pressures on established incumbents, the video delivery business in North America remains overwhelmingly dominated by cable companies, and the local telephone business remains under the tight monopoly control of the telephone giants. Convergence or divergence, the market belligerence was for most of the 1990s a frustrating technological truce.

Competition or Consolidation?

The trends of the 1990s offer a perfect illustration of the Competition-Consolidation Paradox. The industry thrust towards consolidation has elsewhere been called "*keiretsu*," after the Japanese tradition of cartel-like industry collaboration instead of open-market competition.

In the North American media industries, for most of the 1990s, business rhetoric embraced competition as a desirable market outcome that would stimulate economic growth and job creation, encourage innovation and R&D, and lower prices and offer greater choice for consumers. In reality, however, very few of these goals were achieved. Faced with a choice between the demand-side virtues of *competition* and the supply-side advantages of *consolidation*, the big industry players unequivocally chose the latter. As Frances Caincross put it in her 1997 book *The Death of Distance*:

> Competition does not come easily in communications. The opportunities to restrict access and build monopolies have been greater in communications than in many other businesses. . . . In few other industries in the capitalist world has this level of monopoly been allowed and the spirit of competition so crushed.[13]

For critics, buzz-words like "convergence" and "Information Superhighway" have been hollow slogans concealing a business agenda in favour of deregulation. The policy makers, it would seem, got duped by the hype and over-reaching promises of the cable and telephone lobbies, whose industries were more interested in cream-skimming lucrative business markets than running fibre-optic wires to hospitals, libraries, and schools.

In short, the Information Superhighway has been a great deal for Wall Street and Bay Street, but a bad deal for Main Street. A more charitable view would be that political leaders genuinely believed that lighter-touch regulatory restrictions would foster greater competition, lower prices, service innovations, and consumer choice. And if that hasn't happened in the short term, perhaps some patience is necessary.

Towards the end of the 1990s North American communications companies saw their stock prices soar again, thanks mainly to yet another rash of mergers and acquisitions unleashed by legislative and regulatory relaxations. In March 1998 *Broadcasting & Cable* magazine even asked on its cover: "Are Cable Stocks Too High?" In 1998 media industry mergers and acquisitions were expected to exceed $150 billion (U.S.) — or double the $77.7-billion figure for 1997. It is possible, however, that the devastating financial effects of the "Asian Flu" that began spreading globally in late 1998 could have a significant impact on the media industries over the next few years.[14]

The most aggressive consolidation in the U.S. market has been among the Baby Bells. In late 1997 the door to Baby Bell consolidation was opened when a U.S. appeals court judge ruled as unconstitutional provisions in the 1996 Telecom Act that barred the Baby Bells from the long-distance market until they met various local "open-market" tests. After the 1984 dismantling of AT&T, the seven regional Baby Bells had been created: NYNEX, Bell Atlantic, Ameritech, BellSouth, Southwestern Bell, US West, and Pacific Telesis. At the end of 1998 there were only four left.

Bell Atlantic merged with NYNEX to form a telephone powerhouse along the U.S. eastern seaboard. In July 1998 Bell Atlantic added GTE's long-distance, wireless, and Internet strengths in a $55-billion (U.S.) stock-swap merger. Since GTE was the controlling shareholder in BC Telecom and Quebec Telephone, the merger with Bell Atlantic, besides troubling U.S. competition watchdogs, was considered a major blow to Bell Canada. The deal effectively absorbed two of the Stentor telephone companies into a Baby Bell empire controlling one third of the U.S. market. At the same time, GTE-controlled BC Tel and Alberta's provincial telephone company, Telus, were on their way to the altar in a merger that promised to form a Canadian telco powerhouse in the West. The Stentor consortium soon became a victim of this rapid trend towards industry consolidation and transnational alliances. No one was surprised when, in the fall of 1998, Stentor announced — rather like the Third Republic voting for its own dissolution in a Vichy casino — its own dismantling and effective extinction.

Meanwhile, Texas-based Southwestern Bell Communications (SBC),

the most ambitious and best-performing Baby Bell, provoked a highly publicized controversy with its acquisition of two sister Baby Bells, first Pacific
Telesis and then Ameritech. The merger with Chicago-based Ameritech
gave Southwestern Bell control of 57 million telephone lines in thirteen
U.S. states — or roughly one third of the $100-billion annual local phone
market in the United States. For the regional Bells, consolidation has been
a defensive strategy against incursions onto their turf by long-distance
giants AT&T, MCI, and Sprint.

Some Baby Bells, to be sure, have been getting into the cable TV business, though mainly through buyouts of existing cable assets and the
creation of separate divisions. Colorado-based US West, for example,
bought its way into cable TV to form MediaOne Group, which now ranks
as the third-largest cable empire in the United States — after Time Warner
and John Malone's TCI. After US West's $11.5-billion (U.S.) acquisition
of Continental Cablevision, MediaOne counted nearly 5 million cable
subscribers. To date, MediaOne has been the only Baby Bell that seems
determined to make a business out of bundling cable and telephone service
through the same wire to the home. A counter-example is Bell Canada,
which, in May 1998, after much frustration as a portfolio shareholder in
the U.S. cable business, dumped its stake in Jones Intercable in a $500-
million (U.S.) sale to cable giant Comcast.

If the renewed industry consolidation has been good news for the financial markets, it has been received somewhat less sanguinely in Washington. The SBC-Ameritech merger promptly ran into political turbulence as
congressmen expressed grave concern about consumer interests getting left
out of all the merger excitement. As John McCain, Republican chairman of
the powerful U.S. Senate Commerce Committee, put it: "Companies
consolidate when they cannot compete, and consolidation without competition can hurt consumers." Few could argue, indeed, that consumers were
better off with an oligopoly of a few corporate giants. *Business Week* magazine summed it up in August 1998: the net result of industry consolidation
was "Big Mergers, Bad Service." [15]

Consolidation certainly made a mockery of FCC chairman Reed
Hundt's description of the 1996 Telecom Act as "the biggest global effort to
de-monopolize any industry sector that has ever been mounted." Even as
Hundt imprudently blurted out his naive optimism on the first anniversary
of the Telecom Act's passage, there was already a movement afoot in Washington to remedy some of the mistakes made in drafting the widely criticized
legislation. At the FCC, senior officials were wondering whether they had
made a serious mistake by attempting to "choreograph" competition in a

market where technologies and business strategies were so unpredictable.

In early 1998 Hundt's successor as FCC chairman, William Kennard, made several announcements expressing his dissatisfaction with the unrelenting stranglehold of the cable industry in the broadcasting market. The Telecom Act contained provisions to deregulate monthly cable rates starting on April 1, 1999, and it was no April Fool's joke on consumers. Kennard noted, however, there was still not sufficient competition from satellite TV and, consequently, cable companies continued to exercise too much market power over consumers and competitors. The proof was that monthly cable rates had started to skyrocket again — by 8.5 percent in the year after the passage of the 1996 law. In the decade from 1987 to 1997, monthly cable rates in the United States had increased by 107 percent, compared with 40 percent for the Consumer Price Index. In the same period, the price of a movie ticket had increased by only 15 percent.

Besides the FCC, powerful congressmen were expressing exasperation with cable rates. In late July 1998 Senate majority leader Trent Lott gave the cable industry a "stink bomb" warning before the Senate Commerce Committee. "I want to make it clear to the cable industry that you are playing with fire here," said Lott, a Republican from Mississippi. "And if the rates continue to go up the way they've been going up in some areas, I think a major problem will erupt. We cannot have a situation where rates increase several percentages, because our constituents will raise Cain. And when they do, we will take action."

Lott was echoing the statement of his Republican colleague, John McCain, who growled: "I strongly oppose regulation, but I don't oppose regulation as much as I oppose unregulated monopolies."

Even in the face of these political warnings, the U.S. cable industry kept pressing for permission to consolidate further. In mid-1998 the National Cable Television Association lobbied the FCC to relax ownership rules that restricted any one cable company from controlling more than 30 percent of all U.S. cable households. The cable lobby argued that the horizontal-concentration rule should be lifted because cable now faced effective competition from DBS satellite services.

Gene Kimmelman of the U.S. Consumers Union disagreed: "It's astonishing that, in one of the most concentrated industries, anyone would even consider relaxing concentration levels. If anything, we think that the FCC should be cracking down and tightening up."

The cable lobby's manoeuvre was transparent. It was calling for looser concentration rules to help facilitate John Malone's megadeal with AT&T. In June 1998 Malone had announced a $48-billion merger with the long-distance giant. In fact, Malone was selling out to AT&T, which agreed to pay $32 billion in stock and assume all of TCI's debt. It was a brilliant manoeuvre for AT&T, which got instant access to TCI's 22 million cable-ready homes in a dozen U.S. states. AT&T also got access to TCI's large stable of programming properties, such as Discovery Channel and The Learning Channel.

If the buyout of TCI was a tremendous coup for AT&T, the advantages for TCI were less obvious. True, TCI got a badly needed cash injection and could now benefit from the branding appeal of AT&T by bundling cable TV with AT&T's phone service. But what about John Malone? In early 1998, as the U.S. cable industry celebrated its fiftieth anniversary, American magazines such as *Fortune* and *Business Week* had referred to John Malone as the "Comeback Kid." After the AT&T deal only a few months later, though, it looked as if fifty-seven-year-old Malone was vanishing into semi-retirement as a billionaire.

Malone did walk away from the deal with $1.8 billion in AT&T stock, but he was hardly retiring. Not only did Malone join the AT&T board, he committed to run its programming arm, Liberty Media. Hooking up with AT&T brought Malone's career back full circle: in 1963 he had started at Bell Labs, the research arm of Ma Bell. Now he was a "Bell Head" again.[16]

There was another powerful irony to the deal. The man who came to Malone's rescue with the stock offer and cash bailout was none other than Michael Armstrong, the former CEO of DirecTV's owner, Hughes Communications. The hard-charging Armstrong, who had been at the helm of AT&T since replacing Robert Allen in late 1997, was previously Malone's bête noire as the man who plotted DirecTV's "death stars" assault on the cable industry. But on June 24, 1998, Malone was now positively beaming next to Armstrong as the two announced their corporate marriage.

"I've met every AT&T chairman since 1964, and this is the first one that gets it," said Malone.

For some industry observers, the TCI–AT&T deal brought back vivid memories of the failed fusion between TCI and Bell Atlantic. *Business Week* magazine observed:

> We've all seen it before — two powerful executives, presiding over a hastily convened news conference to announce their new world-shaping combination. They stand, gripping and grinning for the cameras, zipping off sound bites for the evening news, and predicting that their mega-merger will be the combination of resources, talents, and technology that finally brings the future into the present.[17]

Undeterred, media giant Time Warner quickly followed the AT&T–TCI deal with a similar announcement. In late July 1998 CEO Gerald Levin said that Time Warner would make its cable plant available to long-distance phone companies like AT&T to offer local telephone service. For Time Warner, an alliance with long-distance carriers was an ideal solution to its embarrassing inaction on convergence. Time Warner, like most other cable empires, didn't want to enter the telephone business itself. So letting long-distance telephone companies use its coaxial wires to offer phone service would allow Time Warner to increase revenues from their networks. Levin evidently was not discouraged by the recent failures of other cable–long-distance alliances, notably a deal between Sprint and a TCI-Comcast-Cox cable group that came undone after disputes over cost and control.

While regulators examined the AT&T–TCI deal, John Malone and Michael Armstrong were focused less on Washington and more on Wall Street. AT&T's stock plummeted after the deal, mainly because the phone giant had taken on TCI's massive debt. Malone stated publicly that he feared AT&T stockholders would veto the deal because of the negative impact on share value. Malone, in fact, was now AT&T's largest individual shareholder with about 1.5 percent of the company's stock. But that wasn't nearly enough for him to have any measurable impact on a shareholder vote on the mega-merger.

As the cable and telephone industries plotted their futures, another revolution was taking place elsewhere — on the Internet. Throughout the first half of the 1990s the Internet had hardly registered on the radar screens of policy makers and industry leaders. But while convergence and the Information Superhighway preoccupied the political and corporate elites, the World Wide Web was quietly extending its tentacles.

As *The Economist* observed in July 1995:

> For the past few years the titans of media and communications have waged a war for the digital future. With great fanfare, telephone and cable TV companies have launched dozens of trials to demonstrate their vision of speedy electronic networks, connecting homes to a boundless trove of information, communication, education and fun. Shambling towards their distant goal of a wired world, they have been too busy to notice the unruly bunch of computer hackers, engineers and students scurrying about at their feet. They should have paid more attention. For while the giants have just been talking about an Information Superhighway, the ants have actually been building one: the Internet. [18]

The cable industry is now staking its future on the Web with new high-speed Internet-access services like TCI's @Home, the brand adopted by both U.S. and Canadian cable companies. The big phone companies have also shifted their focus towards the Internet, as Web access providers and backbone infrastructures. The satellite industry, too, has seized on opportunities presented by the Internet: several global satellite systems have been launched to provide a backbone for Web traffic. As penetration rates for home computers, modems, and Internet hosts have soared, it seems as if the entire global economy has been moving onto the Internet — and the buzz-word "e-commerce" has quickly become assimilated into the language. It now appears that, as few could have predicted in the early 1990s, the Information Superhighway is in fact the World Wide Web.

With the rapid growth and strategic importance of the Internet, market power has been shifting from traditional places like Hollywood and New York to Silicon Valley. Silicon Valley had seen the Internet coming. Indeed, companies like Intel, Microsoft, and Yahoo! were already planning to become the Web's main engines. All they needed were the wires running to people's homes.

CHAPTER 4

Silicon Valley
Building the Infostructure

SILICON VALLEY IS ORGANIZED MUCH LIKE THE INTERNET — IT HAS NO obvious epicentre. If you come here in search of a towering cluster of skyscrapers marking the World Computer Headquarters, you will not find it. The Valley is a loose confederation of small, vaguely interconnected towns running northward from San Jose to San Francisco along a thin ribbon of land once known as the "Valley of Heart's Delight."

Soft Power: Silicon Schmoozing

Baptized as Silicon Valley in 1971 by a local journalist making reference to the silicon chips manufactured in the region, the area has become virtually synonymous with U.S. economic growth and American high-tech power. Once a corridor of apricot and prune orchards, the Valley today boasts more than 7,000 high-tech companies — from small "gazelle" firms to giant powerhouses like Intel and Hewlett-Packard — and countless thousands of start-ups. Eleven new companies are hatched here every week. The Valley's annual economic output is roughly $250 billion (U.S.). [1]

True, not all major computer-based corporations are located in Silicon Valley. Bill Gates and Microsoft are farther up the Pacific coast in Redmond, Washington, near Seattle. The Compaq computer maker is in Texas. And Big Blue IBM's headquarters are in New Jersey. But even these major companies cannot ignore Silicon Valley, where all major high-tech giants must have a presence. Microsoft, for example, has a satellite "campus" in the Valley where battalions of software developers work along-side employees of Microsoft-owned WebTV, e-mail provider Hotmail, and the Macintosh Internet products group. Even the major American television networks have caught Valley fever. The U.S. nets have made substantial investments in Internet-based multimedia companies just in case couch potatoes abandon their TV sets for the Web.

If Silicon Valley's software products promise to make print journalism obsolete, at the moment high-tech coverage is actually fattening newspaper and magazine profits. Major dailies across North America now feature separate sections dedicated exclusively to computers and the Internet: the *New York Times* has "Circuits," the *Globe and Mail* has "Technology Plus," the *Toronto Star* has "Fast Forward." *Fortune* magazine has been particularly aggressive about pandering to Silicon Valley. In 1997 *Fortune* adopted an advertiser-friendly policy of having either Microsoft founder Bill Gates or Intel's CEO Andy Grove featured in every single issue — like rock stars on the cover of *Rolling Stone*.

In magazine journalism, besides the countless titles that have been launched by Silicon Valley's high-tech revolution (*Wired* and *Upside* are the bibles), more traditionally mainstream publications are now migrating to California in the hope of getting in on the high-tech advertising bonanza. In 1998 *Forbes* left its editorial digs in New York City for San Francisco, and celebrated the move with a puffy cover story on the Valley's biggest names called "Masters of the New Universe." The same year, the Knight-Ridder newspaper chain walked away from its headquarters in Miami to move its head office to San Jose.

"There is no doubt some of the best thinking about the future of the information business is in Silicon Valley," explained Tony Ridder, CEO of Knight-Ridder. "And there is little doubt the new technology and emerging power of the Internet will greatly affect how people will get their news and information. Knight-Ridder people simply must be immersed in the kind of futuristic and entrepreneurial thinking found in Silicon Valley." [2]

The key to the Silicon Valley miracle is the competitive advantage of industry "clusters" — new companies constantly spinning off and creating value and wealth through innovation and drive. Moreover, Silicon Valley companies are not weighed down by the psychological sclerosis of rigid hierarchies that characterize traditional corporate and government bureaucracies. In the Valley, management structure is flat. Not even the most senior executives have private offices or dedicated parking spots. Power is based on knowledge, not on artificial constructs like titles and rank. Silicon Valley is a working example of management economist Peter Drucker's prediction that "the factory of tomorrow will be organized around information rather than automation."

Its phenomenal success has earned the Valley the envy of its emulators.

New York City boasts a "Silicon Alley." Austin, Texas, has its "Silicon Hills." Utah created a "Silicon Desert." And Seattle brags about its "Silicon Forest." Closer to home, down the California coast in Los Angeles — where silicon is associated more with cosmetic surgery than with microchip technology — jealous comparisons with the Valley have found their way into local politics. In 1998 the city of Los Angeles, not content with its status as the world's Dream Factory, announced that L.A. and its environs would henceforth be known as the "Digital Coast." The baptism was duly reported, and promptly ignored.

If Silicon Valley has a geographic capital, it is undoubtedly San Jose, the major airport city at the south end of Santa Clara County and home to the National Hockey League team the Sharks. The San Jose local newspaper, the *Mercury News*, would otherwise be an unremarkable daily paper, except that it's the indispensable source of business info and scuttlebutt on the Valley's high-tech machinations. Farther north, the Valley's high-powered venture capitalists are located in Menlo Park, also home to the Institute for the Future, an organization whose name would be absurdly pretentious anywhere else.

Nearby Palo Alto is unquestionably the Valley's intellectual centre. It was in this quaint town that the Silicon Valley phenomenon began as a private-sector spin-off from electrical engineering labs at Stanford University. In the late 1930s two Stanford students, Bill Hewlett and David Packard, got together and founded a little company called Hewlett-Packard, which today is one of the world's biggest computer giants. Stanford may be the only university in the world where faculty members report annual incomes that, thanks to lucrative consulting work, effortlessly exceed the $1-million threshold. The town is also famous for Xerox's world-renowned PARC experiments — an acronym for Palo Alto Research Center.

For the uninitiated, daily life in Silicon Valley can seem strange. Configured as a string of townships stretched over a long sliver of land, even the shortest distances require a twenty-minute drive on the clogged freeway. In the towns themselves, a sense of community is oddly fabricated, or quite simply absent. There are local barbecues, but little genuine social interaction takes place. In the Valley, everything is business. The people here are rational actors; they have little time for community. On the positive side, the Valley pays no heed to factors like race, religion, or sex. Any kind of opportunism is welcome here. And immigration is enthusiastically encouraged, especially when it comes from high-tech Asia. Every year, thousands of computer programmers, engineers, venture capitalists, lawyers, and consultants charge into the Valley looking for a piece of the action. As a result, the real estate market is preposterously inflated. Rent is exorbitant and even modest bungalows can fetch nearly $1 million. But the payoffs can be enormous. As is often remarked here, if you pass a twenty-eight-year-old nerd with a bad haircut, he's probably worth $50 million. This image was evoked comically in the subtitle of Robert Cringely's 1996 book, *Accidental Empires: How the Boys of Silicon Valley Make Their Millions, Battle Foreign Competition, and Still Can't Get a Date*. In short, Silicon Valley is the world capital of the winner-take-all economy.

The most curious idiosyncrasy in the Valley is without a doubt its attitude towards failure. Here, failure is worn like a badge of honour. People switch jobs as often as once a year. The constant movement has the happy effect of keeping a constant inflationary pressure on salaries. If you were involved in a high-tech start-up that tanked, you boast about the experience. In a place driven by a relentless cycle of experimentation and creative rivalry, to try and fail is considered ennobling. If you have failed, you have learned — and you will do better next time. As *The Economist* magazine observed: "In Silicon Valley, bankruptcy is treated like a duelling scar in a Prussian officers' mess."

Even treachery is tolerated in the Valley. In 1957 Gordon Moore was part of the notorious "traitorous eight" who defected from a local high-tech lab to found Fairchild Semiconductor, a little company that eventually spawned thirty-seven different enterprises — including one called Intel.

At Intel's resplendent headquarters, an enormous cube-like glass structure in Santa Clara, it is possible to believe you have just walked into the Pentagon. Intel, whose famous Pentium microchip is fitted into most of the world's best computers, is renowned for two axioms. One is "Moore's Law." In 1965 Moore observed that, with price kept constant, computer power doubles every eighteen months. Moore's Law has been governing Silicon Valley's product cycles ever since. Second, and almost as famous, is Intel's corporate motto: "Only the paranoid survive."

When you walk into Intel's headquarters, you quickly learn that this second motto is rigorously followed and enforced. Intel cheerfully distrusts even the most welcome visitors. Once inside the building, you are never allowed to go anywhere unaccompanied. And when you leave, you are thoroughly inspected.

"Microchips are very expensive — and very small," says an Intel executive as his guest's briefcase is searched. "It'd be no sweat to walk out of here with two or three million dollars in your pocket."[3]

Silicon Valley also distrusts big government, mainly because governments like to impose rules and extract taxes. In this respect, the pervasive

Valley culture is not unlike that which prevailed at the apogee of nine-teenth-century capitalism. The prevailing ethos here is laissez-faire. Silicon Valley is a microcosmic example of Austrian economist Joseph Schumpeter's famous theory of "creative destruction," which asserts that human history is not a linear march forward, but a cycle — a relentless gale-force process of creation, change, adjustments, destruction, and rebirth. Silicon Valley is governed by an abiding belief that this creative cycle should be left to the Invisible Hand. Words like "government" and "regulation" are foreign to the local lexicon.

Ironically, Silicon Valley's local economy has benefitted tremendously from government support. One need look no further than the global phenomenon driving Silicon Valley's worldwide dominance of the microchip, software, PC, and digital-routing markets: the Internet. The Internet, after all, was a creation of the Pentagon, the American taxpayer-supported military-industrial complex. In the 1960s, even before the Internet was born, the U.S. military spent roughly $1 billion for semiconductor research. Xerox's world-renowned Palo Alto research experiments — where the prototype of Apple's Macintosh computer was designed — received 10 percent of their budgets from the U.S. government. American foreign policy also has protected Silicon Valley's interests. In the 1980s, when Japan was dumping suspiciously cheap microchips into the United States, Washington rushed to the rescue with the protectionist Semiconductor Trade Arrangement.

As in most industries, Silicon Valley has learned to accommodate this paradox in its corporate culture. Taxpayer subsidies may not inflate entrepreneurial self esteem or help perpetuate the mythology of creative capitalism. But they are a gift horse rarely looked in the mouth.

In the early 1990s Silicon Valley realized that Washington was a place that could not be ignored. The timing for this conversion turned out to be propitious. The defeated George Bush probably hadn't even heard of the Internet, but incoming Bill Clinton and Al Gore were technophiles whose youth and imagination appealed to the software capitalists of the Valley. Gore in particular was Silicon Valley's kind of guy: a pro-business, limited-government Democrat with a long record of interest in high-tech issues when he was in the Senate. In 1991, for example, Gore had sponsored the High Performance Computing Act.

During the 1992 presidential campaign, Gore fell under the intellectual influence of John Sculley, the dynamic chairman of Apple Computer. At the time, Sculley was actively promoting a high-tech vision that was even more grandiose than John Malone's vaunted 500-channel universe. Sculley predicted that technological convergence would soon merge the personal computer, the telephone, and television to create a multimedia industry that would be worth a colossal $3 trillion annually by the turn of the century. Sculley's vision received endorsements from futurists such as George Gilder, whose belief in the microprocessor as humanity's saviour was almost religious. In his book *Life after Television,* Gilder asserted:

> The computer industry is converging with the television industry in the same sense that the automobile industry converged with the horse, the TV converged with the nickelodeon, the word-processing program converged with the typewriter, the CAD program converged with the drafting board, the digital desktop converged with the linotype machine and the letterpress. [4]

Like Gilder, Sculley believed a technological revolution was causing a dramatic shift of civilization away from the Industrial Age to a new Information Age — from manual power to mental power. Today, his ideas have become commonplace. But in the early 1990s, Sculley's ideas seemed bold and exciting. Al Gore was particularly impressed by Sculley's vision. After a few meetings between Gore and the Apple chief, Sculley became the Clinton-Gore ticket's indispensable high-tech guru on the 1992 presidential campaign trail.

Sculley's involvement in the campaign was not devoid of self-interest. His goal was to bring the politically inexperienced U.S. computer industry's agenda to Washington. He also hoped to boost the sagging fortunes of his own company. At the time, Apple Computer was going through its deepest downturn ever, as it continued its long slide in a losing battle against DOS-based personal computers. In the end, of course, Sculley would fail to rescue Apple — that would be accomplished by Microsoft and the return of Apple founder Steve Jobs. In the short term, however, Sculley succeeded magnificently in mesmerizing Bill Clinton and Al Gore.

Sculley played a key role in scripting the Clinton-Gore team's "New Economy" vision, which underscored the links between high technology and economic growth. During the 1992 campaign, Clinton and Gore memorized Sculley's talking points about the paradigm shift from "Old Economy" models, with their organizational hierarchies and strict work rules, to newer models emphasizing the capacities of workers and firms to adapt and change. Sculley's vision found its intellectual complement in the work of Bill Clinton's old friend and future labour secretary, Robert Reich, who had analysed the effects of globalization in his 1991 book, *The Work of Nations.* These messages naturally played to the vanities of Silicon Valley, which was on the leading edge of the global revolution of industrial reorganization.

Gore, who had long argued that the Democrats' traditional constituencies were changing, felt ideologically comfortable with Sculley's high-tech slogans. Gore understood that unions, ethnic minorities, and New Deal and Great Society liberals were being replaced by knowledge workers, free-trade global entrepreneurs, and Wall Street golden boys. These voters were pro-choice, pro-environment, and anti–capital gains tax. It was this constituency, Gore believed, that would send a Democrat to the White House after the Ronald Reagan experience. In 1992, Gore was proved right.

On election day in November 1992, Silicon Valley had worked hard to deliver California to the victorious Clinton-Gore camp. And Bill Clinton never forgot a friend. At his first State of the Union address as president, seated next to Hillary Clinton was John Sculley.

By the mid-1990s Vice-President Gore was visiting Silicon Valley regularly, often bearing gifts in the form of federal R&D tax credits. Known as an "Atari Democrat" in the Senate, Gore visibly enjoyed the private brainstorming sessions with small groups of the Silicon Valley elite, who quickly became known as "Gore-Tech" advisers. These meetings — likened to graduate seminars on the New Economy — were even structured formally into Gore's official schedule. It wasn't long before he had established a well-oiled political machine in the Valley.

Gore's most trusted high-tech adviser in the Valley was legendary venture capitalist John Doerr, who was actually a registered Republican. A senior partner in the powerful firm Kleiner Perkins Caufield & Byers, Doerr was a New Economy disciple and indefatigable networker famous as the possessor of "the best Rolodex in the Valley." A former Intel executive, Doerr liked to say that Silicon Valley was "a network, not a hierarchy." Doerr was unquestionably the most plugged-in networker in the Valley. One of his partners at Kleiner was William Randolph Hearst III, grandson of the legendary media tycoon.

An engineer by training with an MBA from Harvard, Doerr has been instrumental in establishing a powerful Silicon Valley lobbying presence in the U.S. capital. Through his personal connection to Gore, Doerr — whose directorships include Sun Microsystems and Netscape — enjoys extraordinary access and political influence in Washington. He has convinced major Silicon Valley companies — Netscape, Cisco Systems, Intuit, National Semiconductor, Sun Microsystems, CNET, Marimba, Hewlett-Packard — to shed their anti-government reflexes and start playing the political game. The result is a bipartisan political action committee called Technology Network — or "TechNet" in Valleyspeak. The lobby group was originally created to deal with state tax issues in California, but later shifted its attention to Washington.

The turning point for TechNet came in 1996, when a California ballot initiative called Proposition 211 threatened to make securities fraud suits easier to file in the state's courts. Silicon Valley regarded Proposition 211, which undermined the effect of a law passed by the U.S. Congress in 1995, as a potentially lethal threat to its bottom line. Apple founder Steve Jobs called Proposition 211 a "neutron bomb going off in the boardroom." If the CEOs of Silicon Valley had been only vaguely engaged in lobbying efforts before, Proposition 211 mobilized the Valley's most powerful companies into concerted political action.

"In December 1995, saying 'I hate politics' was very credible Decathlon Club conversation," said Wade Randlett, TechNet's Democrat organizer in the Valley, referring to one of the most exclusive clubs in the Valley. "Saying 'I hate politics' in 1996, you'd look like you were refusing to do your part."

In 1996 Bill Clinton was running for re-election, and he naturally turned to Al Gore's high-tech friends in Silicon Valley to fill up his campaign coffers. But there was one problem: Clinton had publicly supported the principle of shareholder lawsuits. When the president came canvassing for money and support in the Valley during the 1996 election campaign, he was under tremendous pressure to change his position and speak out against Proposition 211. Few were surprised when Clinton flip-flopped. In gratitude, the Valley's political bosses made sure that Clinton did not leave town empty-handed. Seventy-eight high-tech executives publicly endorsed the president, and John Doerr organized a $50,000-a-plate fundraiser for the Democratic National Committee. In the end, the battle against Proposition 211 siphoned $40 million from Silicon Valley's lobbying war chest. But the ballot went down to defeat by a margin of three to one.

Thanks to adulatory media attention, by the mid-1990s the Silicon Valley billionaires were treated like superstars in Washington. Congressmen jockeyed for invitations to boardroom briefings at Sun Microsystems, Netscape, Apple, and Microsoft. And TechNet, though a facilitator of intellectual exchanges between Washington and the Valley, also demonstrated remarkable fundraising talents for friendly politicians. Many politicians were hugely impressed just to be rubbing shoulders with the brightest — and richest — men in the world, the so-called "Masters of the New Universe" according to *Forbes* magazine.[5]

"These guys are the rock stars of the nineties," said one Senate staffer of the Silicon Valley billionaires. "Everybody sees them as an attractive lobby group that doesn't have the baggage that some other interest groups have."

Dan Schnurr, TechNet's Republican organizer, put it more simply: "I've never seen a politician in either party who is against the future. A community that can talk about the future has a cachet that other industries don't have."[6]

As vice-president, Al Gore enjoyed a special status. Valley heavyweights actively sought him out. Many of the Valley's biggest names, whatever the magnitude of their paper fortunes, were still twentysomething or thirtysomething whiz kids. For them, hanging out with the vice-president — and possibly future president — of the United States was an intoxicating experience.

"Gore was already deeply committed to their issues, intellectually interested in the technology, and he understood that this was a political constituency, not a trade group," said Tim Newell, a former White House insider who set up the first TechNet meetings. "He took the executives very seriously. I believed they were natural allies, and once we got them in the room together they'd click."[7]

It was possible to wonder, though, whether Gore was getting captured by the Silicon Valley lobby. Many of the vice-president's speeches on high technology could have been scripted by Silicon Valley gurus. Even Gore's crowd-warming jokes had a Valley spin. His favourite quip for a while was the observation that if cars had advanced as rapidly as computer chips, a Rolls-Royce would hit speeds of a million miles an hour and cost only twenty-five cents.

"But the last time I used that line," Gore would add, "was at a meeting of computer experts. And one of them said, 'Yeah, but that Rolls-Royce would be one millimetre long.'"

Some Democrats were taken aback by John Doerr's unusual access to both Gore and Bill Clinton. In 1997, during a Group of Seven economic summit, Doerr slipped into a high-level meeting merely to ask Clinton to meet with some of his Silicon Valley buddies. Clinton happily obliged. Doerr is also said to have phoned Gore from the Aspen ski slopes to request — and obtain — the professional reinstatement of a White House aide known for his pro–Silicon Valley outlook.

Few doubted that Al Gore would be turning to cash-rich Silicon Valley to help finance his future political ambitions. Some commented that TechNet was in fact an adjunct to Gore's 2000 presidential campaign. At a TechNet gathering in mid-1998, someone was seen sporting a button with a catchy rhyming slogan: "Gore and Doerr in 2004."

The Internet Business Model and the "New Economy"

In early 1997, as Clinton and Gore prepared to commence their second term, the White House's National Information Infrastructure project was producing frankly disappointing results. Worse, the 1996 Telecom Act had been passed almost stillborn. The law was so replete with "safeguards" that, after a year, there was no solid prospect of market competition between the telephone and cable industries, and no fibre-optic wires hooking up schools, libraries, and hospitals. In retrospect, all the high-minded political rhetoric about competition, economic growth, job creation, and lower prices for consumers seemed hollow and embarrassing.

Feeling betrayed by the giant corporations that controlled the wires to American homes, Gore increasingly turned to Silicon Valley, where the computer and software billionaires shared the White House's frustrations with the Under Construction signs hung on the Information Superhighway. Circumstances conspired in Gore's favour, for by the mid-1990s the World Wide Web was taking off as a global medium by extending the capacities of the text-based Internet with multimedia. Since the Web would need an efficient "infostructure," perhaps its phenomenal growth would provide a catalyst for construction of the Information Superhighway.

The Internet indeed was imposing a new paradigm on the global economy. In a widely distributed report called *Digital Tornado*, the FCC predicted the Internet would soon topple all pre-existing market and regulatory models:

> The chaotic nature of the Internet may be troubling for governments, which tend to value stability and certainty. However, the uncertainty of the Internet is a strength, not a weakness. With decentralization comes flexibility, and with flexibility comes dynamism. Order may emerge from the complex interactions of many uncoordinated entities, without the need for cumbersome and rigid centralized hierarchies. Because it is not tied to traditional models or regulatory environments, the Internet holds the potential to dramatically change the communications landscape. The Internet creates new forms of competition, valuable services for end users, and benefits to the economy.

Given these facts, the FCC concluded: "Government policy approaches toward the Internet should start from two basic principles: avoid unnecessary regulation, and question the applicability of traditional rules." [8]

The emergence of the Web fit perfectly into the high-tech agenda of the Clinton-Gore White House. The Web not only gave impetus to the Information Superhighway, it also served as the vehicle for the New Economy of the twenty-first century. The Internet was the perfect technological expression of Gore's belief in "distributed intelligence." Moreover, the Internet's basic characteristics — open, decentralized, participatory, pluralistic, personalized, self-organizing, interactive, empowering — were win-win political messages to American voters.

Silicon Valley shared Gore's high-minded vision, but more bottom-line concerns could not be overlooked. TechNet was particularly active in its lobbying efforts in favour of educational reform and flexible immigration policy — both aimed at providing Silicon Valley with a skilled workforce. More important, TechNet was a vocal opponent of e-commerce taxes on the Internet. And once again, the Valley could count on support from the White House on the issue.

President Clinton chose a technology conference in San Francisco, just north of Silicon Valley, to announce his hands-off approach to the Internet. Cyberspace, he said, should not be taxed. The message was a stark, and well-timed, contrast to a resolution adopted the previous week by U.S. state governors. The National Governors' Association, which claimed states were already losing $4 billion annually in revenue to mail-order sales, estimated lost revenue to Internet commerce at more than $12 billion. The governors favoured a single statewide sales tax rate on all taxable electronic-commerce and mail-order purchases. Clinton disagreed.

"There should be no special breaks for the Internet," declared Clinton in San Francisco, "but we can't allow unfair taxation to weigh it down and stunt the development of the most promising new economic opportunity in decades." Clinton praised the phenomenal growth of Web-based business, estimating that business-to-business electronic commerce in the United States alone would likely exceed $300 billion by 2002.

The title of the White House's e-commerce policy — A Framework for Global Electronic Commerce — revealed its international ambitions. The policy, officially announced on July 1, 1997, was based on the following principles: private-sector leadership; no undue restrictions; state involvement limited to a minimalist legal environment; government recognition of the Internet's unique characteristics; and facilitation of e-commerce over the Internet on a global basis.

"We are on the verge of a revolution that is just as profound as the change in the economy that came with the Industrial Revolution," said Al Gore when announcing the policy. "Soon electronic networks will allow people to transcend the barriers of time and distance and take advantage of global markets and business opportunities not even imaginable today, opening up a new world of economic possibility and progress."

There still remained the tricky question of taxing Internet transactions. Silicon Valley's TechNet found a key supporter for its anti-tax cause in Ira Magaziner, a "Friend of Bill" and the White House's senior adviser on

Internet policy. Like Gore, Magaziner enjoyed close ties to the Silicon Valley elite. He clearly was sensitive to the Valley's position on Internet taxation, for in early 1998 the White House announced a moratorium on taxing business transactions on the Web.

Said Magaziner:

> There are two different models we could have considered for how this industry would develop. The first is the telecommunications and broadcast model, where governments around the world either own or operate the industries and, as in the United States, heavily regulate them. The other model is where buyers and sellers come together freely and do business, and the role of government is simply to set a predictable legal environment for commerce. We've opted for the latter model rather than the traditional model. The reason is because in the telecom and broadcast industries, governments regulated for specific reasons that do not exist with Internet commerce. In broadcasting, there is a limited amount of spectrum to be allocated. In the case of telephony, when the initial infrastructure was built, the size of investment required relative to the size of companies was huge. So governments licensed monopolies and set up regulations around those monopolies. With the Internet, there is almost unlimited bandwidth and massive competition. There is almost unlimited consumer choice. There are companies from computer industries, software industries, telecommunications, broadcasting, satellite, publishing, consumer electronics and utilities all competing to build the infrastructure. So we don't need government regulation. For all those reasons, we went to a market-driven system.

On the specific question of taxing the Internet, Magaziner said: "We spent over fifty years trying to bring down customs duties in the physical world, and we should not introduce them in this new world." [9]

As the White House announced its e-commerce policy at home, U.S. trade representative Charlene Barshefsky attempted to sell the idea of a tax-free Internet abroad. By May 1998 Barshefsky boasted that she had reached bilateral agreements with virtually every Internet-user country on the planet — except Canada. Ottawa had balked at the idea of a tax-free Internet, agreeing only to a moratorium on taxing transactions in cyberspace. The Canadian government, like U.S. state governors, appeared to regard the Internet as a potentially huge revenue source. In late 1998 the U.S. Senate voted in favour of a three-year moratorium on state and local taxes on electronic commerce. Canada, for its part, was attempting to take a leadership position on electronic commerce, and in October 1998 played host to an OECD (Organization for Economic Cooperation and Development) conference on e-commerce called "A Borderless World — Realising the Potential of Global Electronic Commerce." At that meeting in Ottawa, free-market advocates led by the United States called for an unfettered, self-regulated Internet, while European countries took the view that governments needed to take an active role in regulating the Internet in areas such as privacy.

The Clinton-Gore vision of a duty-free cyberspace was, of course, precisely what Silicon Valley wanted to hear. The Valley's warm embrace of the Clinton-Gore vision was expressed in June 1998 by *Wired* magazine, which published a cover story titled "Here Comes the New Economy." The fusion of White House economics and Silicon Valley capitalism was perfect. Silicon Valley indeed provided a textbook case study of New Economy business models. Since so many Silicon Valley companies were only a few years old — Netscape, for example, was born in the mid-1990s — they had no connection to the old models that compelled monopoly incumbents to protect sunk costs by resisting change.

A roster of new concepts, buzz-words, and axioms emerged to describe the workings of the digital New Economy. "Friction-free capitalism," for example, describe how information technology makes transaction costs smoother through the empowerment of consumers, accelerated market development, shorter life spans for products and jobs, and the removal of parasitic intermediaries. The term "disintermediation" describes the death of intermediaries, whose role in the value chain is becoming less and less necessary. "Diseconomies of scale" discourage companies from getting too big and bulky. Big is no longer beautiful because — as IBM learned the hard way — it often means rising production costs and falling productivity. Microsoft dominates the market because, as an organization, it has kept its development teams small and nimble. That strategy is called "adhocracy" — or bureaucracy without structure.

Perhaps the most revolutionary Silicon Valley idea is making money by giving away your products for free. Netscape's early business model, for example, was based on giving away its software as "shareware." Netscape allowed millions of people to download its Navigator browser for free in the hope that they would pay for updates. As a marketing strategy, it might have seemed brain-dead at first. But it worked. Within a few years, Netscape's market value soared — to $2.6 billion (U.S.) in 1998 — and its founders became super-rich. Bill Gates, a Web skeptic until 1995, was obliged to frantically catch up to Netscape by rushing his own Microsoft browser onto the market. Netscape's founders had shrewdly understood that the beautiful thing about selling downloadable products was that production, transportation, and transaction costs were virtually zero.

Rob Glaser, one of the brightest minds in Silicon Valley, adopted the Netscape business model when he launched a company that creates "streaming" products to add sound, video, and other media to the Web. Glaser, a Yale grad from Yonkers, New York, had been one of Bill Gates's top lieutenants at Microsoft, where he was working on experiments in interactive TV. It was during one of his brainstorming sessions on the potential of interactive TV that Glaser realized the future was not interactive TV, but the Internet — and Microsoft had missed it. Glaser left Microsoft to start RealNetworks, which began giving away both its browser and server products with the expectation of making money later through upgrades. Once RealNetworks handed out free software, it had the name and e-mail address of the client, who could later be persuaded to pay for a more powerful version.

The market model was simple: give product away to create a standard and capture market share up front. And the payoff could be enormous. Glaser's RealNetworks, which promised to transform the Internet into a broadcast medium, had a 1998 market capitalization of more than $1 billion (U.S.) and yet counted only $15 million in revenues. The cost of this phenomenal success was that, like Netscape, RealNetworks attracted the consuming envy of Bill Gates, who soon developed a competing Microsoft video "streaming" software called MediaPlayer.

Silicon Valley business models depend, of course, on ever-increasing computer purchases and Internet usage. In the Valley, this is known as "Metcalfe's Law" — named after Internet pioneer Robert Metcalfe — which posits that the value of a network is equivalent to the square of the number of its users. Put more simply, as a network grows, the usefulness of being connected to the network not only increases, but does so exponentially. Needless to say, the growth of the Internet has been spectacular. In 1990 the Web counted about 725,000 core users worldwide, though some 3.4 million people were using the Internet for e-mail. By 1996 those figures had soared to 36 million Web surfers and 71 million Internet e-mail users. Projected figures for the year 2000 are astonishing: 438 million core users, 707 million people using the Web for electronic commerce, and 827 million people using the Internet for e-mail.

When Metcalfe's Law is applied, it can be predicted that the Internet soon will be a marketplace worth hundreds of billions of dollars. And yet, remarkably, nobody owns or controls it.

The Internet poses a potential threat to incumbent delivery systems such as cable TV and telephony. The fact that the Web has been piggy-backed onto existing telephone infrastructure exasperates phone companies, if only because they are extracting a relatively modest portion of value-added revenues from the Internet explosion. If consumers can make low-cost long-distance calls via the Internet, unless a phone company is an Internet service provider it cannot fully exploit the Internet telephony market. Some major phone companies — like Deutsche Telekom in Germany — have responded by moving into Internet-protocol (IP) telephony, which is tech-nological convergence between the Internet and the telephone system. Bill Gates once remarked: "I'm not sure what the Internet is good for commer-cially, but I don't know why you would want to be in the long-distance market with that thing out there." Indeed, the market for Internet telephony is expected to reach $7 billion (U.S.) by 2003. If convergence between the television and telephone industries has been slow, Internet telephony may well prove to be the convergence that few were expecting.

The Internet may also beat the cable and telephone industries to fully deployed technological convergence with television. If people can order movies and TV shows via the Web, why would they wish to subscribe to cable TV? Thanks to new technologies like RealNetworks' video "streaming," full-motion video is already available on the Web and will continue improving to the point that it can offer high-resolution, broadcast-quality images. Streaming technology promises to transform the Web from a point-and-click search engine for nerds and information junkies into the dominant medium of the twenty-first century.

When that happens, the key question will be: Who will be the new medium's gatekeeper? The question is fundamental because it's the gate-keeper — like cable TV today — who exercises market power and siphons off the lion's share of value-added revenues. The major industry players are already frantically jockeying to become the Web's powerful gatekeeper. But it's still too early to say who will triumph in the long term.

The Web was invented in 1989 — twenty years after the Pentagon created the Internet — by Tim Berners-Lee, a British researcher working at the European Laboratory for Particle Physics. Berners-Lee designed a new kind of Internet text called HyperText Markup Language — or HTML. But the Web didn't actually catch on until 1993, shortly after undergrad-uate Marc Andreessen dropped out of the computer engineering program at the University of Illinois and transferred to the university's National Center for Supercomputing Applications. It was there that Wisconsin-born Andreessen and his classmates, subsisting chiefly on chocolate chip cookies and Mountain Dew, created a software program called Mosaic. A browser that made multimedia possible, Mosaic brought the Web to the masses by making the surfing experience visually pleasing and by introducing easy point-and-click navigating. In 1994 the cherubic Andreessen teamed up with Silicon Graphics founder Jim Clark, a high-school dropout turned Stanford math professor, and the two men moved to the Valley to launch a new company called Mosaic Communications Corporation — later renamed Netscape. Farther up the coast in Redmond, Washington, meanwhile, Bill Gates was dismissing the Internet as a passing fad of little consequence.[10]

It is astounding that Gates, the most powerful software billionaire on the planet, actually missed the importance of the Internet. For his critics, there was nothing particularly surprising about Gates's near tragic oversight. Although Microsoft likes to boast that "we set the standard," Gates's success has been based largely on taking other people's ideas and making them better. Microsoft hit the jackpot selling its MS-DOS operating system to IBM and PC-compatible computers, but it had merely bought the software — called "QDOS" — from Seattle Computer Products and tinkered with it to fit IBM's specifications. Similarly, Microsoft's Windows was merely a PC version of Apple's user-friendly operating system. And, in like manner, Microsoft's Web browser was a Netscape Navigator clone, though Gates would later claim that his idea to develop the Explorer browser pre-dated the incorporation of Netscape. Also, the Microsoft Network was a shameless — and less successful — copy of America Online. A sign of Gates's hardball tactics was his infamous threat to AOL founder Steve Case: "I can buy 20 percent of you, or I can buy 100 percent of you. Or I can go into this business myself and bury you." Case stood his ground, and it was AOL that buried the Microsoft Network. AOL's highly publicized takeover of Netscape in late 1998 put Microsoft even further on the defensive.[11]

In the early 1990s Gates wasn't the only one who got blindsided by the Web explosion. Like many other media companies, Microsoft's research efforts focused on the 500-channel universe and interactive TV. Moreover, Microsoft made the tactical error of devoting much of its energies to the marketing launch of Windows 95 at the very moment that the Web was exploding globally. While Microsoft's massive army of techno-wizards and marketing gurus were methodically planning the launch of Windows 95, hundreds of thousands of cybersurfers were downloading the Netscape Navigator browser. To his credit, though, Gates was quick to realize his mistake. In the spring of 1995, fearing that Microsoft could well repeat the folly of IBM in the early 1980s and get clobbered by a series of upstart companies, Gates had a road-to-Damascus technological conversion.

On May 26, he issued an internal Microsoft memo entitled "The Internet Tidal Wave," in which he announced that the company's future depended on its dominance of the Web. "Now I assign the Internet the highest level of importance," Gates wrote. "In this memo I want to make clear that our focus on the Internet is critical to every part of our business."

In December 1995 Gates hosted an "Internet Strategy" briefing for a few hundred analysts and journalists in downtown Seattle. Windows 95 had just enjoyed a stupendous market launch, but Gates seemed uninterested in that product. He told his audience that Microsoft was "hardcore" about the Internet. He also talked openly about Microsoft's plans to beat Netscape at its own game on the Web. How would he do it? Gates announced that he would bundle Microsoft Network and the new Microsoft browser with its Windows 95 operating system, which was built into most of the home PCs throughout the world. That commercial tactic would, of course, prompt U.S. anti-trust officials to take actions against Microsoft.

Companies like Microsoft and Intel had an obvious economic interest in the Web's becoming a global medium. Microsoft's Windows operating system and Intel's Pentium chips were in virtually every computer — hence the name "Wintel" for their powerful, symbiotic duopoly. Both companies were buying into the multimedia content business, too. Microsoft's Advanced Technology Group, with 500 employees and an annual R&D budget of $150 million (U.S.), had been working on a strategy based on producing content for interactive TV. By the mid-1990s the Advanced Technology Group was predicting that, by the outset of the twenty-first century, personal computers would have 100-gigabyte hard disks — 1,000 times the storage capacity of the average PC in 1995. This would allow the average PC to save and replay 100 full-length movies.

Gates, meanwhile, was making the rounds in Hollywood to meet with Tinseltown powerbrokers like Michael Ovitz to discuss joint content deals. There was even a rumour — false, it turned out — that Gates was poised to buy Orion Pictures, which had recently released the hit movie *The Silence of the Lambs*. Some conjectured that Gates was planning to build his own movie studio in Seattle. That too proved ill-founded. Microsoft did announce, however, a joint agreement to develop Internet content with Disney and NBC, and was also deploying its huge cash resources to buy up numerous multimedia content creators. A marriage between Hollywood and Silicon Valley seemed inevitable, though some critics warned that Hollywood was getting "Sili-conned" by the software techies up the coast. [12]

"We're interested in getting together with anyone who might have thoughts about how technology will come together with content," said Gates. "A lot of those people happen to be in Hollywood."

The Web had one major problem, however. Silicon Valley had produced "killer" software applications and created tremendous hardware firepower for computers. But communications *infrastructure* was abysmally inefficient because it lacked capacity. Consequently, sending a multimedia software application over the Web via telephone wires was like firing a cannonball through a garden hose. Telephone networks simply couldn't provide enough wireline capacity to permit the Web to function at high speeds. The cable industry, it is true, was a much more efficient conduit for the Internet, but its "tree-and-branch" network had many built-in disadvantages — notably a lack of two-way capability. Satellite systems, for their part, could offer backbone Internet capacity, and niche telecom players could provide fibre-optic trunks to make a good business of bulk Internet traffic. However, the "last mile" — the connection from the street curb to the home — was constricted because telephone companies had not upgraded their local-loop infrastructure. That segment of the Information Superhighway remained a clogged choke-point. For early cybersurfers, the congested World Wide Web quickly became known as the "World Wide Wait."

Bill Gates understood that an urgent solution to the bandwidth crisis was needed. If sluggish cable TV and telephone monopolies were preventing Microsoft from getting into homes, Gates had the cash to buy his way through the roadblocks on the Information Superhighway. Indeed, Microsoft was rich enough to buy the highway itself.

The Software Billionaires: Cable Guys or Bell Heads?

Bill Gates was not the only convert to the Internet in the mid-1990s. The cable industry, too, had made a strategic decision to bet heavily on Internet access as a new revenue stream. With their relatively high-capacity coaxial wires, cable companies could offer Internet access at much higher speeds than "POTS" — plain old telephone systems.

In Canada, Rogers launched an Internet-access service called "The Wave," starting with a market trial in the town of Newmarket, just north of Toronto. In the United States, Time Warner's cable group came out with a "Road Runner" service. And John Malone's TCI spearheaded another service called @Home, which was launched in 1996 in Hartford, Connecticut. Wall Street was so impressed by @Home's potential that investors gave it a market value of $2 billion (U.S.) at its initial public offering. Not insignificantly, @Home's headquarters were in Silicon Valley.

@Home's business model was classic cable-TV economics. @Home would not own any wires going into households, but would instead be controlled by a consortium of cable operators headed by John Malone's TCI. @Home would take 35 percent of a subscribing cable company's monthly fees, as well as additional fees for premium services. The fees extracted by @Home's owners were considered too high for Time Warner and US West's MediaOne, which decided to merge their cable Internet services — Road Runner and MediaOne Express — to form a rival service provider for non-allied cable systems. In Canada, major cable companies like Rogers and Shaw abandoned The Wave and adopted the @Home brand.

From the outset, @Home's partners knew the service had to offer more than just Internet access. Content was critical to the service's success. @Home therefore developed partnerships with publications in other media — for example, the *New York Times*, *HotWired*, and *USA Today*. Also, CNN was signed up to provide large-screen video feeds. In addition, @Home launched an audio service called "TuneIn," using RealNetworks' "RealAudio" streaming technology to run on @Home's high-speed platform. @Home also signed an agreement with Amazon.com, the on-line bookseller, which had similar deals with America Online and Netscape, a tandem that would soon become @Home's most formidable competitor as a Web content packager.

The telephone companies, meanwhile, were moving expeditiously with technical improvements aimed at speeding up Internet downloads on their twisted-pair copper wires. ADSL technology — for "asymmetric digital subscriber line" — offered some promise as an intermediary so-lution, but there was no denying that coaxial cable wires were much more efficient for high-speed Internet access. Cable's major weakness, however, was its lack of two-way capability. At the end of the 1990s only about 15 percent of the entire North American cable industry could boast two-way digital networks. To get that far, the price tag had been close to $10 billion (U.S.) — a huge cost for an industry already weighed down by crushing debt. If cable hoped to finance costly infrastructure build-outs and digital upgrades needed for high-speed Internet service and interactive TV, a cash injection was badly needed.

Enter Bill Gates, whose cash-rich and capacity-starved Microsoft had been looking for a solution to the bandwidth squeeze.

Gates had been assessing for some time the strategic advantages of entering the television business. In 1993 he had lured RealNetworks founder Rob Glaser back to Microsoft as a consultant to evaluate the advantages of an alliance with the cable TV industry — especially the big cable empires like John Malone's TCI and Time Warner. Glaser drew up a plan for a Microsoft-cable deal called "Cablesoft." It seemed logical that

Microsoft look at cable as an indispensable ally: while fewer than 40 percent of American homes were equipped with a PC, almost all — or 68 million households — were hooked up to cable TV. Gates now seemed to be advancing on both fronts at once — the Internet and interactive TV — and presumably they would converge into the same thing at some point.

As part of its convergence plans, Microsoft developed an interactive TV system called "MITV" (pronounced "My TV") connected to a giant video server called Tiger. By June 1994 the company was ready to showcase MITV in public, and Gates himself chose to run the demonstration. During the demo, however, Gates got a disk-error message as his screen went blank. He paused, dumbfounded, and then quipped: "I think that's the end of the demo."

Undeterred by the setback, Microsoft hyped MITV at a cable-industry trade show later that year, this time corralling the complicity of partners like ESPN and the Home Shopping Network. But once again, the pundits were unimpressed. They observed that Microsoft had succeeded magnificently in delivering "vapourware" to television. Undaunted, Microsoft committed to three interactive TV trials: one with TCI in Seattle, another with Southwestern Bell in Dallas, and the third in Tokyo with the Japanese phone giant, NTT. By the end of 1995, however, the two U.S. trials had been put on hold.

Two years later, Gates was ready to get serious about television, but this time he adopted a different strategy. In June 1997 he plunked down $1 billion (U.S.) for an 11.5-percent piece of Philadelphia-based Comcast, the fourth-biggest U.S. cable company with more than 4.4 million subscribers. Flush with Microsoft's equity injection, Comcast paid $500 million for Bell Canada Enterprises' 36-percent stake in the Colorado-based cable group Jones Intercable, which had 1.4 million subscribers. Only a few months later, Jones Intercable founder Glenn Jones sold his 2.9 million shares to Comcast for $69 per share — or a total of about $200 million. When Jones was asked why he pocketed a premium for his own shares while minority shareholders received only $27 per share, he replied: "It's America."

Gates was unconcerned by the shenanigans that his foray into cable had triggered. Microsoft needed high-bandwidth infrastructure, and the Comcast-Jones deal gave him instant access to the coaxial wires of one of the biggest cable empires in the United States.

"Cable is the most efficient platform for TV and computer services, period," said James Dolan, CEO of Cablevision, one of the biggest cable groups in the United States. "Bill Gates sees it. TCI sees it. We see it. I hope investors see it. I know my consumers are going to see it."

In Canada, Ted Rogers was beaming and boasting after the Microsoft-Comcast deal, which he described as the beginning of a powerful alliance between cable TV and the computer industry. The timing was right for Rogers, who only a few months earlier had been on Wall Street on a desperate mission to raise cash. Showing his customary penchant for hyperbole, Rogers revealed that North American cable barons had recently met with Gates.

"When I left Mr. Gates last week, I said: 'Today is the most historic day for the cable industry since I've been in it,'" Rogers enthused. "We made a real campaign of falling in love with the computer and having them marry us. This is monumental. There's nothing I can compare it to." [13]

Microsoft's investment in Comcast was undeniably a tremendous vote of confidence for the North American cable industry. And cable's spin doctors didn't neglect to hype the deal as if it were akin to the Second Coming. Suddenly, cable's long track record of bad service, price gouging, and broken promises seemed forgotten. The hated cable barons were now in the passing lane on the Information Superhighway. With Microsoft's blessing, cable was now the official pipeline for pumping video and data into people's homes. More important, as James Dolan was hoping, cable stocks shot up by several billion dollars the instant the Microsoft-Comcast deal flashed on the newswires.

Not everybody greeted the Microsoft-cable deal with undiluted elation. Gates's long-time rival, software billionaire Larry Ellison of Oracle, warned that Microsoft's push into content via cable was a sign that Gates was a megalomaniac who wanted to be not only a software giant, but also a Hollywood mogul and cable tycoon.

"He wants it all," said Ellison.

After Microsoft's foray into cable, Gates was indeed at a crossroads. He had to decide what business Microsoft should be in. As *Wired* magazine phrased it: "As the railroads once had to decide if they were in the train business or the transportation business, Microsoft had to decide if it was in the personal-computer industry or something bigger."

In early May 1998 Bill Gates was in Atlanta to attend the annual National Cable Television Association convention. His appearance was — as it was wherever he went — a major event. As the star speaker, Gates did not disappoint his audience of North American cable executives. He praised cable TV, which he called the "gateway" to households. He lauded the industry for its efforts to upgrade the cable plant and expand capacity. And he urged cable executives to keep up the good work and spend more. He almost sounded like a Cable Guy himself.

In truth, Gates was being cautious. He did not say that he'd opted resolutely in favour of cable as the main pipe to the home. He was leaving his options open.

"There are other ways to come in," Gates warned the assembled cable executives. "But if you get out front, you have a chance to be the one that drives all this."

In fact, Gates was already involved in several alternative deals, such as a global satellite system called Teledesic. An "Internet in the sky" system of 840 satellites, Teledesic was planning to provide broadband video, multimedia connections, and videoconferencing. Also, the "Wintel" tandem of Microsoft and Intel was partnered with Baby Bells working on ADSL technology. In January 1998 Microsoft, Intel, and Compaq joined forces with phone companies such as Ameritech, Bell Atlantic, BellSouth, GTE, Southwestern Bell, and Sprint to form a "Universal ADSL Working Group" to create an interoperable standard.

Gates clearly was spreading his risks, and he had lots of cash to do it. His investment in Comcast, while good news to cable shareholders, was less a resounding endorsement of the cable industry than a strategic investment at the right price. Gates was merely taking advantage of cable's low stock values. He was, moreover, not unaware of the vulnerability of major cable companies going through shaky succession planning as their pioneering founders neared retirement or death. Comcast was a classic example of a family-run business attempting to pass control from one generation to the next, as thirty-eight-year-old Brian Roberts was now running the company that his father Ralph had founded. Many believed that Gates was giving the younger Roberts a bear hug. Some industry analysts evoked the familiar saying that business families often go "from rags to riches to rags in three generations."

Canada's Ted Rogers, whose own corporate empire was facing an uncertain future as he approached retirement, felt energized by the Microsoft-Comcast deal.

"Bill Gates has a tremendously innovative mind, and his concept has tremendous value," said Rogers, who had attended meetings between Gates and CEOs of North America's biggest cable companies. "He would be our R&D arm." Rogers called Gates the "smartest man in America," yet remained cautious about the consummation of a deal with Microsoft. "There's a fifty-fifty chance we'll be able to come together on an economic model," he said.

Rogers was naturally delighted by the deal's immediate impact on cable stocks, but he overlooked the deeper structural significance of

Microsoft's cable strategy — in a word, it marked the beginning of the end for family-run cable dynasties. Some, it is true, believed Gates's interest in cable TV was a whimsical indulgence by a software billionaire with lots of money to squander. Others were convinced that Gates was buying up broadband infrastructure so he could control both the pipelines into homes and the content that was pumped through them. In short, they believed that Gates was the John D. Rockefeller of the twenty-first century.

Whatever his motivation, Gates's old friend and Microsoft co-founder, Paul Allen, had been closely following his former associate's corporate manoeuvres. In April 1998 Allen announced that he would spend $2.8-billion (U.S.) in a takeover bid for family-owned Marcus Cable. Allen, one of the richest men in the world with a personal fortune of $20 billion, paid a hefty premium for the Dallas-based cable company with 1.1 million subscribers. As part of the deal, Allen also covered about $1.2 billion of Marcus's debt. Allen therefore paid about eleven times Marcus's annualized cash flow, or more than $2,500 per subscriber.

This time, a software billionaire was not simply investing in a major U.S. cable company, but taking control. If the writing was indeed on the wall for North American cable dynasties, the short-term news seemed to be positive. Allen had signalled his conviction that cable infrastructure was excellent for the delivery of interactive services to consumers, including Internet access, entertainment, and sports. [14]

"Right now, cable is the leading vehicle," said Allen after the Marcus takeover. "That's not to say there will not be others, but right now cable is in the lead position."

Allen's buying spree had only just begun. In July 1998 he topped his Marcus deal with a $4.5-billion takeover of the St. Louis–based cable giant Charter Communications, which counted 1.2 million subscribers in nineteen states. Once again, Allen paid a huge premium for a cable company — $3,700 per subscriber, or fourteen times cash flow. The cash purchase of Charter was a sign either that Allen had too much money to blow, or that his cable acquisitions were part of a long-term strategy. Allen stated that the Charter deal signified "another step in my Wired World strategy, which is a connected future, marked by the merger of high-bandwidth data channels, the power of the personal computer, and the availability of valuable content."

Although Allen had left Microsoft's management team in 1983, he remained the software giant's second-largest shareholder after Gates — and moreover retained a seat on the Microsoft board. In 1985 Allen had founded his own software development company, Asymetrix, and following a successful battle with Hodgkin's disease he expanded his investment strategy in many directions under the aegis of a new company, Vulcan Ventures. Throughout much of the following decade, Allen went on an acquisition binge that did not always seem to follow a coherent pattern. For example, he bought two sports franchises, the Portland Trail Blazers basketball team and football's Seattle Seahawks. He also became the biggest shareholder, with 24 percent, in the Hollywood studio DreamWorks SKG, started by Steven Spielberg, David Geffen, and Jeffrey Katzenberg. And he bought a piece of the USSB satellite TV operator and Barry Diller's USA Networks. More notably, he bought stakes in some forty high-tech companies, including CNET and Starwave. In 1992 he founded Interval Research Corp., a Palo Alto high-tech think tank headed by David Liddle, an alumnus of Xerox's PARC project.

Perhaps Allen's greatest indulgence was his fascination with the late rock guitarist, Jimi Hendrix, who, like Allen, was from Seattle. In the early 1990s Allen decided to construct a Seattle museum, called the Experience Music Project, in honour of the legendary guitarist who released an album in the psychedelic sixties entitled *Are You Experienced?* The museum, scheduled to open in 1999, was built to feature interactive exhibits designed according to Hendrix's own concept of a "sky church" — a place where artists and musicians could work without the constraints of the marketplace. In that respect, the Hendrix museum was much like Liddle's Interval Research project, which was endowed with $100 million (U.S.) for "exploratory" projects. Allen, while not endowed with Hendrix's musical genius, has even been known to take to the stage with a guitar and join jam sessions.

With Marcus and Charter combined, Allen controlled the seventh-largest cable TV empire in the United States, counting some 2.4 million subscribers. Since the two cable groups were not clustered in the same geographical areas, it was widely expected that Allen was planning to expand his interests in cable systems even further until he reached at least 5 million households. In late 1998 there was speculation that Allen was seriously considering a takeover of the MediaOne cable empire controlled by the US West Baby Bell. Allen was facing only one obstacle in that ambition: Bill Gates. The Microsoft billionaire was also thinking about buying MediaOne, the third-largest cable group in the United States.

"We will continue to be aggressive," said Bill Savoy, Allen's chief investment strategist and president of Vulcan Ventures. "Scale matters in the cable business. The assets are in play. A year from now, they could all be gone."

Steven Schultzman, a media analyst at Solomon Smith Barney, offered another explanation for Allen's interest in cable assets: "It's obviously not about scale, it's more about scope. He looks at this business the same way

AT&T and Microsoft look at this business. They need access into the home. He knows there are three outlets on the wall: cable, telephone, and electrical. Currently, only one of those is a fat data pipe."

While Bill Gates was often compared to John D. Rockefeller and Jay Gould, Allen didn't escape the nineteenth-century comparisons either. In a profile of him in *Wired* magazine called "The Accidental Zillionaire," Paulina Borsook observed:

> Allen's acquisitions and investments suggest the cyber-equivalent of the 19th-century tycoon's practice of owning the cattle, owning the stockyard, owning the railroad that transports the beasts, and owning the meat-packing company that delivers the chipped beef to consumers. In the world of digital convergence, he intends to buy part of the pipe that delivers the goods, part of the content being carried, and part of the hardware and software that underlies it all. Playing the part of a venture capitalist, he is investing in many different companies, with the idea that a certain proportion will fail, some will do OK, and some will generate great returns.

Borsook also noted that Allen, who turned forty-five in 1998, was more like a super-spoiled rich kid than a self-made man. His disastrous investment in the Skypix satellite TV venture had demonstrated how impulsive the socially awkward billionaire could be. Allen had gotten jazzed about the potential of satellite TV even before John Malone's 500-channel universe and the launch of DirecTV. But Skypix turned out to be a high-tech boondoggle that collapsed in a flurry of lawsuits in 1992.

"Contrary to the myth surrounding him," noted Borsook,

> Allen has not built a successful company on his own since leaving Microsoft in 1983. While he has recently made some wise purchases, sources within the companies he has started claim another kind of "Allen effect": far from being profitable, these companies are rarely required to come up with products that meet market tests of innovation and timelines. . . . Many of his companies might be better off as foundations than as competitive businesses.

Wall Street nevertheless was intrigued by the corporate strategies of sophisticated investors like Bill Gates and Paul Allen, co-founders of the Information Age's most powerful company. There was even speculation that Gates and Allen were in cahoots. According to rumours, the Comcast and Marcus deals were only the first moves in a major campaign of cable buyouts across the United States.

What was their agenda?

It didn't take long for the mists surrounding Gates's strategy to dissipate. The Comcast deal had come with a straightforward quid pro quo. In return for his billions, Gates wanted the cable industry to let Microsoft build the set-top boxes that would serve as the Information Highway's gatekeeper. In short, Microsoft was pressuring the cable industry to adopt its Windows operating system — as well as Microsoft-owned WebTV display technology — for the digital converter boxes of the twenty-first century.

It was a bold move. Gates was flexing his muscles by attempting to deprive the cable industry of its major strength — gatekeeper power. The cable industry needed Microsoft's cash, but there was a price to pay — market power. The cable industry understood well the strategic importance of gatekeeping. It had usurped that role from the off-air broadcasters, who had reigned supreme for nearly thirty years as the main outlet for TV viewing.

On July 7, 1997, Gates was in New York City to meet with the cable industry's most powerful CEOs assembled in the boardroom at Time Warner's Rockefeller Center headquarters. Gates had come with a deal: Microsoft would supply the cable industry with set-top boxes in exchange for a cut of all future revenues. In short, Microsoft would control the brains of the future consumer electronics, computer, and entertainment industries. The cable industry would merely operate the wires.

John Malone, as the cable industry leader, had seen this coming. Malone had been worried about Gates's winner-take-all ambitions ever since his visit to the Microsoft headquarters near Seattle a few months earlier. Gates had just paid $425 million for the Palo Alto start-up, WebTV. Malone, a master strategist himself, thought for the first time that Microsoft might be seriously contemplating a big move on the cable TV business. Shortly afterwards, when Gates paid $1 billion for a stake in Comcast, Malone was at first happy that cable had piqued Silicon Valley's interest enough to scare up the capital needed to achieve the cable industry's short-term goals. It was what Malone liked to call "stirring my equity." He didn't mind at all that outsiders like Bill Gates were making his paper fortune soar.

At the New York meeting, however, the penny dropped. In the Time Warner boardroom, Malone realized there was a huge price to pay for cable's flirtation with Microsoft. Gates wanted the same lock on TV sets that he already had on PCs. His proposed deal wasn't just a bear hug, it was a squeeze play.

"Bill Gates would like to be the only technology supplier for this whole evolution," Malone said at the TCI annual meeting a few weeks later. "We would all be very foolish to allow this to happen."

Another top executive at the fateful New York meeting said: "Microsoft just overstepped itself. It probably could have got what it wanted if it had been more cautious in how it presented its proposal. Microsoft has been kind of paternalistic. Cable guys have big egos, are self-made men, and don't like to be talked down to."

Suddenly it seemed the Cable Guys and Silicon Valley were better rivals than allies. As *Fortune* magazine observed:

> The mating dance between cable and the Valley brings together two of America's most growth-hungry businesses, and it has intensified over the past year. High-tech companies are banking on fast digital connection into the home to help sell more microprocessors and software — in PCs hooked to online networks and in digital set-top boxes. . . . The attention from Silicon Valley has caused a remarkable turnabout in cable's fortunes on Wall Street. Most stocks have doubled in the past year. It has also heightened the paranoia in this close-knit, dynastic, nepotistic industry that the Valley, and Bill Gates in particular, will figure out a way to soak up all the juice, just as Microsoft and Intel did in the PC business.[15]

Following the New York meeting, Malone decided that he had to stop Bill Gates from usurping cable's strategic direct access to consumers. If he didn't, Microsoft would control the global entertainment industries. And cable TV would be reduced to a mere conduit.

The set-top box war had officially begun.

The Silicon Valley–Cable TV Mating Game

The Consumer Electronics Show in Las Vegas is the annual powwow where the major high-tech players flaunt their latest products and trumpet their megadeals. At the event in January 1998, John Malone was uncharacteristically spending most of his time out of the spotlight. Locked away in his hotel room, he was engaged in an intricate fertility dance with some of the biggest names in Silicon Valley.

After the showdown in New York City, Malone's goal was to have as many high-tech suitors from Silicon Valley as possible to play off Bill Gates. Malone and other U.S. cable barons had announced they would not allow any single software to control their digital set-top boxes, but would bundle several, interoperable standards into their boxes — in effect, so the boxes could double as cable modems hooked up to computers. It was a shrewd strategy, for the jealousies between Silicon Valley and Microsoft were often bitter. At that very moment, in fact, Silicon Valley was lining up behind

Netscape in its epic anti-trust battle against Microsoft in Washington.

Malone's first corporate flirtation was with one of Gates's main rivals, Scott McNealy of Sun Microsystems. It was McNealy who once had said: "There are two camps — those in Redmond, who live on the Death Star, and the rest of us, the rebel forces." At Congressional hearings in Washington, McNealy had warned the world that Microsoft's quest for control of computer operating systems was akin to seeking proprietary ownership of the English language.

McNealy happily responded to Malone's mating call. Over the Christmas holidays, he and Malone had agreed on a tentative deal at TCI's headquarters near Denver. According to the terms of the deal, TCI would put Sun's Java software in its next generation of digital set-top boxes.

McNealy, who relished the deal as an especially gratifying pre-emptive strike against Microsoft, was keen to announce it with fitting fanfare as part of his keynote address to the Consumer Electronics Show. That evening, on January 9, 1998, McNealy was in his twenty-eighth-floor room at the Las Vegas Hilton uncorking a bottle of champagne to celebrate his triumph. Java had been first in the box. To the victor, the spoils.

The party did not last long, however. Only thirteen hours later, McNealy learned the hard way that John Malone was the most accomplished, and canny, dealmaker in the business. Behind McNealy's back, Malone had negotiated a parallel deal with Microsoft. While McNealy was charging around the Las Vegas convention floor boasting of his deal with TCI, Malone was on the phone with Gates, who was in an airplane negotiating frantically on a portable phone so that he could have his own announcement when his jet touched down in Las Vegas. As part of this back-of-the-envelope deal, TCI agreed to license 5 million copies of Microsoft's CE operating system for its set-top boxes.

"We're gratified by Microsoft's willingness to work with other software providers," Malone said. "This is an ecumenical process."

Malone's gratification extended even further. He had negotiated a similar deal with Oracle's CEO, Larry Ellison. Malone's come-one-come-all strategy, by brilliantly playing the software billionaires off one another, ensured that the Cable Guys were still calling the shots. The cable industry needed Silicon Valley to finance its rollout of digital boxes, so Malone offered each big software player — Sun, Microsoft, Oracle — a piece of the box. But not proprietary control.

Malone soon found a brand name for his defensive strategy against Microsoft and Silicon Valley: "OpenCable." Managed by the industry's Colorado-based CableLabs R&D centre, OpenCable was a multi-vendor strategy concocted to ensure that digital set-top boxes, whatever was put inside them, were technologically compatible across the cable industry. In other words, the OpenCable strategy would make it impossible for any one company — notably Microsoft — to dominate digital television or become a new industry gatekeeper.

"The industry is very wary about an approach like the PC industry's proprietary operating system, because that places control in the hands of the suppliers of those components," said Bruce Ravenel, head of TCI's Internet services and a key player in the talks with Microsoft and Sun.

OpenCable was a major setback for Gates. Like McNealy, he wanted an exclusive. Technically speaking, they were justified, because one single standard in a digital box is much easier to operate than a bundle of different software systems. But Malone was intractable. He knew that a single proprietary standard meant loss of gatekeeper power for cable.

"I told Bill, 'Look, we don't have a deal yet,'" said Malone later. "You know, it's always a problem when you try to limit Microsoft to just a piece of things."

A few months later, Malone was still gloating as McNealy and Gates jockeyed for position at the annual cable convention in Atlanta, each insisting that his software was better suited to cable's digital box. Malone compared the task of coupling Sun's Java and Microsoft's Windows CE software to "mating porcupines."

Gates was frankly preoccupied elsewhere throughout 1998. Condemned in the media as a modern-day robber baron, he was fighting the bitter anti-trust suit in Washington in which his accusers were none other than the Silicon Valley clique. While the anti-trust actions had been initiated when George Bush was in the White House, both Bill Clinton and Al Gore refrained from commenting on Microsoft's travails because of their known affinities with Microsoft's rivals in Silicon Valley. There were other sensitivities. Joel Klein, the U.S. Department of Justice lawyer taking the lead on the anti-trust suits, was a longtime "Friend of Bill" who had been deputy counsel in the White House. Also, Netscape founder Marc Andreessen was one of the TechNet circle who often advised Gore on high-tech issues. Moreover, Gore's former domestic-policy adviser, Greg Simon, had left the White House to become a consultant at Netscape. Still, in 1997 Gore had dined privately with Bill Gates at the software billionaire's new Seattle mansion following a Microsoft-sponsored CEO summit. At that event, Gates praised the vice-president: "He's one of the first policy makers to understand technology and information. I have drawn on his wisdom often."

The anti-trust suit against Microsoft could only have been good news for the cable industry. While Bill Gates was appearing before Congress to explain Microsoft's hardball business tactics against Netscape, the once-hated cable industry was happily promoting its "open" concept. There was some irony to the OpenCable gambit, for "open" was not a familiar idea in the closed, control-oriented cable industry. But it was a clever ploy that exploited the prevailing trend towards international protocols and open network systems like the Internet.

Still, the willingness of major U.S. cable groups — Comcast, Marcus, and Charter — to sell out to software billionaires seemed to signal profound changes in the media landscape. Malone himself sold out in the end, not to Silicon Valley but to the long-distance telephone giant, AT&T.

These were seismic changes. Companies like Microsoft and AT&T had lots of cash and plenty of time; cable companies had neither. If cable's coaxial wires could provide the infrastructure for the Information Superhighway, it was far from certain that cable tycoons would be around to build it.

In the final analysis, the battles over infrastructure — whether the 500-channel universe or the Information Superhighway — were marked by profound paradoxes. Industry crisis masqueraded as visionary confidence, and for a brief moment the deception was almost convincing. The rhetoric of competition, in like manner, almost succeeded in masking the reality of rapid industry consolidation. And amidst this complex chemistry of commercial heroism and corporate paranoia, consumers felt a rush of excitement that quickly dissipated. The 500-channel universe was a myth. And the Information Superhighway was still under construction. The Digital Revolution was inevitable, but its early advocates were false prophets.

Meanwhile other battles were being fought on other fronts. The 500-channel universe and the Information Superhighway were *carriage* projects whose ambition was the building of infrastructure. Carriage inspires commercial strategies aimed at appealing to consumers. The matter of *content* raises different stakes and issues. Content is about citizens and culture. And as such, the battles over its commercial control are even more contentious.

PART II

Content

CHAPTER 5

Free TV
Crisis in Lotusland

On Labour Day 1998, baseball slugger Mark McGwire of the St. Louis Cardinals cracked the ball out of his home team's Busch Stadium — tying the sixty-one-home-run record set by Roger Maris in 1961. The following night, McGwire stepped up to the plate against the Chicago Cubs and broke the record with another homer. When he hit the ball out of the park that night, the last thing on his mind was that his historic exploit had sent the Canadian television industry spinning into panic.

After McGwire's record-tying home run, the Fox television network junked its entire prime-time schedule the following night to broadcast the St. Louis–Chicago game in anticipation of the record-smashing home run. Shows like *King of the Hill* and a new comedy called *Costello* sat it out in the dugout while Fox fixed its cameras on McGwire at bat. This was distressing news in the executive offices of Canada's Global TV and CTV networks. Global had planned to simulcast Fox's *King of the Hill* that night, and CTV had scheduled Fox's premiere episode of *Costello*. Now both Global and CTV were forced to fill the empty slots with last-minute filler. Global slotted in an old rerun of *King of the Hill*, and CTV switched to a simulcast of ABC's *Soul Man*. Canadian viewers were utterly confused as they cross-checked their TV guides.

Mark McGwire's moment of glory proved that, in English-language Canadian television, the U.S. networks call the shots. The prime-time schedules of most Canadian television stations are programmed not in Toronto, not in Montreal, not in Vancouver, nor anywhere else in Canada. The decisions are made in Los Angeles by executives at CBS, NBC, ABC, and Fox. The history of Canadian television has been an inglorious saga of colonial dependency. So dependent on American television are Canada's broadcasters, in fact, that even the most modest Canadian success on national TV screens is celebrated like a cultural triumph.

Betting on the Trojan Horse

In the fall of 1998 the CTV network boasted two new Canadian dramatic series: *Flesh and Blood* and *Power Play*. These two shows were added to two returning Canadian series, *Due South* and *Cold Squad*. Global, for its part, started the season with two Canadian dramas: *Traders*, the popular series about financial intrigue on Bay Street, and a new pilot called *Justice*, set in the Ottawa corridors of power. In many respects, this was quite an achievement for Canada's two major private networks: six Canadian series in a single season. But these shows were tiny islands of Canadian content in a vast sea of American prime-time fare — everything from *60 Minutes*, *ER*, *Frasier*, *Friends*, and *Third Rock from the Sun* on Global to *Veronica's Closet*, *Ally McBeal*, *Felicity*, *Wheel of Fortune*, and *Jeopardy* on CTV. Of the 28 hours of prime-time viewing hours per week, Global counted only 2.5 hours of Canadian content in prime time with *Traders*, *Bob and Margaret*, and *Psi Factor*. CTV, for its part, had a measurably better, but still mathematically paltry, record of 6 hours of Canadian programs in prime time: *Due South*, *W5*, *Power Play*, *Cold Squad*, *Earth: Final Conflict*, and *Nikita*. In contrast, the publicly owned CBC counted an impressive 26.5 hours of Canadian shows out of the 28 prime-time hours.

As the 1998–99 television season approached, the *Globe and Mail* published a dismayed front-page assessment of the Canadian prime-time conundrum:

> Shows such as *Earth: Final Conflict* and *Psi Factor*, made to be low-rent filler on U.S. stations, have been plugged into prime-time slots here because they are made by Canadian companies. Such nominally Canadian shows outnumber the recognizably Canadian ones, such as *Traders* and *Due South*, almost three to one. Private networks spend less than 27 per cent of their revenues on Canadian programs, an amount that has dropped almost 4 per cent in five years. As a result, domestic shows tend to be obscure. In England, the top 10 TV shows (in 1997) were all British; in Canada, only *Hockey Night in Canada* and local news shows register regularly in the top 20. [1]

In truth, television in Canada was American even before there was Canadian television. In the late 1940s, when television first arrived in

Canada, the airwaves were 100-percent American, with zero Canadian content. CBC Television didn't go on the air until September 6, 1952, and then in Toronto and Montreal only. As in radio, CBC was several years behind commercial U.S. television, which had made its Canadian debut on May 14, 1948, when Buffalo's WBEN-TV, a CBS affiliate, hit the airwaves and could be received in Toronto and its environs. By 1952, before Canadian television existed, nearly 150,000 Canadians already owned TV sets in order to watch cross-border American channels. A colonial reflex of a different kind inspired many thousands more to rush out to buy TV sets so they could watch the televised coronation of Queen Elizabeth II in 1953.

The creation of CBC Television as a state-owned monopoly found its justification in the principles of public ownership. The Canadian government, like many others, took control of the airwaves on the grounds that spectrum was limited and therefore required regulation. Even the United States had opted for strict regulation of broadcasting when the FCC was created by Franklin Delano Roosevelt. But whereas the Americans rejected outright state ownership of broadcasting, Ottawa opted for the European model of government monopoly over television.

The CBC's status as a single monopoly broadcaster obliged it to schedule programs that would appeal to the greatest possible number of people, much like the mass-audience, private U.S. networks. As a result, from the very start of Canadian television, the CBC operated not as a distinctive non-commercial broadcaster, but as a mass-audience outlet for the same major commercial brands that bankrolled American television — cigarettes, soap powder, razor blades, automobiles, and the like. Thus the CBC was confronted with a profound paradox from the moment it went on the air: its commercialism contradicted the public-service values that inspired public broadcasters in other countries. By the end of the 1950s Canadians were watching CBC variety shows with commercially branded names such as *Chrysler Theatre*, which must have seemed indistinguishable from U.S. network shows like *Texaco Star Theater*, *Philco Playhouse Theater*, and *Schlitz Playhouse*. What's more, CBC Television was built and expanded through private affiliates and much of its program schedule was filled with American shows. The public network, to be sure, produced many excellent Canadian programs. But despite the claims of nostalgic Canadian nationalists today, the CBC was hardly modelled on Britain's non-commercial BBC. From its inception, Canada's public broadcasting network was influenced more by the commercialism of American television than by the values of public broadcasting in the U.K.

Non-CBC-affiliated private television arrived in Canada in 1961 with the licensing of CTV network stations. CTV's flagship station, Toronto's CFTO, was licensed mainly because its financial backers — including newspaper tycoon John Bassett, the Eaton family, and cable baron Ted Rogers — were well-connected Tories whose clout with the Conservative government of John Diefenbaker was an open secret. When CFTO began operations, it promptly became a conduit for popular American television shows. CFTO's owners even attempted to persuade Ottawa to allow the U.S. television network, ABC, to become a 25-percent shareholder. The request was formally denied, but ABC nonetheless provided CFTO with a $2.5-million "loan" and took three seats on its board of directors in exchange for a share of the station's profits.

In the early 1960s there was little popular support in Canada for what would later become known as "Canadian content" on television. The federal regulator — in those days called the Board of Broadcast Governors — did impose on television stations a minimum 45-percent quota for programs that were "basically Canadian in content and character." But that loose definition gave private stations plenty of wriggle room to violate the spirit of the quota. Allowances were made, for example, for "Commonwealth" programs, non-Canadian television specials, and even baseball's World Series.

In 1968 the federal government created the CRTC in a context of emerging national pride and turbulent social change in Canada. Under the leadership of Pierre Juneau, the regulator immediately showed more firmness concerning Canadian content on television. In 1970 the CRTC held highly publicized Canadian Content Hearings during which Juneau sparred with senior executives of the private television industry, notably CTV president Murray Chercover. The most contentious issue was the slavish dependency of Canada's TV networks on American programs. Chercover and his bean-counters marshalled a battery of arguments to justify their lack of patriotism on the airwaves, but they were no match for Juneau's Jesuitical intellect. Still, their tense exchanges were a dialogue of the deaf.

"We believe," stated Juneau, "that the prophets of doom, the messengers of mediocrity, will be overwhelmed by the new generation of competent, creative, confident artisans and by all those of preceding generations who have already demonstrated their freshness of mind, their talent and their capacity for inspired leadership."

History would prove Juneau's assertion naively optimistic. In the meantime, Juneau laid down the law by imposing a general Canadian-content quota of 60 percent for private television from 6:30 p.m. to 11:30 p.m. — the regulatory definition of prime time. After protests by private broadcasters, however, the CRTC lowered the quota to 50 percent. For the CBC, the quota was held at 60 percent.

While private-TV executives grumbled, media reaction to the quotas was overwhelmingly positive. Allan Fotheringham, then a columnist for the *Vancouver Sun*, congratulated the CRTC for taking on the TV executives, whom he called an "avaricious band of bank balances." Author Pierre Berton called the CRTC decision "a landmark in Canadian history." And the *Globe and Mail* published a congratulatory story under the headline: "CRTC stands firm against critics."

"The Commission is arguing," stated Juneau, "that unless we do something about it, Canadians are going to have their choices dictated to them by a distribution system which will inevitably find it more economic to pipe all over Canada an overflow of mass-produced American programs rather than supporting programs that are relevant to Canadians."

When Juneau left the CRTC in 1975, the Commission made a decision whose unintended consequence was the undermining of any potentially positive effects of the Cancon quotas. In 1976 the CRTC allowed Canadian television stations to make profits through "simultaneous substitution" — or simulcasting — which allowed Canadian stations to siphon advertising revenues from U.S. border stations by simultaneously airing, with the technical complicity of cable TV companies, the programs featured on the U.S. stations. For example, if CTV simulcasted an American show aired by, say, NBC in the United States, Canadian viewers could choose to watch the show on either CTV or NBC, but they would see only the CTV signal and its Canadian commercials. The federal government further reinforced the protection of broadcaster revenues by prohibiting, with a law called Bill C-58, Canadian advertisers from deducting as allowable expenses any commercials placed on U.S. border broadcasts.

These measures were a bonanza for Canadian television stations. In effect, simulcasting and Bill C-58 gave Canadian networks exclusive territorial rights to any American programs they aired and to all domestic TV advertising revenues along the Canada-U.S. border. In principle, there was nothing particularly anomalous about national broadcasters buying territorial rights for their domestic markets. But the simulcasting twist meant that Canadian TV stations now had a powerful incentive to fill up their prime-time schedules with popular American shows procured at marginal cost and air them against U.S. border station slots. The result was the rapid colonization of Canadian prime-time schedules by simulcasted American television shows.

It soon became obvious that simulcasting and Canadian content quotas were wholly incompatible, at least in their objectives. The Cancon quotas remained in effect, however, and Canadian television networks were obliged to respect them. Predictably, the networks quickly discovered a way, thanks to the preposterously permissive definition of "prime time," to abide by the letter of the quotas while violating their spirit. They could broadcast cheaply produced Canadian news and information shows until 8 p.m. and later in the evening after 11 p.m., while devoting most of the real prime-time hours between 8 p.m. and 11 p.m. to simulcasted American fare. The Canadian networks were thus spared the obligation of investing in costly domestic shows, notably original Canadian dramatic series, for they could respect the quotas with in-house news shows. If there was any positive effect of this institutionalized delinquency it was that the Canadian television networks developed a strong tradition of news and current affairs journalism. Canada produced excellent broadcast journalism, but failed to promote televised storytellers. Television dramas were imported from the United States at low cost.

In the 1970s the only notable Canadian dramatic series on CTV was *The Littlest Hobo*, a low-budget show whose star was a German shepherd. CTV grew so accustomed to its delinquency, in fact, that it began to regard it as an entrenched right. In 1979, when the CRTC got tough with the network by imposing a specific Canadian-drama quota of twenty-six hours per season, CTV appealed the decision to the Supreme Court of Canada. In 1982, however, the high court upheld the regulator's decision.

When Global TV emerged on the Canadian television landscape in the early 1970s, it was supposed to provide a refreshing antidote to CTV's colonial behaviour. Global won a licence from the CRTC by billing itself as a patriotic showcase for Canadian programs. It was the right button to push in the early 1970s, when Pierre Juneau was attempting to Canadianize the nation's airwaves. The button was also pushed by the right person: one of the lead consultants behind Global's bid for a licence was Seymour Epstein, a former adviser to Juneau at the CRTC who was now working in the television industry.

After obtaining the regulator's benediction, Global went on the air on January 6, 1974. Two months later, Global was in receivership. The problem: a lack of Canadian programming. The station had been losing $50,000 a day, and its main investors, Maclean Hunter and Odeon Theatres, had lost patience and decided to pull the plug. In Ottawa, the embarrassed CRTC had egg all over its face. Canada's newest television station, a promised "showcase" for Canadian programs, had collapsed ignominiously in full view of an expectant public.

The only person to take furtive pleasure in the collapse of Global was Israel ("Izzy") Asper, a wily tax lawyer in Winnipeg. Asper had plans of his own for the stillborn Global. In 1973, when the CRTC announced that it was ready to consider applications for a new Winnipeg TV station, Asper was the frustrated leader of Manitoba's opposition Liberal Party. In those days, Winnipeg was served by only three TV signals — CBC, CTV, and a U.S. border station called KCND beaming in its signal from North Dakota. Asper, ever on the lookout for an opportunity to make a buck, quickly concocted a scheme to win the licence. He believed there was no room for a fourth station in Winnipeg, however, so he fixed his predatory ambitions on the North Dakota station, KCND.

When Asper went down to North Dakota and offered to buy KCND, he was rebuffed by the station's owner, a wealthy Texan named Gordon McLendon. But Asper had a powerful bargaining chip. Seymour Epstein had alerted Asper to the fine print of a bilateral agreement between Canada and the United States that would allow a new Canadian station in Winnipeg to block out the KCND signal once it was on the air. Also, Bill C-58 was making its way through the Ottawa policy machinery, and it sounded the death knell for pirate U.S. border stations. KCND's advertising revenues would be wiped out overnight. The prospect of owning a value-less broadcasting asset in North Dakota forced McLendon to say uncle. He sold the station to Asper for $750,000. Asper promptly had KCND dismantled, piece by piece, and hauled up to Winnipeg in trucks. Re-assembled in a vacant Safeway store, the station was rebaptized "CKND" — the "C" suggesting Canada, but the "ND" still betraying the station's true origins in North Dakota.

While Asper and business partner Paul Morton were christening CKND, the CRTC was desperately seeking a rescue plan for the bankrupt Global TV in Toronto. Seizing an unexpected opportunity, Asper and Morton presented themselves as white knights prepared to relaunch Global, phoenix-like, from the dull embers of its shameful ashes. They brought with them a Toronto ally, radio tycoon Allan Slaight, along with consultant Seymour Epstein.

The CRTC gratefully approved Asper's bailout plan. At first blush, the rescue seemed like an ideal solution. Asper had patriated a North Dakota TV station and therefore seemed like the perfect candidate — a true Canadian nationalist — to buy a Toronto station whose mission was to showcase Canadian programs. The CRTC failed to understand, however, that Izzy Asper was above all a shrewd tax lawyer. Patriotism came after profits. Asper saw in Global TV not a showcase for Canadian dramas, but the first piece in a national television network that would serve as a low-cost, high-profit conduit for American television shows.

When the reborn Global hit the airwaves in 1975, it began airing cheap American fare like *The Gong Show* and *The Love Boat*. Canadian shows, such as *Shh! It's the News* with Don Harron and Catherine McKinnon, were summarily dumped. Global was now culpable of the very problem it had been created to remedy. It ran so many episodes of *The Love Boat* that it was soon scoffingly dismissed as "The Love Boat Network." Still, Global proved that — thanks to CRTC-sanctioned simulcasting — cultural colonialism was a highly profitable business in Canada. As Herschel Hardin observed in his book *Closed Circuits: The Sellout of Canadian Television:* "Global, which was supposed to help defend the cultural border, ended up moving the cultural border northward, with itself on the southern side." [2]

The rapid Americanization of Canadian television did not proceed without controversy, and indeed was frequently denounced by cultural nationalists and supporters of the CBC. In 1996 CBC anchorman Peter Mansbridge employed familiar nationalist discourse when he railed against the Americanized schedules of Canada's private broadcasters like Global and CTV.

"When I hear someone argue that the Canadian television landscape would be no different without the CBC, I'm appalled," said Mansbridge:

> When CTV is running *ER, America's Funniest Home Videos, Cybill* or any one of the dozens of other American programs it runs in prime time, what exactly is that telling you about this country? When CanWest Global is running *NYPD Blue, Seinfeld, X-Files* or any of dozens of other American programs it airs, what exactly is that telling you about this country? Look at the awards programs that run on Canadian networks. They — the privates — run the Grammys; we run the Junos. They run the Emmys; we run the Geminis. They run the Oscars; we run the Genies. Yes, they get bigger audiences, but that simply speaks to the overwhelming influence of American culture in our society. And Canada's private television networks aren't just innocent bystanders of that happening. How do American awards programs — and I haven't mentioned all the others, from "The People's Choice Awards" to "The American Country Music Awards" — how does broadcasting them on a Canadian network contribute to the development of Canadian talent? How are Canadians to appreciate what we grow at home if our best are denied recognition? We often lament that

Canadians have to leave for the United States before we notice them. Surely part of the reason for that is that on all but one regular English-language television channel in this country, homage is paid only to American talent.

Michael McCabe, the private broadcasting industry's chief lobbyist, shot back at Mansbridge in the pages of the *Globe and Mail*. Marshalling a familiar fatalist argument, McCabe stated:

> What we as a country have absolutely no control over is that we live beside the most powerful entertainment machine in the world. The American production industry cranks out thousands of hours of programming a year, and with a population base of 260 million people it can afford to do so. These programs flow with the force of the Fundy tides, unimpeded across the border, where they are distributed throughout the country by cable and satellite. These programs would still be on Canadian television sets even if there were no Canadian private stations, and Mr. Mansbridge knows that. [3]

McCabe hit the problem right on, though he was arguing against himself. If Canadians can watch an American sitcom on ABC or NBC, why do they need Global or CTV to rebroadcast the same show at precisely the same time? Canadian television viewers do not benefit from this. Only Canadian private TV networks like CTV and Global benefit.

Indeed, the longstanding debate between cultural nationalists and neo-conservative continentalists is a red herring that has diverted attention from the real issue. Continentalists, whatever their ideological persuasion, can take satisfaction in the fact that virtually every American television channel is available in Canada. American network television has never been banned here. In fact, the U.S. networks have historically received priority carriage on cable at the lower end of the dial. The real issue is the effect of simulcasting, which has virtually Americanized the schedules of Canadian television stations. The trade-off for simulcasting profits was originally supposed to be investments and screen time for Canadian programs. But Canadian television networks simply reneged on that corollary part of the regulatory bargain. Thus, the simulcasting model has encouraged Canadian television stations to function as mere *schedulers* of popular, ready-made, low-rent American programs, not as *developers* of original Canadian programs.

It didn't take long for the CRTC to realize that simulcasting had back-fired. In 1983 the regulator admitted with some dismay that "Canadian dramatic productions are virtually non-existent on private English television." Simulcasting was a powerful commercial addiction for Canada's television networks. And the regulator would spend the next fifteen years attempting to attenuate its cultural effects on the national broadcasting landscape.

"It's true that, in the past, private broadcasters didn't know how to develop programs," says Ivan Fecan, CEO of the CTV network since 1997. "A lot of the senior people were in sales or accounting. It was a numbers game. Broadcasters really didn't make an effort to bring in new voices. It was too good a business the way things were." [4]

Fecan's analysis is a subtle, yet candid, indictment of his predecessors at CTV. He had spent the 1970s and 1980s moving briskly up the ranks of Toronto's Citytv and the CBC as a dynamic programming wunderkind. He developed a reputation as a creative thinker. If Fecan can be guardedly critical of simulcasting today, it's because he has staked his reputation at CTV on making money with Canadian programs.

Moses Znaimer, the legendary TV maverick at the CHUM Group, agrees with Fecan that Canadian television has been dominated by corporate bean-counters — or "overfed guys in business suits" as Znaimer likes to call them. Znaimer, who founded Toronto's gritty, street-smart Citytv in the early 1970s and later launched hip specialty channels like MuchMusic and Bravo!, began his career, like Fecan, as an innovative producer at the public CBC network.

"To my knowledge, I'm the only television president at this kind of company who's a producer," says Znaimer. "The rest of them are finance guys and sales guys. The creative guys are halfway down the organizational chart, and I think it shows." [5]

Even the CBC was long driven by the same commercial logic as its private rivals, and in the 1980s the public broadcaster simulcasted *Dallas* and many other popular American shows. Ironically, the CBC's commercialism irritated executives at CTV and Global. They wanted the lucre of simulcasting profits all to themselves. In a sense, they had a point. In Britain, the BBC was commercial-free, leaving all advertising revenues to the private ITV network. The U.K. broadcasting model worked wonderfully. ITV stations such as Thames and Granada honoured their part of the bargain by channelling commercial profits into the production of high-quality British television dramas like *Brideshead Revisited* and *The Jewel in the Crown*. The ITV stations competed upmarket against the BBC, not the reverse. In Canada, on the other hand, the CBC aired commercials and thus was under the same programming pressures that CTV and Global were. The result was the opposite of the British experience: the CBC competed downmarket against its private rivals — and indeed became a "simulcast jockey" just like CTV and Global.

Throughout the 1980s there was a great deal of debate in Canada about the direction of the country's television system. With large infusions of taxpayers' money flowing through to producers via Telefilm Canada, many argued that Canada's television networks — public and private — should adopt the British model of producing uniquely indigenous programs. Some excellent Canada dramas were in fact being made, such as Kevin Sullivan's *Anne of Green Gables*. Most programs, however, tended to reflect cultural trade-offs as Canadian producers chased deals with American television networks. CTV's cop show *Night Heat*, for example, was shot in Toronto with Canadian actors, but its setting was scrupulously disguised because the show had been pre-sold to the CBS network. Some shows, like CTV's *Mount Royal*, were embarrassing flops because they tried too hard, with fewer resources, to emulate hit American series of the *Dallas* and *Dynasty* variety.

It was perhaps unfortunate that the first major boom in Canadian television production occurred during the greedy decade of the 1980s. Despite Telefilm's good intentions, the federal agency soon found itself in the uncomfortable role of bankrolling movies and TV programs whose sole purpose was to fatten the fees of Canadian producers and fill up Cancon quotas for indifferent Canadian television networks with only nominally "Canadian" programs. Everybody was getting rich, but Canadian television wasn't getting any better. As the cultural nationalist writer Susan Crean put it in 1986:

> I think what may be happening here is simply that a class of cultural capitalists now exists in Canada that has learned, over the years, how to make a fancy buck out of trafficking in American (or imitation, made-in-Canada American) culture. And they now have high stakes in the status quo. . . . For the artistic community, I think cultural sovereignty is a slyly laid trap.

Crean's remark echoed conservative philosopher George Grant's observation in his 1965 book *Lament for a Nation*: "No small nation can depend for its existence upon the loyalty of its capitalists."

To be fair, Canadian television executives were simply being rational actors. The economic model of simulcasting was so lucrative that Canadian broadcasters saw no advantage in becoming developers of Canadian programs. In the 1980s, for example, an episode of an American hit series like *Dallas* cost roughly $850,000 (U.S.) to produce. Of that amount, a U.S. network paid about $750,000 as a licence fee, and the producer covered the rest by selling the show in the second-run syndication market. Therefore, the entire cost of producing *Dallas* was covered in the U.S. domestic market, allowing the show's producer to sell per-episode broadcast rights in foreign markets like Canada for marginal sums — generally in the $50,000 range. For a Canadian broadcaster, that amount was only a fraction of what it would be obliged to pay for a comparable Canadian drama. For example, a Canadian *Dallas*-style series in the 1980s was *Empire Inc.*, which cost $483,000 per episode to make. Thus, if a Canadian broadcaster paid only 20 percent of *Empire Inc.*'s budget as a licence fee, the cost would be nearly $100,000 — or double the $50,000 paid for an episode of *Dallas*. Moreover, *Dallas* benefitted from a bigger budget and prepaid publicity and therefore was sure to attract bigger audiences for a Canadian television network. While the effect of U.S. program exports to Canada was denounced by Canadian nationalists as cultural "dumping," this cold calculation dictated virtually every programming decision at Canadian television networks with the power of dogma.

What Canadian television executives did not know, however, was that the U.S. networks on whom they depended would soon be facing a crisis of their own. And, predictably, the Canadian broadcasting system would import that crisis as faithfully as it was importing American television programs.

Three Blind Mice: Network Television in Crisis

In the 1970s the "Big Three" U.S. television networks — CBS, ABC, NBC — shared the American viewing audience like a powerful cartel. In 1979 Frank Reel published a book about the networks' triumphant quasi-monopoly power called *The Networks: How They Stole the Show*. Two decades later, however, Ken Auletta wrote a book about the declining popularity of the networks called *Three Blind Mice: How the TV Networks Lost Their Way*. The contrasting titles of those two books provide a measure of the tragic decline of the U.S. networks in only twenty years.

There was no single cause behind the rapid fall of network television in the United States. A number of complex factors were at play. First, the popularity of VCR machines eroded the audience share of network TV by allowing people to tape and "time-shift" their viewing habits. The penetration of VCR machines in U.S. households shot up from zero in the late 1970s to more than 70 percent by 1990. Second, the Big Three were now the "Big Four," after the launch in 1986 of another network rival: Rupert Murdoch's Fox. Third, skyrocketing costs were financially crippling the networks as the bargaining power of stars and producers increased throughout the 1980s. In 1990, for example, NBC agreed to pay the producers of *The*

Cosby Show a licence fee of $3 million (U.S.) per episode — or $75 million a year. NBC was also paying an astonishing $70 million a season for another hit show, *Cheers*.

The most powerful challenge to the dominance of the U.S. networks, however, was the explosive growth of cable TV channels. By the early 1990s nearly 65 percent of American homes subscribed to cable TV, and cable channels were grabbing an increasing share of the viewing audience — and advertising revenues. The 1996–97 season marked the first time in history that the Big Three saw their combined audience share dip below 50 percent of total viewing. In 1998 the Big Three's downward slide continued, dropping to 47 percent — barely more than half of their 91-percent audience share twenty years earlier. While the local affiliates that the networks paid to air their programs were doing well financially, the networks were on the brink of disaster.

In 1997 the Big Four networks had combined revenues of $12.7 billion (U.S.), but their cash flow (earnings before interest, taxes, depreciation, and amortization) was only $697 million. Most of the positive cash flow that year came from one network, NBC. Cable channels, on the other hand, had a cash flow of $2.5 billion on total revenues of $9.4 billion.[6]

The collapse of network dominance made the original Big Three vulnerable to corporate takeovers in the 1980s — General Electric bought NBC, Westinghouse took control of CBS, and Disney bought ABC. But even the deep pockets of these corporate powerhouses could not stop the chronic bleeding. While each network was facing a crisis whose origins seemed to be unique, in the late 1990s they were all plunged into the same soul-searching, budget slashing, layoffs, and general panic as ratings continued to fall and costs kept soaring.

CBS: *The Tiffany Network*

CBS was founded in the late 1920s by William Paley, who ran the network for more than half a century. As a radio network, CBS featured popular stars such as George Burns and Jack Benny. In television, CBS scored in the 1950s with hits such as *I Love Lucy* and gained credibility as a news organization, thanks to anchorman Walter Cronkite and shows such as *60 Minutes*. CBS commanded the top of the ratings from 1955 to 1968, but its performance slumped in the 1970s despite the success of shows like *Kojak*, *The Mary Tyler Moore Show*, *M*A*S*H*, and *All in the Family*. CBS's decline was due largely to its failure to attract young audiences.

With Paley at the helm, CBS diversified in a number of directions, including ownership of the New York Yankees, Steinway pianos, and Fender guitars. Paley resisted, however, more strategic moves into cable TV channels and refused to form an alliance with a Hollywood studio. Before he stepped down in 1983, Paley failed to choose a successor and the network was on a downward slide. In 1985 Ted Turner offered to buy CBS for $5.4 billion (U.S.). The CBS board, which was hostile to Turner, turned to media giants Time and Gannett as rival suitors, but without success. The same year Loews Corp. industrialist Laurence Tisch (hotels, cigarettes, insurance, real estate) bought a piece of CBS. Tisch's move prompted the CBS board to make frantic overtures to several companies about a merger — Philip Morris, Gulf + Western, Westinghouse, Coca-Cola, and Disney. But again the defensive tactic failed. The Tisch family prevailed and took control of CBS.

Under Tisch's control, CBS Records was sold to Sony and the TV network was reduced to bare bones after a massive cost-cutting exercise. Staff dropped from 40,000 in the 1970s to 7,000 in the early 1990s. Revenues declined from $4.8 billion in the mid-1980s to $3.3 billion in 1990. In 1990 the network recorded a $22-million loss. In 1994 CBS suffered a major blow when twelve major network affiliates defected to Rupert Murdoch's Fox Television. CBS also lost lucrative NFL football rights to Fox. In 1995 Tisch suffered a no-confidence vote from the network's institutional investors. In response, he sold CBS for $5.4 billion to the giant industrial group, Westinghouse.

NBC: The Peacock Network

NBC began as the marketing arm of RCA, which was formed in 1919 by General Electric and Westinghouse after the two companies bought the radio assets of British-based Marconi. RCA first pioneered television in the 1920s when the legendary David Sarnoff was running the radio network. In 1941, two years after Sarnoff introduced television with coverage of President Franklin Roosevelt's inauguration of the New York World's Fair, the U.S. broadcasting regulator granted NBC a television licence for a New York City station, WBNT.

NBC was broadcasting in colour as early as 1953, and in the 1960s triumphed with hip comedy shows like *Rowan and Martin's Laugh-in* and the *Man from U.N.C.L.E.* series. By the 1970s, however, the network was lagging behind in the ratings, and NBC's executive suites became a revolving door. By the 1980s NBC was back on top under the leadership of young CEO Brandon Tartikoff, who developed hit shows such as *The A-Team* and *Miami Vice*.

In 1985 the industrial conglomerate General Electric bought NBC's parent RCA for $6.4 billion (U.S.). GE hoped to use NBC's strong cash flow to help finance growth of its defence systems business. Under GE ownership, NBC was put through a severe downsizing exercise. This strategy put the head office in conflict with Tartikoff, who had achieved ratings successes with high-cost shows like *Cheers*, *The Cosby Show*, and *Golden Girls*. Tartikoff soon left for Paramount, and NBC started slipping in the ratings.

By the early 1990s Hollywood mogul Barry Diller and NBC comedy star Bill Cosby were both launching separate takeover bids for NBC. GE chairman Jack Welsh refused to sell, however. In 1995 a merger with Ted Turner's TBS was aborted (TBS instead merged with Time Warner). Throughout the 1990s NBC was buoyed by the success of shows like *Seinfeld*, *ER*, and *Friends*. The most successful of the original Big Three, NBC has been Fox's main rival in bidding wars for costly, but potentially lucrative, sports rights.

ABC: *The Alphabet Network*

ABC was created in 1943 as a spin-off of NBC radio's Blue Network. RCA, which had controlled NBC, was forced by the FCC to divest the Blue Network following a federal anti-trust investigation. In 1952 ABC and United Paramount Theaters merged, and soon Hollywood studios like Warner Bros. were producing popular series such as *Ozzie and Harriet* for the upstart "third" network.

By the 1960s ABC was the most innovative program developer of the Big Three, especially with shows such as *The Fugitive* and *Peyton Place*. ABC lacked a large corporate parent, however, and consequently much of its history was marked by a number of abortive takeover attempts. In 1965, for example, corporate giant ITT came close to buying ABC, and the following year the network fended off takeover bids by both General Electric and billionaire Howard Hughes.

ABC's best years were the late 1970s, when the network ranked number one, thanks to hit series such as *Happy Days*, *The Six Million Dollar Man*, *Charlie's Angels*, and *Dynasty*. In the 1980s ABC shrewdly diversified into cable channels, notably with the purchase of the highly successful all-sports ESPN. The network followed a steady decline throughout the decade, however, and soon fell prey to corporate raiders. In 1984 ABC president Leonard Goldenson approached IBM about a possible buyout, but the computer giant eschewed the overture.

In 1986 Capital Cities Communications, a broadcasting and publishing group much smaller than ABC, bought the network — with the financial backing of billionaire investor Warren Buffett — for $3.5 billion (U.S.). In the following years, ABC's revenues improved, thanks to the performance of ESPN and other cable channels such as A&E and Lifetime. By the early 1990s, however, profits were falling again. In late 1992 ABC took advantage of the FCC's loosened cross-ownership restrictions by announcing its interest in buying a major Hollywood studio — in particular, Paramount. But the Viacom conglomerate (formerly Gulf + Western) pre-empted this ambition with its own successful bid for Paramount.

In 1996 another Hollywood studio, Disney, bought Capital Cities/ABC for $19 billion in order to vertically integrate the TV network into its production facilities. In particular, Disney saw ABC as a broadcast distribution outlet for its vast libraries of movies and cartoons.

Following the Disney example and Rupert Murdoch's purchase of Fox, other Hollywood studios vertically integrated into television. Paramount launched its own network, UPN. Warner Bros. created the WB network. And Barry Diller launched USA Networks with the financial backing of Bronfman-controlled Universal Studios.

The emergence of these wannabe TV networks gave American viewers more channel choice, but they also further eroded the market share of the Big Four. At the same time, the launch of more cable channels — from the Golf Channel to Court TV — fragmented the audience pie even further. Even worse, more and more Americans were simply not watching television at all — especially the younger generation most coveted by advertisers. By the late 1990s the crisis in U.S. network television was verging on catastrophe.

"The pure network television business is basically a low-margin to break-even business," said CBS president Michael Jordan in early 1998.

One problem was that the networks, with the exception of CBS, had become obsessed with capturing the young, upscale 18-to-49 age demographic group, and thus were engaged in a brutal war for the same potentially hit shows. As the networks fought over talent, costs soared. In only a few years, the average per-episode cost of a new series doubled to about $1.5 million (U.S.) by 1998. Sometimes the inflation was reminiscent of the Weimar Republic. NBC's per-episode costs for the hit series *ER* jumped from $4 million to $13 million — or a colossal $300 million for the 1998–99 season (most of the money was bonuses awarded to the show's actors and producers). Other series, like *Frasier* and *Home Improvement*, fetched $4 million per episode in 1998. Sports rights were even more expensive: in 1997 NBC agreed to pay $1.75 billion for an expanded season package of NBA basketball games — double its previous contract.

Fortunately for the networks, the U.S. advertising industry was still paying a 50-percent premium for their mass audiences despite their declining audience share. As *Fortune* magazine put it, the networks "might have gone out of business by now if not for the willingness of their advertisers to pay more and more for less and less, like the kid who plunks down a quarter for a downsized candy bar that once cost a dime." Indeed, by the late 1990s basic cable channels in the United States were capturing 42 percent of viewing time but taking in only 25 percent of TV advertising spending. That market aberration was quickly changing, however. In 1998 it was estimated that $1 billion would shift away from the networks towards cable channels in the following few seasons. [7]

In March 1998 a group of Big Four executives held an emergency summit to find a common solution to their crisis. The meeting was supposed to be secret in order to avoid the appearance of cartel-like industry collusion, but news of the network summit leaked out. At the meeting, ABC, NBC, CBS, and Fox executives agreed to stop fighting amongst themselves and instead face the real enemy. The war was no longer between rival TV networks, but between "free TV" and the burgeoning cable channels. According to the terms of the truce, each network would focus on its own strengths instead of attacking its network rivals. For example, NBC and CBS would stop portraying rival talk-show hosts Jay Leno and David Letterman as mortal ratings foes. The real threat was coming from Comedy Central, The Learning Channel, TNT, Discovery, Nickelodeon, Cartoon Network, and Lifetime.

"The fact that they've been beating each other on the head while the Indians are circling is just plain stupid," said Allen Banks, a media expert at Saatchi & Saatchi [8]

When peace broke out between the networks, it immediately became obvious that network executives were natural belligerents who felt uncomfortable with new marketing approaches. ABC tried out a number of bizarre marketing techniques to win viewer loyalty. The network offered frequent-flyer points to viewers of certain shows, though they had to fill out a questionnaire to prove they had actually watched these shows. ABC also launched a PR campaign whose chief slogan was disarmingly simple: "TV is good." Other ABC publicity pitches were "Without a TV, how would you know where to put the sofa?" and "If TV's so bad for you, why is there one in every hospital room?" Yet another slogan attempted to prevent couch potatoes from abandoning their sofas: "It's a beautiful day. What are you doing outside? Watch TV." What ABC failed to realize was that many viewers were indeed inside and watching TV — but were tuned to cable channels like A&E, TBS, and CNN.

The networks, it must be said, still commanded nearly 50 percent of the U.S. television audience. The drop from 91 percent in two decades unquestionably had been disastrous, but 47 percent was still a large chunk of the television audience. Only the networks could aggregate the mass audience numbers coveted by major brand advertisers. However, the "department store" market model was increasingly being challenged by the "boutique" model of niche television. And if the TV networks did not adapt, they would end up like the Big Three automakers: still in business, but battered by the competition and forced to undergo drastic adjustments to stay alive.

Some saw the network TV crisis as a threat to the time-honoured tradition of "free TV." As the market inexorably shifted in favour of subscription television, many argued that the new TV market model was not merely destroying the mass audience but also separating viewers into well-heeled "haves" and a less privileged class of "have nots" with access to only a few off-air signals. In the 1990s at least 30 percent of Americans did not subscribe to cable TV, many because they could not afford it. "Free TV" was still considered a basic citizenship right, and over-the-air broadcasters remained heavily regulated with social obligations such as right-of-reply, political airtime, and community service programming. In 1998, the U.S. broadcaster lobby estimated the cost of these social obligations at $6.8 billion annually.

"The issue is the future of free television," said CBS owner Laurence Tisch in 1991. "Will citizens have to pay fifty dollars to see the Super Bowl? Or ten dollars to see a made-for-TV movie? That question will be there. And when the crisis comes, it will be too late."

Awaiting resolution of that larger question, the major U.S. networks had to find solutions to their more immediate bottom-line crisis. Besides continued efforts to keep costs down, the Big Four made a number of strategic moves to improve their financial position. First, they argued for lighter-touch regulations permitting the broadcasting industry to consolidate into a smaller number of bigger players. Second, the industry seized on "high-definition" and digital technology as a way to expand their revenue streams. Third, the networks entered the cable TV business themselves by starting up or buying niche channels and thus cannibalizing their fiercest competitors. Finally, the networks sought to exploit the advantages of vertical integration by owning or taking equity positions in the TV shows they aired in their prime-time schedules.

The consolidation of American broadcasting began in radio. In the early 1990s U.S. radio stations were suffering financially and called on the FCC to loosen rules restricting station ownership. In 1992 the U.S. regulator obliged with its "duopoly" rule, which allowed one company to own two AM and two FM stations in any single market. To no one's surprise, the FCC decision triggered a massive consolidation of the U.S. radio industry, which promptly fell under the control of a smaller number of broadcast groups. The 1996 Telecom Act further deregulated the U.S. radio market by lifting the forty-station limit on the number of radio outlets any one company could own nationally.

The Telecom Act also deregulated ownership of television stations. Before the law's passage, broadcast groups were limited to 14 stations and a national audience coverage of 25 percent. In other words, a network like NBC or CBS could own 14 stations with a 25-percent audience reach, and its remaining stations had to be independent affiliates. The 1996 law lifted the numerical cap and raised the audience reach to 35 percent. As in radio, deregulation of the television industry triggered a massive consolidation under the control of a small number of powerful broadcast groups. By 1998 the top 25 groups controlled 432 television stations, or 36 percent of the U.S. television industry — a 49-percent increase in the first two years since the law was passed. The Big Four networks were, of course, in the top 10 broadcast groups. The biggest group, Fox Television, had a national reach of 34.9 percent with its 23 stations — a tiny fraction beneath the maximum 35-percent ceiling. CBS ranked third, NBC fourth, and ABC sixth.

The deregulation of television ownership quickly came under fire in Washington. Larry Irving, assistant commerce secretary in the Clinton administration, said: "This may not even be deregulation. This may be unregulation, and that may be of significantly more concern to us. In television there has been no demonstration that this kind of consolidation is necessary to keep these stations on the air."

As they proceeded with consolidation, the major U.S. broadcast groups also lobbied aggressively for the right to exploit the coming bonanza of "high-definition" television. Although HDTV had been a monumental failure in both Japan and Europe, the U.S. television industry jumped on HDTV in the mid-1990s as a manna-from-heaven solution to their financial crisis. The National Association of Broadcasters, which represents the Big Four networks in Washington, saw HDTV as a winning theme that would allow the industry to appropriate some of the high symbolism of Al Gore's Information Superhighway. When Gore had first announced his National Information Infrastructure project, only the telephone, cable TV, and computer industries were invited to participate. The old-guard broadcasters felt they'd been left on the shoulder of tomorrow's electronic highway. HDTV was their way of zooming ahead in the passing lane.

"We *are* the National Information Infrastructure," said John Abel, vice-president of the U.S. broadcasting lobby. "Nobody has the penetration we have. We're it. We're like the air. We're everywhere! No wire is ever going to achieve the universal service we already have."

Engineers had been kicking the tires of HDTV technology for more than a decade. The Japanese announced their MUSE technology in the 1980s and the Europeans soon followed with their own analogue D-MAC high-definition standard. But in the end neither the Japanese nor European HDTV standards worked. In the 1990s U.S. broadcasters realized that, with the advent of digital compression technology, they could squeeze several wide-screen channels into the spectrum where previously only one channel could fit. This change would allow TV stations to create new revenue streams by "multicasting" a number of channels: data and information services, home shopping, multiplexed blockbuster movies, live sporting events, and so on. It was like having five broadcast licences for the price of one. Moreover, the prospect of an American-led HDTV rollout promised to be a billion-dollar bonanza for big consumer electronics manufacturers such as Sony, Panasonic, and Leitch.

There was only one problem. Congress believed that the broadcasting industry should pay for use of digital TV spectrum. After all, satellite TV and other wireless systems had already paid huge sums in spectrum auctions to help Congress reduce the U.S. government's debt. There didn't seem to be any reason, therefore, why conventional TV broadcasters shouldn't do the same. It was estimated that a digital spectrum auction would raise about $70 billion for federal coffers.

Not surprisingly, American broadcasting executives did not share Congress's debt-reduction enthusiasm — at least not on their dime. They wanted the HDTV spectrum for free. The U.S. broadcasting industry had long enjoyed special favours in Washington. This time, however, there was no valid policy reason why CBS, NBC, ABC, and Fox should be given, at no cost, spectrum for which telephone and satellite TV companies had spent billions.

In a pre-emptive strike against Congress's preference for spectrum auctions, the National Association of Broadcasters launched a $2-million ad campaign accusing Congress of threatening to impose a "TV tax." In newspaper ads, one anti-auction NAB slogan read: "Doesn't a free society deserve free TV?" The NAB also bought thirty-second television spots on stations in Washington and other major American cities. One ad showed a multi-coloured kite floating in the air as a voice-over intoned: "Air is a wonderful thing. Free air lets us send you all the shows you love and local news, sports, and weather. Now Congress has a new idea. They tax everything else. Why not the airwaves?" A telephone number appeared on the screen: 1-888-NO-TV-TAX. About 3,500 calls came in every day while the ads ran. Some 40,000 angry calls passed through to the offices of Congressmen during the NAB negative publicity blitz.

The broadcasting lobby neglected to mention one important fact: the airwaves were owned by the American public, not by the private broadcasting industry. The NAB's ad campaign also failed to note that, in fact, Congress had no intention whatever of taxing "free TV." Congress was merely contemplating putting digital TV spectrum to auction — just as it had done for satellite TV and terrestrial wireless spectrum. Auctions are not taxes. Broadcasters also neglected to reveal that they coveted the digital spectrum not because they planned to offer "high-definition" picture quality to their viewers, but because they wanted to reap additional profits from "multicasting" new channels. Indeed, the broadcasters saw digital TV strictly as a revenue opportunity for themselves, not as a bold new technology for consumers. Their high-definition vision was as hollow as John Malone's over-hyped 500-channel universe.

Bob Dole, the powerful Senate leader and Republican presidential candidate, was resolutely opposed to giving away public spectrum for free. Dole, who like many other Congressmen was infuriated by the scare tactics of the broadcasting lobby, rejected free digital spectrum as "the biggest giveaway of the century."

"Here we are," said Dole in 1996,

> trying to balance the budget, cutting welfare, cutting other programs, and about to give a big handout here to the rich and powerful. For more than 40 years, the American people have generously lent TV station owners our nation's airwaves for free. Now some broadcasters want more and will stop at nothing to get it. They are bullying Congress and running a multimillion-dollar scare campaign to mislead the public.

Undaunted, the NAB stepped up the political pressure on Congress. At the NAB's 1996 convention in Las Vegas, a small plane circled above the casino strip trailing a giant banner that read: "HDTV: Television for the 21st Century." In Washington, lobbyists carrying briefs for the broadcasters covered the Capitol and aggressively twisted arms. Some implicitly threatened election-skittish Congressmen with local broadcaster hostility when they next faced the ballot boxes in their home states.

The hardball lobbying strategy paid off. A sufficient number of nervous

Congressmen caved in and rammed hastily drafted clauses into the Telecom Act which ensured that broadcasters would not be obliged to bid for digital spectrum. To save face for the most embarrassed Congressmen, a fig-leaf compromise was reached whereby Congress promised to revisit the issue at a later date. But the broadcasters had unquestionably won the day on a $70-billion issue.

Newt Gingrich, the powerful Republican, said to his colleague Bob Dole after the cave-in: "You got rolled." Others denounced the spectrum giveaway as "corporate welfare." Senator John McCain, the influential Republican from Arizona, was enraged by the cowering attitude of his fellow Congressmen: "I congratulate the broadcasters and their surrogates here in the Senate and the Congress. I congratulate them on prevailing. I congratulate them for their incredible influence that has prevented us from mandating an auction of the spectrum which belongs to the taxpayers."

The television industry had won a huge giveaway, but they still had not won the battle for HDTV. In October 1997 Al Gore moved in and established an advisory committee to recommend "public interest" obligations that should be imposed on digital HDTV television stations. Also, Congress warned the major U.S. networks that they had better use the digital spectrum to develop HDTV and not merely to multicast a bunch of new non-high-definition channels. A third warning came from the FCC, which ordered the broadcasters to convert to HDTV by no later than 2006.

The U.S. television industry suddenly realized that, saddled with major cost burdens and facing a strict deadline, HDTV was far from a spectrum free-for-all. It was estimated, for example, that each local television station would have to spend between $5 million and $8 million to retool its plant for HDTV. With more than 1,500 stations in the United States, the total cost to the U.S. broadcasting industry would be staggering. Some major stations promised to make needed capital investments in HDTV within a year or two, but the industry as a whole quickly cooled to the idea of billion-dollar upgrades because immediate financial returns seemed doubtful.

The obstacles to a mass-market HDTV rollout were numerous. First of all, high-definition television sets would sell initially for at least $6,000 retail. Second, the Big Four networks couldn't agree on which digital standard to adopt, provoking a battle of network engineering departments. Finally, and perhaps most important, the cable industry opposed transmitting the HDTV signals on a "must carry" basis. Cable's resistance was a death sentence for HDTV. Nearly two thirds of American television viewers subscribed to cable, and therefore the broadcasting industry depended on cable companies for access to consumers. But the cable industry had no incentive to retransmit high-capacity HDTV signals through their coaxial wires, which were already squeezed because the cable industry still had not converted to digital. The mighty cable industry was once again flexing its gatekeeper muscles.

"The arrogance of the cable industry has reached a new high," said NAB president Ed Fritts. "As a national public policy, we would not want 70 percent of the public deprived of the best of digital TV. If digital TV is the national policy, it seems to me it ought to apply to cable."

Decker Anstrom, the U.S. cable industry's chief lobbyist, countered that cable systems could not drop existing channels on their analogue lineups merely to make room for the Big Four's HDTV signals. "I'd love to have the government and broadcasters explain to 99.9 percent of our customers why they have four blank channels so 400 rich people in Washington can watch two hours of programming a week on their $7,000 television sets," said Anstrom.[9]

By the end of 1998 many were betting that HDTV would never take off in the United States — or, at least, would not arrive as a mass-market product before the 2006 deadline. The HDTV saga provided yet another classic example of how hardware hype invariably deflates when confronted with the cruel realities of the market, technology, and regulation.

Even if the Big Four networks never got their HDTV signals through cable wires, they all were moving aggressively into the cable business as owners of specialty channels. From a business point of view, it made sense for the Big Four to get into the niche TV business. Cable channels had stolen much of their audience share, so cannibalizing their most formidable competitors was the best counterstrategy to stop the bleeding.

ABC had been the first network to invest in cable channels. In 1984 it bought the all-sports channel, ESPN, which quickly became the most prodigious cash cow on the cable dial. ABC later created ESPN spin-off channels such as ESPN2 and ESPNEWS. It also bought stakes in popular cable channels such as A&E, Lifetime, and History Television. In 1997 ABC teamed up with the Comcast cable group to buy E! Entertainment, which features shows on the lifestyles of the rich and famous, for $321 million (U.S.). And the Disney Channel is controlled by ABC's parent company. By the late 1990s ABC's revenues from its cable channels totalled about $1.2 billion, much of it from ESPN.

NBC made an aggressive foray into the cable business in the 1990s with its CNBC, a twenty-four-hour channel devoted to business and political talk. CNBC also started channels in Asia and Europe. NBC's all-news partnership with Microsoft, MSNBC, was dismissed as a hobby farm for

Bill Gates, but its future as a potential CNN rival looked promising following Gates's billion-dollar investment in the Comcast cable empire. NBC also took minority positions in seventeen cable channels, including Court TV, National Geographic Channel, Bravo!, and American Movie Classics, and launched a channel in South America called Canal de Noticias NBC. The total value of NBC's cable assets has been estimated at $2.5 billion.

CBS, having failed to invest early in cable channels, has been frantically attempting to catch up. In early 1997 CBS paid $1.5 billion for two cable channels: The Nashville Network and Country Music Television. CBS also owns the regional sports channels, Home Team Sports and MidWest Sports. The network had less success with its Eye on People channel, which stalled shortly after its launch in 1997. The following year John Malone's Discovery Channel moved in and took a 50-percent share and creative control, though CBS remained a partner in the channel.

Rupert Murdoch's Fox Television expanded into cable programming with a focus on news and sports — the same areas where Murdoch's British broadcasting interests are strongest. In the United States, Murdoch has been particularly aggressive in his acquisition of broadcast rights for the regional sports channels that he jointly controls with John Malone's Liberty programming subsidiary. After a controversial battle with Time Warner, which controls one of the biggest cable empires in the United States, Murdoch finally succeeded in getting his Fox News channel onto major U.S. cable systems by paying substantial per-subscriber inducements, or "launch fees."

By the late 1990s the Big Four networks had learned a lesson from John Malone, who never hesitated to use his market power to muscle his way into ownership positions in cable channels. But while the cable industry sought the advantages of vertical integration through program ownership, the major TV networks had moved into the cable business as a way of recapturing the eyeball defections from "free TV" to niche TV. The most lucrative revenue opportunity for the U.S. networks, however, has come from vertical integration with Hollywood studios.

In the 1950s and 1960s, the Big Three networks had controlled vertically integrated production arms, and thus exercised enormous leverage over non-allied producers because they could self-deal within a closed supply-and-demand cycle. To counter the market power of the Big Three, the FCC imposed in 1970 the so-called Syndication and Financial Interest Rules (called "fin-syn" rules), which prohibited the TV networks from producing their own programs. The networks thus were forced to commission programs from outside producers — mainly the Hollywood studios.[10]

In the 1980s the U.S. networks fought these restrictions in a favourable climate of deregulation, arguing they were no longer an oligopoly because of the rise of cable networks and home video. In the early 1990s the FCC agreed and modified the fin-syn rules by allowing the Big Three networks to hold an interest in the programs they aired and to produce up to 40 percent of their schedules. In 1995 the FCC lifted the restrictions altogether, opening the door to mergers between the Hollywood studios and the TV networks. The result was a rapid reintegration of networks and production studios: Disney/ABC, Paramount/UPN, Warner Bros./WB network, 20th Century Fox/Fox Television. Also, in 1998, Hollywood mogul Barry Diller was cobbling together yet another TV network with the backing of Montreal-based Seagram, which controls Universal Studios.

Vertical integration has allowed the Hollywood studios to use TV networks as guaranteed "shelf space" for their vast libraries of content as well as new productions. Vertical integration has its risks, however. The networks are under pressure to schedule shows produced by their parent Hollywood studios, and therefore might neglect, or even reject, a future hit show merely because it was produced by a non-allied producer. NBC incurred major opportunity costs by reserving a choice prime-time slot — between *Friends* and *Seinfeld* — for a couple of mediocre NBC-owned shows, *The Single Guy* and *Union Square*. Disney, for its part, blocks out certain nights of the week on ABC for its own programs, and has even been criticized for censoring ABC news reports that are critical of the Disney empire. Fox so far has been lucky, scoring big with its own hit series such as *Ally McBeal* and *King of the Hill*.

By 1998 there was strong evidence that the Big Four networks were taking vertical integration to the point of abuse of market power. Specifically, the networks were demanding from non-allied producers equity positions in the shows in exchange for a prime-time slot. DreamWorks, for example, got involved in a bitter spitting match with NBC over the network's insistence on acquiring an ownership position in DreamWorks' comedy, *Nearly Yours*. NBC also muscled in on producer Brillstein-Grey's hit series, *NewsRadio*, which returned to the network's prime-time schedule in 1998–99 in exchange for an NBC equity position.

Some observers noted that the Big Four's hardball tactics were provoked by the excessive financial demands of arrogant producers of hit shows like *Seinfeld* and *ER*. Instead of paying huge sums for broadcast rights, the networks are increasingly demanding equity stakes in order to participate in the "back end" — the huge profits derived from syndication and other ancillary rights.

"The future of network programming is going to be more ownership of programming, more internal control," said Jamie Kellner, chairman of Warner Bros.' WB network.

An analysis of the twenty-seven new shows premiering in the fall of 1998 on the Big Four networks revealed that twenty shows were selected because of a backroom co-venture deal between the network and the show's producer. According to TV critics, the result was the worst television season in memory — everything from a kick-boxing-cop show to a series featuring has-been sex queen Bo Derek playing a struggling cattle-ranch matriarch in Hawaii. There were, it is true, some notable exceptions. the WB network network picked up *Felicity*, a series about a cute pre-med college student who ditches her studies to follow her boyfriend to New York City. The series was produced by Disney-owned Touchstone, but although Disney-controlled ABC actually passed on the show, it nonetheless became a critical success and one of the season's best offerings.

The WB network is not available on cable TV in Canada, and consequently *Felicity* could not be simulcast by a Canadian TV network. CTV picked the show up anyway, but without a simulcasting slot against a U.S. border station its profits from airing *Felicity* were reduced, which doubtless explains why CTV buried the show by scheduling it at 7 p.m. on Sunday nights, where it was up against Global's simulcasted ratings topper, *60 Minutes*. Thus the best new series on American television, unavailable in Canada on the WB network, was sabotaged by CTV merely because there was no room for the show during the week, since CTV's simulcasted prime-time schedule was already largely pre-programmed by the Big Four.

Felicity, like Mark McGwire's record-smashing home run, furnishes a perfect illustration of the Canadian television conundrum. When CTV and Global can reap fat profits from simulcasting, they are exposed to the whims of the U.S. networks that make all the programming decisions. When CTV and Global cannot simulcast, they buy the American programs anyway to prevent their Canadian rivals from airing them. Either way, Canadian television networks cannot avoid the inherent frustrations of their utter dependence on the U.S. television system.

The Canadian networks have grown so frustrated, in fact, that they are now looking for new approaches. And, predictably, they are importing them directly from the United States.

Colonial Convulsions in Lotusland

Izzy Asper, the founder of Global TV, is a study in paradox. Asper, who runs his international broadcasting empire from his home town of Winnipeg, claims to be a passionate Canadian nationalist. His patriotic convulsions have indeed been numerous. In 1983, when he suffered a major heart attack at age fifty, it was suggested that he fly to the famous Mayo Clinic in the United States for top-quality medical attention. Asper wouldn't think of it. He would get treatment in his own country.

"I wasn't going to the United States, I'm a Canadian, damn it," Asper later recalled. "I trust the system, so I had my surgery in Winnipeg, even though I had to wait around for six weeks, doing nothing."

It would be unduly cynical to doubt Asper's love for his country. There can be little doubt, however, that Asper is the most prodigious agent of Americanization in the history of Canadian television. It might be wondered, indeed, why Asper has never awakened one morning and said to himself: *I'm not an American, I'm a Canadian, damn it. I trust the system in Canada. I'm tired of using my television stations merely to rebroadcast American prime-time soaps and sitcoms. I'm going to finance a great Canadian television drama — set in my beloved Manitoba!*

There is no evidence, to date, that Asper has ever been seized by any brainwave of the sort. His patriotism seems to be a private matter. Patriotism is one thing, profits something else altogether.

Asper has made little effort to conceal his vision of Global as a cash machine whose profits are derived chiefly from importing American television shows. He has unashamedly compared the television business to "selling soap," and he appears to be impervious to the ceaseless onslaught of derision and criticism of Global as a low-rent "Love Boat Network."

At Global TV, executives talk almost reverently about simulcasting as if it were a complex and mysterious art form whose secret is known only to a happy few. Boarding a plane to Los Angeles and outbidding CTV for the simulcast rights to *NYPD Blue* doubtless requires extraordinary mental acuity. In the final analysis, however, Global's self-satisfaction is based on the comforting knowledge that, however limited its programming autonomy may be, Global still makes more money than any other broadcaster in Canada.

"If you take the Rubik's cube of performance, no matter how you spin it, we're making the most money," asserts Global TV president Jim Sward.[11]

Sward is right. It's hard to argue with success, however unpatriotic. Global is undeniably successful, both in ratings and on the bottom line. And Global executives certainly share the spoils of that success. In 1996 Izzy Asper paid himself $1.6 million in salary and bonuses plus $2.2 million in options. The same year Jim Sward, who had scrambled up the ladder in Ted Rogers's radio and cellular phone groups before joining Global, earned a salary of $774,480 plus $866,250 in bonuses.

Global's success is not limited to Canada. Its CRTC-protected profits have helped Asper finance an aggressive strategy of global expansion, including broadcasting assets in Australia (where it controls Network Ten), New Zealand (where it owns TV3 Network), and Ireland (where it has launched a new TV network with co-owners including the pop group U2). In the late 1990s Asper was openly expressing interest in buying TV stations in the United States, but those ambitions were blocked by U.S. foreign-ownership restrictions. Canada's own foreign-ownership ceiling of 33 percent protects domestic broadcasting groups from takeovers by U.S. and other foreign companies, and thus has facilitated the consolidation of broadcasting groups like Asper's CanWest Global. These rules, while helpful in the past, have put Asper on the horns of a dilemma. He knows that Canada will have to lift its ownership ceilings before U.S. regulators ever allow Canadian broadcasters to expand south of the border.

Asper controls his family-owned company and therefore is not vulnerable, like CTV, to a hostile takeover. This might explain why, in 1998, he discreetly hired a raft of high-priced lawyers in Washington and Ottawa to press for loosened ownership rules in both countries. Global's prime-time schedule was already largely American. Now Asper wanted to build a genuinely North American television group over which he could amortize his insatiable appetite for U.S. soaps and sitcoms.

"We don't think a company like ours can be in one country," said Asper in early 1997. "If I dared tell you my view of where the world was going, I'd probably get locked up. But I honestly believe that we haven't even begun to feel what globalization is all about."

Asper, who paid himself $2.7 million in 1998, had other reasons for deploying his profits outside Canada. By the mid-1990s, the Canadian television industry was plunged into convulsions of uncertainty about its future. The U.S. television industry was going through a brutal shake-out in the wake of deregulation, consolidation, and vertical integration, and the aftershock was being felt in the boardrooms of Canadian television networks. For the first time in decades, Canadian networks like Global and CTV could not count on simulcasting profits from hit shows aired on the Big Four. Canadian networks, like their U.S. counterparts, were growing frustrated by the soaring prices of American programs. Moreover, in the 1990s the U.S. and Canadian broadcasting markets were increasingly becoming "North American," particularly with the rise of cable channels such as A&E and Ted Turner's TBS. These channels could easily buy North American rights for programs, thus depriving Canadian networks of local simulcast rights.

In short, the cosy Canadian market was suddenly a less protected and predictable place for Global and CTV. Competition was looming everywhere: from U.S. border stations, from American cable channels, from Canadian specialty channels, from grey-market satellite services, and now from the Internet.

In response, Canada's private TV networks at first resorted to the predictable reflex of fiercely defending the old paradigm. The Canadian Association of Broadcasters lobbied the CRTC, for example, to sanction unworkable variations of simulcasting — "non-simultaneous" substitution, program deletion, and "strip" substitution. In effect, Canadian broadcasters asked the CRTC for the right to patch their own advertisements over the signals of any American network show, whatever time of the week it aired on a U.S. border station. For example, if ABC aired *NYPD Blue* on Wednesday nights but Global wished to broadcast it on Tuesday, Global wanted permission to have ABC's broadcast of the show blocked out in Canada. As newspaper columnist Terence Corcoran put it: "One can imagine the message to viewers: 'Sorry, you can't see *NYPD Blue* on ABC channel 7 tonight, you should have caught it on Global last night.'" This time, however, the CRTC refused to indulge the special pleading of Canada's private networks. [12]

The private networks soon adopted a less original lobbying strategy by simply borrowing their survival strategies directly from the U.S. networks. First, they lobbied for industry consolidation. Second, they jumped on the digital HDTV bandwagon. Third, they moved aggressively into cable specialty channels to cannibalize competition. Finally, CTV and Global lobbied for vertical integration and the right to take equity positions in the programs they aired.

The Canadian lobby campaign for radio deregulation, for example, was a straightforward Me-Too tactic. The American broadcasting industry had won radio-ownership deregulation, so Canadian radio owners wanted it too, even though the Canadian industry was different, both structurally and financially, from U.S. radio. The U.S. radio industry was highly fragmented and pluralistic, whereas in Canada private radio was dominated by a clutch of major broadcasting companies — CHUM, Rogers, WIC, and Radiomutuel. Also, unlike the money-losing U.S. radio industry, Canadian radio had recovered from a slump and was highly profitable after 1996.

The CRTC evidently could not resist the appeal of a policy fashion. In late April 1998 the regulator announced that Canadian radio stations would henceforth be allowed to consolidate with multiple ownership in the same market. That was the carrot. The stick was that radio stations would see their Canadian-content quota increased by 5 percent to 35 percent. The media coverage of the landmark decision focused on the Cancon issue, doubtless because the implications of more Canadian songs on the airwaves were easier to understand than the structural implications of industry consolidation. Just the same, the net effect of the CRTC decision was to bring less competition and greater concentration to the Canadian radio industry, which was already highly concentrated and doing exceptionally well financially.

The consolidation of the Canadian television industry would be much more complicated. By the mid-1990s a bitter war was raging between Canada's two main private television empires: Global and CTV. No longer was the Canadian television industry divided by a schism between the publicly funded CBC and a coalition of private broadcasters. The CBC had virtually Canadianized its prime-time schedule, and consequently the private networks had no reason to whinge about having to compete for U.S. simulcast rights against a taxpayer-supported broadcaster. The battlelines were now clearly drawn between CTV and Global.

Global was strong in the lucrative southern Ontario market and in most of western Canada but was shut out of Alberta and Quebec, leaving two large vacancies in Izzy Asper's dream of owning a consolidated national television system. Asper had attempted to win Alberta licences in 1994, but the CRTC rejected his applications. In 1996 Global got another chance when the CRTC announced its intention to license a new television station in Alberta. Most observers believed that, this time, Global would have little trouble winning its coveted Alberta licence. But again, the CRTC rebuffed Global by awarding the licence to Craig Broadcasting's A Channel proposal.

Global's Jim Sward, who had worked on the Alberta strategy for three years, was infuriated. He reacted to the CRTC rejection by angrily threatening to cancel Global's Canadian-made series, *Traders, Jake and the Kid*, and *Ready or Not*.

"There is nothing encouraging in the decision, absolutely zero that recognizes any of the work we've done," complained Sward. "Our Canadian shareholders will say, 'Why bang your head against the wall?' So yes, the future of *Jake, Traders*, and *Ready or Not* is in jeopardy. I don't think we'll be renewing them." [13]

Tactically, Sward's intemperate outburst was positively stupid. In effect, he had attempted to blackmail the CRTC by threatening to withdraw Global's Canadian programs unless the regulator approved its Alberta expansion plans. More fundamentally, Sward's claim that the CRTC had not recognized Global's past good deeds was preposterous. If anything, the regulator had been too indulgent toward Global, which had built an impressive broadcasting asset in Canada while giving precious little back to the country whose regulatory system had fattened its profits and financed its global expansion. Moreover, Global had commissioned *Traders* and *Jake and the Kid* not because it was committed to Canadian drama, but as part of its sales pitch to the CRTC in order to get its broadcast licence renewed. In a word, without the implied threat of regulatory constraint, neither show would have made it onto Global's schedule.

Sward knew he'd goofed. He made an ambiguous attempt to backtrack: "I said I didn't think we were going to be able to support the kind of indigenous, high-budget, high-quality national programming we were supporting." [14]

On the Quebec front, Global's executives once again showed their baffling lack of diplomatic skills. In 1996 Global sought to buy, in partnership with Montreal's French-language TV station Télé-Métropole, the assets of the CBC's bankrupt Quebec City affiliate, CKMI. Global planned to use the mothballed CBC station to beam its own signal into the lucrative Montreal market and thus extend its network reach into Quebec. But Global required CRTC approval for the deal.

The CRTC hearings examining Global's Quebec ambitions took place at the end of 1996 — in the immediate wake of the Alberta licence imbroglio. Jim Sward's impetuous threats were still echoing in the minds of CRTC commissioners. Worse, Global had just appealed the CRTC's Alberta decision to the federal Cabinet, a manoeuvre that, while formally legal, surely must have intensely annoyed the regulator. Asper, moreover, had hired two top Ottawa lobby firms — Hill & Knowlton and Government Business Consultants — to press Global's case against the CRTC while Global wrapped itself in the flag with newspaper ads about the success of *Traders*. In truth, *Traders* was successful despite Global. The network had effectively sabotaged the show by airing it on Thursday nights against CTV's simulcast of the hit American series *ER*.

In December 1996 the CRTC seemed ready to punish Global for its appalling arrogance and high-handedness. The tension was palpable in the room as CRTC commissioners listened to Global executives make their pitch for the Quebec licence. At one point, Global's regulatory lawyer, Glen O'Farrell, referred to his company's intention to "buy" the CBC's Quebec City licence. This semantic slip was a tactical error that CRTC commissioner Andrée Wylie pounced on.

"Broadcast licences are not saleable," snapped Wylie. She reminded the embarrassed O'Farrell that the airwaves in Canada are owned by the public and that broadcast licences are temporary privileges, not permanent private property rights.

The CRTC's interrogations also seemed to cast some suspicion on the precise nature of Télé-Métropole's role in the deal. The CRTC was not unaware that a common industry ploy was to bring in palatable straw partners for optical reasons in order to win regulatory approval. The CRTC seemed unconvinced that Télé-Métropole — owned by the big cable company Vidéotron — was anything more than a Montreal partner intended to give Winnipeg-based Global's Quebec ambitions more local credibility.

Following the hearing, the Global team was so dispirited by the apparent hostility of CRTC commissioners that Izzy Asper couldn't contain his anger.

"I just don't understand the attitude of the CRTC," said Asper. "We just got our second national licence to operate in New Zealand in four years, and I have been trying to do the same thing in Canada for the past nineteen years. It's not just the business — it's emotional. I'm pathologically Canadian. But if I can't grow here, I'll go to Ireland."

In the end, the CRTC was only exacting a subtle revenge on Global by making its executives eat humble pie in public. In late January 1997 the federal Cabinet upheld the CRTC's decision to award the Alberta licence to Craig's A Channel. A month later, the CRTC, emboldened by the Cabinet's support, magnanimously granted Global its coveted Quebec licence. Asper, while still shut out of Alberta, was getting closer to realizing his dream of building a trans-Canadian television system.

Ivan Fecan understood that Global's consolidation represented a potentially lethal threat to the CTV network. CTV had long been outraged by the disparity between its onerous "network" regulatory burdens and the relatively light-touch obligations imposed on the non-network CanWest Global television "system." Now Global, which had become more profitable than CTV, was benefitting from the strategic advantages of consolidation. Fecan believed a counteroffensive was urgent.

A concerted strategy would be difficult to marshal, however, because CTV was a loose confederation of regional affiliates with no central control. Fecan was CEO of CTV's biggest member, Baton, but he did not control the entire network. He gave some thought to withdrawing Baton from CTV in order to configure Baton — like Global — as a national "system" with reduced regulatory burdens. The company's name, Baton Broadcasting System (BBS), was the most obvious sign that Baton was thinking about emulating the Global model.

But Fecan rejected this option for a more ambitious plan. He convinced Baton's owners, the Eaton and Bassett families, that the best counteroffensive against Global was for Baton to consolidate its control over the entire CTV network. To achieve this, Baton would have to buy out

CTV's disparate affiliates owned by CHUM, WIC, and Electrohome. Control of CTV would allow Baton to rationalize its operations under one management structure and become a unified network, instead of a vulnerable empire of regional broadcasting baronies.

Fecan made his bold move in late February 1997 — precisely the same moment that Global was celebrating CRTC approval of its Quebec licence. In a complex deal that involved asset swaps and buyouts of CTV affiliates, Toronto-based Baton took effective control of CTV. Anointed by the Eaton and Bassett families, Fecan became the boss of CTV, pushing out CTV president John Cassaday and other top executives who quietly left before they were shown the door.

"Welcome to CTV — not BBS, not Baton, not Baton/Electrohome, but at last, the new CTV," declared Fecan in mid-1998. "We are now, for the first time in thirty-seven years, a fully integrated and unified network speaking with one voice. . . . This is the powerhouse that is now CTV."

Suddenly it looked as if Ivan Fecan, still in his early forties, was the most powerful man in the Canadian broadcasting industry. He also seemed determined to show that he was different from other CEOs of private broadcasters in Canada. Arriving at CTV with a raft of loyal stalwarts from the CBC, Fecan strenuously affirmed his commitment to developing high-quality Canadian dramas for CTV's prime-time schedule. It appeared that CTV's embarrassing past as a simulcast jockey was over. Some even believed CTV was being colonized by a public television CBC culture.

The media thundered their approval of Fecan's ascendancy to the throne of Canada's premier private TV network. Fecan had his detractors, though. Skeptics said his programming patriotism was calculated posturing to win regulatory approval for Baton's takeover of CTV. John Haslett Cuff, television critic for the *Globe and Mail*, observed that Fecan was in fact a bean-counter like so many other television executives. Cuff credited Fecan with developing a number of excellent shows at CBC — *Codco, Kids in the Hall, North of 60* — but he argued that Baton's takeover of CTV would only give Fecan more financial muscle to compete with Global for American television fare:

> With the increased stake in CTV and improved market penetration, the network will be able to bid higher for those immensely profitable U.S. shows, such as *America's Funniest Home Videos, Melrose Place, Men Behaving Badly, Ellen* and *Dr. Quinn, Medicine Woman,* beloved by shareholders and mass audiences alike. Much of what Baton has produced that qualifies as Canadian content under the CRTC's arcane and flexible conditions of

licence is either homogeneous, U.S.-flavoured pap (*Poltergeist: The Legacy, Lonesome Dove, FX: The Series, Two*) or bargain-basement, mass-cult drivel (*eNow, Camilla Scott, Dini*).[15]

Judged purely as corporate strategy, Fecan's takeover was a stunning coup de théâtre that signalled to Global that CTV was serious about competing as a consolidated network force. Fecan was nonetheless determined to put an end to Global's regulatory holiday due to its convenient non-network status as a broadcasting "system."

At the end of 1997 the CRTC held hearings examining the need for a "third network" in English Canada. The target of the hearings was unmistakably CanWest Global, whose "system" status was now exposed to open public scrutiny. CTV and other major industry players stepped forward to argue before the CRTC that Global should be recognized for what it was — a full-fledged television network — and that its Canadian-content obligations therefore should be adjusted upwards.

Robert Lantos, the legendary movie producer, appeared before the CRTC to decry the lack of domestic programs on Canadian television: "Our broadcast landscape remains today the most colonized of the major industrial nations, and it is in our cultural, industrial, and national interest to change that." Lantos, the producer of the series *Due South*, liked to remind Canadian television executives that, if they believed they couldn't make money on Canadian programs, they should step aside and let him run their networks. This challenge usually had the effect of stunning television beancounters into an awkward silence.

Appearing before the CRTC, Lantos rejected Global's call for a more hands-off, free-market approach to regulating television content. "Either you regulate or you don't," he said. "But you can't regulate on the one side — i.e., protect broadcast licensees, limit competition, not allow a free market — and not regulate on the content side."

The vise was tightening on Global. Two separate consultants' reports found a major discrepancy — as much as 50 percent — between the levels of spending on Canadian programs by CTV and Global.

"If this is correct, it's indefensible — and grounds for immediate action by the Commission," said Ian Morrison, the feisty head of the Friends of Canadian Broadcasting. In his appearance before the CRTC, Morrison quoted the Bible as a reminder to Global about reinvesting profits in Canadian programs: "St. Luke said it best: 'Where a man has been given much, much will be expected of him; and the more a man has had entrusted to him, the more he will be required to repay.'"

While fighting these regulatory wars in Ottawa, Izzy Asper was engaged in another test-of-nerves battle against Shaw Cable for control of the Vancouver-based broadcasting group, WIC. Shaw had grabbed control of WIC from the feuding Griffiths family, which had failed to produce an heir capable of running the business. But Asper was also a major WIC shareholder, and what's more he had long coveted the vulnerable B.C.-based broadcasting empire. After several months of legal belligerence, Shaw and Asper called a truce. A carve-up of WIC's assets was unavoidable. In August 1998 Shaw and Global announced that Global would get all of WIC's television assets — including stations in Alberta and Quebec.

After the WIC deal, it seemed Izzy Asper had needlessly locked horns with the CRTC to take Global into Alberta and Quebec. The asset swap with Shaw accomplished that with one stroke of the pen — though regulatory approval was required for it. With stations in Alberta and Quebec, Global would become the biggest private television network in Canada. The CanWest Global "system" was now unquestionably a national network, though Asper was the last to admit it.

"I want to congratulate Izzy for finally getting what he's wanted all along, a national network," taunted Fecan.

Asper shot back: "I think Ivan should focus on his company and make it better. He's certainly got enough to do. He should worry about his own company and leave mine alone. I don't know what he thinks he has to gain by trying to hurt his competitor like this. I mean, really, what good does it do for him?" [16]

In the fall of 1998 the CTV-Global hostility escalated into a full-scale war during the CRTC's landmark hearings into the future of Canadian television. At the hearings, Canada's television producers found the symbolic high ground by calling on the CRTC to "reclaim prime time" for Canadian programs — that is, to remedy the American colonization of the Canadian television landscape. Unmoved, Global stubbornly insisted that there was no money to be made in airing Canadian drama series.

"Frankly, I don't think it's the Commission's business in the private sector," Jim Sward told the CRTC. "We all got where we are on our own . . . . God bless private enterprise. That's the juice. And if we decide to stomp on it, then it will lose all its liveliness."

Andrée Wylie, who was chairing the CRTC hearings, stiffly reminded Sward and his fellow Global executives that their richly flowing profits owed largely to regulatory protections, not to free enterprise.

"The train you are on is regulated and it has worked very well for you," said Wylie. "You can mention private enterprise as many times as you want."

In the backrooms, it appeared Ivan Fecan had forged an alliance with Canadian television producers to establish CTV's pro-Canadian credentials and isolate Global as the contemptible simulcast jockey. As part of its patriotic publicity blitz leading up to the regulatory hearings, CTV began airing a sixty-second spot whose slogan was "CTV: Canadian Television." There was only one problem with the promotional clip, however: it featured the faces of several American television stars, from *Ally McBeal's* Calista Flockhart to *Felicity's* Keri Russell. John Allemang, the *Globe and Mail's* television critic, wryly observed in a critique of CTV's curious form of cultural nationalism: "Canadian Television is not the same thing as Canadian programming." [17]

While CTV and Global battled for market dominance through the strategic advantages of consolidation, they seemed united in their ambiguous attitude towards high-definition television. In fact, it was the CBC, with its long history of technological nationalism and battalions of in-house engineers, that took the lead on HDTV in Canada.

Ottawa frankly didn't know what to do about HDTV. In late 1995 the government had set up an industry-led task force to come forward with proposals. The task force, headed by CBC executive Michael McEwan, was composed of a wide cross-section of names from virtually every corner of the industry — television broadcasters, hardware manufacturers, cable and telephone companies, film producers, technical standards experts and engineers, and government bureaucrats. Like the Information Highway Advisory Council, its membership gave the impression of industry-wide consultation. But in truth, there was little agreement on what to do, if anything, about HDTV.

Hardware manufacturers like Sony and Leitch, which anticipated huge profits from HDTV manufacturing runs, were naturally gung-ho about high-definition television. Canada's television networks, like their U.S. counterparts, were more interested in HDTV as a generator of new revenue streams from multicasting. They contemplated with decidedly less enthusiasm the cost implications of the necessary capital upgrades to offer HDTV picture quality. Besides the CBC, the only Canadian broadcaster that showed some interest in HDTV was Global, mainly because Izzy Asper was planning to buy television assets in the United States and therefore had some interest in ensuring that his Canadian stations were lockstep in sync with the U.S. industry. Indeed, Global's ever-present Jim Sward played a leading role in the task force deliberations throughout 1997.

The HDTV task force submitted a report to the government in October 1997. Predictably, it asked for everything the U.S. broadcasting industry had been given, including free spectrum and automatic digital licences for every TV station in the country. The task force also recommended that the deadline for full conversion to HDTV in Canada be set at 2007, one year after the U.S. deadline. In short, the Canadian approach to HDTV would be a straight copy of the U.S. industry's approach, including the hidden agendas.

As in the United States, the chief obstacle to HDTV in Canada was the cable industry. Since about 75 percent of Canadian homes subscribed to cable TV, it would be impossible to deploy HDTV in Canada without the co-operation of the cable industry. But like their American counterparts, Canadian cable companies did not want to be forced to carry the HDTV signals of conventional broadcasters.

The federal government's muted reaction to the HDTV task force report seemed to reveal utter confusion as to the best course of action. The only concrete step the government took was the creation of a non-profit, public-private group called Canadian Digital Television, headed by Michael McEwan, who left the CBC to set himself up as a consultant. McEwan's mission was to catalyze and co-ordinate industry efforts towards a Canadian HDTV strategy. This task was virtually impossible, however. Most of the major Canadian broadcasters had cooled to HDTV for the same reasons as their American counterparts: the conversion costs were too high, the revenue potential was too uncertain, and the cable industry wasn't on-side. HDTV provided yet another textbook case of muddle, foot-dragging, U-turns, and non-decision. A heroic technological project quietly faded into embarrassed silence while the engineers worked on the glitches.

While the prospect of digital multicasting profits seemed far off, Canadian broadcasters moved more aggressively into ownership stakes of specialty channels on cable TV. True, some broadcasters — like CHUM with MuchMusic and CBC with Newsworld — had launched specialty channels in the 1980s. But most Canadian television networks had not diversified into cable channels with the same ambition that the major U.S. networks had. In Canada, the CRTC controlled the number of new cable channels that would be licensed and, more important, who would be awarded the licences. And with a few notable exceptions, television networks had been kept out of the niche TV market.

In the mid-1990s Canadian networks were losing audience share and advertising revenues much like the Big Four south of the border. It was doubtless this fact that led the CRTC to extend a helping hand to Canada's conventional broadcasters. In 1996, when the CRTC awarded a roster of new specialty licences, the television broadcasters emerged as the big winners. CTV won a handful of licences, including a headline news channel,

The Comedy Network, CTV Sportsnet, Talk TV, and stakes in Teletoon, Outdoor Life Network, and History Television. CHUM, too, added several new channels to its existing stable of boutique program outlets: Space: The Imagination Station, MuchMoreMusic, CablePulse 24, Canadian Learning Television, Star TV, and the French-language Musimax. Vancouver-based WIC won a licence to launch Report on Business TV as the *Globe and Mail's* partner. Global was awarded a licence for Prime TV. And in Quebec, the Montreal broadcaster Télé-Métropole won an all-news licence for Canal Nouvelles.

After this triumph, Canada's private television networks soon were mimicking moves by the U.S. networks to vertically integrate into production and grab equity stakes in the Canadian programs they aired. Global made the first move in June 1998, when it paid $40 million in cash for Fireworks Entertainment, an independent producer of mainly "industrial" (i.e., not identifiably Canadian) programs suitable for the export market.

Global's takeover of Fireworks immediately sounded alarm bells in Ottawa. The federal government's 1983 broadcasting policy had been aimed at structurally separating television networks from program production. That policy had been a great success, but now the spectre of vertical reintegration threatened to undermine fifteen years of achievement — including the making of Canadian TV dramas such as *Traders, Due South, Anne of Green Gables, North of 60,* and *Black Harbour.* The TV networks, for their part, claimed that increased costs, declining simulcasting profits, and a reduced share of the advertising pie gave them no choice but to own and control the programs they aired.

In fact, Canada's private networks were merely aping the convulsions of the Big Four while putting a Canadian spin on their demands. Canadian television networks not only depended on American programs, they depended on American lobbying tactics, too.

Public Broadcasting: The Death of Distinction

The subject of public broadcasting invariably stirs strong emotions. Many regard taxpayer-supported broadcasters — like Britain's BBC, Canada's CBC, and the American PBS networks — as indispensable instruments of citizen engagement and social cohesion. Others denounce public broadcasters as irrelevant white elephants erected by socialist or New Deal governments, and call for their prompt dismantling or privatization.

The first public broadcasters were the institutional offspring of nineteenth-century nation-states and their paternalistic social elites. Designed in the early twentieth century by middle-class Britons with residual Victorian values, public broadcasting offered a comforting solution to the two main obsessions of the nation-state: political legitimacy and territorial integrity. When John Reith (later Lord Reith) created the BBC in the 1920s, he saw the public broadcaster as an instrument to create "a more intelligent and enlightened electorate," thus making a direct link between electronic communications and democratic citizenship. Today, this high-minded mission, while wholly admirable, seems to many as archaic as the Victorian values that formulated it.

The supporters of public broadcasting are loath to acknowledge it, but the principles underlying state ownership of television can make no claim to absolute values. As Michael Tracey put it in his Gibbonesque book, *The Decline and Fall of Public Service Broadcasting*:

> Public service broadcasting was very much an idea constructed within one moment in time, the early part of the twentieth century, on patrician and governmental principles from another, the nineteenth century. As we approach the twenty-first century, it becomes clear that the sets of principles through which the idea of public service broadcasting was articulated have a precarious social, political, economic, and cultural anchorage.[18]

Tracey's linkage of public broadcasting and Victorian values is accurate, but not all state-owned broadcasting systems embraced the social-responsibility model adopted in Britain. In continental Europe, for example, state ownership of broadcasting was often imposed by governments whose major preoccupation was not cultural paternalism, but straightforward political control. In some countries, such as Holland, religious denominations controlled television. In Portugal, the Catholic Church controlled broadcasting jointly with the state. In Italy, the television spoils were cynically carved up among the three dominant political parties — Christian-Democrats, Socialists, and Communists — each getting its own TV network. In the United States, which was devoid of a noblesse oblige tradition and stridently committed to market forces, state-owned broadcasting was rejected in favour of an advertising-driven medium. The creation of PBS in 1967 by Lyndon Johnson was largely the result of efforts by the private Ford and Carnegie foundations, and its public funding was paltry from the outset.

In short, no broadcasting model — whether "public trustee" or purely "commercial" — has ever established itself with absolute authority. Television systems reveal a wide variety of social constructs based on relative values. The only common element that can be found among disparate broadcasting systems is that, in recent years, virtually all of them have been transformed by the combined forces of technological change and free-market liberalism. In a world of trans-border technologies and commercial globalization, the autonomous power of states over broadcasting — and over many other things — has been significantly attenuated, if not severely eroded. Public broadcasters, at least in their current design as mass-audience programmers, have lost their legitimacy in a world where spectrum is no longer scarce, competitors can provide substitutable services at no direct cost to taxpayers, and national borders are increasingly irrelevant in the media industries. Whether one likes it or not, the paternalistic sensibility of Lord Reith has been superseded by the commercial ambitions of Rupert Murdoch.

No one knows this more than public broadcasters themselves. As the logic of commerce increasingly dominates the television business, public broadcasters have become more and more commercial.

In the United Kingdom, even the venerable BBC has been forced to revamp its orientation towards a more commercial approach. The BBC once dominated and influenced Britain's private ITV network, known for its regional stations such as Thames and Granada. The two networks, though competitors, were linked by a common corporate culture and, more important, bonded by a duopolistic pact that gave all advertising revenues to ITV while the non-commercial BBC benefitted from a generous licence-fee support system. The BBC–ITV symbiosis was the inspiring formula for what has long been considered the best broadcasting system in the world. It worked because the BBC and ITV, run by an Oxbridge elite instead of hard-nosed bean-counters, were exempt from a downmarket competitive rivalry. In his book on the BBC, Tom Burns echoed the famous anti-Pentagon speech by Dwight Eisenhower when he described the BBC–ITV system as a "social-industrial complex." It may have been paternalistic, but everybody was kept happy: *Brideshead Revisited* for the chattering classes and *Benny Hill* for the masses.

The ideological swing towards radical neo-conservatism in the 1980s dealt a major blow to the BBC. Margaret Thatcher, who had come to power in 1979, was determined to dismantle the BBC–ITV system, which she resented as a "cosy duopoly." In 1983 even the old-guard establishment newspaper, *The Times*, published an article that asked the heretical question "Do We Really Need the BBC?" Ironically, the Iron Lady had more success smashing apart the private ITV network than she did demolishing the state-owned BBC. In 1990 Thatcher revoked the licences of the ITV stations and auctioned them off to profit-seeking entrepreneurs, some of them her political friends.

Under director-general John Birt, the BBC has been going through

Left: John Malone, father of the 500-channel universe, with Bell Atlantic CEO Ray Smith. Malone and Smith announced their corporate nuptials in October 1993 as the "perfect information age marriage." A few months later, the marriage was on the rocks. *(AP/Wide World Photos)*

Below: Caricature of a callous cable baron by Anthony Jenkins of the *Globe and Mail.* *(reprinted with permission from the* Globe and Mail*)*

Above: Phil Lind, the longtime Rogers lieutenant, was a master lobbyist whose backroom skills produced predictable results from the CRTC. Lind left Rogers after suffering a stroke in July 1998.

Right: Cable baron Ted Rogers was concerned about the death stars threat from satellite TV. Some wondered whether the eccentric billionaire was up to the challenge. *(photo by Peter Caton, Gerald Campbell Studios)*

Right: Joel Bell, possessed of a brilliant intellect and indefatigable drive, spearheaded Power DirecTV's attempt to enter the Canadian market.

Below: Power Corp. billionaire Paul Desmarais flanked by sons André (left) and Paul Jr. (right). The fact that André Desmarais was married to Prime Minister Jean Chrétien's daughter made the satellite TV saga highly sensitive in Ottawa power circles. (*courtesy of the* Financial Post)

Above: André Bureau, president of Astral Communications, left the chairmanship of the CRTC in 1989 to run a company whose broadcasting interests were governed by CRTC regulations.

Left: Michael Neuman, CEO of ExpressVu. When Neuman was promoting his satellite TV service in Calgary, Alberta-based cable baron Jim Shaw Jr. snorted: "Basically, what we're dealing with, with Michael Neuman, is big hat, no cattle, and he wants to start ranching." (*courtesy of Canapress photo service*)

Right: Al Gore and his father, Albert Gore Sr., who died in late 1998. Gore Sr. had been a prime mover in the U.S. Senate behind the Interstate Highway System. His son was the driving force behind the Information Super-highway. *(courtesy of the* Financial Post*)*

Below: Keith Spicer, chairman of the CRTC from 1989 to 1996, lacked patience for the details of regulation. *(courtesy of the* Financial Post*)*

Above: The road ahead on the Information Super-highway according to *Globe and Mail* caricaturist Brian Gable. *(reprinted with permission from the* Globe and Mail*)*

Left: John Manley, federal industry minister, was Al Gore's counterpart in Canada where he promoted his vision for a Canadian Information Highway. The pro-market bureaucrats in Manley's ministry, Industry Canada, were often at loggerheads with regulatory officials at the CRTC and the culture-crats in the department of Canadian Heritage. *(courtesy of the* Financial Post*)*

Right: Paul Allen, the unlikely "zillionaire" who founded Microsoft with Bill Gates, has amassed an enormous cable TV empire in the United States. Allen's real passion is emulating his rock guitarist hero, the late Jimi Hendrix. *(courtesy of the* Financial Post)

Below: AT&T president Michael Armstrong (left) with John Malone announcing the phone giant's buyout of Malone's cable empire. *(courtesy of the* Financial Post)

Above: Charles Sirois, CEO of Teleglobe. The brilliant telecom wunderkind has used his monopoly profits from Teleglobe's international long-distance business to build a diversified media company. *(courtesy of Réjean Meloche Photographe)*

Left: Software billionaire Bill Gates, the John D. Rockefeller of the Information Age, began investing in U.S. cable companies in order to control the wires running into American homes. *(courtesy of the* Financial Post)

Left: Izzy Asper, founder of CanWest Global, with his three children (from left to right) David, Gail, and Leonard, all of whom work at Global. As head of "The Love Boat Network," Asper maintains a strict separation between profits and patriotism.

Below: Moses Znaimer, the brilliant media maverick and founder of MuchMusic, was one of the first TV executives to understand that the "mass audience" was dying. (*photo by Mia Klein*)

Above: Picture from *Due South*, featuring Paul Gross as Mountie Benton Fraser and Keith Rennie as detective Stanley Kowalski. The Alliance series was set in Chicago and pre-sold to CBS. When the U.S. network pulled the plug, *Due South* retreated to its spot on CTV in Canada. (*photo by Jeffery Newbury, courtesy of Alliance Communications*)

Right: Ivan Fecan masterminded Baton's take-over of the CTV network. The former top CBC executive threw a gauntlet in Izzy Asper's face by promising to make a profit with Canadian programs. (*courtesy of the* Financial Post)

Left: Robert Lantos is the closest thing Canada has to a bona fide movie mogul. Lantos cashed out in 1998 by selling Alliance to Michael MacMillan's Atlantis and has since returned to his passion for producing feature films. *(photo by David S. Eisenberg, courtesy of Alliance Communications)*

Below: Michael MacMillan, the low-key CEO of Alliance Atlantis, built Canada's biggest television production company after graduating from the film program at Queen's University in the 1970s. *(courtesy of Alliance Atlantis)*

Above: Ian Morrison, head of the Friends of Canadian Broadcasting, is an effective broadcasting watchdog who has hounded the cable industry for its monopoly tactics.

Right: Linda Schuyler, founder of Epitome Pictures, transformed her experience living in Toronto's east-end Riverdale area into the popular Degrassi Street TV series. *(courtesy of Epitome Pictures Inc.)*

Right: Hollywood lobbyist Jack Valenti. Valenti, who got his start in Lyndon Johnson's White House, has been Hollywood's international enforcer, and the bane of cultural nationalists, for more than three decades. *(AP/Wide World Photos)*

Below: Allan Gotlieb with Ronald Reagan in Air Force One. Gotlieb, one of Ottawa's most powerful mandarins, was Canada's ambassador in Washington throughout the 1980s, when Tory minister Flora MacDonald launched her "Flora's Folly" crusade against the Hollywood studios. *(courtesy of Allan Gotlieb)*

Left: As these French and German posters illustrate, Europeans publicly opposed the global domination of the Hollywood studios even in the early days of cinema.

Right: Françoise Bertrand, chairperson of the CRTC. Bertrand provoked concern in the industry by stating publicly that the Commission should regulate Canadian content on the Internet. *(Michael Bedford Photography)*

Below: David Colville, CRTC vice-chair for telecommunications. Colville opposed a $600-million regulatory giveaway to the cable industry on the grounds that the money belonged to cable subscribers. He was overruled. *(Michael Bedford Photography)*

Above: Andrée Wylie, CRTC vice-chair for broadcasting. Wylie, an intellectually rigorous commissioner, warned that the cable industry's combination of gatekeeper power and control of new channels would lead to market abuses. *(Michael Bedford Photography)*

Left: Steve Case, chairman of America Online. AOL bought CompuServe and then Netscape. Bill Gates once said to Case: "I can buy 20 percent of you, or I can buy 100 percent of you. Or I can go into this business myself and bury you." Case didn't flinch, and AOL is now going after Microsoft. *(courtesy of the* Financial Post*)*

a veritable commercial revolution. In the past two years the BBC has created five new over-the-air channels, including a round-the-clock news service called News 24, an ambitious Internet service, and five new commercial channels launched jointly with the U.S. Discovery Channel. This year, Birt also created a commercial subsidiary, BBC Worldwide, whose mandate is to pursue commercial joint-ventures and exploit the BBC's vast library of content. In a word, Birt is modelling the BBC on the major U.S. television networks.

Birt, who is thoroughly detested by the BBC's "Aunty knows best" old guard, remains convinced that Beeb's survival in the digital universe depends on a more commercially-oriented business strategy. The new-look BBC strategy is equally contested, however, by its private competitors. The BBC is funded, after all, by a tax imposed in the form of a licence fee on television sets. Why, then, should the BBC be permitted to deploy its public funding to compete commercially with private broadcasters who can't develop new business strategies on the Queen's shilling?

Rupert Murdoch's Sky News, for example, reached about 2.5 million British homes via cable until the BBC started offering its News 24 free of charge to U.K. cable operators. The result? Sky News has since lost some 700,000 subscribers and the BBC's all-news channel now reaches more than 2 million cable TV homes in Britain.

In France a long and powerful tradition of *dirigisme* has been unable to withstand the technological and ideological assaults on public broadcasting. Until the 1980s the centralized state politically controlled French television. The three television networks — TF1, Antenne 2, and FR3 — were directly run out of the Minister of Information's office, which routinely exercised a veto on items scheduled to appear on the evening news. The French president not only hand-picked the senior executives at the networks, but also hired and fired on-air personalities on the slightest whim or pretext. Charles de Gaulle, frustrated by the hostility of Parisian newspapers, once comforted himself with the knowledge that he still controlled television: *"Toute la presse est contre moi. J'ai la télévision. Je la garde."* [19]

Ironically, it was a socialist government that created France's first private television network, Canal Plus. Launched in 1984, the hugely successful pay TV channel was privately owned, but indirectly controlled by the Elysée Palace. Canal Plus was headed by André Rousselet, a close friend and longtime *chef de cabinet* of President François Mitterrand. In 1985 Mitterrand created two more private networks, La Cinq and M6. The following year, Mitterrand's conservative prime minister, Jacques Chirac, privatized the major state-owned network, TF1, which immediately transformed itself into a commercial broadcaster along the American model. Soon the two remaining public networks, Antenne 2 and FR3, were chasing the privatized TF1 downmarket into increasingly populist excesses.

France's two remaining public TV networks, merged under one corporate aegis called France Télévision, today face a declining audience share and reduced advertising revenues. And like many other public TV networks in Europe, France Télévision is engaged in a desperate soul-searching exercise as it attempts to deal with creeping marginalization due to increased competition in a fragmented broadcasting market.

The latest blow to public TV in France came from Lionel Jospin's socialist government, which in 1998 tabled a bill that would scale back France Télévision's dependency on ad revenues. Jospin wanted France Télévision to curb its growing commercialization and start acting like a bona fide public broadcaster. Not surprisingly, executives at France's private networks applauded the proposed law, while France Télévision's top mandarins were decidedly less enthusiastic about the legislation.

France's broadcasting bill was drafted with one eye fixed on the European Commission in Brussels. The EC's Television Without Frontiers directive, first adopted in 1989, took aim at Europe's numerous state-owned TV monopolies by encouraging competition and transnational signal distribution. An updated version of the EC broadcasting policy is now going after Europe's state-owned networks that are using public funds to compete unfairly against private broadcasters.

The British and French experiences are instructive for the Canadian broadcasting system because they are reminders of what the CBC had already gone through two decades earlier. The CBC never knew the luxury of being a purely public broadcaster along the British or French models. While the CBC produced many excellent programs, it would be difficult to argue that it has been markedly distinctive — except in radio — from what is available from the main private networks, CTV and Global. Indeed, the CBC is driven by the same twin obsessions of ratings and advertising dollars that preoccupy the bean-counters at Canada's private networks.

In Quebec, there is virtually no difference whatever between the public Radio-Canada and the private Télé-Métropole: both compete for large audiences with popular *téléromans* and *téléséries*. In many respects, the Quebec television industry has been a populist version of Britain's BBC–ITV duopoly. This model can work when the number of available channels is limited and the viewership is culturally homogeneous. But when viewers have access to fifty or a hundred channels and audiences are fragmented, public television as a mass-audience broadcaster increasingly becomes regarded as unnecessary as a practical matter and illegitimate in principle.

In the Digital Revolution, the only possible way public broadcasters can survive is by reasserting a new form of legitimacy. That can be accomplished only if public broadcasters reinvent themselves. In Canada, no more royal commissions, parliamentary hearings, or commissioned reports are needed. Muddling through and incremental change will not do. Public broadcasters must realize what they have long failed to acknowledge: in a cluttered landscape of commercial television, their greatest strength is their distinctiveness. Public television must stop emulating its private rivals; it must exploit the advantages of differentiation. Public television must appeal to citizens, not consumers.

In Canada, this idea is given lip-service support within the CBC, but in reality it's regarded with deep suspicion by entrenched bureaucratic interests. Too many corporate fiefdoms have too much to lose by profound change. Journalist Barbara Amiel seized the essence of the problem within the CBC when she wrote: "The CBC has hired some of the best people in the country and then hired some of the worst people to be in charge of them." [20]

Today, only revolutionary leadership at the CBC can transform the public broadcaster's sclerotic corporate culture. Remarkably, the CBC has suffered from weak leadership at precisely the moment the public broadcaster needs to be galvanized by a new vision.

If the portraits of past CBC presidents were hung side by side in a gallery, they would be contemplated as an intriguing collection of figures whose efforts, some more impressive than others, have reflected no particular sense of continuity or defining vision about the role of public broadcasting. The last strong CBC president was Pierre Juneau, a brilliant autocrat who ran the "Corp." from 1982 to 1989. Juneau, who was engaged in a guerilla war with the Tory prime minister Brian Mulroney for much of his tenure, managed to reduce the CBC's bloated unionized staff to some degree. Yet when he stepped down, the CBC was still very much the same organization it had been when he arrived. As head of the CRTC in the early 1970s, Juneau had challenged CBC presidents to offer a more distinctive service to Canadians. But as CBC president himself, he left no better record. It was on Juneau's watch that CBC Television was airing simulcasted episodes of *Dallas* in prime time.

Juneau was succeeded by Ottawa mandarin Gérard Veilleux (1989–94) and longtime CBC executive Tony Manera (1994–95). Both were competent and well-meaning, but neither managed to impose a coherent vision on the CBC. Veilleux left the CBC for a top executive post at Power Corp. Manera stormed out of the CBC, guns blazing, and levelled bitter accusations at Brian Mulroney's government for slowly bleeding the public broadcaster to death with budget cuts. When Perrin Beatty became CBC president in 1995, the appointment was baffling. Beatty, the scion of a wealthy small-town Ontario family who had been elected to the House of Commons at age twenty-two, was a longtime Tory politician. This fact alone made his appointment by Liberal Prime Minister Jean Chrétien somewhat indecipherable. Some read it as proof of the Chrétien government's complete indifference to the fate of the CBC.

When he arrived at the CBC, Beatty was widely considered an earnest, immensely likeable man whose good intentions could not be doubted. Yet he soon found himself uttering all the familiar homilies about the role of public broadcasting in the new broadcasting universe. In reality, however, there was little evidence that Beatty was committed to anything other than the status quo.

Beatty arrived at the CBC joined at the hip to Guylaine Saucier, who was appointed CBC chairperson. Saucier, a tough-minded Quebec businesswoman, saw her job as more than ribbon-cutting and rubber-stamping. She was strong-willed, but she also had a clear vision for the CBC — something that Perrin Beatty seemed to lack.

"The CBC will survive and prosper only if it can differentiate itself from other broadcasters," Saucier told a Senate committee in 1997. "Our programming, therefore, must be both unique and marketable and complement that of private broadcasters."

Saucier not only proved to be a hands-on CBC chair, she quickly came to the view that Beatty had to go. She cordially despised Beatty so intensely, in fact, that in late 1995 she went to the Prime Minister's Office and requested that he be fired. The PMO refused. So Saucier decided simply to act as if she, not Beatty, were running the CBC.

Saucier's ambition and tenacity cast Beatty in the unenviable role of the bumbling, impotent Louis XVI dominated by the intelligent and cunning Marie Antoinette. Beatty was even derisively dismissed as the "Saucier's apprentice." In 1998 Saucier had her term as CBC chair renewed, apparently on the condition that Beatty's term *not* be prolonged beyond March 1999. The peculiar spectacle of animosity between Beatty and Saucier provided such intriguing gossip in the Ottawa power circles that it was easy to forget that, while knives were drawn and glinting, the fate of the CBC was hanging in the balance.

Advice should always be furnished with caution. The enunciation of a panacea might have the virtue of simplicity but possibly the vice of over-simplification as well. Nonetheless, any future leader of the CBC would be well advised to adopt as a general operating principle: *programming over infrastructure, software over hardware.*

In the language of economics, the justification of the CBC as a producer of high-quality, culturally significant programs can be found in the notion of "merit goods." It could be reasonably argued that, in a small country like Canada, market forces alone cannot produce merit goods in broadcasting; therefore this market failure can justifiably be corrected through government intervention. The notion of merit goods might be opposed by pro-market neo-conservatives. Their arguments are not without some foundation and they deserve serious attention. One argument, for example, is that merit goods — whether public broadcasting or public museums — tend to be consumed mainly by the affluent and educated and hence should not be financed by all taxpayers. It nonetheless can be assumed that, as in many European countries, there is general support for the principle of public broadcasting in Canada.

If the CBC wishes to survive — and its survival should not be taken for granted — it should focus its mission on the production and programming of merit goods. By any definition, that should not include simulcasted American soaps and sitcoms, sports matches, or game shows. The more practical question relates to means of achieving the goal of transforming the CBC into a producer of pure merit goods. First, the CBC should retreat entirely from advertising and sustain itself on long-term public financing so it can make long-range plans. Second, it should withdraw from its heavy bricks-and-mortar infrastructure and devote its resources to programming only. To accomplish this, the CBC might consider Britain's Channel 4 model. At a minimum, the CBC should emulate the BBC's "producer choice" model and break itself into structurally separate units — broadcasting and production — to encourage more input from independent producers.

The CBC's obsession with technology and infrastructure is a residual hangover from the technological nationalism that has driven the Canadian broadcasting system for decades. Even in the 1990s, when the CBC's very existence was being called into question, the broadcaster treated itself to a spanking new Broadcast Centre in the shadow of Toronto's CN Tower. Perhaps the CBC was attempting to assert its existence materially in a time of crisis. The construction of the Broadcast Centre also demonstrated the extent to which the CBC was still stuck in the old technology-and-infrastructure paradigm.

As Richard Collins, a London School of Economics professor who spent many years studying the Canadian broadcasting system, observed about the CBC:

Its new Broadcast Centre on Front Street is a monumental indictment of the CBC's inability to read obvious trends. At a time of resurgent commissioner broadcasting, of rapid innovation in cost-saving production technologies, of incandescent anger from outside the charmed triangle of Toronto-Ottawa-Montreal, not only does the CBC build a temple to the production methods and Pharaonic pretensions of broadcasting in the 1960s, but it put the television studios on the top floor of the building! The contrast to CFTO's unpretentious facilities within sight and sound of the [highway] 401 and Citytv's snappy lean-and-mean operation round the corner can only add to the despair with which contemporary advocates of public broadcasting contemplate the pyramid of Front Street. The CBC's record of recent operational decisions is so inept as to tempt this commentator to recommend a Carthaginian solution — demolish the entire structure, burn the ruins, and spread salt over the land so the monster will never rise again. [21]

The evocation of Carthage should be taken by the CBC as an ominous warning. What the public broadcaster needs is an enlightened dictator. Failing that, it may well end up with a Roman general. If so, the once vital Corp. will become a pale "Corpse," consigned to the dustbin of Canadian history.

CHAPTER 6

Me TV

The Decline of the Mass Audience

"REMEMBER THE NINTH COMMANDMENT," SNAPS MOSES ZNAIMER IN A tone of amiable reproach, smiling imperiously at his puzzled interlocutor.

Znaimer, wearing his trademark buttoned-up black shirt and sporting a ponytail, is seated Zen-like in his spacious corner office at Citytv, the funky Toronto TV station he founded in the early 1970s. Citytv's white mock-Gothic headquarters, located in the heart of Toronto's fashionable Queen Street West district, have become the cultural epicentre for the city's Gap Generation. And Znaimer, who launched Citytv's MuchMusic pop-video channel in the mid-1980s, is that generation's high priest — or "executive producer," as he calls himself.

Znaimer's influence extends far beyond Queen Street West and the teenagers across Canada who are permanently plugged into the pulsing MuchMusic culture. Today, MuchMusic is available in the United States on DirecTV and ersatz MuchMusic channels have been launched in Scandinavia, continental Europe, and South America. Znaimer has concocted an admirably provocative slogan for his success: "Canadian cultural imperialism."

It's difficult to believe that Znaimer actually gets any work done in his office, which is part techno-museum, part gadget-cluttered toyland, part temple of self-adulation. Along one wall stands a dwarfish statue of Znaimer himself, crowned comically like a midget emperor. The resemblance is uncanny, and presumably Znaimer approves of its presence. Every artifact in the spacious office seems to be a reverential offering to the legend, mystique, and personal aura of its sole occupant, known universally as simply "Moses," who is undoubtedly one of the most controversial, brilliant, notorious, inspiring, and enigmatic figures in television. Like his Biblical namesake, Moses has founded, and cannily promoted, his own personal mythology on the hard rock of a certain number of received truisms — the Ten Commandments of the Television Age.

"The ninth commandment?" his guest asks quizzically.

The mind catapults back in time to summon forth vaguely etched memories of Old Testament wisdom, making a quick detour via the technicolour images of Cecil B. DeMille. Moses has descended from the mount, and the mind's eye attempts to scan down the chiselled imperatives engraved on a great stone tablet. But the roster of ancient interdictions is a blur. Only "thou shall not commit adultery" comes into focus. That would be a highly pertinent piece of advice in the television business, even right here at Citytv. But sexual morality is not the topic of discussion on this bright spring morning.

"The ninth commandment. Hmm. I give up."

Znaimer attempts to conceal a slight twinge of disappointment, and perhaps wounded vanity. His guest, unlike the hundreds of young, ambitious employees hustling briskly through the corridors of the Citytv building, has not indelibly memorized the tenets handed down by Moses from Media Mountain. Znaimer fixes his visitor with a bemused stare and articulates, slowly, the words of the "ninth commandment" as if reading from Scripture:

"There never was a mass audience, except by compulsion." [1]

MuchMoreMoses and the Rise of Niche TV

Znaimer was one of the first television executives to stake his career on the death of the mass audience. And so far his instincts have been proved right. When conventional TV networks were selling soap detergent by broadcasting *The Young and the Restless*, Johnny Carson, and the Super Bowl, Znaimer was creating a hip rock 'n' roll TV station that took the pulse of the Toronto streets. He quickly discovered that an entire generation had been disenfranchised by the conservative, white-bread WASP mentality that prevailed in the boardrooms of Toronto's established television stations. Znaimer understood that, in the coming multi-channel world, television did not have to be a mass ritual. Just as department stores surrendered to boutiques, broadcasting was becoming "narrowcasting," "free TV" was being transformed into "Me TV." The mass audience was being splintered into multiple psychographic categories. And that, Znaimer believed, was a good thing.

"Crowds make me nervous," Znaimer asserted in June 1998, stunning a Toronto audience of broadcasting executives with his characteristically bold assertions. "For me, more than ten people, that's the Nuremberg rally.

I think it's long gone when three corporations can dominate the mind."

The cold numbers confirm Znaimer's instincts. In the United States, the Big Four networks today attract less than half of the viewing audience, and in Canada the performance of the major networks — CBC, CTV, and Global — is not much better. True, a 50-percent share is a huge chunk of the viewing audience, but it's a lot less than the nearly 100 percent that TV networks commanded only two decades ago. Today, it can no longer be argued that the major TV networks are "weapons of mass distraction."

Znaimer nonetheless rejects the concept of "fragmentation" promoted by advertisers. "I don't like the word," he says. "It's a word from the mouth of a monopolist. For me it isn't fragmentation. It's liberation, precision, democratization."

Over at the rival CTV network, CEO Ivan Fecan does not entirely agree with Znaimer, who was once his boss at Citytv. "I believe there will always be a mass audience," says Fecan, who left Citytv for the CBC and then did a stint at NBC in Los Angeles before landing in the top job at CTV. "People have a need to be part of a community. There will always be a Top Ten because people want one."

Fecan knows, of course, that the television landscape is rapidly splintering. Indeed, he has aggressively moved CTV into the niche TV business with new specialty channels in narrow interest areas such as comedy and sports. But Fecan prefers to see these channels as "brand extensions" or "drill downs" that attract the deeper interests of CTV's mainstream mass-audience viewers. He believes that, in the final analysis, the couch potato is here to stay.

Znaimer, on the other hand, believes there never was a mass audience — except "by compulsion." For him, the explosion of new TV channels permits us, finally, to plug into interests and communities of our choice. We are "compelled" only occasionally — by political assassinations, World Cup soccer matches, Princess Diana's death, Bill Clinton's zipper problem — to join a billion eyes fixed on a single event.

Both views are undoubtedly valid to some extent. But the recent history of television shows a seismic shift away from mass-audience programming and a rapid fracturing of viewing into increasingly specialized and advertising-targeted "communities of interest." In the United States, niche cable channels have toppled the Big Four networks. In Canada, specialty channels have been growing in number, enjoying greater audience share, and attracting a bigger piece of the advertising pie every year. By the year 2000, Canada's conventional TV broadcasters are expected to capture only 52 percent of the television audience. Specialty channels — U.S. and

Canadian — will take 35 percent, and the rest will go to other forms of TV viewing such as U.S. network television and pay TV.

The growing popularity of specialty channels is not reflected, however, in their share of advertising revenues. While specialty channels win roughly one third of audience share in Canada, they grab only about 15 percent of the $1.2-billion advertising pie. True, the advertising gap is compensated for by robust subscription revenues from cable and satellite TV. In 1997 total revenues (advertising and subscriptions) for Canadian specialty channels were $589 million, on which they earned an average profit margin of 18 percent. Advertising revenue for specialty channels in Canada has been growing by about 17 percent every year since 1993. In contrast, conventional broadcasters like CTV and Global now regard an ad-revenue increase of 8.9 percent a boom year.

Znaimer's MuchMusic is one of the most profitable cable channels in Canada, with a profit margin of 27.5 percent on revenues of $26.8 million. Only the TSN all-sports channel is more profitable, with a profit margin of 36 percent. TSN, however, receives a $1.25 monthly per-subscriber wholesale fee from cable companies, while MuchMusic gets only 11 cents per month for its roughly 6 million subscribers. That translates into $8 million in subscriber fees, or less than half of the $19 million MuchMusic earns from advertising. MuchMusic's success, therefore, is based on the channel's ability to charge a premium on advertising for targeting the coveted youth market. The channel also keeps operating costs down by hiring young, energetic kids who work for low pay. Znaimer's emoluments, by contrast, are exceedingly liberal. According to annual reports by the CHUM Group, which owns Citytv and its specialty channels, in 1997 Znaimer earned $1.4 million in compensation plus $754,800 in fees paid by CHUM to his personal company, Olympus Management Limited, for "management of production and performance services." In 1998, his compensation was $1.5 million.

Most would say Znaimer richly deserves his generous remuneration. He has shrewdly piggybacked an impressive stable of niche TV channels — MuchMusic, Bravo!, Space: The Imagination Station, CablePulse 24, MuchMoreMusic — onto the existing infrastructure of the original Citytv station. True, the success of MuchMusic and MuchMoreMusic has been ensured by protectionist regulations that ban competing U.S. channels like MTV and VH1 from the Canadian market. Still, MuchMusic is arguably better than, or at least as good as, MTV. Its international popularity and the growing number of franchise MuchMusic channels around the world seem to confirm that.

Znaimer's mother station, Citytv, actually began as a local off-air

Toronto station that hit the airwaves in the early 1970s when cable TV was still taking off in Canada. In its early days, Citytv was chronically underfinanced and operated on a shoestring budget in its digs on Queen Street West. The station's founders — including Znaimer himself, Phyllis Switzer, Ed Cowan, and Jerry Grafstein — quickly resorted to airing soft-porn flicks to kick-start the ailing upstart station. The station's "baby blue" movies, a daring programming gamble in the staid Toronto of the early 1970s, brought controversy but not profits. The station was still floundering.

After a brainstorming session with American media consultant Jacques de Suze, Znaimer decided to transform Citytv into a gritty, urban, ultra-hip TV station. The emerging aesthetic of rock videos was later superimposed onto Citytv's news reporting and virtually every other type of program. Znaimer had found his formula. pop music and urban chic. Citytv was, and remains, an essentially *local* Toronto channel. The ethos of localism has been codified in one of Znaimer's Ten Commandments. Number five states: "The best TV tells me what happened to me, today."

With the launch of MuchMusic in the mid-1980s, Znaimer took a different approach. MuchMusic would not be limited by the constraints of space and time — the local Toronto market. Localism is essentially vertical: everybody watching is in the same place at the same time. With Much-Music, Znaimer adopted a horizontal approach: he created a lifestyle culture that ingeniously exploited the local trendiness of its Toronto setting to fashion a demographic community of interest well beyond the city limits. MuchMusic thus marked the merger of Citytv's localism and MTV's global ambitions. It exemplified the familiar slogan: Think globally, act locally. To Znaimer's credit, he was one of the first television executives to understand the dynamic of media "glocalization."

Znaimer has his critics, to be sure. If he can justifiably boast that he was ahead of his time in putting people on the air whose skin was not British-stock white, he also has shown a decided predilection for the non-WASP skin of pretty, sexy, and unbelievably young girls who not only look good on camera, but also don't demand big salaries. It is possible to walk into the Citytv building — called the "environment" — and believe you have inadvertently stepped into an eye-popping party thrown by Hugh Hefner. Some critics have murmured that, despite the meticulous maintenance of the Moses mythology for the optics of image-making, Znaimer has actually been out of the loop in recent years. It's said that the CHUM Group, which bought Citytv in the late 1970s, has sent in corporate bean-counters to contain Znaimer's over-reaching creative drive. CHUM lets Znaimer brand the Citytv empire with his vision and style, it is said, but the "suits" are there to make sure the trains run on time and the place turns a tidy profit.

Znaimer's critics dismiss his vainglorious talents for self-promotion, yet his admirers point to an undeniable courage and genius. He is unquestionably a complex figure, driven by the conflicting impulses of certitude and insecurity. In mid-1998 *Toronto Life* cruelly mocked Znaimer's sartorial tastes, which the magazine described as "shirts buttoned to the collar; large, tinted glasses that evoke a 1970s porn magnate." Yet in the very same issue of *Toronto Life*, critic Robert Fulford praised Znaimer for his creation of Bravo!, the high-brow arts channel. Bravo! even turns a handsome profit, thanks largely to cable subscription fees. In 1997 the channel made a 16.5-percent profit on total revenues of $14.3 million — $12.2 million from cable subscriptions and $2 million from advertising.

Though time's winged chariots have been catching up with Znaimer, he keeps racing forward. His dream of building an informal network of Citytv-like stations throughout North America has failed to materialize, though competitors like CTV have not hesitated to copy the hip Citytv formula to launch new affiliates in cities like Vancouver. Znaimer's greatest strength is his knack for developing new specialty channels. After the launch of MuchMoreMusic in the fall of 1998, he began preparing to launch Star TV and Canadian Learning Television. He would even like to see a bundle of CHUM channels sold as a package to cable and satellite TV subscribers. Znaimer has long complained that Canada's broadcasting regulator allows more and more American channels into Canada on cable — CNN, A&E, Speedvision, Ted Turner's TBS superstation — while shackling the creative energies of producers like himself.

"How old will I be before the cable industry in this country banks on a Moses Znaimer channel instead of a Ted Turner channel?" he says.

If Znaimer has an American counterpart, it is undoubtedly Ted Turner, another egocentric genius whose success has been inextricably linked to his excess. Turner was one of the first American television entrepreneurs to understand the decline of mass-audience television. In a speech to advertising executives in 1978, Turner warned that they would ignore at their peril his new Atlanta-based superstation, WTBS, which he planned to deliver to cable systems via satellite. Turner's all-news channel, CNN, would soon follow.

"Where you have idiots watching idiot shows, I guess you can sell them idiot products," Turner bluntly told the advertisers. "Not us."

His vision — and it was a bold assertion in 1978 — was that the Big Three networks would decline rapidly in the 1980s and be eclipsed by cable TV.

"Your TV sets will become something on which you can see anything you want to see whenever you want to see it," said Turner. "Not just what three nincompoops in New York decide for you."

When CNN first went on the air in 1980, it had only 1.7 million cable subscribers in the United States. In its first five years, CNN lost money. By the early 1990s, however, some 136 million viewers were watching the all-news channel. In 1992, CNN earned $155 million (U.S.) profit on revenues of $536 million. The Gulf War had given a tremendous boost to CNN's fortunes. Its coverage of the war made CNN the best-known television channel on the planet. Some even said that CNN had become an adjunct of the U.S. State Department. It certainly had become an indispensable media conduit for the conduct of global diplomacy.

Turner learned the hard way what he could have figured out after spending a day at Znaimer's Citytv: there is no such thing as "global" television. In television, as in art, everything is *local*. Turner had understood the horizontal logic of niche TV, but he had failed to appreciate the compulsions of space and time — the bonds of locality. At first, he resisted the pressure to transform CNN into a non-American news channel. He believed that what worked in Atlanta would be consumed without resistance in Germany, Australia, and India. He was wrong. Turner was forced to admit that, in television programming, there was no such thing as globalization — only *glocalization*.

It was the threat of competition that forced Turner to adjust his thinking about CNN. In 1985 he expanded overseas with CNN International. By the early 1990s, however, CNN was facing international competition from the BBC and Rupert Murdoch's Star TV in Asia. In response, Turner hired dozens of ethnic and non-American journalists to give CNN a stronger local appeal around the world. He also started taking ownership stakes in foreign news channels — in Germany and Russia, for example — and paying for the unrestricted rights to use material from other national broadcasters. And in a move against Murdoch's Star TV, Turner developed a relationship with China's Central Television.

After more than a decade, Turner was basing CNN's strategic growth on the wisdom of Moses' fourth commandment: "As worldwide television expands, the demand for local programming increases." Znaimer, for his part, was proving that glocalization and Canadian cultural imperialism could be the same thing.

Cable TV Goes to the Movies

Niche TV did not start with local or global news. Nor does it owe its beginnings to pop music videos. It began with Hollywood blockbusters and American sporting events.

In the early 1970s the U.S. cable industry was still operating on the margins of the American broadcasting industry. Time Inc., the magazine publisher, had bought up a number of cable systems in New York City, including a company run by Charles Dolan and Gerald Levin. The two men had struck on the idea of driving cable penetration nationwide with an all-movie-and-sports channel. The new channel would be called Home Box Office.

First launched in 1972, HBO did not become a success until 1975, when it became available to U.S. cable systems via satellite — thanks, ironically, to Canada's Anik satellite, which was used to beam HBO into American markets. In the mid-1970s the major U.S. television networks didn't believe HBO would make money, and therefore ignored the threat of pay TV on cable. Even the Hollywood studios doubted HBO would ever take off. They were wrong. When HBO started being transmitted via satellite to cable systems across the United States, cable penetration soared to more than 9 million households in a single year. By the end of the 1970s, HBO had almost single-handedly driven U.S. cable TV penetration to about 15 million subscribers, most of them attracted by the channel's combination of uncut Hollywood movies and live sporting events.

The phenomenal success of HBO in the late 1970s made the U.S. cable industry the powerhouse it is today. In 1998 nearly 66 million American households subscribed to cable — about 67 percent of U.S. television homes. The rapid penetration of cable TV led to the explosive growth of more than 100 cable networks, generating more than $30 billion (U.S.) in annual subscription revenues. HBO was the engine that drove that growth. Its success also catapulted Gerald Levin into the executive suites of Time Inc., which is now Time Warner. Levin today is CEO of the global media giant.

After its success was established, HBO became a major financing source for movies — *Sophie's Choice*, *First Blood*, *The King of Comedy*, to name a few. HBO put money into film production as "pre-buys" to obtain exclusive pay TV rights. It wasn't long before HBO's market power over cable systems and Hollywood movie studios was becoming worrisome. A war soon broke out between Hollywood and HBO over rights to movies — or over money.

In 1980 four major Hollywood studios — Columbia, 20th Century Fox, Universal MCA, and Paramount — combined their efforts in a counter-strike against HBO. The Hollywood majors launched, along with Getty Oil (which owned the ESPN sports channel at the time), a rival pay TV movie channel called Premiere. Anti-trust officials in the Justice Department of President Jimmy Carter took a dim view of the Hollywood combine, however, and a suit was promptly filed against Premiere. A U.S. court ruled that Premiere was a price-fixing and illegal boycott cartel that could exercise abusive power against HBO. After the court ruling, Premiere folded, stillborn, at a $20-million loss to its owners.

In 1982 Hollywood challenged HBO's dominance once again when Paramount, Universal, Warner Bros., and American Express announced plans to launch The Movie Channel. Viacom soon joined the consortium by merging its Showtime channel with The Movie Channel. Again, U.S. anti-trust authorities promptly initiated an investigation of the venture. At the time, HBO commanded 60 percent of the pay cable market. It was estimated that The Movie Channel/Showtime would take about 30 percent. Thus, the two channels together clearly would form an oligopoly. The merged channel responded to the threat of an anti-trust suit by restructuring Paramount and Universal out of the deal so the merger would include Viacom, Warner Bros., and American Express only. By the end of the 1980s HBO and Showtime controlled 84 percent of the U.S. pay TV market just the same. But as the U.S. cable market matured, HBO's bargaining power attenuated and the channel began diversifying beyond movies into family entertainment, comedy, and boxing matches. In the 1990s HBO would become famous to television viewers as the producer of *The Larry Sanders Show*.

In Canada, an experimental pay TV system owned by the Famous Players movie chain had been tested in the Toronto suburb of Etobicoke from 1960 to 1965. In the mid-1970s cable barons like Ted Rogers were not indifferent to the phenomenal early success of HBO. Rogers actually had applied, unsuccessfully, for a pay TV licence in 1972, and he continued to lobby Ottawa to fast-track pay TV's arrival in Canada. In 1975 the CRTC announced it would hold public hearings to examine the possible introduction of pay TV in Canada.

The Canadian cable industry's enthusiasm for pay TV was hardly a mystery. In a small domestic market like Canada, there could be no HBO-style channel that could finance the movies it aired. There was no Canadian movie industry to speak of. Pay TV in Canada therefore could be only one thing: a conduit for American movies. As Hershel Hardin put it:

> Canadian pay TV was a contradiction in terms. You could hold public hearings on it for a lifetime, around the clock and on weekends, accepting and discussing submissions and boosting broadcasting lawyers' incomes, and what would come out at the end would be: (a) another extension of the American distribution

system; and, (b) an increase in our balance-of-payments deficit with the United States.[2]

During the CRTC hearings in 1975, some forty briefs were submitted to the regulator. Conventional broadcasters, who felt threatened by an HBO-like service in Canada, naturally opposed pay TV. Many others shared their concern about the possible negative effect of pay TV on the Canadian broadcasting system. Nearly half the briefs submitted, however, came from cable TV companies strongly urging the regulator to give an immediate green light to pay TV. Ted Rogers lobbied hard for a pay TV licence with promises of investing 15 percent of gross revenues in Canadian movie productions. The cable lobby promoted the idea as "Canadianization through Americanization" — a semantically alarming, though at least honest, twist on the familiar cross-subsidy nostrum.[3]

"We see two kinds of people making money with pay TV," said Colin Watson, a top Rogers executive at the time. "One, the cable operators. Second, the Canadian production community. And the cost of that is inundating pay TV with American programming. If there isn't recognition of that, there isn't going to be pay TV."

In December 1975 the CRTC issued its verdict: there was "little enthusiasm" for pay TV in Canada and therefore it would not grant any licences. The decision was a setback for the Canadian cable industry, which felt intensely frustrated watching HBO drive cable cash flows in the United States while regulatory foot-dragging delayed pay TV's commercial launch in Canada.

The cable lobby soon shifted its attention away from the CRTC and towards the Liberal government. While the Canadian cable industry was notoriously Tory, one important cable investor at the time was Jerry Grafstein. Later a senator, in the 1970s Grafstein was a top adviser to Prime Minister Pierre Trudeau. As it turned out, the Trudeau government proved decidedly less reluctant than the CRTC when it came to the introduction of pay TV in Canada.

In June 1976 Jeanne Sauvé, the communications minister in Trudeau's Cabinet, described pay TV as a "watershed in broadcasting" and declared that its introduction in Canada was "inevitable." Interestingly, Sauvé made this declaration at a meeting of the Canadian Cable Television Association, the cable industry's powerful lobby group. The minister's speech was inspired by a concern among government officials that pay TV would run ahead of government policy. Already, a closed-circuit movie service was operating in Toronto apartment complexes. There was concern, moreover, that Ted Rogers might start his own pay TV service willy-nilly as a test of regulatory resolve.

Sauvé's announcement had the desired effect on the CRTC. Only a few weeks after the minister's "pay TV is inevitable" speech, the CRTC launched yet another public consultation on the issue. This time, the regulator was singing from the same hymn book as the cable industry. CRTC chairman Harry Boyle called pay TV a "national policy of cultural security for Canada" and a chance for the Canadian broadcasting system to "convert technical systems to a national purpose." Many believed Canada should hurry up and launch its own national pay TV channels before HBO arrived via satellite. The *Toronto Star* called pay TV "an opportunity Canada has been waiting for." And *Maclean's* stated that "once tamed, pay TV may be the best friend Canadian culture ever had." The *Globe and Mail* warned, on the other hand, that pay TV was an American Trojan Horse wrapped in a Canadian flag.

Rogers Cable interpreted the new CRTC process as the cue that, this time, pay TV was imminent in Canada. Rogers was convinced that, like cable-owned HBO south of the border, it would soon be launching its own HBO-like all-movie channel, which it planned to offer to its subscribers for $6 per month. The Rogers-led cable lobby even announced the creation of "Pay Television Network," and produced a slick brochure that was distributed to cable subscribers with exhortations to write to Ottawa and clamour for pay TV. Rogers executive Colin Watson was so confident that the "Pay Television Network" would win a licence that he changed the licence plates on his Mercedes. They now read "PAY SIX."

Watson was rushing his fences. The cable industry underestimated the hostility toward pay TV manifested by conventional broadcasters, who feared that an all-movie channel on cable would erode their audience share. CTV, for example, said it would oppose pay TV in Canada unless the movie channel was owned by itself. As a compromise, the cable industry proposed to launch two movie channels — one dedicated to American movies, the other serving as a showcase for Canadian films. Few were duped by this ploy. The two-channel idea was a transparent attempt to get a Hollywood-fed pay TV channel into Canada wrapped in a flimsy Canadian flag.

In 1977 the CRTC declined again to license pay TV services in Canada. However, it bent to industry pressure by announcing a licensing policy for pay TV in the near future. The regulator stipulated that any pay TV channel operating in Canada would have to serve as a showcase for "high quality" and "predominantly Canadian" programming. The CRTC also said it favoured a national pay TV service which, to appease the fears of broadcasters and producers, would have a board of directors representing cross-industry interests. Interestingly, the CRTC's pay TV policy statement was issued by its new chairman, Pierre Camu, a Liberal insider who had arrived at the Commission from a job as the top lobbyist for Canada's private broadcasters.

It took three more years of bureaucratic foot-dragging on pay TV before the CRTC — now chaired by Queen's University professor John Meisel, a rumpled caricature of the absent-minded academic — finally decided to expedite the introduction of a Canadian pay TV service. The justification that was marshalled was the CRTC's mission to develop national satellite services for remote regions in Canada. The spectre of Canadians using illegal C-band satellite dishes to pick up HBO directly was sufficiently alarming to scare the CRTC into action. Ted Rogers led the charge on this theme. He warned that, unless Ottawa acted fast by licensing Canadian pay TV, the cable industry would lose thousands of apartment blocks to satellite dishes picking up HBO and other unauthorized American channels. After nearly a decade of delays, the CRTC now set about to fast-track pay TV in Canada.

In 1981 the CRTC called for applications for pay TV licences. A total of thirty-seven bids came in and public hearings were scheduled. Several high-profile industry groups submitted applications for a coveted all-movie licence. One group, called Astratel, was headed by André Bureau and financially backed by Montreal movie mogul Harold Greenberg and Bureau's old boss at Télémedia, Philippe de Gaspé Beaubien. Another group, called Premiere, was put together by Citytv's Moses Znaimer, Jerry Grafstein (a Citytv investor), cable executive Gordon Keeble, former CRTC vice-chairman Jean Fortier, and a roster of arts and media personalities such as Jack McClelland, Anna Porter, Peter Gzowski, Peter Newman, Norman Jewison, and Patrick Watson. A third group called First Choice Canadian, put together by lawyer Peter Grant and fronted by broadcasting executive Don Macpherson, was a consortium of business interests including the wealthy Sobey family from Nova Scotia. A company called Superchannel, financed by Alberta's Charles Allard, also applied for an all-movie licence. The CTV network, Conrad Black's Standard Broadcasting, and a group led by former CBC executive Jack MacAndrew also put in bids.

In deference to the customary regulatory ritual, most of the applicants indulged in grandiloquently patriotic declarations about Canadian cultural sovereignty, as if pay TV were a philanthropic endeavour and the future of the country depended on it. Robert Fulford aptly wrote in *Saturday Night* that the CRTC's pay TV hearings were characterized chiefly by "rhetorical overkill," and that the whole affair had "an aura of chicanery and dissimulation." Ian McCallum, who was operating a small closed-circuit pay TV service in Saskatchewan, warned the CRTC that pay TV was a bust and would never generate enough revenues to support program production in Canada. Nobody listened to this curious bit player among a cast of Canada's biggest broadcasting players, all mesmerized by HBO's robust cash flows in the United States.

Within the CRTC, senior officials were impressed by Bureau's Astratel application and recommended that it be accorded a licence. But Bureau's backer, Harold Greenberg, had recently produced a juvenile high-jinx film called *Porky's*, which in the eyes of some CRTC commissioners was frivolous cinematic garbage. The internal politics within the Commission thus soured against the Astratel bid. It was vetoed — against the recommendation of the CRTC staff — for reasons of artistic snobbery.

In March 1982 the CRTC announced the winners of the pay TV beauty contest: First Choice and Superchannel were awarded competing all-movie licences, and C Channel won a licence as an arts programming service.

"It's our last chance to get Canadian content right," declared John Meisel. "What we are doing is helping the genie out of the bottle so that Canadian productive genius and skill will be fully employed to delight Canadians."

The CRTC didn't "get it right" at all — it got it wrong, very wrong. The new pay TV channels went on the air in February 1983. Four months later, C Channel went into receivership. Meanwhile, First Choice and Superchannel were engaged in a furious bidding war for Hollywood movies. Both channels were desperate to win the Canadian rights for *Star Wars* to drive subscriptions before their opening launch. Thus, all-movie pay TV in Canada began much as had been predicted — not as a showcase for Canadian content, but as a Canadian export window for Hollywood blockbusters.

By the mid-1980s the CRTC's pay TV debacle was a full-scale disaster. First Choice and Superchannel, fatigued by the rigours of market competition, had failed to attract enough subscribers to make money. First Choice soon went bankrupt, despite company president Don MacPherson's earlier assurances that his financial backers had "deep pockets." Ironically, Harold Greenberg — the movie tycoon whose Astratel bid had been dismissed by the CRTC because of his low-brow movie *Porky's* — suddenly emerged as the white knight in a buyout rescue of First Choice. It was difficult to overlook the fact that the man who had fronted Greenberg's failed bid for an all-movie channel was none other than André Bureau, now the chairman of the CRTC that was authorizing the Greenberg buyout.

The relaunch of Canadian pay TV marked a return to a familiar reflex in the Canadian broadcasting system. This time, there would be no more ruinous competition. The country would be divided into two regional monopolies. First Choice took Ontario, Quebec, and parts east; and Superchannel took western Canada. Not only did the CRTC approve of this plan, the regulator went further by lowering the Canadian-content quotas imposed on the two pay TV services. First Choice originally had been licensed with a 50-percent Cancon quota plus an obligation to invest 45 percent of gross revenues in Canadian programs. First Choice's idea of abiding by these Canadian cultural obligations had been to co-produce, using Canadian talent, soft-porn movies with Playboy Enterprises and promote itself as a "Playboy Channel." The plan was undoubtedly seductive, but it was never consummated. In 1986 André Bureau reduced First Choice's 50-percent quota to a 30-percent quota in prime time and to only 20 percent overall, plus an expenditure commitment of only 20 percent for Canadian programs. Cultural nationalism was ceding to continental pragmatism. The first worked wonderfully at CRTC hearings; the second imposed its law in the marketplace.

In the end, the pay TV affair was awash in bureaucratic bumbling, furtive ambitions, and crass opportunism. And the CRTC was cast in the unenviable role of *chef d'orchestre* with André Bureau — who had cleverly straddled the line between private interests and public service — holding the baton.

It is easy to imagine Harold Greenberg's satisfaction with the decision. First Choice — later renamed The Movie Network (TMN) — now could fill up its schedule with Hollywood movies and keep spending on Canadian productions to a minimum. When Bureau stepped down from the CRTC chairmanship in 1989, he first joined the prestigious Montreal law firm Heenan Blaikie. But soon Greenberg appointed him to the presidency of Astral Broadcasting, which controlled The Movie Network, and other broadcasting interests that depended on the CRTC's regulatory favour. Ted Rogers bought a piece of Astral and later became a 25-percent shareholder in Astral's pay-per-view channel, Viewer's Choice. Bureau also joined the board of directors of Shaw Communications, the Calgary-based cable group.

If pay TV and pay-per-view were a tremendous career opportunity for André Bureau, neither have been commercially successful in Canada. The Movie Network, with only about 450,000 subscribers on cable, has performed poorly. Viewer's Choice pay-per-view, for its part, has been limited to only a few channels on cable systems and its "buy rates" consequently have been embarrassingly low since the service was launched in the early 1990s. The dirty secret at Viewer's Choice is that buy rates for its porn movies are six times higher than for other films. Viewer's Choice has the advantage of exceedingly permissive Canadian content rules: only about 5 percent of the movies available on the pay-per-view service are Canadian. That figure is roughly equivalent to the paltry amount of screen time occupied by Canadian films in movie theatres — a situation that Astral executives have publicly decried as Canada's "feature film disaster."

The modest 5-percent Cancon quota imposed on Viewer's Choice did not escape the Friends of Canadian Broadcasting. When Ian Morrison, head of the public-interest advocacy group, was once appearing before a Senate committee, he followed an earlier presentation by Astral executives, including the late Harold Greenberg, Bureau, Francis Fox, and Lisa de Wilde. Greenberg made an impassioned speech before the honourable senators, proclaiming his profound attachment to Canada and the need to protect Canadian culture. Bureau joined in the nationalistic chest-pounding with glowing descriptions of the commitment of Viewer's Choice, The Movie Network, and other Astral-owned channels to Canadian culture. When Morrison stepped forward and took his seat as a witness before the same Senate committee, he accused the Astral executives of "wrapping themselves in 5 percent of the Canadian flag."

Pay TV in Canada was a bust. But Canada's cable barons had managed to build out their networks and consolidate their market power in the national broadcasting industry even without a popular Canadian version of HBO.

Cable Power: The Logic of Vertical Integration

The CRTC had shut cable barons like Ted Rogers out of the pay TV market for a reason. During the 1970s and early 1980s, the strict separation of "carriage" and "content" was elevated to the status of dogma by regulators.

The separation was founded on a reasonable assumption about market behaviour. In the 1970s it was clear that cable TV systems were quickly emerging as the powerful gatekeepers of the entire broadcasting industry, and thus could exercise enormous power over other market players. Most vulnerable were program suppliers and channels that depended on cable for access to viewers. The most obvious danger was that cable companies would exploit their market power to take control of programming and thus end up dominating both content supply and distribution in the broadcasting system.

In the United States, the government had been concerned about the potentially abusive power of cable TV as far back as the early 1970s. President Richard Nixon established a Cabinet Committee on Cable Communications, and its 1974 report — commonly called the "Whitehead Report" after its author Clay Whitehead — proposed a complete divestiture of cable systems from program suppliers. The Whitehead Report accurately predicted that cable TV would soon dominate the broadcasting industry and succumb to the temptation to cement its power and reduce risks through vertical integration.

The Whitehead Report's recommendation to ban vertical integration was never implemented. In the following two decades, many of the most popular "basic" and premium channels on U.S. cable television — from HBO and The Learning Channel to Ted Turner's superstation TBS and the all-news CNN — were vertically integrated under the control of large cable empires. In the 1980s media conglomerates such as Time Warner and Viacom controlled both cable empires and program channels. Viacom, for example, owned Nickelodeon, Nick at Nite, QVC Network, MTV, and MTV's all-music sister station VH1. And Time Warner's cable division held stakes in CNN, Headline News, TBS, the all-movie TNT, Comedy Central, E! TV, Cinemax, Court TV, Cartoon Network, and Viewer's Choice, to name only a few.

John Malone, whose TCI cable group counted more than 10 million subscribers, was by far the most aggressive predator on cable channels. By the early 1990s Malone held interests in a vast stable of programming interests: Discovery Channel, Black Entertainment Television, Family Channel, Court TV, American Movie Classics, Home Shopping Network, Starz, The Box, Encore, and a string of regional sports networks. By the mid-1990s TCI and Time Warner, the two biggest cable empires in the United States, together accounted for 47.4 percent of all U.S. cable subscribers and were vertically integrated with more than forty nationally distributed cable channels.

Malone's hardball tactics to gain control of program channels were legendary. He grabbed control of The Learning Channel, for example, by thwarting its sale to a rival consortium with threats that he would take the channel off his TCI cable systems. The consortium — made up of Hearst Corporation, Viacom, and ABC/Capital Cities — was forced to withdraw its $39-million (U.S.) bid for TLC because the channel depended on John Malone's cable empire for access. After the consortium withdrew, Malone snapped up TLC for only $30 million. Viacom filed a lawsuit against TCI charging that Malone had violated U.S. anti-trust laws by denying competitors access to his cable systems. In its complaint, Viacom asserted:

> Malone's scheme to monopolize cable television begins with his empire of cable systems. . . . Without access to Malone's systems, cable network programmers cannot achieve the 'critical mass' of

viewers needed to attract national advertising or a sufficient number of subscribers required to make the network viable. As a result of Malone's unique control over this life-line, he can — and does — extract unfair and anti-competitive terms and conditions from cable programmers, including Viacom.

These battles were not without some irony. In 1989 Viacom had filed an anti-trust suit against Time Inc. (before the Time Warner merger), charging that Time's cable systems, in order to promote Time-owned Home Box Office, refused to carry Viacom's Showtime and The Movie Channel. Yet Viacom itself was notorious for using its all-music MTV channel to drive competing pop video channels into bankruptcy. For example, Viacom refused to carry on its cable systems Time's music channel, The Box. Viacom nonetheless won its lawsuit: the newly merged Time Warner agreed to pay Viacom $75 million and co-operate in a joint marketing campaign to promote Showtime on Time Warner's cable systems. Viacom sold its cable systems to John Malone in 1995, thus exempting itself from any further charges of exercising undue market power due to the advantages of vertical integration.

But Viacom's MTV has continued to be ruthless in its business dealings — not only with cable companies, but also with the music, video clip, and advertising industries. Despite its commanding global reach, MTV has been curiously paranoid about getting toppled by rival music-video channels. It therefore has insisted on long-term contracts with major cable and satellite TV systems, frequently demanding that its sister channel VH1 be carried as part of the deal. These "tied" deals aimed at promoting VH1 have driven potential VH1 competitors out of business. Hit Video USA, for example, was blocked from 80 percent of U.S. cable systems because of exclusive MTV contracts, and eventually went out of business in 1990. Similarly, MTV has lobbied the FCC, though not always with success, to prevent local stations that carry pop videos, such as New York's WWHT, from gaining mandatory "must carry" status on cable systems.

In Canada, MuchMusic is protected by the CRTC from competition from MTV. But Moses Znaimer fought for years to keep Black Entertainment Television (which airs pop videos for black people) from getting widespread cable carriage in Canada. Znaimer succeeded in the short term, but BET is now widely available on cable in major Canadian cities where black viewers can defect from MuchMusic.

Only channels with strong brands and unshakeable viewer loyalty like MTV can dare to twist the arm of the powerful cable industry. Like MTV,

Ted Turner's CNN is a channel that no cable system wants to be without. CNN's appeal has given Turner tremendous bargaining power. In the early 1980s, after CNN's contracts with major cable systems expired, Turner announced that monthly fees charged to cable companies would be tripled upon contract renewal. In retaliation, John Malone encouraged NBC to launch an all-news channel to increase his bargaining leverage on the rates charged by CNN. Malone's tactic produced the desired result: CNN cut its rates. Even better, Malone ended up buying a stake in CNN.

When Time Warner bought CNN, Turner insisted that both Malone's TCI and Time Warner refuse to carry any all-news channel that might compete with CNN. One of Turner's emerging enemies in the all-news business was the formidable Australian-born media mogul, Rupert Murdoch. Murdoch's upstart Fox Television had ambitious cable plans in the United States, including an all-news channel. Murdoch realized from the get-go that, for the Fox News Channel to succeed, it would need cable carriage on Time Warner's systems in the lucrative New York City market. But with Ted Turner installed as vice-chairman of Time Warner, there was little chance that Fox News would ever get cable carriage in New York. Indeed, Turner insisted that Fox News be barred from all Time Warner cable systems. Turner's blackballing infuriated Murdoch, and soon a full-scale war broke out between the two moguls.

Murdoch ignited the feud by using the complicity of his newspaper, the tabloid *New York Post*, to take swipes at Turner. Murdoch also stated publicly that CNN was boring because it was too repetitive and ran too many commercials. Turner riposted by dismissing Murdoch as a "schlockmeister," undoubtedly a reference to Murdoch's racy British tabloid, *The Sun*, and the tabloid-style programs, such as *Cops*, featured on the Fox network.

In February 1996 Murdoch gave a speech to the National Press Club in Washington in which he pleaded guilty to Turner's insult "if your idea of a 'schlockmeister' is *The X-Files*, *The Times* of London, NFL football, *The Simpsons*, Sky or Star broadcasting, our Fox educational children's programs, NHL hockey, feature films like *Waiting to Exhale*. . . . That's what we do." And then, taking aim at Turner's TBS superstation and CNN, Murdoch added: "We do, however, draw the line at professional wrestling and brown-nosing to foreign dictators. You'll have to turn to one of Ted's channels to see that."

Fortunately for Murdoch, Time Warner was bound by FCC regulations to include at least one competing all-news channel as an alternative to its own CNN. In late 1996 Murdoch believed that Time Warner chairman Gerald Levin had no choice but to invite Fox News onto the media giant's cable systems, especially in Manhattan. But under pressure from Turner, Levin instead did a deal to carry the less threatening MSNBC, the all-news channel launched by NBC and Microsoft. Fox News was blocked again.

Murdoch was livid. He promptly intensified his lobbying campaign, starting with the mayor of New York, Rudolph Giuliani. Murdoch promised the mayor that, if Fox News were offered on New York cable systems, the channel would create 1,475 new jobs in the city. Predictably, Giuliani appealed to Time Warner to carry Fox News on its Manhattan cable systems. Time Warner refused. Soon New York governor George Pataki intervened on Murdoch's behalf. Neither Giuliani nor Pataki was indifferent, of course, to the fact that Murdoch's popular *New York Post* was an influential shaper of public opinion in the Big Apple, particularly during election campaigns.

As Murdoch's lobbying intensified, Turner jumped into the fray by comparing Murdoch with Adolf Hitler because he used his newspapers as propaganda tools. When Murdoch shot back that Turner had cheapened the Holocaust, Turner apologized and simply called Murdoch a "scumbag." The *New York Post* responded on Murdoch's behalf with a front-page headline: "Is Ted Turner Nuts? You Decide." Shortly afterwards, Turner was at New York's Yankee Stadium to watch a World Series game between the home-team Yankees and the team he owned, the Atlanta Braves. Murdoch, whose Fox network was broadcasting the game, hired a plane to fly over the stadium with a message streaming behind in huge banner letters: "Hey Ted. Be Brave. Don't Censor the Fox News Channel." At the same time, Murdoch's *New York Post* began publishing censorious articles about Turner's wife, Jane Fonda, including an unflattering photo of the actress in her radical "Hanoi Jane" days during the Vietnam War. Turner later remarked: "This is a battle between good and evil."

In the end, Murdoch resorted to bribing the cable industry with cash-per-subscriber inducements to carry Fox News. Murdoch agreed to pay John Malone $20 per subscriber for an initial Fox News launch on the 10 million cable households controlled by TCI. Murdoch moreover gave Malone an option to buy a 20-percent stake in the Fox News Channel. He also paid $10 per subscriber to Cablevision and Comcast, which had some 8 million subscribers between them. In mid-1997 Time Warner finally agreed to offer Fox News to 8 million of its subscribers in New York and elsewhere by 2001. The price: $10 per subscriber — or roughly $80 million as key money just to get in the door. Each side claimed that the other had folded first.

This bold way of doing business turned the cable TV market on its head. Normally, cable companies paid channels a wholesale fee for the right to include their signals in program packages. But with so many new channels hoping to launch commercially, the major cable companies could exploit their bottleneck market power to extract — some would say extort — up-front "launch fees" for access to viewers.

In Canada, the warnings of the U.S. Whitehead Report were taken more seriously, at least in the short term. In the 1970s the CRTC rejected attempts by cable interests to enter the pay TV business, and its policy of strict carriage-content separation was applied to the first round of licensing of specialty cable channels in 1984. That year, the regulator licensed CHUM's MuchMusic video channel and the TSN sports channel, as well as Telelatino and a Chinese-language channel. Rogers had been Znaimer's rival for the all-music licence, but the CRTC ruled in favour of the non-cable-affiliated MuchMusic proposal. In 1987, however, the CRTC — chaired by André Bureau — broke its carriage-content rule by letting Rogers and other cable interests take a stake in the YTV children's channel. The other channels licensed that year were Newsworld, Weather Network, Vision TV, TV5, and French-language versions of MuchMusic, TSN, and Family Channel.

If Canadian cable companies could not control new Canadian channels outright, they could at least get carriage access to popular American cable channels to give "lift" to the program packages they were selling to their subscribers. In truth, Canadian cable companies have never been particularly enthusiastic about carrying new Canadian channels — especially if the cable industry can't own them. Cable operators in Canada agree to carry new Canadian channels because, in accordance with CRTC rules, they can "link" them with American channels like A&E, The Learning Channel, and CNN. The assumption is that Canadian audiences are not interested in Showcase, Life, and Women's Television Network, but the attraction of new American channels drives penetration of cable TV subscriptions and thus increases the industry's cash flow and profits — and therefore artificially creates a market for Canadian channels.

The CRTC has long been exceedingly complicit with this commercial strategy of bringing in American channels as "linkage" partners with Canadian channels. In the 1980s the regulator allowed cable companies to offer as many as *five* American channels with a single Canadian pay TV channel. In the early 1990s the ratio was 2:1 in favour of U.S. channels linked with Canadian specialty channels. More recently the CRTC finally imposed a 1-to-1 ratio to even the playing field — only one American (or foreign) channel can be included in a cable package for every new Canadian specialty channel offered.

The only American channels that have not been allowed into Canada are those that resemble — or "duplicate" — Canadian channels. For example, the internationally popular music video channel MTV has never been authorized in Canada because it would compete with Moses Znaimer's MuchMusic. Likewise, the American sports channel, ESPN, has never been authorized for cable distribution in Canada because TSN already occupied the all-sports field. In effect, however, both MTV and ESPN export their programs into Canada, but they have to go through the monopoly intermediaries, MuchMusic and TSN. In 1984 the CRTC in fact licensed MuchMusic and TSN as Canadian-based outlets for MTV and ESPN, which is why their Canadian-content quotas were set low - only 10 percent and 18 percent respectively.

The CRTC's regulatory protection of Canadian program monopolies has been controversial. Cultural nationalists, whose arguments are expediently embraced by the Canadian broadcasting industry, claim that without the "non-duplication" rule — when there's MuchMusic, MTV is banned - - there simply would be no Canadian specialty channels at all. Canadians would have only CNN for news, MTV for music, ESPN for sports, Nickelodeon and the Disney Channel for kids' shows, Court TV for programs about the justice system, and HBO for movies. There would be no Newsworld, MuchMusic, TSN, Family Channel, Teletoon, or TMN for movies. At a minimum, claim cultural nationalists, Canadian channel monopolies broadcast American programs to make profits that are reinvested — as a sort of cross-subsidy — in Canadian program production. It's a different spin on the old "Canadianization through Americanization" nostrum that was propogated by Rogers Cable when it was seeking a pay TV licence in the 1970s — and, moreover, that is the basis of the entire Canadian broadcasting system.

However well-intended, the CRTC non-duplication rule lacks consistency. By targeting only certain types of channels to protect Canadian monopolies, the CRTC has allowed many American channels into Canada while banning others. A&E and The Learning Channel are allowed into Canada, unrestricted, but channels like MTV and ESPN can't get into the country except as mere program suppliers for Canadian intermediaries. Also, the CRTC authorized A&E despite the fact that this popular U.S. channel buys "North American" rights for its programs, thus preventing Canadian channels from buying national rights for the same shows. Ironically, the chairman of the CRTC when A&E was authorized for distribution in Canada was none other than André Bureau, who has since become the most outspoken critic of "North American" program rights in order to protect the specialty, pay TV, and pay-per-view channels that he runs as president of Astral Broadcasting. Pragmatism and opportunism are strange bedfellows indeed.

Columnist Terence Corcoran, now business editor of the *National Post*, has railed against the CRTC's "banana republic" rules that ban channels like HBO despite its Emmy award–winning shows. "Others banned by the CRTC," observes Corcoran,

> include Bloomberg Television and the U.S. versions of Discovery Channel, The Comedy Network, the Disney Channel, and scores of other program services deemed too subversive for Canadians to watch in their original form — unless, of course, the same programming passes through the hands of a Canadian middleman or monopolist who will culturally sanitize the programming by skimming off a fat profit.

It is difficult to argue with Corcoran's point. Even if one accepts the CRTC's rationale for banning certain U.S. channels — to ensure that at least some Canadian programs get on the screen — the non-duplication rule is, at best, based on a dubious better-than-nothing logic. The non-duplication ban is merely a twist on the simulcasting problem: the main beneficiaries are the Canadian middlemen monopolists who siphon profits from airing American programs. The benefits to Canadians, or to Canada as a nation, are more elusive.[4]

Ironically, when the non-duplication ban has not been applied, Canadian channels have thrived. A good example is the CBC's Newsworld. When the CRTC licensed Newsworld in 1987, some believed that CNN should not be allowed into Canada because the CBC now "occupied the field" in the all-news format. The licensing of Newsworld actually met a storm of protest from powerful friends of Prime Minister Brian Mulroney. One was Alberta broadcaster Charles Allard, whose company Allarcom had been seeking an all-news licence itself. Tory MPs from Allard's home turf in the West, many of them virulently hostile to the CBC, quickly rallied around Allard. The prime minister, no friend himself of the CBC, was not unsympathetic to Allard's indignation.

"Instead of hammering us two hours a day, they will have twenty-four hours a day," Mulroney reportedly said when informed that the CBC had won an all-news licence for Newsworld.

In early 1988 Mulroney's communications minister, Flora MacDonald, wrote a letter to CBC president Pierre Juneau informing him that the government wished Newsworld to have a private-sector partner and to offer its service in both French and English. The CBC ceded to the government pressure by making a cosmetic promise to establish a partnership with the *Globe and Mail* and the *Financial Post*. Newsworld was also forced to accept the cable industry's importation of both CNN and CNN Headline News — both all-news channels like Newsworld. In other words, Newsworld quietly agreed to accept a derogation of the non-duplication rule. MuchMusic and TSN would have raised hell if the CRTC had authorized MTV and ESPN for cable distribution in Canada. But Newsworld, facing a barrage of political hostility against its very existence, was obliged to bite its lip and accept competition from CNN. In the end, Newsworld turned out to be an excellent, distinctively Canadian all-news channel, much like CBC Radio.

It was only a matter of time before the non-duplication rule landed the CRTC in political trouble. In the early 1990s Canadian cable companies included the U.S. Country Music Television in one of their channel packages. In 1994 the CRTC licensed an all-Canadian country-music channel called New Country Network. Now that Canada had its own channel in this musical genre, the CRTC retroactively banned CMT from the Canadian broadcasting system. Not surprisingly, the move provoked a swift and unequivocal reaction from the U.S. government, which denounced the CRTC decision as "unjust expropriation" that violated the national-treatment test in Canada-U.S. trade. In retaliation, CMT stopped airing videos of Canadian country music stars on its U.S. network. Also, the U.S. government challenged the CRTC decision under the North American Free Trade Agreement and threatened immediate countervailing measures.

The Liberal government, which was already fighting with the CRTC over satellite TV, was furious with the regulator for the country music provocation. In the end, a last-ditch compromise was reached when CMT's owners were offered a 20-percent stake in New Country Network, which was relaunched in 1996 under the CMT brand. When the bilateral storm subsided, the CRTC had egg on its face for applying an outdated and unworkable policy to a rapidly changing broadcasting market. And yet the hypocrisy of the non-duplication rule persists. Canadian channels like MuchMusic and Newsworld are available in the United States as part of the DirecTV service, but in Canada the CRTC still officially bans many American channels — including MuchMusic's counterpart, MTV.

Moses Znaimer calls it "Canadian cultural imperialism." Others might call it Canadian cultural protectionism.

The Revenge of the "New Consumer"

In 1987 the CRTC licensed a new round of cable channels, including Newsworld, Vision, YTV, Weather Network, MusiquePlus, and TV5. The regulator also announced that, henceforth, monthly cable rates for so-called discretionary channels — those channels not included as part of the "basic" package — would be deregulated.

In Canada, the CRTC had always regulated cable TV rates for the same reason it regulated monthly phone charges: cable companies were a monopoly provider of an essential service and therefore consumers had to be protected against price gouging. But in the 1980s the winds were blowing in favour of deregulation. In the United States, cable rates had been deregulated in 1984 by the Cable Act, which sent monthly cable rates soaring. In Canada, the CRTC proposed that the basic package continue to be subject to "rate of return" regulation, but rates for premium channels would be deregulated.

The CRTC decision gave the cable industry an extraordinary opportunity to make massive profits. By shifting as many channels as possible from "basic" to the "discretionary" portion of their packages, cable companies could charge unregulated prices for non-basic channels. The CRTC decision also gave Canadian channels like MuchMusic and TSN a powerful incentive to abandon their cosy spots in the basic package to become discretionary channels sold at premium prices. Since the cable industry could "link" American channels at a 2-to-1 ratio with any Canadian discretionary channel, MuchMusic and TSN suddenly had tremendous bargaining power because they knew that big cable companies like Rogers and Shaw desperately needed to link them with U.S. channels in non-basic packages.

But MuchMusic and TSN were already reaching many more viewers on the basic service than they could ever hope to reach as part of a discretionary package. Thus, cable companies were forced to offer them the inducement of wholesale fees that were not only substantial, but artificially reflected 100-percent subscriber penetration. TSN, for example, received a monthly wholesale fee of more than $1 per subscriber at 100 percent of cable's entire subscriber base — an unbeatable deal that quickly made TSN the most profitable channel in the country. The French-language Canadian channel TV5 was picked up by cable for a paltry monthly wholesale fee of five cents per subscriber. Its appeal in English Canada might have been limited, but it allowed Rogers and Shaw and other cable companies to link it with two U.S. channels. Thus, while TV5's massive exposure in English Canada undoubtedly did much for the cause of bilingualism, its presence on most cable dials was motivated by a desire to make money from importing U.S. cable channels.

The main challenge for the cable industry was to market the new unregulated channel packages in a way that made it seem to consumers that these channels — though their prices were no longer controlled — were still part of the basic service. The marketing trick employed was a semantic fudge. The cable industry lumped the new deregulated package in with the basic service by calling it "extended basic" — or "full-cable service." The ploy came perilously close to false advertising, but the CRTC tacitly condoned it by looking the other way.

The marketing of extended basic was a spectacular success. While channels like MuchMusic and TSN profited enormously from their lucrative displacement to discretionary packages, big cable companies like Rogers and Shaw made huge margins from selling unregulated packages. In 1987 only 294,000 subscribers were paying for "full cable service" offered by only 25 cable systems. By 1992, the year extended basic was massively marketed by 258 cable systems, that figure shot up to nearly 5 million subscribers — or a 95-percent penetration rate. The jump from 1991 to 1992 is particularly revealing: in 1991 some 1.7 million Canadians subscribed to full cable, and the following year the figure reached nearly 5 million. By the mid 1990s Canadian cable subscribers were paying on average $21.86 a month for the basic cable service, plus $7.22 extra for extended basic. The cable industry's markup on the extended basic package (after paying wholesale fees to the channels) was at least 100 percent — a markup rate rivalled in its audacity only by the perfume and cosmetics industries.

"With that extended-basic trick, the cable industry raised its profit margins by 15 percent overnight," says a former cable executive. "Margins shot up from about 30 percent, which is already very high, to unbelievably high margins in the high forties. It was a master stroke."

The creation of extended basic was an undeniably clever, if not altogether transparent, marketing strategy. Not content with its profit windfall, however, the cable industry also exploited an opportunity to get increases on basic rates, which were still rate-of-return regulated. To make their case for a rate increase on basic, cable companies excluded revenues from their extended basic channels when calculating their overall rate of return, counting only revenues from the basic service. In short, the cable industry used an incremental — instead of fully allocated — cost-accounting method that artificially bundled most costs into the basic service. This artificially inflated costs and depressed profit figures for the basic service, which justified calls for monthly rate increases. And, astonishingly, the CRTC bought it — hook, line, and sinker. The cable industry thus got a double-whammy windfall from the CRTC: extra profits from deregulated extended basic channels, and rate increases for the basic service due to a questionable accounting method.

"The cable industry completely flummoxed the CRTC," recalls a long-time CRTC insider. "The Commission was simply naive. On the broadcasting side, there were few economists or accountants with the background to understand what was going on. There were many on the telecom side, but at the Commission there was a brick wall between the broadcasting and telecom divisions."

The "two solitudes" within the Commission indeed had long been a problem. The telecom division tended to hire accountants, lawyers, engineers, and other highly trained professionals, whereas the weaker broadcasting division hired mainly generalists with little or no training in quantitative analysis. Many senior bureaucrats in the CRTC broadcasting division had worked their way up the system over the years from junior clerical jobs and had little, if any, university education at all. Those who did have abilities often tended to be poached away by big private broadcasting companies — few ever left for the CBC or public-interest groups — and these defections only further weakened the regulator's brainpower. In many respects, the CRTC broadcasting division was simply outgunned by private lobbyists — many of whom were ex-CRTC staffers lured away by bigger salaries, fancier titles, and a belief that the real power was in the industry anyway. Still, most quickly learned that they had been hired away only to make phone calls to former CRTC colleagues every day.

Canadian cable subscribers, it must be said, did not revolt when they received their monthly bills for unregulated channels like TSN, Much-Music, A&E, and CNN. It could even be argued that a total monthly rate averaging about $16.85 was not excessively high. However, the cable industry was still a monopoly in the late 1980s and early 1990s, and thus the CRTC's deregulation of extended basic channels was highly questionable. If Canadians had an alternative — from satellite TV, for example — the stimulus of price competition on discretionary channels might have justified rate deregulation. But this was not the case. The marketing of the extended basic package was a clever ploy that exploited the ignorance and inertia of Canadian cable subscribers. The CRTC, moreover, had the recent lesson of skyrocketing deregulated U.S. cable rates, yet it opted for rate deregulation nonetheless. For the CRTC, the decision was in fact quite easy. Cable subscribers were not the CRTC's clients; the cable industry was.

In the early 1990s cable TV subscribers were getting wiser — thanks in part to the excitement generated by John Malone's 500-channel universe and "death stars." Marketing hype about the Digital Revolution was a mixed blessing for the cable industry. On one hand, the industry was delighted to be perceived as marching at the front of the digital parade. On the other hand, North American cable executives knew they had no intention of actually making the billion-dollar investments needed to bring digital television to consumers. In the meantime, consumers believed, falsely, that the Digital Revolution was just around the corner and soon they would have "pick-and-pay" options, thanks to new technologies and open competition between cable and satellite TV.

In Canada, the cable industry's digital bluffing could count on the CRTC's indulgence. In June 1993 the CRTC announced two major decisions aimed at helping the cable industry compete with digital DBS systems. First, the CRTC allowed cable companies to charge their subscribers, through rate increases, up to $150 each for the cost of putting digital decoder boxes in their homes. In addition, the CRTC extended a "sunset scheme," initiated in 1990, that allowed cable companies to pass through to their subscribers the cost of capital upgrades. This second regulatory favour came with a tradeoff: the cable industry would channel half the "capex" amounts collected into a fund earmarked for the financing of Canadian television programs. According to the CRTC's calculation, the monthly rate increases imposed on subscribers would generate some $600 million over five years, half of which would go towards Canadian program production. At the same time, the CRTC complied with the cable industry's request to license another round of specialty channels. The cable lobby had insisted that its ability to compete in the new digital universe "will not rest solely on its ability to offer Canadians a technically superior distribution system: it will also need more distinctive, quality domestic programming to distribute."

The CRTC could not indulge in such a generous giveaway to the cable industry without some public justification. So a high-minded theme was found to legitimize the backroom bargains. Thus was born the "new consumer." The CRTC claimed that the Canadian cable industry needed more money for digital upgrades and more channels to appeal to the discriminating, technology-empowered "new consumer." Specifically, the CRTC stated that

> the communications environment now emerging will largely be in place by the year 2000. Movement towards this new environment is being driven primarily by three intersecting environmental

forces: changing technology, increasing competition and what has been described as the "new consumer." The most significant technological factor is the digital revolution. Digital technology has given birth to "digital video compression" (DVC), a technology that, for existing television formats, will simultaneously permit an increase in channel capacity and reduce transmission costs per channel. It will also enable the introduction of high definition television systems.

The CRTC's new-consumer-wrapped gift to the cable industry was controversial, to say the least. Even within the Commission itself, some officials suspected that the public interest had, once again, been neglected in a bargain between the regulator and the cable industry. Indeed, three commissioners — David Colville, Beverly Oda, and Rob Gordon — protested the decision in a dissenting opinion, saying that the Commission and the cable industry had robbed Canadian cable subscribers of about $600 million. The three commissioners stated:

> We cannot accept breaking a commitment made to [cable] subscribers that the capital expenditure component of their rates would decrease after five years. The value of these rate reductions would have been up to $85 million beginning in 1995, totalling approximately $600 million for the period 1995–1999. These funds, which were intended to be returned to subscribers as rate reductions, will flow instead half to cable operators and half to Canadian program production. [5]

This three-member dissent was an extraordinary move that revealed a profound division within the Commission. Colville, an engineer who was perhaps the brightest and most competent commissioner, had come from the telecom side of the regulator and was evidently skeptical about the CRTC's collusive behaviour with industry players on the broadcasting side. The media paid little attention to the pro-cable new-consumer boondoggle, doubtless because it had been buried in the dense, impenetrable text of the Commission's decision. No protest came from the television industry, either. The silence of broadcasters and producers had been bought with the promise of $300 million in the form of a new Cable Fund. To a few observers, however, it was frankly scandalous that the regulator had arbitrarily injected hundreds of millions of dollars into the monopoly cable industry so it could compete with satellite broadcasters. The CRTC should instead have been actively promoting the emergence of satellite competitors to monopoly cable TV companies in the interest of consumers, not protecting cable assets from digital DBS competition. But once again, the regulator's first loyalties were to its powerful client — the cable industry.

In June 1994 the cable companies got their new specialty channels. The CRTC licensed a handful of new Canadian channels that could be packaged with U.S. channels: Bravo!, Discovery Channel, Life Network, Women's Television Network (WTN), Showcase, New Country Network, and a French-language Newsworld called Réseau de l'information (RDI). Former CRTC chairman André Bureau, now head of Astral, walked off with two licences: one for an all-movie channel devoted to film classics, the other for a French-language documentary channel called Arts et divertissement.

At the outset, the CRTC's choices appeared quirky, even ill-advised. Observers noted that the CRTC had decided to bring in new players to the broadcasting industry, notably film and TV producers. Robert Lantos's Alliance Communications won a licence for Showcase, which was essentially a rerun channel for Canadian television programs (many of them produced by Alliance). And Michael MacMillan's Atlantis made a winning bid for the Life Network.

"We deliberately and purposefully loaded the dice in favour of Canada," said CRTC chairman Keith Spicer when announcing the winning applications.

For the cable industry, that was precisely the problem. Channels for women, the cultural elite, country music, and Canadian drama reruns seemed like an impossible sell. It must have been particularly galling for cable marketers to learn that channels they had strenuously recommended — comedy, cartoons, and hockey — had been turned down.

"It's going to be a tough sell with consumers," said Ken Stein, president of the Ottawa-based cable lobby. Stein, who today is a top executive with the Shaw cable group, was being exceedingly diplomatic. The buzz in the cable industry was that the CRTC had licensed a bunch of dogs.

The new Canadian channels did look shaky for a while, but in the end they actually began winning better ratings than their American linkage partners. The quality of the new channels was not the problem. The problem was the way the cable industry decided to market them.

The new cable package was launched in January 1995. Rogers, by far the biggest cable company in Canada with more than 2 million subscribers, made a tactical error by remixing its channel packages so that subscribers who didn't want the new channels would be deprived of existing American channels like CNN and A&E. Rogers offered its subscribers a new package that bundled CNN, A&E, TSN, The Nashville Network, the Learning

Channel, TV5, MuchMusic, and Headline News with the newly licensed channels (except Women's Television Network) in a package called New Cable Plus. The new package was, in effect, a bloated extended basic package. Rogers fixed the price of New Cable Plus at $8.10 a month, or $2.65 more than the existing extended-basic package, bringing the total monthly cable bill to $27.39 plus tax.

The Rogers marketing ploy might have worked, but this time media coverage unexpectedly criticized cable's customary "negative option" marketing technique. Negative-option marketing works only when consumers remain passive and uninformed, as they unknowingly pay for rate increases passed through without their prior consent. With the new cable package, subscribers would be billed for the new channels after a free trial period unless they contacted the cable company directly to say they didn't want the new package, which was offered on an all-or-nothing basis.

Negative-option marketing had worked well in the past, and indeed had been instrumental in driving cable penetration in Canada to about 75 percent of all cable-wired households. In 1995, however, that assumption was no longer valid in a context of media hype about the Digital Revolution, the 500-channel universe, "pick-and-pay" channels — and indeed the CRTC's new consumer. While monopoly power was still the market reality, consumers believed they had been liberated by new technologies. In short, there was a gap between facts and values. The Canadian cable industry failed to understand this, even though it had loudly promoted much of the hype about the technological revolution. As a result, Ted Rogers was hoisted on his own petard when his subscribers loudly revolted against the negative-option marketing of the new cable package.

The consumer revolt started in Toronto, where the local newspapers took up the cause with considerable zeal. Just three weeks before the channels were launched on January 1, 1995, the *Globe and Mail* published a front-page story exposing the details of cable's negative-option marketing tactics. Since the main cable company in Toronto was Rogers, Ted Rogers immediately became a target for consumer outrage and indignation.[6]

The CRTC also became a lightning rod for public anger over the fiasco. Keith Spicer was on holiday in Europe when the controversy broke, so a high-level emergency meeting without him was held at the Commission to decide on the most appropriate action. Bud Sherman, the affable telecom vice-chairman, insisted that the CRTC hold a press conference and apologize to Canadians for the negative-option disaster. Fern Bélisle, the cable-friendly vice-chairman of broadcasting, adamantly opposed Sherman. Bélisle insisted that the CRTC say nothing. But Sherman, as acting chairman in

Spicer's absence, overruled Bélisle. Infuriated, Bélisle stormed out of the room and slammed the door.

At the CRTC press conference, Sherman tried his best to explain the foul-up to Canadians. At the same time, Rogers executive Colin Watson was holding a press conference of his own to apologize abjectly to cable subscribers. Watson left Rogers shortly afterwards. Other less lofty heads within Rogers rolled in the wake of the negative-option catastrophe.

In Ottawa, Liberal backbencher Roger Galloway zealously took up the negative-option cause and drafted a private member's bill banning the detested practice. To almost everybody's surprise, Bill C-216 went through the House of Commons like an express train. The bill received particularly enthusiastic support from a number of Liberal ministers (especially those from ridings in Toronto and southern Ontario where the anti cable feelings were the most vocal). By the time the bill reached the Senate, however, the politics of the issue had changed dramatically. For one thing, the cable industry and broadcasting executives such as André Bureau had mobilized and were frantically lobbying the government. Bureau, who as president of Astral Broadcasting controlled several French-language cable channels, was worried that the ban on negative-option marketing would harm his new channels in French-speaking Canada. He was also closely allied to the cable industry through board directorships — Phil Lind from Rogers sat on the Astral board and Bureau sat on the Shaw board.

Determined to kill Galloway's bill, Bureau and his allies found the government's Achilles' heel in Quebec. In late 1996 the Chrétien government was still in shock after the near defeat in the referendum on Quebec sovereignty. Ottawa was paranoid about Quebec and wished as little confrontation as possible with Lucien Bouchard's Péquiste government. Bureau and his allies, inspired more by business interests than by political passions, saw an opportunity in this sensitivity. They cleverly fired up compliant Bloc Québécois MPs who were only too happy to be handed live ammunition and fire it at the Chrétien government. The separatist MPs in Ottawa stood up in the House and claimed, somewhat ludicrously, that the Galloway bill, if passed, would deprive French Canadians of new television channels in the French language. Soon Quebec's separatist culture minister, Louise Beaudoin, joined in the protest and began shrieking from the same scripted text. Even the Quebec Consumers Association adopted Bureau's perverse logic, according to which English Canadian consumers deserved to be protected from negative-option marketing but French Canadians did not deserve the same consumer protections.

In the end, politics prevailed over common sense. Francis Fox, the former Liberal minister now working for Ted Rogers and André Bureau, was the hired gun sent to Ottawa to make sure Bill C-216 did not get through the crimson chamber of sober second thought. The hapless Roger Galloway's bill died in the Senate. The cable industry had won yet another round in Ottawa.

Shortly after the negative-option kerfuffle, the Canadian cable industry called on the CRTC to license a new round of specialty channels so it could expand its service — and thus protect its turf. DirecTV now had about 250,000 subscribers and two new Canadian satellite systems, Star Choice and ExpressVu, were set to launch in 1997. Once again, the threat of a differentiated channel offering from satellite TV mobilized the cable industry into action. It needed more channels to seduce its disaffected subscribers.

The cable industry told the CRTC, however, that it had room for only about eight new channels while awaiting its digital upgrades. The industry therefore recommended that only four Canadian channels be licensed for analogue carriage, allowing cable companies to link them with four U.S. channels. The cable industry added a proviso, though: if the Commission wished to license more than four Canadian channels, they could be designated for *digital* carriage in the future. The cable industry might decide, however, to negotiate with these digital channels to carry them immediately if analogue capacity could be found.

The cable industry's position was a brilliant tactic. It was an open secret in the Canadian broadcasting industry that cable companies systematically exaggerated their capacity constraints — that is, when they said they had only eight spare channels left, they usually had many more vacant channels. Therefore, if the Commission licensed only four Canadian channels as "must carries" on analogue and several others as optional "digital" channels, cable companies would have enormous bargaining power over the hopeful channels on the digital waiting list.

Many in the industry understood the cable industry's agenda, and publicly warned the CRTC not to fall into the trap. But remarkably, the Commission followed the cable proposal almost to the letter. In September 1996 four English-language channels were licensed for immediate analogue carriage: History Television, The Comedy Network, CTV's headline news, and Teletoon. Another thirteen were relegated to the digital list: Treehouse TV, Talk TV, Star TV, Home and Garden Television, MuchMoreMusic, CP 24, Outdoor Life, Prime TV, Headline Sports, Space: The Imagination Station, CTV Sportsnet, ROB TV, and Canadian Learning Television. Also, two ethnic channels were licensed: Greek-language Odyssey and South Asian Television. In French, the CRTC licensed an all-news Canal

Nouvelles, a Canal Vie lifestyle channel, an all-music channel Musimax, and a francophone version of Teletoon.

"We are convinced that there is a clear demand for all genres of Canadian programming approved today," said CRTC chairperson François Bertrand when announcing the licensing decisions.

Bertrand, who had only just arrived as chair of the CRTC, didn't appear to grasp the real issue. It wasn't consumer demand. No one doubted that Canadians would welcome having more television channels that appealed to their special interests, so long as they were marketed in a transparent fashion. The real issue was whether Canadians would ever get to see the new digital channels at all. The cable industry had been promising to offer digital service for more than five years, but there was still no 500-channel universe in sight — and certainly no "new consumer."

The CRTC's two-tier licensing decision didn't help matters, as it gave the cable industry a powerful incentive to exercise market power over the new digitally licensed channels. The CRTC had even allowed the cable industry to take equity stakes in a number of the successful applicants — Treehouse TV, Outdoor Life, The Comedy Network, and CTV Sportsnet. If the U.S. experience was a reliable example, the Canadian cable barons wouldn't stop there.

CRTC commissioner Andrée Wylie did grasp the real issue. Wylie, a sharp and well-connected lawyer, wrote a lengthy dissenting opinion that echoed the protests of David Colville, Bev Oda, and Rob Gordon in 1993. In her dissent, Wylie stated that she opposed the licensing of so many channels for digital distribution because it gave the cable industry excessive market power in negotiations over which channels would get immediate carriage on their systems. Wylie stated that, in her opinion, the CRTC's decision was inconsistent with the Commission's official policy and, moreover, was not in the public interest.[7]

Wylie's warning proved prescient. The following summer during the ramp-up towards the launch of the new channels, rumours began circulating about the cable industry's plans to offer as many as sixteen new channels — eight more than their stated maximum number of vacant channels. In July 1997 the *Globe and Mail* revealed in a front-page article that major cable companies had added three new Canadian channels to the lineup — Home and Garden Television, Space: The Imagination Station, and Outdoor Life. The last of these three was part-owned by Ted Rogers. Shortly afterwards, two more channel additions were announced: CP 24 and Prime TV. With an almost 1-to-1 linkage of Canadian and American channels, that brought the total to at least sixteen channels. Soon the question was being asked: Why did certain of these "digital" channels get selected and not others?

Ian Morrison, president of the Friends of Canadian Broadcasting, said: "Who's making the real decision about who's going to be on the air? The three biggest cable companies who have 75 percent of the cable subscribers. The CRTC in effect is delegating to these people, who are still monopolies, to make those decisions as to what we're going to see."

It soon became apparent that big cable companies like Rogers were not only dictating which new channels would get priority, they were also bullying the new channels desperate for carriage into accepting low wholesale fees. The cable consortium told the channels that the new package would be sold for only $1 retail, and therefore that all wholesale fees paid to the channels would have to be very low.

"It was kind of preposterous the way they did it," recalled one channel executive. "They said, okay, we'll leave you in the room. You write on a piece of paper what you're willing to take. And if it's not good enough, you're out of the game."

This scare tactic had the effect of driving down wholesale fees. One can only imagine the indignation of the specialty channel executives who had nervously scribbled a paltry few cents on the piece of paper when, later, they learned that instead of selling the new package for a dollar, the cable industry had decided to market it at $5.95. Thus the cable consortium had strong-armed the new channels to accept an artificially low wholesale fee to maximize their own retail markup, which this time was way above the customary 100 percent.

"Many felt that the cable industry had pulled a fast one on the CRTC," said Mark Rubinstein, a senior executive at CHUM-Citytv who was forced to swallow his pride to get Space: The Imagination Station and CP 24 into the new package. [8]

The cable industry also imported the "launch fees" model from the United States. Having accepted low wholesale fees, the new channels were also forced to pay $2 million in so-called marketing fees to get fast-tracked onto the cable dial as part of the new Me TV package. True, the $2-million fees-for-carriage were paltry compared to the hundreds of millions paid by Rupert Murdoch to get his Fox News onto U.S. cable systems. But whatever the price extracted, it was still an abuse of market power. The channels added to the Me TV package in October 1997 knew well they were being forced to pay a pound of flesh, but they calculated that it was better to pay up and have a channel on the air than refuse to submit and languish in digital limbo.

Juris Silkans, president of Atlantis Broadcasting, went to his board of directors to seek the $2-million key-money payment to the cable industry to get Home and Garden Television launched. Like other program executives, Silkans was baffled by the CRTC's passive inaction when so many of the new channels were clearly unhappy with the cable industry's hardball tactics.

"It was a bit surprising, to say the least, to see the CRTC do absolutely nothing when the cable industry suddenly decided to launch sixteen channels, including a bunch of American channels, when the same cable industry had told the Commission that it had room for only eight channels," Silkans said.[9]

Cable giants like Rogers did not stop at $2-million launch fees. They also extracted equity stakes from desperate channels. Shaw already owned Treehouse outright and Rogers had stakes in Outdoor Life, The Comedy Network, and CTV Sportsnet. Soon Shaw announced a takeover bid on Headline Sports, and Rogers applied to have its 20-percent stake in CTV Sportsnet increased to 40 percent. Rogers also muscled in on an ownership stake in CHUM's CP 24 local news channel in Toronto. The "CP" in CP 24 had originally stood for "CityPulse," after Citytv's local news show. But when the bean-counters at CHUM sat down with Rogers executives, the name mysteriously changed to "CablePulse" — a name that would be difficult to get included in a satellite TV package. In the end, Rogers extracted cash, equity, and branding appeal from CHUM.

Moses Znaimer prefers not to talk about these backroom deals. "Let's just say we have some talented pragmatists in this company," he says with a smile.

The Me TV package was launched on October 17, 1997. The package included the four "must carry" channels designated by the CRTC (History Television, Teletoon, The Comedy Network, and CTV's headline news channel) plus the secondary group of channels that paid key money to be included (Home and Garden Television, Outdoor Life, Space: The Imagination Station, Headline Sports, Prime, and Treehouse). The Family Channel, which had been languishing with the struggling Movie Network as a pay TV service, was also added to the Me TV package. Finally, the U.S. channels added were Black Entertainment Television, CNBC, The Golf Channel, Food Network, Speedvision, and Ted Turner's WTBS superstation. CHUM's CP 24 was later offered in Toronto. The monthly fee for the new package was set at a minimum of $5.95. It was good value for the money. Competition from satellite TV seemed to be working. But it was also a great deal for the Cable Guys.

Shortly after the Me TV launch, some complained that cable had included U.S. channels of questionable merit while many Canadian channels were stuck on the digital waiting list. At CHUM, despite the fast-tracking of Space: The Imagination Station and CP 24, Znaimer had three other channels — Star TV, Canadian Learning Television, and MuchMoreMusic — waiting for cable carriage. Meanwhile, U.S. channels like Speedvision, which is devoted to automobile racing, had been fast-tracked into Canadian homes.

"Getting a licence for a television channel in this country is like getting a licence to beg," says Znaimer. "I wouldn't mind if cable brought in good stuff from the U.S. Nobody is against that. But they bring in a lot of crap and then say there is no room for Canadian channels. The cable companies have brought in this numbskull channel Speedvision. Congratulations to the Canadian cable industry. They have let in imported U.S. channels that reach more viewers here than they do in the United States!"

From cable's point of view, it could be argued that there are just as many car-racing fanatics in Canada willing to buy the new package to get Speedvision as there are thirtysomething pop music fans interested in MuchMoreMusic. True, but the reason Speedvision was included in the new package had more to do with backroom deals than with consumer tastes. Ted Rogers is a shareholder in Outdoor Life, which is part-owned by U.S.-based Outdoor Life Network. The U.S. channel is owned by a consortium of major American cable companies, including John Malone's TCI. In early 1998 Malone paid about $100 million (U.S.) for a stake in Outdoor Life Network and Speedvision, both of which were floundering commercially. In the United States, the two channels were marketed jointly — and they were twinned in Canada as well. The U.S. cable owners of Outdoor Life Network insisted that its sister channel, Speedvision, be included in the Me TV package. And since Rogers was a co-owner of Outdoor Life, he had little incentive to resist.

If Znaimer thinks that broadcast licences in Canada are licences to "beg," then he is a brilliant beggar. In the spring of 1998 CHUM pulled out all the stops at the cable industry's annual convention in Montreal with an all-star bash to promote MuchMoreMusic. The seduction campaign worked. A few months later, Znaimer happily announced that MuchMoreMusic was set to launch in the fall of 1998, and the channel was launched on schedule in October. Znaimer might have detested cable's bullying tactics, but he was more than willing to play the game. So was CTV, whose channel CTV Sportsnet went on the air in October 1998. The fact that Ted Rogers owned 20 percent of the channel — and wanted to move up to 40 percent — was, of course, a mere coincidence. Ted Rogers clearly had learned a thing or two from John Malone. You start with a 20-percent equity stake in a channel and later move in for control. As a top American telephone executive once said of the cable industry: "Working with the cable industry is like picnicking with a tiger. You might enjoy the meal, but the tiger always eats last."

Global's new channel, Prime TV, presented an entirely different sort of problem. When Global pitched the Prime concept to the CRTC in 1996, it said the channel would be tailored to appeal to the "fifty-plus" age group — that is, the ageing baby boomers and people moving into retirement. At the CRTC hearings, Global enlisted the services of silver-haired broadcaster Michael McManus to front the application. McManus dutifully made an impassioned plea to the Commission to license a channel that would serve the needs of Canada's ageing population. The CRTC was understandably impressed by the idea, for older people are indeed systematically neglected by television's youth-obsessed advertising market, which is indefatigably in search of the Holy Grail of the eighteen-to-thirty-nine demographic group.

When Global's Prime went on the air, however, it promptly abandoned its fifty-plus target group and billed itself as "Canada's superstation," featuring endless reruns of the flossy American shows associated with the main Global network. Months later, Prime TV lowered its demographics even further and rebaptized itself "Canada's Entertainment Network," this time featuring a steady stream of American programs about Hollywood stars and vapid U.S. lifestyle shows. A show called *Grumps* featuring off-the-cuff grousing and debating by retirement-age personalities was revamped to appeal to a younger demographic, with singer Murray McLauchlan as host. Yet Prime's formal conditions of licence stated explicitly that the new channel was obliged to offer programming for people older than fifty years. Canadians in this unenviable age bracket were cynically left out in the cold by the Global bean-counters. One can only admire the testicular fortitude of the Global executives who pulled off this scam. It might be asked, though, why the CRTC stood by and did nothing. In a digital world of unlimited capacity, such delinquency might be pardonable because there would be room for all channels and everybody would have the right to go broke. But in a quasi-monopoly market where cable capacity is limited and competition is still restricted, shenanigans of this sort should not be tolerated. The CRTC should have promptly revoked the licence of the rejuvenated Prime.

Shortly after licensing the Me TV channels, the CRTC announced that cable companies could link Canadian channels with channels in a new roster of U.S. and other foreign cable networks: America's Health Network, ART America, BBC World, Court TV, Deutsche Welle, The Filipino

Channel, Fit TV, The Golf Channel, Speedvision, TV Food Network, TV Japan, TV Polonia, WMN-TV: Russian-American Broadcasting Company, American Movie Classics, Game Show Network, Turner Classic Movies, and Playboy TV. For the moment, however, it is unlikely that cable TV will be able to offer most of these channels. Even if cable exaggerates its capacity limitations, it certainly does not have enough room for all these channels — nor for the more than seventy specialty applications the CRTC received in 1997. Indeed, the greatest obstacle to the full realization of niche TV's potential has been the stubborn refusal of the cable industry to digitize its coaxial networks to make room for the 500-channel universe.

Rogers and Shaw paid for their hollow digital promises in late 1998 when the CRTC rejected their respective moves on CTV Sportsnet and Headline Sports. No to Roger's bid for 40 percent of CTV Sportsnet. And no to Shaw's takeover bid on Headline Sports. The CRTC also went after Rogers and Shaw in early 1999 for their arbitrary rate hikes on the basic cable service.

It's only a matter of time, though, before the broadcasting landscape becomes fully digital. Satellite TV already offers digital service, and the cable industry is now obliged to respond with a massive rollout of digital set-top boxes by 2000. New channels will soon be jostling to be the first to occupy the digital real estate and gain head-start marketing advantages, just as CNN and Canada's TSN reaped the benefits of being first in the field on analogue cable lineups in the early 1980s. In the United States, the first digital channels have been spin-offs of incumbent channels such as Discovery Channel and MTV. In Canada, Rogers is hoping to launch new channels based on Rogers-owned magazines such as *Chatelaine, Flare,* and *Modern Woman.* Another type of channel that is an obvious candidate for digital carriage is pay TV or pay-per-view. The cable industry could well move these high-interest niche services to digital in order to drive the commercial rollout of digital boxes.

Will digital "pick-and-pay" ever liberate consumers from the servitude of pre-selected packages that oblige them to take it all or get nothing? Satellite TV services like ExpressVu already offer theme packages such as all-sports, kids' channels, and movie packages. Still, while channel-specific pick-and-pay is a consumer-friendly marketing model, it does not sit as well with suppliers — not just delivery systems such as cable TV but also channel owners. Bundled packages not only drive penetration of more channels and thus increase cash flow for cable companies, they also guarantee financial security to limited-interest channels that, if sold as stand-alones, would almost certainly go bankrupt. It could be asked, for example, whether channels like Bravo! or WTN would survive in a pick-and-pay world.

From a free-market point of view, we should not care whether Bravo! and WTN go bankrupt. But in a country like Canada, we have guaranteed these channels business viability to achieve certain cultural objectives, even if they have been difficult to define. The tension between these two logics — cultural policy versus business logic — will determine the pace of the transition from a regulated market model based on "packages" to a world where consumers can pay for single channels — or indeed order up single programs for a specified cost via new delivery systems such as the Web.

The emergence of interactive TV and the explosion of the Web will indeed pose a serious challenge to the old market paradigms that in the past have sustained the rigid monopoly power of the cable TV industry. Power is shifting from suppliers to consumers, from distribution systems to content. The new consumer, empowered by technology, will soon make their long-delayed arrival.

CHAPTER 7

The Promise and Perils of Hollywood North

THE BROADCASTING INDUSTRY IN CANADA IS REGULATED, WHICH INSU-
lates its major players from the vagaries of the market. Making movies and
TV dramas is a much more precarious business, to say nothing of the
subtler issue of artistic merit. In a colonial country like Canada, with its
conservative culture, aversion to risk, and grudging dependency on all
things American, it should not be surprising that the history of Canadian
film production has been a continuing conundrum that has never fully
escaped these basic realities of the Canadian experience.

Limiting the Canadian experience to the preoccupations of the Greater
Toronto Area is a provocative proposition. But while non-Torontonians are
loath to admit it, Toronto is without a doubt the financial and cultural
capital of Canada. It is also the movie-making centre of the country. Torontonians have even become somewhat blasé about their city's transformation
into a perpetual movie set — even when the city doubles for Manhattan
complete with scruffy ersatz New York cops and big yellow cabs. When
encountering yet another Winnebego-cluttered corner of their city used as
a film location, the mild resentment of phlegmatic Torontonians is invariably mixed with aloof curiosity. They are long accustomed to the hassles
that go with the territory when your city is known as "Hollywood North."

Big Picture, Small Screen

Hollywood North is big business. It's so big, in fact, that Toronto is now the
third-largest movie-production centre in North America — after Los
Angeles and New York. The city ranks number two in television production,
after Los Angeles. The low value of the Canadian dollar provides incentive

enough for the Hollywood studios to head north to shoot feature films and TV shows. Today, the rivalry amongst Canada's major cities — mainly Toronto and Vancouver — to attract the economic spin-offs of Hollywood activity has become so fierce that Canadian politicians are now tripping over one another as they race down to Los Angeles to bow and curtsy before Hollywood moguls while making extravagant offers of generous tax breaks.

In 1997 American director Jeff Freilich was in Toronto to oversee the shooting of *Naked City*, a made-for-television movie scheduled for broadcast on the U.S. cable channel, Showtime. The Naked City in question was, of course, New York. Freilich chose Toronto for purely economic reasons — especially the low Canadian dollar — and the happy compliance of local authorities.

"We'll use Toronto for the tight exterior shots and for interiors," said Freilich, who is based in Los Angeles. "I love New York, but in terms of how much time it would take to shoot this film there, the money it would take, the availability of locations, and the question of co-operation, it's still easier to do it here. With our means, this is the place."

The same hard economic logic lured American television series like *McGyver* and *The X-Files* to Vancouver, though both shows eventually moved back to sunny California when their stars grew bored with life in rainy British Columbia. Vancouver has also served as the backdrop for movies such as *Millennium*, *Poltergeist*, *Jumanji*, and *Deep Rising*. Clint Eastwood might have been impressed by the landscape of the Canadian Prairies when he came to Canada to shoot the western *Unforgiven*, but he could not have been indifferent to Canada's anemic currency, either.[1]

The real Hollywood North, less powerful and celebrated than the Tinseltown-in-Toronto phenomenon, is Canada's own domestic movie and television industry. The Canadian production industry has grown up, rather like an eager apprentice, in the shadow of the overwhelming Hollywood presence in Canada, but is finally coming into its own. Total economic activity in Canadian film and television production now exceeds $1.5 billion — more than double that figure when U.S. and other foreign productions shot in Canada are included. Thanks to the strength of its domestic television production industry, Canada is the second-biggest exporter — after the United States — of audiovisual products in the global market.

In a business driven by big egos and major stars, Canada has produced many of both. Robert Lantos, the larger-than-life movie producer whose film *The Sweet Hereafter* garnered Academy Award nominations, is a contemporary throwback to Hollywood tycoons like Louis B. Mayer and Samuel Goldwyn. In television, Canadian production houses like Alliance

Atlantis, Nelvana, Salter Street, Cinar, Epitome, and True North are filling television schedules not only in Canada but throughout the world. No longer a marginal industry of small players scrambling for paltry subsidies, Canadian producers today hold their heads high in places like Cannes, Venice, Berlin, Sydney, London, and even Los Angeles.

And yet, paradoxically, Canada's film and TV industry is still regarded, and constantly debated, as a nagging problem that seems to defy a solution. At best, Canada's movie and TV output is like a critical *succès d'estime*: many are raving about it, but few are making any money at it.

The structural factors that have long disadvantaged the Canadian audiovisual industry are well known. Canada suffers from "thin market" syndrome because of the country's relatively small population of 30 million people, about a quarter of whom are native francophones. Without the enormous U.S. advantage of a massive domestic market, it is difficult, if not impossible, for Canadian producers to amortize the cost of making movies and TV programs over their home market alone. This basic reality has led to an export-or-die logic that, while not without its merits, has put pressure on Canadian producers to fashion the qualitative aspects of their products to the tastes and dictates of other places. Thus, while Canada's producers boast identifiably Canadian shows like *Anne of Green Gables*, *Black Harbour*, *North of 60*, *Traders*, *This Hour Has 22 Minutes*, and *Power Play*, they still pay the bills with commercial fare such as *Psi Factor*, *Earth: Final Conflict*, *Scandalous Me: The Jacqueline Susann Story*, and *Legacy*, a drama set in the bluegrass hills of Kentucky.

There is no shame, to be sure, in being prodigious exporters of cultural products. But Canada imports so much from Hollywood that any foreign sales of domestic products only marginally offset a massive balance-of-payments deficit in the entertainment industries. The familiar mantra of statistics that demonstrate the extent of Canada's colonization by the United States can only be dispiriting for cultural nationalists: 96 percent of cinema screen time in Canada is taken up by foreign movies, mostly American; 75 percent of television watched in Canada is foreign, mainly American; 70 percent of music on Canadian radio stations is foreign, mainly American; 65 percent of books purchased in Canada are foreign, mainly American; and 80 percent of magazines sold on Canadian newsstands are foreign, mainly American.

The Canadian television production industry's performance is actually considered a remarkable success story, and in many ways it is. By contrast, the Canadian cinema industry has never been able to claim anything more than a tiny sliver of Canada's domestic market. Measured by box-office receipts, Canadian movies take in only 3 percent of total revenues in

Canada, while about 95 percent of box office goes to Hollywood movies. If Quebec statistics were removed from these figures, English Canadian movies would have a box-office share of less than 1 percent. There may be some comfort in the fact that the Canadian experience vis-à-vis the Hollywood empire, though relatively pitiable, is not unique. In Australia, domestic movies claim only 10 percent of the national box office. In the United Kingdom, the figure is 23 percent. In Germany, domestic films take 17 percent of the total box office. Italian movies claim a 33-percent of share of Italy's national box office. Even in France, with its powerful arsenal of quotas and subsidies, French movies account for only 33 percent of total box-office revenues.

Ironically, Canada has produced some of the world's major cinematic talents and most successful box-office stars. Directors Norman Jewison, David Cronenberg, Ivan Reitman, and James Cameron are Canadian. So are actors Christopher Plummer, William Shatner, Jim Carrey, Dan Ackroyd, Martin Short, and Michael J. Fox. But most of these famous show-biz celebrities work in the United States and their work is financed by the Hollywood studios. As in any other sector, when a country loses its best talent in a structural brain-drain, the unavoidable negative effect is the weakening of the domestic industry. The Canadian talent migration southward is even more dramatic among offscreen talent such as writers and animators. Even those Canadians who remain at home often work for the major Hollywood studios that have set up in Canada. Disney, for example, has built its own animation studio in Toronto to exploit an abundant supply of highly trained local talent produced by nearby Sheridan College.

Besides the allure and domination of American culture, another structural cause of Canada's weak cultural production capacities has been — with the exception of some sectors, such as publishing — the country's obsession with technological nationalism. Canada built highly efficient telephone networks, cable television infrastructure, and satellite systems through central planning, government protection, and even state ownership. The government treated the deployment of satellites and cable as a high-priority policy dogma. The government failed to realize, however, that new delivery systems were useless in themselves. The important thing was the content they transmitted. And yet cultural production was virtually ignored. Obsessed with hardware, Canada neglected to focus on software. The country has produced world-beating national champions like Nortel in the telecom industry; but content, readily available from foreign sources, has never been king in Canada.

Canada's reflex of technological nationalism has not, to be sure, been without some benefits. Indeed, it has been to some extent responsible for the relative success of the national television industry. In the early 1980s the Canadian government realized that little could be done to counter Hollywood's cartel-like domination of the national movie market, so policy makers turned instead towards the television industry as the preferred outlet for Canadian stories. Broadcasting was regulated in Canada, so the government could assert more control over what was offered to viewers.

There was one problem, however: Canada's television networks were, like the Hollywood studios, vertically integrated closed circuits with little interest in anything but their own products. At the public CBC, for example, programs were produced in-house by unionized talent. Likewise, the private networks — CTV and Global and TVA in Quebec — supplied themselves with programs through owned or affiliated production houses, especially in low-cost categories such as news and current affairs. Some senior network executives, while still on the job, formed their own production companies and commissioned work to line their own pockets. It might not have been illegal, but it most certainly was corrupt. More expensive shows, such as dramatic series, were acquired in the United States and simulcasted. In effect, Canada's television networks functioned as closed systems of supply and demand.

The main effect of vertical integration in the Canadian broadcasting industry was the retarded emergence of an independent production sector. For decades, cultural production remained largely concentrated in government agencies, notably the National Film Board and the CBC, which had large bureaucracies to support battalions of state-employed filmmakers. The Canadian situation was, to be sure, not wholly unique. In European countries, program production was likewise owned and controlled by broadcasters. This was especially the case in countries such as France, where broadcasting monopolies were state-owned, or in Britain, where a public-private duopoly existed. However, in these countries high national quotas were in effect. In the United Kingdom, for example, the private ITV network honoured an 86-percent British quota established in the early 1950s by agreement with in-house production unions. The publicly owned BBC informally abided by the same quota. Consequently, while vertical integration prevented the emergence of a thriving independent production sector in Britain, cultural policy objectives were still being achieved because low-cost American program imports were effectively banned by the high quota. A strong independent production industry finally emerged in the United Kingdom with the creation of Channel 4 and the obligation imposed on established broadcasters to outsource production.

In the United States, the Big Three networks also controlled vertically integrated production arms from the earliest days of television. This came to an end in 1970, however, when the FCC imposed the structural separation of broadcasting and production with its Syndication and Financial Interest Rules, or "fin-syn" rules. The new regulations, which came into effect in 1972, were aimed at preventing domination of program production by the Big Three. The fin-syn rules were in fact considered a regulatory favour to the Hollywood studios, which were seeking to become program suppliers to the TV networks at a time when the rise of television appeared to threaten the theatrical movie business. The Big Three bitterly denounced and fought the FCC rules. Still, there could be no doubt that, whatever their rationale, the fin-syn rules triggered a tremendous flourishing of American television production throughout the 1970s and 1980s. Indeed, the 1970s today are looked back on as the golden age of American television, thanks chiefly to the emergence of many creative, thriving independent production houses. [2]

In 1983 Ottawa decided to follow the U.S. example and get tough with Canadian broadcasters. By creating Telefilm Canada, the government effectively forced broadcasters to help develop Canadian program production through commissions to non-allied, independent producers. The main engine of this new policy was Telefilm's Broadcast Fund, established through a tax on monthly cable TV bills to help subsidize the production of Canadian films and television programs. Telefilm promised to invest 33 percent in television program budgets — the level was increased to 49 percent after 1985 — thus creating an incentive for broadcasters to secure Canadian program supply through licence-fee payments to independent producers. Half of Telefilm's taxpayer-supported largesse was earmarked for production sponsored by the CBC.

Telefilm Canada thus achieved the same objective as the U.S. fin-syn rules: vertical integration of TV production and exhibition was effectively banned, at least for ambitious high-cost programs in the drama category such as movies and series. By focusing Telefilm's mandate on television, the government hoped to ensure that Canadian films and TV programs would actually get exhibition, which was highly precarious in the theatrical movie market due to Hollywood's control of Canadian movie theatres. By shifting the emphasis towards television, Telefilm could create an incentive for broadcasters to secure Canadian program supply through licence-fee payments while the CRTC imposed on TV networks specific spending commitments and Canadian-content quotas for first-run Canadian drama.

While several successful Canadian producers had already been active in the 1970s, the boom triggered by Telefilm in the 1980s put them on the map. Robert Lantos, for example, was able to graduate from soft-porn and low-budget features to ambitious movies such as *Joshua Then and Now* and regular series such as *Night Heat* and *ENG*. Similarly, Michael MacMillan had started Atlantis in the late 1970s, but his fortunes didn't start soaring until the mid-1980s.

"Telefilm had $30 million in its first year — that was a lot of money in those days," recalls MacMillan.[3]

Not all the shows that got made were critical successes. Many flopped with television viewers, and there were cases of scandalous abuse of Telefilm's funding regime as American producers laundered their own productions through the Canadian subsidy system by using the letterhead of compliant Canadian proxies. The production boom of the 1980s nonetheless produced some high-quality Canadian programs. MacMillan's Atlantis, for example, won an Oscar in the best dramatic-short category for *Boys and Girls*, based on a story by Alice Munro. That would be only the first of many triumphs for Atlantis, which today, after its merger with Lantos's Alliance, is the twelfth-biggest independent production house in the world.

Despite the tremendous burst of Canadian film and TV production activity in the 1980s, the amounts paid by Canadian television networks to acquire domestic programs remained exceedingly low. For example, in 1984–85 Canadian private television stations paid licence fees that averaged only 5.2 percent of total production budgets, while the CBC kicked in approximately 21.4 percent of budgets. This intransigent parsimony was easily explained. The business logic of vertical integration had been highly advantageous for Canadian television networks, as self-dealing reduced costs and gave broadcasters more control over product supply. TV networks like CTV and Global — and even the CBC — stubbornly stuck to their business plans as mere schedulers of simulcasted American TV shows despite government subsidies, tax incentives, and regulatory obligations. In the United Kingdom, by contrast, independent producers covered virtually 100 percent of their costs through licence fees from broadcasters such as Channel 4, Granada, and the BBC. In the United States, too, financing for made-for-television movies and dramatic series was provided by a television or "cable" network, which typically covered the entire cost of production — one third up front, another third on completion, and the final third on delivery.

"The television networks see Canadian content as a 'cost centre,' not as a 'profit centre,'" says Michael MacMillan. "In business, when you have a cost centre, there is only one thing you want to do with it — lower costs."

Another problem during Canada's production boom years was the temptation to get into bed with Hollywood at any cost. In the 1980s Canadian producers were frantically attempting either to sign a co-production deal with the Americans or make a pre-sale to a U.S. television network. The result was that, while doing deals with the Americans invariably made the financing easier, the inevitable qualitative pressure either sanitized — or simply Americanized — the final product.

Some, like Robert Lantos, saw this as an opportunity to exploit. "Our advantage is our proximity to the U.S. and our shared mass culture and language," said Lantos. "We can sell into the U.S., something Europeans have great trouble doing." [4]

Lantos was right. In many ways, it made sense for Canadian producers to stretch their ambitions southward. The problem, however, was that the rash of deals in the 1980s often had more to do with making money than with making movies. And it was always the Canadian taxpayer who paid the bill. For example, *Joshua Then and Now*, based on Mordecai Richler's novel, was produced by Lantos, directed by Canadian-born Ted Kotcheff, and featured a number of Canadian actors. But there was no escaping the fact that it was a Hollywood movie that, in order to access Telefilm money, was extended into a two-part Canadian television drama. In the end, neither the film nor the television version worked artistically. Lantos likewise cranked out the television series *Night Heat* in Toronto for a New York producer who had pre-sold the show to CBS. The show was shot in Toronto and aired on CTV in Canada, but its Canadian location was never identified in the series. In fact, there was no onscreen association with Canada whatever. Offscreen, the producers could count on Telefilm to subsidize the series with the money of Canadian taxpayers.

John Haslett Cuff, the *Globe and Mail's* television critic from 1986 to 1997, was particularly critical of the legacy of the 1980s in the Canadian television industry. "Compared to the best programs from the U.S. and Britain (and even Australia), Canadian television series still lag lamentably in quality and sophistication," he wrote. "Despite the enormous growth in domestic television production, much of what is produced here still reflects the sort of cultural schizophrenia that is both a product of economic realities and a failure of confidence and imagination." [5]

By the early 1990s the Canadian movie and TV industry had matured considerably, though Hollywood "service" productions shot in Canada remained an important part of total economic activity. Ottawa's creation of the Cable Fund, which was established in 1993 from a direct surcharge on monthly cable bills, helped "top up" stingy broadcaster licence fees. In 1996 the Cable Fund was folded into a new funding mechanism, called the

Canada Television and Cable Production Fund (CTCPF). The new fund was launched with a substantial budget of $200 million to be allocated by two separate entities. First, an Equity Investment Program, managed by Telefilm, was essentially an extension of the Broadcast Fund. Second, a new Licence Fee Program, administered separately, was based largely on the Cable Fund. The federal government added $100 million of new money to be divided between Telefilm and the Licence Fee programs. The CTCPF, today called simply the Canadian Television Fund, has been the principal subsidy-funding engine of the Canadian production sector since the mid-1990s.

Today, Canadian television networks have followed the example of the U.S. networks by returning to the model of vertical integration through wholly owned production companies. In the 1980s, during the favourable climate of deregulation in Washington, the major U.S. networks called for the repeal of the fin-syn rules on the grounds that they were no longer an oligopoly because of the rise of cable networks and home video. In the early 1990s the FCC finally agreed. The U.S. regulator modified the fin-syn rules by allowing TV networks to hold an interest in the programs they aired and to produce up to 40 percent of their schedules. In 1995 the fin-syn restrictions were lifted altogether, opening the door to mergers between U.S. production studios and TV networks. Today, as previously noted, most of the major Hollywood studios own their own television networks — Disney/ABC, Paramount/UPN, 20th Century Fox/Fox, Warner Bros/ the WB network, and Universal/USA Networks. The only two networks that are not vertically integrated with a major Hollywood studio are NBC and CBS, owned respectively by the two industrial giants General Electric and Westinghouse.

In Canada, pressure for structural reintegration predictably resurfaced following the U.S. example. In Canada, however, vertical integration has occurred in the reverse direction. Whereas in the United States, the Hollywood producers now control their own TV networks, in Canada the television networks are buying their own production houses. In 1998, for example, Izzy Asper's CanWest Global paid $40 million in a takeover of Winnipeg-based producer Fireworks Entertainment, which specialized chiefly in so-called industrial projects aimed at the export market.

This inversion is a symptom of Canada's preference for hardware over software. In the United States, a strong production industry was built in Hollywood before the advent of television; but in Canada the production sector remained the poor cousin of infrastructure. It should not be surprising, for example, that in a country driven by technological nationalism, film and

TV producers depended on subsidies disbursed by a "Cable Fund." When Global bought Fireworks, the purchase was a sign of the same hardware-over-software market logic.

After the Global-Fireworks deal, Canadian producers expressed concern over the return to vertical integration, as it would inevitably create an incentive for TV networks to buy programs exclusively from the production arms they owned. The television networks pointed out, however, that producers like Alliance and Atlantis were vertically integrated into broadcasting with specialty channels like History, Showcase, Home and Garden Television, and Life.

"What they call 'self-dealing' when talking about us they call 'synergies' when talking about themselves," remarks Ivan Fecan, CEO of CTV. "Vertical integration is not just an American trend, it's a worldwide trend. In Canada, there has to be industry integration in some form because it is happening all over the world. And so if we don't do it, we'll miss it." [6]

True enough. But vertical integration can sometimes backfire on television networks when they feel compelled to feed their broadcast schedules with shows — no matter how good they are — produced by affiliated companies. The U.S. television industry learned that lesson in 1998–99 when the closed-system logic of vertical integration produced the worst TV season in memory. Self-dealing removed the competitive — and creative — dimension from the production process, and it showed on the air. NBC found choice prime-time slots for two of its own properties, *Single Guy* and *Union Square*, which were duds that likely would never have been bought if they'd been produced by a non-allied production house. ABC blocked out entire nights for programs made by its parent company, Disney.

"Sometimes vertical integration means you just get to lose twice," says Kerry McCluggage, chairman of the Paramount Television Group. "It can hurt your network business if you're not open to diverse suppliers."

In Canada, Global now has a structural incentive to favour shows produced by Fireworks, and consequently it could neglect or reject better shows produced by Alliance Atlantis, Epitome, True North, Salter Street, and other highly successful Canadian production houses. If CTV follows the Global example and buys a Canadian producer, both of Canada's main private networks will be vertically integrated. Even the CBC, while it is obliged to commission work from outside producers, tends to favour in-house projects if only to appease its labour unions.

Some major Canadian production houses are now sufficiently large and powerful to buy a television network. The mega-merger between Alliance and Atlantis, for example, created one of the biggest production forces in

North America — on a par with Hollywood-based companies like Spelling. The deal also thrust the low-key Michael MacMillan into the hot glare of the media spotlight. MacMillan's personal style is a study in contrast to the high-flying, hard-living Hungarian, Robert Lantos, who cashed out in the deal by selling Alliance. Lantos, known for his love of big homes, fat cigars, beautiful women, and single-malt scotch, returned to his first love of making movies. After walking away from Alliance to set up his own company, Serendipity, he already had several projects on his plate: David Cronenberg's *eXistenZ*, Denys Arcand's *15 Moments*, an adaptation of Michael Ondaatje's *In the Skin of a Lion*, and a movie version of Mordecai Richler's *Barney's Version*. That left MacMillan in charge of a production colossus with assets worth about $850 million in 1998. While only in his early forties, the unassuming MacMillan already had two decades of production experience under his belt.

"Twenty years ago, the decision to produce a television show or movie was based on whether or not you could arrange the financing to cover your production costs," says MacMillan. "It wasn't based on whether the project was good or whether there was a market for it. Today, it's the other way around. We could get financing for a lot of projects that we don't produce. We produce projects that are based on how good they are, what broadcaster will be interested, what the best time slot for them is, and what kinds of audiences they will interest."

With the acquisition of Alliance, MacMillan is no longer just a television producer, but Canada's biggest movie mogul. Given the traditional weakness of the Canadian feature film business, it is likely that MacMillan will find movies more of a challenge than the regulated, and less unpredictable, television industry. In Canada, competing with Hollywood has never been easy.

The Power and the Glitter

Canada has been a colony of Hollywood from the earliest days of cinema. After the First World War, most of the nascent Hollywood studios already had organized their affairs as vertically integrated companies that controlled production, distribution, and theatrical exhibition. Adolph Zukor's Famous Players–Lasky Corp., for example, was a Hollywood producer that, through its distribution arm Paramount, acquired movie theatres throughout the United States to ensure guaranteed outlets for its movies. In those early days of cinema, Hollywood viewed Canada not as a separate market, but as a territorial extension of the U.S. domestic market. That attitude would stubbornly persist for the rest of the century.

As early as 1918 the Ontario government had contemplated imposing a prohibitive tax on imported American movies. The Hollywood studios didn't even have to lobby against the proposed tax. Canadian-owned movie theatres, organized as the Motion Picture Exhibitors' Protection Association, fought the tax because their profits depended on a reliable supply of popular American movies featuring stars such as Charlie Chaplin and Buster Keaton. Canadian theatre owners did not realize, however, that their dependency on Hollywood would be their own undoing, for soon the big, vertically integrated U.S. studios would drive them out of business.

In the early 1920s Paramount-owned Famous Players extended its reach into Canada, where the major theatre chain was family-owned Allen Theatres. When the Allens refused to sell out to Famous Players, the Hollywood major deprived Allen Theatres of all movies made by Paramount. The Allens soon relented and sold out. With the addition of the Allen movie houses, Famous Players counted more than 200 cinemas in Canada by 1930. The only serious competition to Famous Players was in Toronto, where another Hollywood company, Loew's, also operated movie theatres.

In 1924, when Charlie Chaplin was shooting *The Gold Rush*, the Hollywood majors established a lobby presence in Canada through an association called the Motion Picture Distributors and Exhibitors of Canada. An offshoot of the U.S.-based Hollywood lobby, the association was run by compliant Canadians with political connections and establishment credentials in Canada, a strategy that continues to this day. The first head of the Hollywood lobby's Canadian branch-plant was Colonel John Cooper, founder of the Canadian Club of Toronto. Under Cooper's leadership, the Hollywood lobby fought amusement taxes, import duties, and all other Canadian regulations that might affect the bottom line of major Hollywood studios — such as Paramount and MGM — that had a commercial presence in Canada.

By the early 1930s Hollywood's domination of the Canadian movie market was becoming a concern to political leaders in Ottawa. In the United States, the major studios were coming under increasing anti-trust suspicion for their combinations and abuse of market dominance. In Canada, however, anti-Hollywood hostility was inspired more by a cultural resentment towards the alleged cheapness of American movies. In 1931 *Saturday Night* magazine grumbled: "The monarchs of Paramount Public are in themselves alien in sentiment and spirit to the finer element of civilization in their own land. . . . Their interest lies exclusively in endeavouring to ascertain how far entertainment can be cheapened and vulgarized in order to yield a big turnover." *Saturday Night*'s proposed remedy was itself rather curious. The magazine proposed that the government force Famous Players to open its movie houses to plays performed by Canadian live theatre companies.[7]

While the mood in Canada might have been anti-Hollywood in some quarters, in the 1930s most Canadians were unfamiliar with the sentiments of cultural nationalism. The only proactive Canadian policy tool for motion pictures was the state-controlled Motion Picture Bureau. Its role was limited, however, to attracting Hollywood studios to shoot movies in Canada. Canadians who were opposed to Hollywood films did not believe that Hollywood's domination of the Canadian market was at the expense of a thriving domestic movie industry. These Canadians simply preferred the movies of the British Empire to which Canada belonged. The Imperial Order of the Daughters of the Empire, for example, took the extraordinary measure of striking a film committee, which publicly complained about the paucity of British movies in Canada. *Maclean's* magazine, in an article titled "The Battle for Canadian Film Control," observed: "General interest seems to centre on British films and the possibility of seeing them. This is a more widely discussed topic than the matter of purely Canadian ones."[8]

The pro-British sentiment was inspired by more than colonial attachment. Canadian movie exhibitors suffering under the monopolistic practices of Famous Players were now crying foul when threatened with Hollywood product boycotts, and open letters were written to Prime Minister R. B. Bennett demanding action. Many believed the solution was to import more British movies to offset the Hollywood boycott. Ray Lewis, a Canadian importer of British films who also happened to be editor of *Canadian Moving Picture Digest*, made the transparently self-interested recommendation that a minimum 25-percent quota on British films be fixed. In 1931 the Ontario government legislated a screen quota, fixing minimum percentages of screen time, to promote the exhibition of British films in the province. The wording was so loose, however, that the quota was never enforced. The same year Ontario's attorney general initiated an anti-trust action against the Hollywood cartel. But an Ontario Supreme Court judge acquitted the defendants on the grounds that there was no evidence of an anti-competitive combination between Famous Players and the Hollywood distributors.

The Hollywood studios were encountering similar resistance to their monopolistic tactics in other countries as well. In France, despite a government-imposed tariff on imported movies, the Hollywood studios were taking in 82 percent of France's national box office by 1925. Three years later, French movie producers lobbied the Third Republic government to establish a quota system: four American movies would be allowed into France for every French movie exported to America. Infuriated, the Hollywood lobby threatened to boycott the French market if this quota was implemented. Needless to say, French movie theatre owners, fearing a loss of product supply, vociferously supported the Hollywood studios. The French government finally watered down the quota with a compromise solution: for every domestic movie produced in France, import permits would be issued for seven foreign films. The damage had already been done, however. France's major movie producers — Gaumont, Pathé, and Éclair — had already stopped making movies in order to concentrate instead on theatrical exhibition.

Germany proved slightly more successful in resisting Hollywood's domination. In 1921 the Weimar Republic imposed a quota limiting the importation of foreign movies to 15 percent of all films screened in Germany. The quota was not respected, but domestic films still commanded about 40 percent of screen time throughout the 1920s. This period was the apogee of the expressionist movement in German cinema, whose notable film masterpieces included *The Cabinet of Dr. Caligari*. The main structural reason for the success of German cinema was the existence of large, vertically integrated German movie companies that could rival the dominance of Hollywood. Universum Film AG — called "UFA" — was not only Germany's biggest producer of movies, but also controlled a major circuit of movie theatres. By the end of the 1920s German movies counted for 27 percent of the total European market, behind Hollywood, whose European market share was 60 percent.

The success of German cinema was only relative to failures elsewhere, and it proved short-lived. Hollywood eventually conquered the German market, thanks to U.S. economic aid aimed at helping the defeated Germany fight hyperinflation in the 1920s. With U.S. loans and investments came Hollywood movies and American jazz music. By 1924 UFA was on the verge of bankruptcy. It was rescued by a $4-million (U.S.) loan from two Hollywood studios: Paramount and MGM. Soon Charlie Chaplin was more famous in Germany than Nosferatu. Even Adolf Hitler watched the parody of himself in Chaplin's *The Great Dictator*.

In Britain, the domestic movie market was almost entirely controlled by Hollywood starting in the 1920s. U.K. movie directors pressured the British government to introduce quotas, but, as elsewhere, they met the fierce opposition of domestic movie theatre owners who relied on popular Hollywood fare. In 1927 the British government passed the Cinematograph Films Act, which established an exceedingly modest quota of 5 percent —

to be increased to a minimum of 20 percent within ten years — on domestic movies. Interestingly, the U.K. quotas had an effect on colonial Canada, for the U.K. definition of a "British" movie included any film shot in the British Empire — including Canada. This opened up a backdoor opportunity for Hollywood studios. Soon they were shooting "quota quickies" in Canada to flood the British market with cheap films. The main goal of the quota quickies wasn't to make money in Britain, but rather to demonstrate to the British government that quotas did not work.

Just as the Allied Victory in the First World War opened up European markets for Hollywood movies in the 1920s, so the Allied victory in the Second World War proved to be an enormous boon for American motion pictures after 1945. Once again, the United States was well positioned to reinforce its hard-power military triumph with a soft-power onslaught of Hollywood cultural products that would, it was believed, disseminate democratic values in fascist Europe. The Marshall Plan was in some respects the Mogul Plan. The two strategies — economic aid and cultural influence — worked in tandem.

France, while officially one of the victorious nations, was in a state of ruinous economic collapse in 1945. The country was also in a state of moral anguish after its catastrophic flirtation with the patriotic fascism promoted by the Vichy regime. In 1946 former French prime minister Léon Blum — a left-wing Jewish intellectual who had led the short-lived Front Populaire government in 1936 — was dispatched to the United States to negotiate an economic aid package with U.S. Secretary of State James Byrnes. As part of the France-U.S. agreement — dubbed the Blum-Byrnes Agreement — the United States wiped out France's war debt and offered France $650 million in aid. In exchange, Blum made a single concession on which the White House strongly insisted: the elimination of import quotas on American movies in France.

The Blum-Byrnes Agreement doubtless helped war-torn France get back on its feet, but it virtually crippled the French cinema industry. By 1947, only a year after the agreement was signed, many of France's movie studios had been driven out of business by the juggernaut of Hollywood movies that invaded the country. In 1948 the French government took measures to counter the Hollywood assault on French culture by introducing import quotas and creating a fund to finance French movies through a tax imposed on box-office tickets and movie distribution revenues.

In the United Kingdom, victorious Britons elected a left-wing Labour government immediately after the Second World War and the new prime minister, Clement Attlee, set about constructing the Welfare State. The government quickly discovered that some $47 million (U.S.) was flowing out of Britain to America every year due to the commercial popularity of Hollywood movies in the United Kingdom. The Labour government had already cut imports of food and other essential goods in order to maintain an acceptable level of hard currency. Now something had to be done about the currency flowing to Hollywood. In 1947 the Attlee government imposed a punitive 75-percent customs duty on all imported movies.

The U.K. movie import tax — called the Dalton Duty after Britain's chancellor of the Exchequer, Hugh Dalton — was received in Hollywood almost as a declaration of war. On August 7, 1947, the day after the Dalton Duty was unveiled in London, the Hollywood majors announced a boycott of British movie screens. But Hollywood went even further. A blitzkrieg advertising campaign for a fictitious new Hollywood movie hit London in a blanket of posters that covered the city. The posters featured the image of an American bald eagle and the word "Unconquered" emblazoned across the top. Thus the British public was made aware of Hollywood's ire.

Incensed by Hollywood's hardball tactics, Attlee's government dispatched industry minister Harold Wilson — the future prime minister — to negotiate with Harry Truman's administration. A compromise was reached whereby Hollywood would remit at least $17 million back home to the United States. Wilson, who had negotiated with Allen Dulles (later head of the CIA), was angered by the hostility he encountered during the negotiations. Members of the Hollywood lobby had distributed in American cinemas extracts of his speeches to smear him as a socialist menace. Wilson put up a brave face, though, because he knew he had to secure a deal. Many British cinemas were simply screening reruns of old American movies, anyway.

"We were paying out not $17 million but $50 million for the privilege of seeing *Hellzapoppin'* for the third time and *Ben Hur* for the twenty-third," said Wilson.

In 1949 Wilson saved face for his compromise in Washington by creating the National Film Finance Corporation, which was given £5 million to subsidize U.K. movie production. The British government followed the French example by slapping a tax — called the Eady Levy after a senior treasury mandarin named Sir Wilfrid Eady — on British box-office tickets. Part of the proceeds of the Eady Levy was funnelled into a new British Film Production Fund, which the Hollywood studios soon began tapping to finance movies they shot in Britain using local talent and technicians.[9]

Hollywood always had a reliable ally in the White House. In 1948 the

Truman administration helped Hollywood repatriate revenues drawn from European markets by creating a government program called Informational Media Guaranty (IMG), which was run out of the U.S. State Department. Through the IMG, the U.S. government gave Hollywood studios dollars for soft foreign currencies earned in Europe. There was one proviso: to qualify for the currency conversions the Hollywood movies shown abroad had to present a favourable picture of American life. In effect, the U.S. State Department was subsidizing the distribution of Hollywood movies in countries — such as Germany and Poland — where the local currency was blocked by foreign-exchange restrictions.

Ironically, the Hollywood cartel had more difficulty asserting its monopoly power in its home market than in passive foreign countries. Congress had passed strong anti-trust legislation in the late nineteenth century — notably the Sherman Act of 1890 — to counter the monopoly power of robber barons such as John D. Rockefeller. A half-century later, this legislation gave U.S. anti-trust officials legal ammunition to aim at the Hollywood cartel's anti-competitive business practices. In a 1948 decision known as the Paramount Decree, the U.S. Supreme Court ruled that the Hollywood majors were indeed a cartel that restrained trade because of their vertically integrated control of production, distribution, and exhibition. The Supreme Court found that the Hollywood majors were a "conspiracy" whose chief intent was to maintain a "monopoly in exhibition" of movies. The high court thus forced the Hollywood studios to divest their movie-theatre circuits in order to promote market forces in the procurement of movies shown to the public. Specifically, the Paramount Decree put an end to "block booking" — a practice that obliges theatres to guarantee screen time for several movies, whatever their quality or commercial potential — by separating distribution from exhibition. Henceforth, U.S. movie exhibitors could bid for Hollywood movies with no obligation to take packages of movies.

"Hollywood is like Egypt, full of crumbling pyramids," lamented mogul David Selznick after the Paramount Decree was rendered. "It'll just keep crumbling until finally the wind blows the last studio prop across the sands."

Selznick was wrong, of course. Hollywood would survive forced divestiture in the United States. In foreign countries, including Canada, the Hollywood studios continued to operate as vertically integrated cartels. Thus, the illegal behaviour of the Hollywood cartel in the United States remained perfectly legal — or at least condoned — in countries with less appetite for vigorous anti-trust actions. Indeed, the Hollywood studios would learn quickly that the most effective way to compensate for setbacks at home was to turn the screws even tighter in passive foreign markets. And they could always count on the White House's support.

In Canada, the dynamic of the domestic movie market — caught between British colonialism and North American continentalism — ensured the retarded development of a national cinema. After the Second World War, the main engine for filmmaking in Canada was the government-owned National Film Board. The NFB was a fertile creative environment for many highly talented Canadian filmmakers, particularly in French Canada, which produced Gilles Carle, Denys Arcand, Jacques Godbout, and Claude Jutra. In English Canada, directors such as Don Owen emerged from the NFB while others, like Budge Crawley, managed to raise private financing for respectable films such as *The Luck of Ginger Coffey* (1964), based on the Brian Moore novel.

The Directors Guild of Canada, a lobby group created in 1961 to represent Canadian film directors, began calling on Ottawa to formulate a national feature film policy. The Directors Guild put forward specific proposals: the creation of a fund to be financed in part by a tax on box-office receipts of Hollywood movies shown in Canada; an increased role for Canadian movie distributors in the Canadian market to counter the stranglehold of the Hollywood majors; and an obligation imposed on the CBC to broadcast twelve Canadian movies a year. Other groups argued for a screen quota. In the turbulent 1960s it seemed that a national film culture in Canada was finally emerging and making demands that reflected policies already in effect in European countries.

In 1967, Canada's centennial year, Ottawa responded to these pressures by creating the Canadian Film Development Corporation (CFDC) with a budget of $10 million. The CFDC's midwife was Judy LaMarsh, the outspoken Liberal Cabinet minister who was secretary of state in Lester Pearson's government. There was some concern at the time that the Hollywood majors would attempt to soak up the CFDC's funding by establishing Canadian subsidiaries. This prompted LaMarsh to make a memorable, albeit regrettable, retort that Hollywood would not likely rush into Canada to chase "a miserable $10 million." In another statement that would be echoed many years later, LaMarsh said: "We should be under no illusions about the difficulties which Canadian producers will face in building up a commercially viable industry in this country. They will have to make it commercially viable by exporting their work."

By most accounts, the CFDC was not a great success. In some cases, concerns about Hollywood meddling proved to be well founded. The

CFDC wrote cheques that pumped additional funding into movies made in Canada by the Hollywood studios. More controversially, the federal agency began bankrolling a series of soft-porn flicks with titles like *Love in a Four-Letter World* and *L'Initiation*, many of which were made in Quebec. These titillating movies were dubbed "maple-syrup porn" flicks. The CFDC did fund a number of excellent movies: Don Shebib's *Goin' Down the Road*, Claude Jutra's *Kamouraska*, Peter Carter's *The Rowdyman*, Gilles Carle's *La vraie nature de Bernadette*, and *The Apprenticeship of Duddy Kravitz*, based on Mordecai Richler's novel and starring Richard Dreyfuss.

Still, in the 1970s there was a feeling that Canada had not done enough to promote its domestic movie industry. In 1973 Liberal secretary of state Hugh Faulkner negotiated a "voluntary" quota with Famous Players and Odeon to secure more screen time for Canadian movies. The quota did not work, however, mainly because Famous Players and Odeon simply ignored it. Faulkner's successor, John Roberts, was no more successful. Roberts attempted to impose a 10-percent levy on the box-office receipts of Hollywood movies in Canada. But the measure was nixed by the Cabinet. Clearly, Ottawa did not have the stomach to apply European-style measures as a remedy for Hollywood's structural domination of the Canadian movie industry.

In 1975 Ottawa took an approach that was less openly hostile to Hollywood: fiscal incentives in the form of a 100-percent capital cost allowance for movies produced in Canada. The tax-shelter solution shifted film policy towards a more commercial approach. Canada would renounce its obsession with artistic movies and start playing the movie game like the Americans. It was an interesting twist to the cross-subsidy model: artistic films would be financed by profits made on unabashedly commercial movies.

"Artists cannot survive on art alone," said John Roberts. "Schlock, to use an inelegant word, is necessary as a solid base for creativity. It provides employment for talents which would otherwise not be able to survive, and therefore not be available for projects of higher artistic value."

Politically, the fiscal approach was an abject retreat. From a public-policy point of view, the tax shelters were an unqualified disaster. Worse, the Canadian government had had plenty of opportunity to understand that tax shelters presented serious risks. Indeed, the tax-shelter solution was borrowed directly from the U.S. government. And the U.S. experience had unequivocally demonstrated that, when 100-percent write-offs are lavished on movies, they invariably attract as much bad money as good money.

Hollywood was in a severe crisis in the early 1970s. The U.S. economy was in a downturn and Hollywood had accumulated collective losses of about $100 million. Part of the problem was simply bad creative decision making: a number of high-profile Hollywood movies had no legs at the box office, and the major studios were attempting to make up for theatrical losses by muscling into television with the complicity of the FCC's fin-syn rules. At MGM, the studio tried to raise money by auctioning off hundreds of memorable costumes and props, including Judy Garland's ruby slippers from *The Wizard of Oz*. They fetched $15,000, hardly enough to turn around the fortunes of a major studio that would know even worse times in the years ahead.

It wasn't long before the Hollywood studios, thanks to the well-connected lobbyist Jack Valenti, would seek assistance from the White House. Valenti, a longtime friend of fellow Texan Lyndon Johnson, had followed LBJ to the White House to work for the vice-president. When Johnson unexpectedly became president after John F. Kennedy's assassination in November 1963, Valenti became special assistant to the new president. Valenti's close relationship with LBJ was known everywhere. He was even married to LBJ's personal secretary, Mary Margaret Wiley. Valenti was LBJ's strategic conduit to Congress, the guy who cut deals between LBJ and Congressmen looking for presidential favours in exchange for their support of White House initiatives. Valenti was LBJ's man on Capitol Hill. While LBJ was still president, the diminutive Valenti left the White House to become Hollywood's chief lobbyist and spokesman. It was the beginning of a long relationship that cemented Valenti's power in Hollywood and Washington over several decades. Presidents would come and go in the White House, but "Jack" was still Hollywood's guy in Washington.

In 1971 Senator Thomas Kuchel put forward a piece of legislation, called the Domestic Film Production Incentive Act, that could have been written by Valenti's own pen. The bill proposed a 20-percent tax exemption on the production or export of any film made in the United States. At the same time, Congress held hearings examining the "unemployment problems in the American film industry." The impetus in favour of a taxpayer-subsidized rescue of the Hollywood majors was vigorously supported by the ambitious governor of California, Ronald Reagan, a former Hollywood movie star and ex-president of the Screen Actors Guild. Reagan's successor as head of the Guild was Charlton Heston, who argued passionately in Washington that Hollywood was "in desperate need of federal assistance."

The proposed Domestic Film Production Incentive Act never became law. Hardly anyone noticed, though, because Jack Valenti, MCA-Universal chairman Lew Wasserman, and the Hollywood lobby machine in Washington had scored another major victory with the Nixon White House. In

1971 Valenti and Wasserman convinced Richard Nixon to include the movie industry as a sector qualifying for the 7-percent tax credits provided for in the new Revenue Act. At Nixon's behest, the Internal Revenue Service allowed movies shot in the United States to be captured by the tax credit. The Revenue Act also allowed U.S. studios to create subsidiaries called Domestic International Sales Corporations (DISCs), which were allowed to defer paying tax on half of profits earned from exports. Above all, individual investors were allowed to claim a 100-percent tax exemption on investments in American movies. This latter tax proved to be enormously useful to non-Hollywood studios. Critically acclaimed feature films such as Milos Forman's *One Flew Over the Cuckoo's Nest*, Bob Rafelson's *Five Easy Pieces,* and Martin Scorsese's *Taxi Driver* were all financed thanks to this generous tax shelter.

The U.S. tax shelters boosted the fortunes of the Hollywood studios almost immediately. *Variety* reported in March 1972 that, at Universal Pictures, some 97 percent of the company's profit increase was directly attributable to the new tax credits. Walt Disney cleverly applied for retroactive tax credits back to 1963, when the fiscal incentives originally had been introduced as part of another law. Thanks to this loophole, Disney and other Hollywood studios won $400 million in back tax credits. Charlton Heston was quick once again to make a passionate case for the government handouts to Hollywood. The famous movie star said the tax credits had been "of inestimable help in our desperate predicament." Heston failed to mention that Jack Valenti and his fellow Hollywood lobbyists routinely denounced foreign governments for subsidizing their own domestic film industries.

While the U.S. tax shelters undeniably helped get some excellent American films made, they also led to abuse that was ethically questionable, to say the least. The fiscal bonanza produced many deals, but fewer movies. As David Puttnam, the British-born producer who headed Columbia Pictures in the 1980s, put it: "This was tax fraud pure and simple. Some even blamed the shelters for a surge in the output of pornographic films produced in the 1970s." [10]

The U.S. government abolished the DISCs in 1976. Meanwhile, in the U.S. Senate, Ted Kennedy called for the 100-percent investment tax shelters to be abolished too. He argued that the tax shelter was an "outright tax subsidy" for the profitable Hollywood industry and therefore should be terminated. Other senators, most of whom enjoyed more complicit relations with Hollywood lobbyists, claimed that the U.S. movie industry was an "American institution" and therefore merited taxpayer support, particularly as a response to threats by foreign movies subsidized in like manner by their taxpayers. The sight of American politicians performing ideological somer-saults to justify socialistic handouts for the Hollywood studios was a bizarre spectacle indeed.

The excesses of the U.S. tax shelters sounded no alarm bells in Ottawa, where the 100-percent tax write-off was simply purloined from the Amer-ican policy and announced as the main pillar of Canada's new feature film policy. Predictably, the same frenzied greed descended on the Canadian movie industry, though the dollar figures were much more modest. Canada's tax-shelter boom attracted countless "Mississauga dentists" looking for highly advantageous tax write-offs on investments with poten-tially huge upsides. Some doubtless were seeking the psychic validation that is procured from close proximity with the glamorous world of movie producers, directors, and actors.

Many Canadian movies got made, thanks to the tax shelters. In the early 1970s only about ten feature films were being made annually in Canada, most with exceedingly modest budgets of about $250,000. By the end of the decade nearly eighty features were being produced each year, most with budgets of about $2 million per picture. Most of these movies, however, featured mainly foreign movie stars — *Running* (1979) starred Michael Douglas, *Circle of Two* (1980) starred Richard Burton, *The Last Chase* (1981) featured Burgess Meredith and Lee Majors, and Vanessa Redgrave starred in *Bear Island* (1980). Worst of all, very few of Canada's tax-shelter movies ever made it to cinema screens because the Hollywood studios still controlled exhibition circuits in Canada.

The impresario of Canada's chaotic tax-shelter film boom was Michael McCabe, who a decade later would become the chief lobbyist for Canada's private television networks. In the 1970s McCabe was a former Ottawa mandarin with close ties to the ruling Liberal government, particularly to ministers such as Mitchell Sharp and John Roberts. McCabe became head of the CFDC at precisely the moment the film industry was overheating due to the tax-shelter excesses, and consequently he took much of the blame for the greed-driven shenanigans triggered by the fiscal bonanza.

"The government and the economy dictate a results-orientated approach, so I propose to be not a filmmaker but a banker and a market," said McCabe when describing his mission at the CFDC.

McCabe's critics blamed him for fuelling the fiscal feeding frenzy with a financing strategy based on turning the Canadian movie industry into a U.S. branch plant. Film critic Martin Knelman let loose in *Saturday Night* with a scathing assessment of the tax-shelter boom: "What could have better filled the Canadian need for self-denigration than the flowering of a schlock movie industry? The insults Canada has endured from Hollywood begin to look like petty mischief compared with the abusive treatment Canada has been getting from its own filmmakers." [11]

Like most booms, Canada's movie boom went bust after only a few short years of frenzied greed. Ottawa was left with a horrendous bureaucratic mess to clean up. One solution was the creation of Telefilm Canada, which diverted film production towards television as a more reliable outlet. But there still remained the seemingly insurmountable problem of Hollywood's domination of the Canadian movie distribution and exhibition business through Famous Players and Cineplex Odeon. The irony was embarrassing. The Canadian movie market was characterized by the same monopoly domination that had provoked the U.S. Supreme Court to issue the Paramount Decree in 1948. And yet nothing had ever been done in Canada to break up the same Hollywood cartel.

In Quebec, the short-lived Péquiste government of Pierre-Marc Johnson engaged in a showdown with Hollywood in late 1985. But the Quebec government backed down from tough anti-Hollywood legislation when Jack Valenti threatened to pull all American movies from Quebec movie theatres (the same Hollywood boycott threat made in Britain in the late 1940s).

In Ottawa, Brian Mulroney was now prime minister and his government was clearly pro-business and pro-American. Mulroney and Ronald Reagan moreover seemed to enjoy a close personal friendship. Politically, the initiation of negotiations aimed at establishing free trade between Canada and the United States made it clear that Mulroney was not particularly interested in taking on the Hollywood majors.

Mulroney must have been intensely annoyed, to put it mildly, to discover in 1987 that his combative communications minister, Flora MacDonald, had decided to introduce a nationalistic piece of legislation aimed at curbing the commercial influence of the Hollywood majors in Canada. Specifically, MacDonald sponsored a bill that would have limited the Hollywood majors to the distribution of movies for which they held world rights. It was estimated that the proposed legislation, if passed, would have handed about 7 percent of the movie distribution business in Canada to Canadian-owned distributors.

MacDonald, a mummified Red Tory relic from the anti-American Diefenbaker era, was perfectly cast in the role of anti-Hollywood crusader. She was also the wrong person at the wrong time for the wrong job. She was the wrong person because her boss, Brian Mulroney, did not support her and in fact disliked her personally. MacDonald had run against

Mulroney for the Tory leadership in 1976 and later supported his rival, Joe Clark. In Clark's short-lived government in 1979–80, MacDonald had held a senior portfolio as minister of External Affairs. Her deputy minister was Allan Gotlieb, the powerful senior mandarin from the Trudeau era. MacDonald and Gotlieb cordially despised each other immediately, and MacDonald even asked Joe Clark to fire Gotlieb. Clark, who respected Gotlieb's competence and influence in Ottawa, refused. This episode came back to haunt MacDonald several years later when, as minister of communications in Mulroney's government, she went to war against Hollywood. Canada's ambassador in Washington at the time was none other than Allan Gotlieb. But, in truth, Gotlieb did not have to sabotage MacDonald's film distribution policy. Brian Mulroney was not about to let Flora MacDonald's anti-Hollywood legislative campaign ruin his bilateral trade agreement with the United States.

Neither were the Americans in any mood to accept legislative restrictions on Hollywood films in the domestic market of their biggest trading partner. In Washington, the "declinist" school had convinced America's political elite that the country was losing influence and prestige throughout the world. The declinists persuaded many that the United States had to reassert its power abroad, which called for a tough, no-nonsense stance on bilateral and multilateral trade issues — including the entertainment industries. In 1984 a Congressional subcommittee had issued a report titled *Trade Barriers to U.S. Motion Pictures and Television, Pre-recorded Entertainment, Publishing and Advertising Industries*. Canada was at the top of the U.S. list of countries whose trade policies were irritants and hostile to American interests. The United States had a number of beefs with Canada — everything from copyright payments for U.S. broadcast signals retransmitted by Canadian cable companies to quotas on Canadian television.

The Reagan White House was largely deaf to pious Canadian claims about the country's "cultural sovereignty," especially since big Canadian cable companies were stealing American TV signals and reselling them to their subscribers without paying royalties. Allan Gotlieb encountered the firmness of the U.S. position one day while meeting with George Shultz, the U.S. secretary of state. Shultz pulled out of his jacket pocket a piece of paper and showed it to Gotlieb. It featured a list of all the American newspapers owned by Canadian media barons such as Ken Thomson and Conrad Black. Shultz had a point. While Canadians owned media properties throughout the world, including the United States, Canada insisted on protecting its own domestic market with a patchwork of incoherent policies whose chief motivation appeared to be anti-American sentiments.

In mid-1987 Reagan personally raised the subject of Flora MacDonald's nationalistic crusade in a meeting with Brian Mulroney. Shortly afterwards, MacDonald realized she would never get her film distribution policy passed — not, at least, while Mulroney and Reagan were negotiating a free-trade treaty. MacDonald quickly retreated. A watered-down version of the policy obliged American distributors merely to prove they had purchased separate Canadian rights for movies, something that could be done easily by lawyers writing up contracts while paying little heed to the intent of Canada's policy. In a word, MacDonald's policy ended in capitulation. It was even dubbed "Flora's folly."

As a face-saving gesture, MacDonald announced that Telefilm would be given an additional $17 million for Canadian distributors to subsidize their acquisition of rights to foreign movies. The money was welcomed by Canadian distributors, though its most obvious effect would be to fatten the wallets of Canada's big film distributors and bid up the prices they paid for Canadian rights to foreign movies.

Once again, the U.S. studios had triumphed. Ottawa's stance vis-à-vis Hollywood had been nothing more than popgun policy making.

Fortress Europe and Canada's Cultural Conundrum

In recent years, Canada has been a relatively passive adjunct of the U.S. domestic market for Hollywood movies. The Hollywood majors have been more preoccupied by a possible counterthreat from "Fortress Europe." The main threat to Hollywood's influence in Europe has been the emergence of the continent as a rival power bloc, whose interests are defended with a single voice by the European Commission in Brussels. Hollywood can no longer adopt its old divide-and-conquer tactic on the Old Continent.

In 1989 the European Commission adopted a Television Without Frontiers directive whose main weapon against Hollywood was a 60-percent minimum quota on European films and programs on television. The directive didn't deal with cinema screens, but television in Europe — such as Britain's Channel 4 and France's Canal Plus — is a major outlet for movies. The main force behind the Television Without Frontiers policy was France, which traditionally has had a powerful film and TV industry, thanks to massive government subsidies. A stiff quota limiting the inflows of Hollywood movies promised to open up Europe-wide markets for French audio-visual products.

The French had been fighting American "cultural imperialism" with renewed vigour since socialist François Mitterrand became president in 1981. Mitterrand's flamboyant culture minister, Jack Lang, was the darling of the French cultural elite and his anti-American speeches were particularly vociferous. Disney's plans to build a EuroDisney theme park just outside Paris gave Lang and his supporters a symbolic target for their tirades against the vulgarity of the Hollywood Empire.

"Our destiny is not to become the vassals of an immense empire of profit," declared Lang, who pointed out that Europe had a $3-billion negative trade balance with the United States in the entertainment industries.

Hollywood was becoming increasingly dependent on foreign markets, and a major setback in Europe threatened to have devastating consequences on the bottom line of American media giants. In 1986 U.S. domestic revenues for movies was $4.4 billion, while foreign sales were $2.3 billion. Five years later, Hollywood dependence on foreign markets had increased dramatically: domestic U.S. revenues were $7.1 billion, while foreign revenues had shot up to $6.3 billion. The annual growth rate of U.S. domestic revenues for Hollywood movies was only 10.3 percent from 1986 to 1991, while the growth rate for sales in foreign markets was more than double that figure: 21.7 percent. Hollywood executives don't always make good movies, but they do know how to count.

Jack Valenti spearheaded the U.S. counterattack against the European quotas, which in his characteristically grandiloquent fashion he denounced as based on a "maimed, disabled theory which honours restriction above public choice." Valenti argued that the quota would do more harm to Hollywood than it would help European cinema: "Is a thousand, two thousand years of an individual nation's culture going to collapse because of the exhibition of American TV programs? The quota is there, it hangs with Damoclean ferocity over the future. And it will, in time, as its velocity increases, bite, wound, and bleed the American television industry."

Valenti naturally could rely on support from the White House, and he was even quite matter of fact about it. "The President of the United States, the secretary of state, the secretary of commerce, and the U.S. trade representative have all been supportive. They have made it clear to the chancelleries of Europe that the imposition of this quota is an intolerable thing for the United States." [12]

The Americans found a useful ally in Britain in its battle with Brussels. In contrast to many other European countries, Britain had a pro-market, pro-American leader in Margaret Thatcher. It was far from certain, however, that the British film and television industry shared the pro-American affinities of 10 Downing Street. So the U.S. government resorted to tacit threats: if Britain supported the Television Without Frontiers policy, its television shows from the BBC, Thames, and Granada would be boycotted in the

United States. Since PBS's *Masterpiece Theater* acquired most of its drama programs — such as "Brideshead Revisited" and "Sons and Lovers" — from the United Kingdom, the British production industry, understanding where its own interests lay, fell into an embarrassed silence as its colleagues on the continent continued to rail against U.S. cultural imperialism.

The Hollywood studios acted as a cartel in Europe, much as they did in Canada. Three studios — MGM, Paramount, and Universal — operated jointly in Europe as United International Pictures (UIP), which was established in 1970. The European Commission had long complained that UIP was a de facto cartel and therefore violated the European Union's founding charter, the Treaty of Rome. But like the Canadian government, the European Commission was highly indulgent towards the very same companies that had been broken up in their home U.S. market by the Paramount Decree. In 1988 the European Commission granted UIP a five-year exemption from anti-trust actions on the grounds that it provided "economic benefits" to the European cinema industry through investments. This claim was vociferously disputed by European film industry leaders, who pointed out that the Hollywood majors had invested virtually nothing in European film production. When the exemption expired in 1993, the European Commission remained paralyzed on the UIP issue, and so extended the exemption until 1998, when Brussels renewed attempts to break up the cartel.

In 1993 the European Commission was conducting talks with the United States as part of the General Agreement on Tariffs and Trade negotiations, which had begun in 1986 to extend the multilateral trade treaty from goods to services. Film and television quickly became a hotly disputed topic in the GATT talks. The United States insisted that movies and TV programs should be included in the negotiations because they were captured by the definition of a "service." Europe, on the other hand, demanded an exemption on cultural products, and backed up its demand by citing the similar exemption accorded Canada in the 1987 Free Trade Agreement. But the White House remained adamant: it demanded that European countries dismantle their generous fiscal and subsidy regimes supporting film and TV production. Otherwise, the White House insisted, American movie studios and television producers should have access to these subsidies under the "national treatment" provisions of the GATT.

In Europe, the prospect of giving the Hollywood studios access to taxpayer-supported subsidies seemed preposterous. The European Commission had a generous subsidy system in place through a program called MEDIA, which granted funds to European producers for scripts, development, training, distribution, dubbing, and other activities. The focus of subsidies in Europe has been on the creative end of the business — such as directors and producers — hence Europe's *auteur* tradition in cinema. In the United States, the 1948 Paramount Decree had given tremendous market power to Hollywood distributors, which imposed a marketing orientation on the American film industry. If negotiations between Europe and the United States on film and TV was a dialogue of the deaf, it was partly due to this fundamental opposition: Europeans saw film as an art form, whereas in the United States movies were regarded as a business.

Pressured by France, the European Commission refused to allow film and television to be captured by the GATT. Europe was thus sending a powerful message to the United States: there would be serious distribution consequences now that the European Commission was speaking for the entire continent. Europe was not a mere adjunct of the U.S. domestic market like Canada, but was a separate and rival power united in purpose.

Europe's intransigence on GATT infuriated the U.S. administration. Bill Clinton was now in the White House and his trade representative was Mickey Kantor, a seasoned Hollywood lawyer. Negotiating for Europe was Sir Leon Brittan, a loyal Thatcherite who had left the Iron Lady's cabinet for the European Commission. Brittan shared Kantor's pro-market and anti-protectionist views, but he was under tremendous pressure in Europe to show his mettle by besting the Americans in the GATT talks. While Brittan and Kantor negotiated in Geneva to meet a self-imposed deadline of December 15, 1993, Jack Valenti and his Hollywood cohorts were in the Swiss city following the talks closely — indeed, they were in the same hotel in a nearby room. When it appeared obvious that Brittan and his European colleagues would give up nothing on film and television, the Hollywood lobby urged Kantor to adopt a scorched-earth strategy.

"Blow up the deal," said one Hollywood studio executive. "Have the President go to the American people and explain what happened. Tell him to blame it on the French!"

Valenti, who was seventy-two years old during the GATT battles, had pulled out all the stops with Clinton. A few days earlier, Clinton had attended a $50,000-a-plate fundraiser at the Los Angeles home of billionaire financier Marvin Davis. Valenti had prepped all the Hollywood moguls who attended the event, and they all privately lobbied Clinton about the irksome Europeans with their quotas and cultural policies.

On December 15 Mickey Kantor broke away from his Geneva talks with Leon Brittan to phone the White House for instructions. Clinton had been calling European leaders on the phone to get the sticking point of audiovisual products resolved. To Kantor's surprise, Clinton instructed him to back off from movies and TV programs and sign the deal. Europe would get its cultural exemption.

When he heard the news, a furious Valenti lashed out with unrestrained indignation.

"In a global treaty supposed to reduce trade barriers, the European Commission erected a great wall to keep out the works of non-European creative men and women," said Valenti. "This negotiation had nothing to do with culture, unless European soap operas and game shows are the equivalent of Molière. This is all about the hard business of money."

Europe had stared down the Americans in the GATT talks and, incredibly, the mighty White House–Hollywood cultural-industrial complex had blinked. What's more, after its GATT setback Hollywood adopted an entirely different commercial approach towards the European market. Instead of treating Europe as a dumping ground for its movies and TV shows, Hollywood began investing in European projects through partnerships with local producers. Time Warner, for example, invested in satellite TV in Scandinavia and in pay TV in Germany. Disney, for its part, formed joint ventures to produce children's programs in France, Germany, Italy, and Spain. Warner Bros. studio announced a joint movie deal with France's pay TV outlet, Canal Plus, and News Corp., controlled by 20th Century Fox owner Rupert Murdoch, operated Britain's BSkyB satellite TV service. Murdoch's Fox also backed British hit films such as *The Full Monty*. Sony, which controls Columbia, built a movie studio in Germany to produce German-language films for the local market. Some successful European producers signed output deals with Hollywood studios. For example, David Puttnam (*Chariots of Fire, The Killing Fields, Midnight Express*) negotiated an output deal with Warner Bros. The U.S. studios also began setting up European operations, such as the new animation units opened by Walt Disney in Paris and Warner Bros. in London. [13]

Hollywood evidently realized that, while the North American cinema business was approaching saturation, Europe promised tremendous growth, as former state monopolies in television were being smashed apart by deregulation and market forces. Shooting movies in Europe also helped Hollywood's bottom line, particularly as labour costs back home in the United States were skyrocketing. *Mission Impossible*, starring Tom Cruise, and Oscar-winner *Braveheart*, starring Mel Gibson, for example, were shot in Europe to reduce costs. The tradeoff for Hollywood's newfound Europhilia has been a sincere effort to localize the content of movies so they can appeal more readily to non-American audiences. Hollywood's lesson in Europe has been that it must treat the continent like an opportunity to be seized, not like a stubborn obstacle to be crushed.

In Canada, on the other hand, it's business as usual. In 1997 heritage minister Sheila Copps found herself cast in the same unenviable role that Flora MacDonald had been in a decade earlier. Like MacDonald, Copps was a strong-minded, outspoken minister who, in the culture portfolio, quickly embraced the cause of her major clients, including Canadian movie distributors. Unfortunately for Copps, she inherited the contradictions of Flora's Folly and quickly found herself obliged to defend them. For one thing, Flora MacDonald's film policy had "grandfathered" the major Hollywood studios — Paramount, Columbia, Time Warner, Fox, MCA-Universal, Disney, and MGM — which were allowed to continue to conduct business in Canada much as they had been doing since the 1920s. Non-Hollywood companies, on the other hand, were banned from distributing independent movies in Canada. This effectively barred Dutch-based PolyGram from operating in Canada as a distributor of films that it did not produce itself.

The Canadian policy was inspired by the political cowardice that begets all grandfather clauses. The film policy, in effect, rewarded those who had done nothing or little for Canadian cinema and punished those, like Poly-Gram, with an admirable track record for investing in local movies wherever they do business. Indeed, PolyGram invested in quality European films such as *Trainspotting* and *Four Weddings and a Funeral*, and promised to do the same in Canada. Hollywood, by contrast, had never shown much interest in investing in Canadian movies. Ottawa stubbornly refused to understand, however, that policies based on grandfather clauses are unjustly discriminatory and hence indefensible. The split-run magazine controversy provided another illustration of this policy muddle. *Time* and *Reader's Digest* were grandfathered, while *Sports Illustrated* was banned in Canada. Likewise in telecoms, U.S.-based GTE was accorded a grandfathered exemption from ownership restrictions and hence could maintain majority control of BC Tel. Yet no other foreigners could own more than 33.3 percent of a Canadian telecom company — thus protecting Canada's local phone monopolies (and their executives) from hostile foreign takeovers.

Darryl Iwai, president of PolyGram Filmed Entertainment subsidiary in Canada, pointed out that, in the music industry, his company had backed Canadian recording stars such as Bryan Adams and Shania Twain. "Poly-Gram's audio philosophy is now being translated into the film division," he said.

Canada's distribution ban on PolyGram provoked an official protest from the European Union on behalf of the Dutch-controlled firm. The spat between Ottawa and Brussels over PolyGram was rife with irony, contradictions, and hypocrisy on both sides of the Atlantic. The irony was that

Canada and Europe had previously been mutually reinforcing allies against Hollywood's so-called cultural imperialism. When the European Union was fighting the United States for a "cultural exemption" in the GATT talks, it evoked the similar exemption won by Ottawa as part of the Free Trade Agreement. The trans-Atlantic solidarity against Hollywood engendered a great deal of warm feelings between Ottawa and Brussels for a few years — until, that is, PolyGram attempted to set up shop in Canada to distribute independent movies in the Canadian market.

The Europeans were no less hypocritical in the PolyGram affair. If access to the Canadian market was what the European Union was seeking, that goal was achieved when, in May 1998, Canada's Bronfman family bought PolyGram for $10.4 billion (U.S.) and made it, with the stroke of a pen, a Canadian-controlled media giant. But suddenly the Eurocrats weren't so preoccupied with market access to Canada. The real issue was the loss of European control of a cherished media company whose movie unit, PolyGram Filmed Entertainment, had benefitted from years of generous subsidies as a Brussels-sponsored "national champion."

Even more embarrassing for the Europeans was their unpatriotic paralysis before the unexpected chance to regain control of PolyGram Filmed Entertainment. That opportunity came when Edgar Bronfman Jr. decided to put PolyGram's money-losing movie unit on the auction block and keep the music business. Some European media companies, it is true, stepped forward as potential bidders for PolyGram's movie library. First in line was France's Canal Plus, a pay TV channel that has become a veritable movie studio, thanks to years of political support and massive subsidies from the French government. But Canal Plus refused to pay the $400-million (U.S.) asking price for PolyGram's film library.

It soon appeared that PolyGram's movies would fall into decidedly non-European hands. In October 1998 Hollywood studio Metro-Goldwyn-Mayer offered $250 million for a portion of PolyGram's movie library. A few weeks later, the billionaire Saudi prince Muhammad Bin Bandur Bin Abdul Aziz also expressed interest in buying PolyGram's movie unit. It appeared, however, that Bronfman-controlled Seagram would merely fold PolyGram Filmed Entertainment into Universal Pictures, which the Bronfmans also controlled.

While the PolyGram affair preoccupied diplomats in Ottawa and Brussels, Sheila Copps opted for a window-dressing approach to remedy Flora's Folly. First, in early 1998 Copps announced a comprehensive review of Canada's feature film policy. Second, in June 1998 Copps sponsored a global cultural summit in Ottawa called "At Home in the World:

An International Forum on Culture and Co-operation." The summit was a snub to the Americans, who were not invited. They didn't miss much, for the meeting turned out to be nothing more than a series of courteous exchanges from which no resolutions or concrete commitments emerged.

Hollywood might not have been at the table at the Copps summit, but the major U.S. studios enjoyed a special invitation in Canada that no European, South American, African, or Asian film producers could boast. The Hollywood studios were drawing on direct and indirect subsidies for their projects shot in Canada — all thanks to the taxpayers of Canada.

Hollywood's interest in shooting films in Canada had begun in the 1970s and 1980s, when Ottawa started handing out millions of dollars to movie and TV producers. The U.S. majors shrewdly saw that Telefilm was a potential boondoggle that would allow them to launder their own U.S. productions through Canada's funding system. Later, the U.S. majors were attracted to Canada by the low Canadian dollar. A $50-million Hollywood movie can be shot in Canada for $35 million. By the late 1990s it could be asserted confidently that the most powerful man in the Canadian entertainment industry was Gordon Thiessen, governor of the Bank of Canada. There could be little doubt that any significant upward adjustment of the Canadian dollar by Canada's central bank would provoke a massive retreat of Hollywood studios back to sunny California.

Hollywood's presence in Canada brought, to be sure, some measurable benefits. When Hollywood studios shoot in Canada, they hire lots of Canadian camera operators, makeup girls, best boys, gaffers, and gofers who get paid and pay taxes. They do not, however, hire many screenwriters, cinematographers, or directors. A decade ago, Hollywood movies shot in Canada were called "below-the-neck" productions. The conceptual and artistic work was done in Los Angeles or New York. Canadians were the grunts hired on location to lift cables, pour coffee, and run errands. The Hollywood studios also bid up the price for film crews, which had the effect of increasing the cost of genuinely Canadian productions — and thus put a further strain on the Canadian subsidy system.

Dan Johnson, former president of the Canadian Association of Film Distributors and Exporters, said gratitude towards Hollywood would be naive. "The idea of being saved by Hollywood studios coming and doing production in Canada is the Blanche DuBois syndrome," he said. "It's relying on the kindness of strangers."

Today, the Hollywood studios have found yet another reason for shooting in Canada. In late 1996 Ottawa replaced a film-production tax shelter for Canadian producers with a tax credit allowing refunds of

25 percent of labour costs for Canadian film and TV productions. In 1997, after intense lobbying by Hollywood and its proxies in Canada, Ottawa extended its fiscal generosity to Hollywood and other foreign producers shooting in Canada. A new Film and Video Production Services Tax Credit offered foreign producers an 11-percent tax refund on labour costs, or a maximum of about 5 percent on the entire production's budget.

Federal bureaucrats would not say how much Canadian taxpayer money was being used to bankroll the major Hollywood studios, which have combined annual revenues of about $30 billion (U.S.). Ottawa bureaucrats have remained tight-lipped about the giveaway to Hollywood because the total figure is colossal — estimated between $50 million and $100 million annually — and thus potentially controversial. This bureaucratic wall of silence was tantamount to the federal government refusing to reveal the amount taxpayers pay for the CBC.

For Canadians residing in Ontario and British Columbia, the taxpayer handout to Hollywood is even higher. Glen Clark, the socialist premier of British Columbia, and Ontario's ultra-conservative premier Mike Harris have radically different views on the role of the state in the economy. But they resemble quarrelling twins when it comes to sucking up to Tinseltown. Indeed, Clark and Harris have been indulging in an absurdly obsequious spectacle of bowing and scraping at the feet of Hollywood moguls as a prelude to offers of generous tax write-offs in exchange for using Canada as a movie backlot. It's called cash for cameras.

In March 1998 Harris became the first provincial premier to make a trip to Los Angeles. The schmoozing was lubricated by Canada's greatest Hollywood director, Norman Jewison, and former prime minister Kim Campbell. As Canada's consul-general in Los Angeles, Campbell hosted a private dinner for Harris and a clutch of Hollywood tycoons at her sumptuous L.A. residence. Among those who attended the dinner to meet the Ontario premier were studio heads including Sherry Lansing from Paramount, Terry Semel from Warner Bros., and top executives from Dream-Works, Disney, and Imax. Canadian-born director Ted Kotcheff, who made the first *Rambo* film, was also on hand. So were the Roots people, very anxious to foist their logos on the rich and famous, with free goodybags for all those present.

Harris, who was accompanied by provincial treasurer Ernie Eves, was positively starstruck in Hollywood. "If we don't get a production shot in Ontario, I want to know why," he said, expressing his satisfaction that Hollywood movies like *Good Will Hunting* had been shot in Ontario.[14]

"We talk the same language," Harris said of his meetings with the

Hollywood moguls. "And if Ontario can't compete today, we'll fix it. As far as I'm concerned, the sky's the limit."

Indeed, there seemed to be no limit to Harris's generosity. While normally against government handouts, particularly welfare cheques, Harris did not disappoint Hollywood. He matched Ottawa's fiscal incentives, dollar for dollar.

Harris's gambit was a gauntlet thrown in the face of Glen Clark. Hollywood spends about $425 million a year in British Columbia, which has served as the backdrop for well-known American TV series such as *McGyver* and *The X-Files*. In April 1998 Clark jumped on a plane and headed south for a two-day session of schmoozing with executives at Paramount and MGM. Back in B.C. several weeks later, Clark must have felt somewhat ridiculous jammed into a futuristic sports car whizzing around the set of a Hollywood TV show called *Viper*. He had chosen that ludicrous location as the backdrop for his announcement that he would match Mike Harris's tax offer to Hollywood. Annual bill to B.C. taxpayers: about $20 million minimum. [15]

"We know this is a classic footloose industry," said Clark. "It can evaporate overnight."

Meanwhile, the California state government was steaming over the frenzied Hollywood migration northward in search of Canadian taxpayer subsidies. Pete Wilson, the California governor at the time, struck a committee to come up with a state fiscal scheme to prevent the defections. The state was also considering filing a formal trade complaint against Canada and there was talk of U.S. bilateral retaliation against Canada.

In Canada, the preposterous pandering to Hollywood studios by Canadian politicians has been coming under closer scrutiny. Robert Lantos, Canada's legendary movie producer, said about the tax gifts to Hollywood studios: "This happens to be a nice little handout they can take home. How come we have taxpayer money to put on Time Warner's bottom line but we're closing hospitals?"

Handouts to Hollywood studios will not likely inspire Paramount, MGM, Columbia, Disney, or Fox to make Canadian movies. Not even Universal Pictures, which is controlled by Montreal's Bronfman family, has shown any interest in making Canadian movies. Unlike Europe, which is relatively insulated from American cultural influence by geography and language, Canada continues to be regarded by the Hollywood studios as an adjunct of the U.S. domestic market. That fact is not likely to change in the foreseeable future.

Canada therefore will have to find its own solutions to building a viable feature film industry. Measures like screen quotas, box-office levies, with-holding taxes, and investment obligations have been tried with some success in Europe, but they have never proved workable in Canada, partly because of a lack of political courage in Ottawa, where the Hollywood lobby enjoys tremendous influence, thanks to well-oiled social and political networks. There is also a fear that punitive measures would be met with a Hollywood boycott and thus provoke a public outcry by indignant Cana-dians deprived of the latest blockbuster movie. Canadian politicians simply don't have the fortitude to stare down the White House–Hollywood tandem. Unlike Europe, Canada is one small country standing alone — and moreover attached to the United States by culture and geography.

Other instruments must be found if Canada expects to foster its national cinema industry. Direct and indirect subsidies — through bodies like Telefilm Canada or through tax credits — are the most effective way to stimulate the production of Canadian movies. The disadvantage of subsi-dies is that they do little to remedy structural problems such as the grip on Canadian movie theatres — notably by the Famous Players and Cineplex Odeon chains — of the Hollywood studios. The advantage of subsidies, however, is that they don't offend anyone — except, perhaps, some Cana-dian taxpayers — and they promote the development of a domestic industry from the production side of the business.

At present, the main problem with Canada's position vis-à-vis Holly-wood is the lack of consistency and coherence in Canadian cultural poli-cies. Canada does not heavily regulate the inflow of books or videocassettes, yet it imposes Canadian content quotas on television and radio. No restric-tions are placed on the ownership of cinemas or video stores in Canada — hence Famous Players, Cineplex Odeon, and Blockbuster do business with impunity. And yet ownership restrictions apply to television and radio stations and telephone companies. In short, Canada has a complex arsenal of restrictive policy instruments that show no discernible coherence: restriction of inflows, ownership rules, direct subsidies, cross-subsidization schemes, eviction of foreign firms, government ownership, and special treatment under trade agreements. If these policies were applied evenly across all the cultural sectors, the Canadian government could at least claim conceptual clarity and coherence of purpose. But no such coherence exists. Canada's policies are a jumble of tools that reflect muddling through, crisis management, bureaucratic gridlock, and favours to special pleading and vested interests.

The decision to grandfather the Hollywood majors while applying a prohibition on non-Hollywood movie distributors like PolyGram illustrates the contradiction of Canadian policy. If the policy muddle persists, Ottawa is doomed to lose trade disputes before the World Trade Organization — just as it did on the *Sports Illustrated* case. The politics of realism appears to be prevailing in Ottawa these days, however, and this is an encouraging sign.

Art Eggleton, Canada's minister of international trade, delivered a speech at Toronto's York University in 1997 entitled "Can Canada Maintain Its Cultural Identity in the Face of Globalization?" Eggleton cited the familiar statistics of foreign domination of the Canadian market in film, television, publishing, and music. He wondered whether, given Canada's unimpressive performance, the arsenal of the government's traditional cultural policies was worth maintaining.

"Many of the federal government's cultural policies were designed three decades ago," said Eggleton. "Then, the national concern wasn't access to world markets, but Canadian access to the Canadian market. Since then, times have changed. The worlds of technology and trade are not recognizable from a decade ago, yet the instruments that we use to promote Canadian culture have not changed."

Movie producer Robert Lantos remains optimistic:

> As the Hollywood studios go more and more into blockbuster over-drive, risking bigger and bigger budgets on safer and safer formulas, they leave the making of films that tell strongly felt stories, by filmmakers with a personal vision, more and more to us. . . . Unquestionably, it would make more economic sense simply to join the United States and forget all this anxiety about who we are. But for me, I believe that's too big a price to pay. If we are going to remain a country, and I am convinced that we will, then we must have pride and dignity. This we can only have if we have our own identity. Mass culture is the currency of national identity. It's not something static, to be stored in a museum. It's a living, breathing, organic thing, part of our daily lives. And it costs money. If we are to continue as a nation, then we must have the resolve to invest in our culture, and the heart to protect it.[16]

New technologies and future consumer habits just might come to the rescue of non-American film and TV production industries. Increasingly, filmed entertainment is being delivered to consumers via new distribution techniques such as pay TV, pay-per-view, video-on-demand, and digital video discs. There will always likely be some attraction to watching a movie in a traditional cinema setting. Indeed, the major theatre chains are building their complexes to provide a theme-park-like experience that creates a dazzling environment for movie-goers. This form of entertainment will be particularly appealing to people who work at home and wish to leave it for distraction. But the percentage of total box-office revenues from theatrical releases is declining as consumers shift their viewing habits to other media.

The cold numbers bear out the decline of old media and the rise of new forms of entertainment consumption. In 1997 videocassette sales in the United States totalled $16.5 billion — $7.6 billion in sales and $8.9 billion in rentals. That figure was nearly three times higher than total box-office receipts of $6.3 billion. The video market has been declining since the mid-1990s, however, and it is only logical that the $16.5 billion in spending will go somewhere. It will likely shift towards television outlets, where cable and satellite TV can offer pay-per-view and video-on-demand. Video-on-demand in particular could well be worth billions if its status in the commercial release chain bumps it up to second place after theatrical cinema release, ahead of videocassettes, pay-per-view, pay TV, and regular TV.

Some believe the Web will be the next mass medium. For many, the multimedia revolution has already begun.

CHAPTER 8

The Multimedia Revolution

"IN THE SHORT TERM, WE HAVE OVERESTIMATED ITS IMPACT," SAID BILL Gates about the Internet. "In the longer term," he added, "we have dramatically underestimated it."

The Internet is the Book of Apocalypse in the communications revolution. The design, logic, and social usage of the Internet have turned all existing paradigms upside down.

The Internet as New Paradigm

Before the emergence of the Web, communications infrastructures like telephone and cable systems were designed as "smart" networks feeding "dumb" terminals — telephones and TV sets. The Internet, in contrast, is a "dumb" network that connects "smart" terminals. Intelligent networks traditionally have had to be controlled and regulated because capacity was scarce. The Internet, on the other hand, assumes unlimited capacity and thus renders regulation unnecessary. Conventional networks have been assets fixed in defined territories. The Internet is non-territorial and thus cannot be restricted geographically. Conventional broadcasting systems have been used to transmit scheduled content to mass audiences. The Web, on the other hand, is essentially a personalized medium that facilitates transactional exchanges that do not spill into the public domain. Traditional network systems have been closed, controlled, and regulated as natural monopolies. The Internet is an open-architecture system that defies control and facilitates pluralism.

These differences are profound. It should not be surprising, therefore, that the explosion of the Web has been both denounced and embraced.

There is much gnashing of teeth among the pessimistic techno-Luddites who fear its negative social consequences. To them, the Internet is a lawless frontier, a technological Wild West whose chaotic commercial logic threatens to undermine established values based on community. Their denunciation of the Web — a global forum for kiddy pornographers, prying computer hackers, techno-savvy gangsters, and cyber-smart terrorists — is essentially based on moral reproach. They want the Internet regulated, monitored, and taxed. Web optimists, filled with passionate intensity about the Internet's potential, embrace the new medium with messianic zeal. For them, the Internet is synonymous with liberty, openness, dialogue, communication, and global peace. The Internet is the ideal technological facilitator of pure democracy: fully participatory and interactive with a low cost of entry into the discussion. The Web is a libertarian paradise free from government interference and meddling — and, it is hoped, from taxation, too.

That the Internet will have a profound effect on civilization cannot be doubted. Yet what the Internet's principle social functions will be remains uncertain. Will it serve as a telephone — or "videophone"? Will it be a television? A home movie theatre? An information-gathering device? A global e-commerce shopping mall? An international e-mail network? An instrument of education and enlightenment? A new form of publishing with computer-downloaded books? A global conduit for pornography and hate literature? All of the above? At present, no one knows for sure. Yet hundreds of millions of dollars are being invested on the basis of these various scenarios.

If anything is certain, it's that the Law of Unintended Consequences will likely impose its quirky logic on the Web just as it has on so many other new technologies. Those who have a fixed vision of the Web's potential, or limitations, should be reminded of what Ken Olsen, the founder of mainframe computer maker Digital Equipment Corp., asserted confidently in 1977: "There is no reason anyone would want a computer in his home." Today, like-minded skepticism is commonly expressed about the Web's potential as a mass medium capable of delivering television and other services to the home.

While couch potatoes are the stubborn reactionaries of the Digital Revolution, the pro-Internet techno-Cassandras are irrepressible, many of them inexorably — and ironically — slouching back towards the future to focus their surpassing visions. The idea of the "smart home," for example, has been revived and repackaged to make room for "Information Age appliances." In the smart home of the future, every household appliance — from toothbrush to toaster — will be a mini-computer that can be connected to the Internet. Media gurus like Nicholas Negroponte have pushed this vision even further with predictions about "human-computer interfacing."

According to Negroponte, we all may soon be wearing technological jewelry — rings, bracelets, and earrings that will connect us to the Web via satellite. The invention of "palm-top" computers seems to offer early confirmation of this vision. Whether Web-friendly wristwatches will become mass-market consumer products is another question. As for the smart home, its imminent arrival was first predicted in the late 1960s. More than thirty years later, the only person who appears to possess one is Bill Gates, who could well afford to build his own multi-million-dollar computerized residential complex near Seattle. The rest of us are still waiting for the real estate market to catch up with the Information Age. [1]

As previously noted, Gates actually dismissed the Web as a marginal phenomenon when it first emerged circa 1993–94. He quickly realized his error, however, and after his road-to-Damascus conversion redirected Microsoft's future ambitions to the Web. Today he says: "Microsoft is betting that the Internet will continue to grow until its popularity is as mainstream as the telephone is today." [2]

For that to happen, two preconditions must be met: universal penetration and unlimited capacity. Neither is present today.

For the Web to function as a global medium, Internet access must be as ubiquitous worldwide as the telephone and the television. Today, however, Web usage is restricted largely to industrialized countries, with North America far ahead of the others. Consequently, the Web is dominated by the English language and culture. To be even more precise, the Web so far has been an electronic extension of the commercial empires of Hollywood and Silicon Valley. In the late 1990s about forty of the most accessed one hundred Web sites were located in California. Most of the others are were the United States. In Europe, the Internet has been slower to take off because, unlike North America, where local phone rates are based on a flat monthly fee, local rates are billed per minute. In Germany, for example, Web-surfing rates of about $5 per hour provoked an Internet users' group, called DarkBreed, to boycott the Web in protest of Deutsche Telekom's billing system. Given the explosive growth of the Web, it can be predicted that European and other countries will soon be forced to harmonize their telephone billing regimes with the North American system of fixed monthly rates. A special Internet tariff may even emerge worldwide.

The cultural and linguistic imbalance in favour of the English language, the United States, and California will undoubtedly change as Internet penetration spreads throughout the world. And the Internet has been growing at a spectacular rate. In 1998 more than 100 million people were surfing the Web. In the United States, about 45 million households were hooked up to the Internet and 27 million people were surfing the Web at the office. In Canada, about 4 million households will likely be connected to the Internet by the year 2000 — half the number of cable TV subscribers in Canada.[3] In the first few years of the twenty-first century, scarcely a decade after the Web emerged, more than a billion people worldwide are expected to be plugged into the Internet. Compared with previous media, the Web's soaring growth and pervasive influence have been staggering. Consider, for example, that after the radio was first invented, it took nearly forty years for the "wireless" to reach 50 million households. Television reached 50 million viewers after thirteen years. The Web reached the same figure in only four years.

Even with these phenomenal growth figures, the Web is still constrained by bandwidth limitations — in a word, wireline "pipes" that are too constricted to pump high-speed data to end terminals. The delayed construction of the Information Superhighway has been to blame for most of the frustration on the "World Wide Wait." But with massive infrastructure investments by software giants like Microsoft and global telecom players such as WorldCom and Qwest, it can be expected that the electronic highway will finally be built in the first decade of the next century. According to some estimates, by the year 2000 fibre-optic cables will be able to transmit 1 trillion bits per second — or the simultaneous transmission of 200 million faxes or 660,000 video conferences per second.

In the meantime, the "dumb" television set may provide the Web with a solution to the challenge of universal penetration. By plugging into television sets, the Internet can bypass the problem of relatively low household penetration of home computers and modems. Virtually every home has a TV set, if not two or three. For the Web to become a mass medium in the short term, therefore, it will have to make a strategic displacement from PCs in the office towards the TV set in the living room. The mass-marketing of WebTV — a product owned by Microsoft — marks the first manoeuvre in the Web's territorial ambition towards the living room. If this shift gains acceptance, manufacturers of TV sets will soon be under enormous pressure to build sets that are no longer dumb TVs, but smart computers that merely look like TV sets.

George Gilder calls the computerized TV set the "teleputer." In his 1994 book, *Life after Television*, Gilder predicted that the "teleputer" would soon become an indispensable part of our daily lives: "Just as the TV, once an exotic tool of elites, became even more ubiquitous in America than the telephone or the automobile, the teleputer will end the decade not as a luxury but as an indispensable appliance."

Gilder was over-optimistic by a few years, for the "teleputer" still has not arrived as a mass-market consumer electronics product. His warning for those stuck in the old TV paradigm should nonetheless be taken seriously:

> It is the companies that shun the PC today in order to cater to the TV, consumer electronics, and telephone industries that will end up in luxury backwaters. They will resemble companies catering to mainframe trade early this decade or the horse business early this century. They may find exotic or intriguing niches. But just as the real action was not at Churchill Downs or the Peapack Hunt Club, but in Detroit, the real action today — the source of wealth and power — is not at Nintendo or Sega, Sony or QVC; it is in the cores of thousands of computer and software companies comprising the industrial fabric of the Information Age — the exhilarating new life after television. [4]

Already, the stubborn conservatism that Gilder warned against has attempted to shape and appropriate the Web according to the dictates of the old television paradigm. Conventional television stations are struggling to find a business model for the Web as a broadcast medium – called "webcasting" — that can be advertiser-supported. These conservative approaches are wholly predictable. Experience has proven that, whenever a new medium appears, those who control incumbent technologies attempt to capture the potential of the new rival by imposing the logic of the old paradigm. When television was newly invented, for example, RCA president David Sarnoff gave a demonstration of a TV prototype at the 1939 World's Fair in New York City.

"Now we add radio sight to sound," declared Sarnoff, who believed the new visual medium was an extension of radio.

Today, we know that TV killed the radio star. Tomorrow, it could well be that the Web will kill the suited television executive of the present. The television industry got a wake-up call in 1998 when Procter & Gamble, one of the world's major advertisers, held a series of high-level meetings under the acronym FAST — for Future of Advertising Stakeholders. The aim of the meetings was to assess Internet advertising opportunities. Television executives, if they are too old to understand the fundamental logic of the Web, are smart enough to know that when advertising dollars shift towards the Internet, they shift away from television.

Advertisers are moving resources towards the Internet because more people are spending more time surfing the Web. A U.S. survey taken in 1998 revealed that increased time spent in front of home computers means time spent away from other forms of electronic media. In the

United States, 18 percent of Americans said they read fewer magazines due to time spent on the Internet, 18 percent said they spent less time reading books, and 11 percent said they read fewer newspapers. The big loser, however, was television. Of those surveyed, 78 percent said they spent less time watching television due to time spent on the Internet. In 1998 the proprietary on-line service, America Online, counted some 11 million subscribers in North America. Most were spending nearly an hour a day surfing the Web on AOL — a dramatic increase from only fourteen minutes per day in 1996.[5]

Rob Glaser, who left Microsoft where he was Bill Gates's lieutenant to start up RealNetworks, has been spearheading the Web's push towards a mass medium. Glaser brought radio to the Internet with RealAudio technology, and is now taking on the $125-billion (U.S.) television industry with RealVideo. In a recent speech entitled "The Internet as the Next Mass Medium," Glaser declared, "You talk about the 15 hours a week that people spend listening to the radio, or 20 hours watching TV. Four or five years from now we'll talk about the 10 or 15 hours a week that people spend experiencing audiovisual information over the Internet. It'll be just a standard part of the media fabric of people's lives."

Are TV executives nervous? The frenzy of mergers attests to that. The Disney-owned ABC network paid a reported $80 million (U.S.) for the Web-based supplier Starwave. NBC jumped into bed with Microsoft to form MSNBC. And CBS paid $100 million for the Internet service SportsLine. The deals in the other direction are conducted with more self-assurance: witness Microsoft co-founder Paul Allen's $500-million investment in DreamWorks, and the $425 million that Allen's partner, Bill Gates, casually kicked into WebTV. Even the biggest TV ratings service, AC-Nielsen, responded to a threat from Web-based ratings companies by merging in late 1998 with NetRatings. In competition with another merged Web-ratings service controlled jointly by Media Metrix and Relevant-Knowledge, they are battling to impose their own ratings-measurement techniques for the Web.

But what will people be watching on the Web? If distribution is reduced to a commodity because of unlimited capacity, market power will shift from suppliers to consumers. And this shift should, finally, prove the threadbare axiom that "content is king." As *The Economist* magazine pointed out in a survey of the Internet: "Providing Internet access may soon become a tough commodity business. . . . Yet the best business prospects lie not in carrying other people's bytes or running their stores, but in having something to sell yourself."

George Gilder describes the coming content cornucopia in *Life after Television*:

> The medium will change from a mass-produced and mass-consumed commodity to an endless feast of niches and specialties. A new age of individualism is coming, and it will bring an eruption of culture unprecedented in human history. Every film will be able to reach cheaply a potential audience of hundreds of millions.

Rob Glaser agrees that niche interests will drive the future of content. "Aggregators who are all over sports," he says, "or all over news, or all over music, or kids' stuff, or French impressionism, or cooking, or something that may not even have an economic model in the 36-channel world, but which has a deep and committed community — that's who will do great."

Conventional TV broadcasters may not die and vanish, but they are going to be squeezed. "There will still be broadcast television," says Glaser. "There will be cable television, and there will be satellite. But the underlying consumer mechanism for delivering choice will be Internet-based. There's no question about it. There is no competitor."

Thanks to new digital technologies, content itself is being completely transformed. Not only does the Web have a relatively low cost of entry but new technologies have also made content-production costs much lower. Video games and animated movies can be produced on desktop computers and distributed, at virtually no cost, via the Web. Pop music stars like David Bowie and The Artist Formerly Known as Prince are selling their music via the Web from personalized Web sites. In late 1998, Bowie invited fans plugged into his Web site (www.davidbowie.com) to submit lyrics for one of the pop star's newest songs, "What's Really Happening," promising the chosen wordsmith a $15,000 (U.S.) publishing contract and a trip to New York City to sit in on Bowie's recording sessions. Anyone has a shot at stardom on the Web. Take unknown singer Ani DiFranco, for example. She recorded an album, *Righteous Babe*, on low-cost digital audiotape, stamped out her own CDs for about $1 per unit and started selling them on the Web. *Righteous Babe* soon sold 250,000 copies and shot up to number 22 on the Billboard chart, the music industry's bible. DiFranco now has her own fan club that operates on the Web. The secret to her success, besides artistic talent: low production and distribution costs and no middleman.

The "Big Five" music giants — PolyGram, Sony, Warner, EMI, and Bertelsmann — are not indifferent to this phenomenon. Indeed, the Big Five are worried that their market share will be seriously eroded by the growth of independent record labels on the Internet. According to an industry study, between 1998 and 2008 the Big Five will see their global market share drop from 78 percent to 64 percent, while the market share of independent labels will increase from 22 percent to 36 percent. That loss for the Big Five will be from legal competition. They will likely lose even more money from music piracy on the Web.

David Bowie, Prince (now called "The Artist"), and Ani DiFranco are real human beings made of flesh and blood. But the Web is already producing digital superstars for the world of virtual reality. In Japan, a computer-generated androgynous singer called Kyoko Date climbed to the top of the pop charts with a single, "Love Communication." Today, the virtual star, also called "DK-96," has legions of fans in Japan. The stardom of DK-96 is the virtual realization of the fantasy in William Gibson's novel *Idoru*, in which a computer-generated singer becomes a superstar in Japan. The Web has also produced the world's first "cyber-opera," called *honoria in ciberspazio*, in which cyber-personalities play out the love story of a heroine who finds true love with a cyborg. In cinema, movies such as *Toy Story*, *Antz*, and *A Bug's Life* have also used computer-generated characters as stars. One advantage of cyber-stars is that, unlike Tom Cruise and Arnold Schwarzenegger, they don't demand $10-million fees.

According to *Wired* magazine, the emerging entertainment industry will soon render irrelevant current notions of geography and centralized production:

> Studios are not studios: feature films are created on desktop computers for less than $1,000. Theaters are not theaters: the cinema experience is being transferred to theme parks and onto massive video murals that will forever change our cityscapes. Film is not film: celluloid is going the way of vinyl records as movies are distributed digitally. And Hollywood is not Hollywood: the industry has gone global as fiber-optic cables allow simultaneous work on the same movie by creatives working from Cannes to Calcutta.

For consumers, all this change is great news. Content can now be delivered to Web users on an on-demand basis. A Silicon Valley–based company called TiVo has launched "on-demand TV" that delivers time-shifted television programs via the Web. TiVo stores television programs on servers that allow subscribers to develop their own customized, personalized program choices, which are suggested by the service based on previous selections. TiVo subscribers pay $400 (U.S.) up front for a set-top box, including a search engine and a hard drive that stores twenty hours of television programming. Subscriptions to TiVo cost $10 per month.

"Our mantra is that life is too short for bad TV," says TiVo vice-president Stacy Jolna.

TiVo, which was founded by former Silicon Graphics executives, has signed program-supply deals with channels such as Home Box Office. The service might take off, and it might tank. But it illustrates where the industry is going. Another sign is a new magazine, *TV Online*, launched in January 1999. The magazine, created to push Internet users towards video-based "channels" on the Web with entertainment stories, signed up 350,000 subscribers before it published its first edition.

"Sometimes it takes a publication to anchor a new technology," says *TV Online* editor Philip Swann. "The Internet is still such a jungle of information that people are looking for a little guidance and more focus."

The emergence of program guides for Web-delivered content demonstrates that — for all the talk of "disintermediation" — the function of packaging will not completely disappear on the Internet. New intermediaries will emerge and make money from new forms of packaging. In the old broadcasting paradigm of passive "lean back" television, content aggregators were television channels and cable TV companies. Channels preselected programs for their broadcast schedules, and cable TV companies packaged channels in bundles and sold them on a monthly basis to subscribers. The viewer was a passive couch potato who had little bargaining power in the transactional process with monopoly cable TV companies. Nor did the viewer have any choice as to when particular programs could be watched (unless they were taped on a VCR machine). The Web, on the other hand, is an interactive "lean forward" medium. Programs can be stored on servers and delivered on an on-demand basis to viewers willing to pay a fixed cost to watch a show according to their tastes — and, most important, *when* they want to watch it. The only question is whether viewers will have the energy and inclination to lean forward and interact with a Web-based delivery system.

If the Web does become a mass medium, there is no reason to believe that Web-based content aggregators will be the same content packagers that have dominated the television paradigm. Already, on-line services like America Online are emerging as content packagers with enormous market power. Other new players like Yahoo!, Lycos, Infoseek, and other search-engine "portals" are also rapidly becoming the Web's gatekeepers. Their rise to power in the value chain is not unlike cable TV's displacement of conventional off-air television as the industry gatekeeper in the 1970s. But the cable industry, having once been the technological usurper, won't likely relinquish its gatekeeper power without a fight.

Portal Pandemonium: The New Gatekeepers?

Like so many Silicon Valley successes, Jerry Yang and David Filo were blue-jeaned, pizza-addicted computer geeks when they struck an idea that would make both of them billionaires while still in their twenties.

In 1993, ancient history in Web time, Yang and Filo were engineering students at Stanford University in Palo Alto, the brainpower centre of Silicon Valley. The Web had just been invented, thanks to Mosaic software, and Yang and Filo were surfing on the new medium and collecting hundreds of "bookmarks" to tag their favourite sites. Soon Filo and Yang had each accumulated about 200 bookmarks and their frustration was growing as they attempted to keep track of them. In those days, Mosaic — which would later become Netscape — could not sort bookmarks into convenient onscreen folders. So Yang and Filo applied their software engineering knowledge to the task of creating a program that would permit them to create a "hot list" in different subject categories. They called the list "Jerry's Guide to the World Wide Web" and posted it on the Internet for anybody to use.

To their surprise, Yang and Filo began getting e-mails from around the world from appreciative Web surfers thanking them for bringing some order to the chaos of the emerging realm of cyberspace. Yang and Filo realized their idea might be the beginning of something big. They were right. The Stanford classmates put their doctoral dissertations on hold and perfected their Web search engine. They rebaptized it Yahoo!, a parody of Silicon Valley's obsession with acronyms — Yet Another Hierarchical Officious Oracle — and added the exclamation point for dramatic effect.

Yahoo! caught on so quickly on the exploding Web that soon both Netscape and America Online were making extravagant offers to buy the software. Yang and Filo shrewdly resisted. Instead, they dropped out of Stanford altogether and created their own company in Santa Clara. John Doerr, Silicon Valley's most powerful venture capitalist, wanted Yahoo! to merge with another Web search engine called Architext (later Excite), which had also been developed by Stanford grads. But Yang and Filo turned instead to Sequoia Capital, which had helped finance Apple Computer and Cisco Systems. Sequoia put up $1 million (U.S.) for a stake in the company. When Yahoo! made its initial public offering (IPO) in 1996, its valuation was $300 million. Yang and Filo were instant multi-millionaires. That was only the beginning.

Today Yahoo! is by far the most popular portal on the Web. In a typical month, about 30 million people use Yahoo! as an entry point to the Web.

Yahoo!'s success is spectacular by any standard. More people visit the Web via Yahoo! than through Netscape or AOL. More people use Yahoo! than watch MTV. More people check out Yahoo! than read *Time* or *Newsweek* in any given week. In 1997 Yahoo! and Netscape joined forces to develop a topic-based Internet navigation service bundled into Netscape's browser. Yahoo! also acquired the Four11 on-line phone book for $95 million. And in 1998 Yahoo! moved into the Internet-access business with Yahoo! Online, a partnership with telecom giant MCI.

In late 1998 Yahoo! had a market capitalization of more than $13 billion — an awesome figure for a company whose revenues were only $115 million. Sequoia's initial $1-million stake was worth nearly $1 billion at the end of 1998, and shareholder return on Yahoo! stock was a staggering 416.7 percent. Today, Yang and Filo each own 13 percent of the company — putting their personal fortunes at about $1.5 billion each. They brought in a CEO, Timothy Koogle, to run the company while they work on the creative side of the business. In typical Silicon Valley fashion, Yang and Filo eschew formal titles: their business cards identify each of them as Chief Yahoo.[6]

The spectacular success of Yahoo! owes largely to its strategic position as an indispensable gateway connecting Web users to content. For Web surfers, there are three different layers of service. First is the on ramp service provided by an Internet Service Provider (ISP), whether local dial-up services or proprietary on-line services like America Online. Second, portals like Yahoo!, Lycos, and Excite are gateways that Web users encounter once they are hooked up to the Internet. (America Online, which has 14 million paid subscribers, is in fact a hybrid service that is at once an ISP and a portal.) Third, Web destinations are the Web sites that users are attempting to find, whether for information, entertainment, or commercial transactions.

The value of a portal is its role as a sorting mechanism — a packager, in effect — that leads users to their desired destinations. Web portals attract customers by offering one-stop access to destinations on the Internet. In fact, the word "portal" is somewhat misleading, because portals like Yahoo! do everything they can to keep users from leaving their domains and moving through to other sites.

Industry experts attribute the huge popularity of Web portals to a deep-seated need for shared experience, which the chaotic, pluralistic, and fractious nature of the Web has exacerbated. Starting the journey from a single, reliable, and familiar gateway is highly desirable — hence the enormous value of portals like Yahoo! that occupied the field early and branded their names among early-adopter Web surfers.

"Consumers are lazy," says Patrick Naughton, chief technology officer of Disney's Buena Vista Internet Group. "They want convenience. They don't want to type in URLs. And bookmarks were never a good idea." [7]

At present, Web portals capture about 15 percent of total Internet traffic. While that figure is relatively modest as a percentage of total traffic, portals are still the most visited sites on the Internet. This has given portals like Yahoo! tremendous market power, and they can command huge premiums from advertisers. To date, about 59 percent of on-line advertising — estimated at $2 billion (U.S.) for 1998 — goes to a small number of branded portals.

Old media players are faced with a frustrating dilemma as they watch the value of upstart companies like Yahoo! soar into the billions. Established companies can set up their own portals, though they are already late into the game. Or they can buy existing portals to assert gatekeeper power. Both strategies are being pursued. The main obstacle to the second option is the staggering valuation figures Wall Street has given to portals like Yahoo! Some industry experts believe that portals will back into broadcasting through takeovers or partnerships with old media companies such as television networks.

The first convulsion in the so-called portal pandemonium occurred in the spring of 1998. In May the Excite portal paid Netscape $70 million in advertising revenue in exchange for an exclusive spot on the Netscape home page, called Netcenter. For that privilege, Excite had outbid rival portals Infoseek and Snap! The same day, Lycos inked a deal with phone giant AT&T that included an agreement to produce a CD-ROM containing a browser that automatically links users to the Lycos site via an AT&T Internet connection. The AT&T–Lycos deal was a defensive counterstrike against a similar deal between Yahoo! and long-distance phone company MCI. Meanwhile, NBC paid $32 million for a minority stake in the Silicon Valley new-media publisher, CNET, which owns the portal Snap! A week later, Disney bought a 43-percent stake in the portal Infoseek. Disney appeared to be looking for a single gateway to direct Web surfers to the disparate sites of Disney-controlled media brands, including ABCNews.com, Disney Blast, and ESPN.com. Disney later launched its own web service, called Go Network.

In June 1998 AT&T made an offer to buy America Online for an amount "comfortably above" its $19-billion market value. But AOL founder Steve Case rejected the offer, just as he had spurned the overtures of Bill Gates several years earlier. Case clearly had ambitions of his own. AOL had already bought CompuServe, and in late 1998 Case announced a $4.2-billion takeover of Netscape in a stock deal that also involved Sun Microsystems.

Though it failed to win AOL, AT&T understood that the key to a portal's success is branding. AOL is a familiar brand name that, moreover, generates robust cash flows from 14 million subscribers. The power of branding has played in favour of traditional aggregators of content — TV networks, Hollywood studios, news organizations, sports leagues. For example, the ten most popular U.S. Web sites in 1998 were (1) CNN.com; (2) ZDNet.com; (3) MSNBC.com; (4) weather.com; (5) Disney Online; (6) ESPN.com; (7) Pathfinder.com (Time Warner's site); (8) USAToday.com; (9) digitalcity.com; and (10) ABCNews.com. Other companies whose Web sites are among the top twenty-five are CBS Sportsline, Sony Online, NFL.com, Warner Bros. Online, broadcast.com, and washingtonpost.com. Most are either major brands or serve a useful function, like weather.com.

Portals have also provided an additional source of revenue for major computer makers. Compaq, for example, owns a stake in the Alta Vista portal, which appears on Compaq computer screens as a default menu. Likewise, owners of Dell computers — many of which are sold on the Internet — see the Excite portal when they start up their computers. Portals are happy to pay millions of dollars for access to computers whose brand names enjoy mass-market appeal.

In Canada, the cable industry's Internet-access service, @Home, is attempting to add content and other value-added services to its main function as a high-speed on-ramp. Likewise, giant phone companies like Bell Canada have their own Internet-access services such as Sympatico. Major Canadian media groups such as Southam, controlled by Conrad Black, are also well positioned to enter the portal business. Southam's Canada.com Web site could become an important portal site benefitting not only from the Southam brand, but also from the territorial association with its home country. Indeed, Canada.com's slogan reinforces the notion of territory: "Start Your Search from Home." The Sun Media group and Bell Canada Enterprises likewise have developed a portal site called CANOE (Canadian Online Explorer), which features, among other things, links to Sun-owned newspapers. In 1998 the *Globe and Mail* partnered with the Chapters bookstore chain to establish a rival Canadian service to U.S.-based on-line bookseller Amazon.com. The challenge for Canadian portals is to win the loyalty of Web users who might otherwise be attracted by Canadian affiliates of U.S. portals — Yahoo! Canada, AOL Canada, and a Canadian version of the Microsoft Network.

Some industry observers, like Esther Dyson, believe the power of portals is exaggerated.

I think the whole concept of portals is overrated, because the more difficult it is to pass through a portal, the less attractive it will become to consumers. Each would-be portal will have to negotiate carefully between being too broad and too specific, between exercising too much editorial quality control and losing value-added branding and personality. The broader a portal gets, the less value it brings to consumers. The more customers the portal attracts to the vending machines — for fees — the less each individual consumer is worth.[8]

Dyson is also worried that leviathan companies like Microsoft and AOL will end up controlling all portal access points, much as cable TV has become the powerful gatekeeper of the television industry. Bill Gates's attempt to buy AOL and the subsequent creation of the corporate colossus AOL-Netscape-Sun would appear to justify Dyson's concern about consolidation in the portal business.

Gates's own portal, the Microsoft Network (MSN), so far has been only a modest success. MSN has only 2 million paid subscribers despite the fact that Microsoft has been bundling the MSN software with its Windows operating system in most computers. Microsoft's new Web strategy is based on building MSN as a portal and owning destination commercial sites — notably in real estate, car sales, and travel bookings — that will become the Wal-Marts of the Web. After experimenting with "content" projects like the on-line magazine *Slate*, Gates is convinced that perhaps content is not king on the Web — commerce is. And so Microsoft is going after the $1-trillion (U.S.) market in home mortgages, the $447 billion spent on cars every year in the United States, and the $502 billion that Americans spend annually on travel. Gates is betting that a lot of those transactions will soon be taking place on the Web. So Microsoft has created Web sites like Home-Adviser, CarPoint, and Expedia to capture those revenues. The AOL-Netscape-Sun triumvirate has the same ambition.

Some believe that Microsoft's strategic shift towards becoming a Web Wal-Mart is a sign that the computer geeks never understood television in the first place, even though Gates has been spending billions buying up cable systems and companies like WebTV. Microsoft's new strategy appears to be: less glitz, more bits. Microsoft's new e-commerce strategy will be competing more with newspapers for classified ads than with television networks. Some say that joint television ventures like MSNBC are little more than a hobby farm for Gates, though he is certainly not unaware that ownership of cable TV channels gives him the power to shape public opinion. Indeed, while Gates was facing anti-trust charges levelled by the Clinton administration, MSNBC seemed inordinately interested in the sexual scandals undermining the president's reputation.

"Microsoft may lack the entertainment gene," says William Bass of Forrester Research, which estimates Microsoft's on-line revenues at $2 billion (U.S.) by 2001.

Rob Glaser, founder of RealNetworks, puts it another way:

> While Microsoft has had a good success in better network applications, like client-server databases, Microsoft has never been a media or communications-centred company. If you look at the results Microsoft has achieved on its interactive media side, and how it's organized off to the side — it never felt deeply integrated. There were a number of people I knew at Microsoft who prided themselves on not watching television because they found it a distraction. To me, that's a perfectly valid opinion, and it may be — from a child-rearing standpoint — a superior way of looking at the world. But if you want to be in the media business, there's no substitute for having a gut feeling for what the medium is.

Bill Gates himself doesn't deny that Microsoft is not an entertainment company. "The notion that Microsoft is a media company is a strange thing to say," he said in 1997.

America Online's Steve Case does not share Microsoft's ambivalence about television. Case believes the Web will become the next mass medium. AOL's strategy is not merely to be a shopping mall, but to become an aggregator of content much like cable television today. That is precisely why AOL, while merging with titans like Netscape, has been pressuring U.S. regulators at the same time to ensure that AOL and other on-line services are guaranteed non-discriminatory access to the cable industry's wires into the home.

Case began demanding access to the cable plant in mid-1998, when he took his claim to the FCC to argue that cable's infrastructure for Web traffic should be treated as a "common carrier" just like telephone wires. Case told the FCC that if companies like AOL can lease access to telephone wires, the same non-discriminatory access should be ensured with respect to cable's coaxial wires, particularly major U.S. cable systems like TCI and Time Warner. The cable industry, for its part, argued that the cable plant is not a utility like the phone system and therefore should not be subject to the same common-carrier access rules. In truth, the cable industry was determined to block AOL's popular service from killing the market penetration of the cable industry's own Internet-access services, @Home (which bought the Excite portal for $6.7 billion (U.S.) in January 1999) and Road Runner. The cable industry, a traditionally closed shop long used to monopoly gatekeeper power, understood that AOL's attempt to bypass its exclusive billing relationship with cable subscribers could be a lethal blow to cable's strategy to shift its business to the Web.

In late 1998 Case told the FCC that the cable industry's professed commitment to an open broadband system was bogus, because the major cable companies were insisting that consumers would "have to go through us" to get the Internet service provider of their choice. In short, the cable industry was fiercely defending its gatekeeper power.

Case argued that cable's basic business model — its "DNA" — does not favour openness and competition. "If cable's DNA does not change," he said in a speech to the National Press Club in Washington in October 1998, "cable-broadband services will never become a major Internet player, and the Internet will not reach its full potential."

Michael Armstrong, president of the phone giant AT&T, which now controlled John Malone's TCI cable empire, shot back at Case in early November 1998 with a warning that AOL would not get a "free ride" on cable systems. "Getting a free ride on someone else's investment and risk is really not the way to do it," said Armstrong. "It's not fair and it's not right."

Armstrong's comments were somewhat ironic given that, as CEO of DirecTV and AT&T before the phone giant bought out TCI, he too had denounced cable as a closed-system monopoly. Now, as head of the company that controlled the biggest cable empire in the United States, he was talking like a veteran monopolist determined to deny access to potential competitors. A possible strategic partnership between cable services like @Home and AOL would be a sign that the cable industry recognizes AOL's market power and is willing to share some of the revenue pie with the world's most popular proprietary on-line service.

Case's determination to deliver AOL via cable wires reveals his conviction that on-line multimedia services are destined to become just like television. Many continue to argue, however, that the Web will never become a broadcast-like mass medium because people are essentially couch potatoes who desire a "lean back" experience — not a "lean forward" interactive challenge every time they switch on their television-cum-computer.

One former Silicon Valley naysayer, CNET founder Halsey Minor, is now a convert to the potential of the PC-TV. In 1997 CNET had included the PC-TV in its list of "Ten Technologies That Don't Stand a Chance." The following year, however, CNET changed its mind and put the PC-TV in the number six spot on its Top Ten list of "Ten Technologies That Will Take Over." CNET is particularly gung-ho about products like WebTV.

"The new WebTV Plus's picture-in-picture capability lets you watch TV while a slow page loads, or surf the Web during a commercial," said CNET. "You can even browse TV show listings on-line. Innovations like these are winning over more fans. . . . But Web sites showing up on TV really aren't a big deal. The real advance will come when TV shows start behaving like Web sites."

CNET predicts that it will take about five years — circa 2003 or 2004 — for television and the Web to merge completely: "Remember the 500 channels? Well, they're here — only a lot of them are Web sites. . . . With a digital cable set-top box atop your boob tube, the day of interactive TV has dawned. Okay, it's about eight years late according to most pundits' original predictions. But that doesn't mean that we're wrong this time."

Among the conventional old-media TV networks, NBC has been the most aggressive about shifting its business strategy towards Web-based delivery. NBC started off with strategic partnerships: the creation of MSNBC with Microsoft and its minority stake in CNET and its Web portal, Snap! More recently, NBC, which is owned by General Electric, has made a major push into multimedia using video and audio-streaming technology for a service called InterVU. NBC plans to supply Web-based content to an "Interactive Neighborhood" network of some 100 affiliate stations. Microsoft, which is a partner in Interactive Neigborhood, has created "Sidewalk" city guide sites for the affiliated stations. Among the television programs featured on the Web service are shows such as *Homicide: Life on the Street*, *The Tonight Show with Jay Leno*, and *Late Night with Conan O'Brien*.

An upstart company that has created one of the most popular video-based Web sites is broadcast.com, a commercial Web-based broadcaster with links to 35 Internet Service Providers. Some 370 radio stations and 30 television stations are available on the site daily as well as live coverage of more than 420 sports teams on the Web. Its most lucrative business, though, is the live broadcast of business events such as analysts' conferences and earnings announcements. But it was Bill Clinton's sexual escapades that made broadcast.com a bona fide hit. More than a million people visited the broadcast.com site to watch President Clinton's testimony about his extramarital affair with White House intern Monica Lewinsky. When the company went public in mid-1998 after being in business for only three years, its market value after the initial public offering was nearly $1 billion (U.S.) — giving its two founders, Mark Cuban and

Todd Wagner, personal fortunes of about $200 million each. In late 1998 broadcast.com counted about 520,000 daily users.

At AOL, Steve Case's belief in the Web's potential as a television-like medium was affirmed when he hired Bob Pittman, formerly head of the MTV music video channel, to run his company. Under Pittman's leadership, AOL has set its sights on television as its main competition. AOL already has a prime-time audience of about 700,000 simultaneous users, a figure that is roughly equivalent to audience figures for CNN and MTV. According to Nielsen Media Research, America Online subscribers watch less television because they are plugged into AOL for about 46 minutes per day — a dramatic increase from 14 minutes in 1996. Rob Glaser's Real-Networks video-streaming technology will help AOL offer broadcast-quality video to its subscribers. RealNetworks' new product, RealPlayer, has been bundled into AOL's latest software on its CD-ROM, giving AOL immediate access to streamed multimedia content such as video games. In late 1998 Netscape joined AOL and other Web portals by bundling the RealNetworks video streamer with its new "Communicator" browser. With the rush towards streaming-technology deployment, it cannot be long before AOL and Web portals can package and sell real "channels" much as cable companies do.

Canadians cannot subscribe to U.S.-based cable companies or satellite services like DirecTV, mainly because these services offer CRTC-banned channels such as MTV, HBO, and ESPN. Canadians can subscribe freely to AOL, however. The obvious question, therefore, is what would happen if AOL began offering MTV, HBO, and ESPN to its subscribers?

If the Web does indeed become a mass medium, Canada's regulatory restrictions will be severely put to the test.

The Regulatory Temptation

In June 1993 Canada's broadcasting regulator announced the arrival of the new consumer. The CRTC declared that digital technologies would soon empower consumers, who would henceforth exercise more discrimination and control when choosing forms of distraction on television.

The CRTC's new consumer was little more than an over-hyped vision of a digital zapper in John Malone's 500-channel universe. When Malone's hype was exposed as hollow rhetoric, the CRTC's new consumer vanished from sight — or at least from the CRTC's press releases.

Five years later the CRTC decided that the time had arrived to exhume the new consumer and outfit him for the new realities of cyberspace. In July 1998 the regulator announced an ambitious examination, including public hearings, of the impact of "new media" on the traditional communications environment. The regulator seemed to have learned a few lessons since 1993. Originally, the new consumer was a symbolic diversionary tactic evoked in public while the regulator schemed to protect the asset base and bottom line of the cable industry from the competitive threat of digital satellite TV. In 1998 the regulator seemed to be asking the right questions, including whether regulators should — or could — exercise any control at all over global networks and delivery systems like the Web.

The CRTC wasn't the only regulator examining the impact of the Web and new media on existing commercial models and policy frameworks. In the United States, the FCC published a report called *Digital Tornado*, which predicted that the Web would undermine old-media regulatory models. "The chaotic nature of the Internet may be troubling for governments, which tend to value stability and certainty," observed the FCC report:

> However, the uncertainty of the Internet is a strength, not a weakness. With decentralization comes flexibility, and with flexibility comes dynamism. Order may emerge from the complex interactions of many uncoordinated entities, without the need for cumbersome and rigid centralized hierarchies. Because it is not tied to traditional models or regulatory environments, the Internet holds the potential to dramatically change the communications landscape.

The report concluded that, when establishing policies for the Web, governments should avoid unnecessary regulation and question the applicability of traditional rules.[9]

The European Commission also published a Green Paper on technological convergence and new media. The EC called for a light-touch approach to regulating the Web: "The development of new services could be hindered by the existence of a range of barriers, including regulatory barriers, at different levels of the market." The OECD, too, has published an ambitious report, *Webcasting and Convergence: Policy Implications*, in which the Paris-based international think tank argued in favour of deregulation of the Web. "It would be highly impractical, if not impossible and not desirable in the case of privacy concerns, that all multimedia Internet content should be monitored or regulated by governments in the same way as traditional broadcasting media," stated the OECD report.[10]

Supranational organizations like the European Commission and the OECD naturally tend to call for deregulation, or light-touch rules, for new communications technologies. These organizations, which have no direct authority or legitimacy vis-à-vis national populations, favour transnational market forces over cultural policy and state intervention. The explicit mission of the OECD is to break down national barriers and promote free-market forces. And the European Commission has always been inspired by a pro-market ethos, if only because deregulation at the national level among its member countries reliably translates into more supranational power for the EC in Brussels. For the EC and the OECD, globalization is good and should be encouraged. National governments, which must manage the social and cultural consequences of transnational technologies and commercial globalization, do not always share the deregulatory zeal of supranational bodies.

At the national level, regulators often embrace the discourse of free markets and consumer empowerment. Their actual decisions, however, sometimes reflect an entirely different predisposition — especially when transnational technologies and new delivery systems like the Web threaten to undermine their own institutional legitimacy. In Canada, the CRTC has been careful to ask the right questions, but it's less certain about what the right answers to those questions might be. Many suspect that, given the choice between regulation and bureaucratic suicide, regulators would not be naturally inclined to choose the latter option — no matter where the public interest lies.

Françoise Bertrand had been chairperson of the CRTC for only a few months in 1996 when she alarmed many industry players with her assertion that the Commission might have to regulate content on the Web.

"I think it's very important, on those new modes of communication, that there is Canadian content, Canadian producers as well," said Bertrand in an interview on CBC's Newsworld. "I see it as a definite possibility that I will be exploring with the staff here, but also with the players and the consumers, so that we have a clear picture on how we can go about it."

Bertrand's remarks triggered quick responses from Web-based operators like Internet service providers, who feared they would become subject to government regulations.

"In terms of Canadian culture and promotion and content, the traditional rules and regulations just don't apply," said Margo Langford, general counsel for iSTAR and head of the Canadian Association of Internet Providers. "If they could re-examine the policy behind the regulations, I think their arguments would pretty quickly dissipate."

Bertrand's comments doubtless explain why the CRTC subsequently, when announcing its New Media hearings in 1998, insisted that the regulator "brings to this proceeding no preliminary views with respect either to how new media should be defined, or to what role, if any, the Commission should play in their regulation or supervision." Still, the Canadian public remained suspicious.

The McLuhan Program's E-Lab at the University of Toronto collected and collated the public submissions that poured in to the CRTC in response to the regulator's call for public comment on new media. The general sentiment expressed was overwhelmingly anti-regulation, anti-monopoly, pro-market, and passionately in favour of freedom of expression. The McLuhan E-Lab noted: "A tone of resentment and outrage is evident, an attitude that seems driven by the suspicion that the CRTC, a regulatory agency, has already made up its mind to regulate new media. The CRTC's call for comments specifically denies this, but many new media forum participants remain skeptical."

Some respondents sent in unmistakably hostile messages to the CRTC. One message exclaimed: "Get out of my computer, you jerks!" Another one read: "Stay out of my mind." Among the more dispassionate responses, a majority stated their belief that the Web was not "broadcasting" and thus should not be regulated as such. Many asserted that the Web was more like publishing, which is not regulated in Canada or in any other democratic country.

Summing up the public input to the CRTC consultation on new media, the McLuhan E-Lab observed:

> Most participants have high expectations of what an unfettered Internet can deliver for Canadians. The Internet itself is viewed as allowing more people access to education, a kind of gigantic library without walls. The resources of the world are available at the touch of the keyboard for many in this "medium without borders." Left unrestricted, the Internet may contribute to the "future development of the human race." The Internet has the potential to equalize Canadian participation in the global communications system, to develop world citizens in a global village. This New Media forum demonstrates that the average citizen who does not attend government hearings can be heard.

The CRTC, like most regulators, does not have a tradition of giving much consideration to the views of average citizens, even when their opinions are sent in on the Internet. Regulators are concerned mainly with the interests of their "clients" — the major players in the industries that they regulate. One does not have to be a cynical advocate of the theory of "regulatory capture" to understand this truth. Industry players, not ordinary citizens, implement regulatory policy. Industry players are involved in the symbiotic relationship with regulators that trades recognition of institutional legitimacy for legal protections. The Web threatens to smash apart this entrenched complicity because it is utterly indifferent to the triple logic of bureaucracy, territory, and legitimacy.

David Colville, the highly regarded CRTC vice-chairman, gave a clue as to the regulator's thinking about new media in September 1998 when he dismissed the notion that the Commission would assert its jurisdiction over the Web as a matter of bureaucratic survival.

"We're not trying to invent new things for the Commission to do," said Colville. "The real issue is how can we make sure that there's a Canadian presence, that Canadians can turn to see themselves, to see the Canadian culture, the Canadian identity on new media."

Colville appeared to be echoing the statement of his boss, Françoise Bertrand, in 1996 when the CRTC chair said that content regulation on the Web was possible. Colville even went as far as to say that the notion that the Web could not be regulated by states is "a bit of a myth."

"I don't know whether it's possible or not," he said. "But when you think about it, radio and television transmissions are just spewing through the ether and you could ask who could ever capture that sort of thing and regulate it." [11]

Much of the discussion before the CRTC in late 1998 focused on the normative question of whether the CRTC *should* regulate the Web. Regulation, however, has always tended to focus on more practical matters. State regulation of radio and television, for example, found its justification in the material fact of limited spectrum capacity. Limited spectrum allowed governments to assert their role in allocating and co-ordinating the use of radio frequencies. The Internet imposes a radically different logic. Transmission of data and images on the Web does not rely on "signal" distribution. Instead, Internet communication is based on a common, universal computer language — software protocols — that permits the transmission of "bits" from one point to another, rather than "signals" from one point to many points in the public domain. Unlike cable television, software protocols on the Web dissociate the service from the means of transport and thus reduce distribution to a commodity. In short, those who control distribution capacity for the Internet cannot extract the same monopoly rents from Web traffic in the way that cable TV owners have done in the past. The reason is simple: the Web is an open-architecture network system, not a bottleneck system controlled by a rent-seeking gatekeeper. Cable TV systems are centralized, monopolistic, closed, and controlled. The Internet is decentralized, pluralistic, open, and uncontrollable.

Given these basic facts, it is extremely doubtful, as a practical matter, that states can assert their control over Web-based forms of entertainment, especially through traditional mechanisms such as licensing. In traditional broadcasting, regulators accorded licences to particular persons or companies and often promoted their economic viability by protecting them from competition. On the Internet, however, virtually anyone can be a "programmer," which renders the principle of licensing utterly irrelevant.

Against this backdrop, which regulatory regime should apply to the Web? Is it "broadcasting"? Is it "telecommunications"? Should competition policy alone be sufficient as a legal means of restraint for market behaviour on the Internet? Or, perhaps more pertinent, should some converged legal regime that combines all three be constructed? Many lawyers have been getting rich from crafting arguments on all sides of these questions.

Traditionally, broadcasting has been regulated primarily from a content perspective, and the values of cultural identity have been central to broadcasting policies in many countries, particularly in Europe. Telecommunications regulation, on the other hand, is based on "common carriage." The focus of telecom regulation therefore has not been on the content of what is transmitted (voice messages) but on the terms and conditions of the transmission of phone calls (rates, tariffs, inter-exchange fees, and so on). The Web by definition escapes traditional regulatory tools.

Some legal precedents can help clarify this issue, whose financial stakes for industry players cannot be underestimated. A U.S. federal Court of Appeals, in the case of *ACLU* v. *Reno*, has ruled that the Internet is not broadcasting. The U.S. court decision based its distinction between "broadcasting" and "telecommunications" on the fact that, on the Web, users seek out Web sites and "pull" down what they are interested in viewing. Broadcasting, on the other hand, is "push" transmission. The U.S. court also found that the Internet is characterized by no capacity scarcity, low entry barriers, and moreover is protected by freedom-of-speech rights.[12]

The European Commission has gone one step further by defining video-on-demand as "telecommunications." In its directive, Television Without Frontiers, the EC stated that: "Video-on-demand services, like all genuinely inter-active services, are classed as telecommunications in that transmission is in response to individual demand." No Canadian court has ruled on this issue. If the CRTC adopts a broad definition of "broadcasting" that would include services like video-on-demand and Web-based multimedia content, court challenges to the regulatory ruling would be highly likely.

At present, the CRTC seems uncertain what to do about Web-based content, whether audio or video. More generally, the entire Canadian policy apparatus is rife with inconsistencies, applying specific rules for some sectors and other rules — or no rules at all — to other areas. The CRTC's most predictable reflex, as the "death stars" satellite TV saga amply demonstrated, is to assert its jurisdiction over communications technologies that can effectively bypass its authority and over foreign market players who can similarly bypass the CRTC's chosen monopoly middlemen in the Canadian market.

The spectacular success of the Internet bookseller, Amazon.com, has shown how innovative forms of electronic commerce are challenging traditional intermediaries, whether small bookshops or major chains. In the compact disc market, on-line companies like U.S.-based CDnow offer similar examples of how the Internet is being used to market and sell millions of units of cultural products that, until now, have been sold through bricks-and-mortar retail chains. The success of wholesale operations like Amazon.com and CDnow is largely due to the efficient bypassing of conventional intermediaries.

A distinction must be made, however, between on-line wholesalers like Amazon.com and owners of intellectual property who distribute their products digitally, directly to consumers via the Internet. When you buy a book or a CD on the Internet, it is no different from buying a shirt or a computer from a consumer catalogue. These products are hard goods that, once ordered, are delivered to your door. To employ Nicholas Negroponte's familiar distinction, Amazon.com sells "atoms," not "bits." Buying or renting a downloadable movie or song on-line is a different, more direct, form of distintermediation. The transaction is immediate and digital delivery is made at virtually no additional cost.

At present, digital delivery of cultural products faces a number of major obstacles. Most Hollywood studios, major record companies, and other players in the entertainment industries have established New Media divisions and are testing consumer habits with Web sites offering all manner of services, games, and distractions. Still, these same companies are exceedingly reluctant to start selling, or renting, their intellectual property as digital products on the Internet.

There are two main reasons for this circumspection. First, owners of intellectual property are, as noted, worried that their products will be copied, at marginal cost, by individuals and distributed in millions of units throughout the world on the Internet. Most copyright holders will not start selling digital cultural products on-line until a fail-safe encryption system for encoding and decoding digital signals is universally adopted. Second, a number of critical technical obstacles must be overcome. For example, downloading video and music takes a long time, and the quality is often erratic, and therefore networks must be expanded to increase bandwidth capacity.

It is only a matter of time, however, before both these problems are resolved — the copyright issue by international treaty and the market adoption of reliable encryption systems; and the technical issues by the build-out of digitized networks and the mass-market introduction of video-streaming technology. It can be confidently predicted that, with the emergence of major brands on the Web, the sale and rental of cultural products on-line will become a billion-dollar industry within the next decade.

A decade is a very short period of time. Yet policy makers still seem uncertain about how digital cultural products should be regulated, if at all. In Canada, the confusion and inconsistency in this area are remarkable. The CRTC, for example, does not regulate Internet radio stations and other forms of audio-on-demand, but has decided to license and regulate video-on-demand. The regulator also has defined video-on-demand as "broadcasting" and yet remains silent on the definition of on-line music. Are radio programs not "broadcasting," too? If so, why are they not subject to the same regulatory rules?

The debate over video-on-demand offers an illustration of how the CRTC tends to respond to conceptual ambiguity by asserting its own authority in areas where there is some doubt on the matter. On July 2, 1997, the CRTC issued video-on-demand (VOD) licences to several Canadian applicants — all of them major players in the Canadian broadcasting system. The CRTC took a light-touch approach when granting these VOD licences, insisting only on guaranteed "shelf space" for Canadian products and financial contributions for Canadian content production. In issuing the VOD licences, the CRTC followed the same approach it had adopted in the past: granting licences to a limited number of established Canadian players so they could "occupy the field" before an incursion of foreign-based operators.

There is no reason to believe, however, that the market logic of VOD will necessarily respect national territories and obey national regulations. A computer server from which on-demand movies are retrieved does not have to be located on Canadian soil. Consequently, there is no reason why those who control foreign-based digital retrieval systems will feel compelled to gain access to the Canadian market through CRTC approval. This would put pressure on the CRTC-designated intermediaries, the VOD licensees.

In Canada, the dispute over video-on-demand and multimedia services has been part of the ongoing battle between the cable TV and telephone companies. Cable companies and other established players in the Canadian broadcasting system have been fighting for a broad definition of broadcasting in order to capture on-demand services and thus limit the impact of competition by imposing regulation and market-entry barriers. The phone companies and computer industry — both new players in the provision of content to homes — have been seeking a restrictive definition so they can exploit VOD and other multimedia services with no fear of onerous regulations and other market-entry barriers.

As noted, the European Commission considers video-on-demand to be telecommunications, not broadcasting. The EC considers VOD to be switched, point-to-point communications — not point-to-multipoint broadcasting. Some have argued that the CRTC could avoid past pitfalls by acknowledging, like the European Commission, that services such as video-on-demand and multimedia cannot be considered broadcasting — and therefore should not be subject to regulation. This argument, however valid, neglects two powerful factors: the CRTC's defensive tendency to assert its jurisdiction broadly to validate its own legitimacy; and the tremendous pressures exerted on the CRTC by established players fearing that unregulated media services will pose a serious competitive threat to their market dominance in Canada.

It should not be surprising, therefore, that the CRTC has insisted to date on a broad interpretation of broadcasting as it appears in the 1991 Broadcasting Act. The regulator similarly has interpreted "program" very broadly. By doing so, the CRTC has asserted its jurisdiction over video-on-demand — and thus, as noted, justified the issuance of VOD licences to a group of major players in the Canadian broadcasting system. The function of this "picking winners" approach is to neutralize the impact of new types of cultural products by bringing them under the regulatory control of the CRTC, which authorizes designated Canadian players the right to exploit them commercially.

The CRTC was no doubt aware of respected legal opinions arguing that video-on-demand is not in fact a broadcasting activity, and therefore should not be regulated. As explained earlier, video-on-demand entails a point-to-point transaction between a supplier and a particular individual. Broadcasting, on the other hand, entails a point-to-multipoint sending of pre-scheduled signals to the general public. The original version of the current Broadcasting Act, when it was being debated in the late 1980s as Bill C-136, stated explicitly that programs "made on the demand of a particular person for reception only by that person" would be excluded from the definition of broadcasting. That particular clause was removed, however, after intense lobbying by major Canadian industry players whose regulated commercial interests were threatened by a narrower definition of broadcasting that might have encouraged competition from unregulated video-on-demand operators.

The removal of that clause was a strategic error that, if avoided, might have prevented the current ambiguity over how to deal with on-line services. Today, Internet-based services like America Online are starting to offer video and music and other multimedia products that, according to the CRTC's broad interpretation, clearly would be considered broadcasting and hence would require regulation. Yet the CRTC cannot assert any regulatory control over these services. When the provincial phone company, SaskTel, openly defied the CRTC by offering video-on-demand service without regulatory approval on the grounds that VOD is point-to-point communications, the CRTC backed down. When foreign-based VOD operators emerge, the CRTC's impotence in this area will likely become even more obvious. These inconsistencies cannot be maintained without making a mockery of the entire communications policy and regulatory structure in Canada.

A solution to this ambiguity calls first for some conceptual clarity. Buying video-on-demand is precisely like walking into a bookshop or a video store — only the method of delivery is different. The CRTC itself evoked the bookstore analogy when discussing video-on-demand in its 1995 *Convergence Report*: "True VOD, on the other hand, is not scheduled. These services will be akin to a book store or library, where individual programs are stored on electronic shelves and customers access the titles they want by navigating through a series of menus."

Neither bookstores nor video stores are regulated for the purposes of Canadian cultural policy. Yet the CRTC has decided to regulate video-on-demand. The CRTC's rationale: "Because of their nature and scale, however, certain mass-appeal, on-demand applications such as movies can and should be regulated where this would contribute materially to the cultural objectives of the Broadcasting Act."

Do books, magazines, videocassettes, and CDs not have mass appeal, too? In truth, the CRTC has decided to regulate VOD merely because its delivery system — wires to the home — is owned by companies under its regulatory authority. By focusing on the delivery system, the CRTC has once again fallen into the trap of putting its own legitimacy and the commercial interests of its major clients before the rigours of conceptual consistency and good public policy.

The federal government, happily, is not so encumbered. A recent speech by Art Eggleton, the federal trade minister, imposed some conceptual clarity on the debate. "Our cultural policies were historically designed to support 'hard' cultural goods, like magazines, books, sound recordings and film," said Eggleton. "But increasingly, cultural products are taking the form of 'soft' electronic transmissions. Magazines, including such Canadian publications as *Maclean's* and *Saturday Night*, are appearing on-line. Newspapers, books, films, and sound recordings can be distributed electronically. How are we to treat these on-line cultural products? Are they cultural goods or a service? It makes a difference in trade agreements. How can these products be regulated? How can contents of cyberspace even be monitored, let alone controlled?" Eggleton was asking the right questions, though Ottawa still had no workable answers.

What is the solution? The CRTC itself has recommended a legislative amendment to exclude services like "commercial on-line multimedia services," "interactive courses" offered by accredited schools, and "educational multimedia materials." This recommendation appears to be exceedingly conservative. However, it could be argued that America Online, Microsoft Network, and any other Internet-based service could be described as "commercial on-line multimedia services." These Internet suppliers of multimedia content soon will be offering video-on-demand and many other digitally delivered cultural products. Does that mean that some VOD services in Canada need a licence, while the CRTC admits it cannot regulate others?

If policy makers do not move quickly to clarify these issues, the realities of the marketplace will impose their own facts — and, once again, the policy process will be exposed to the old criticism of "lag" as it attempts to play a losing game of catch-up with the real world. As astounding as it might seem today, when the Broadcasting Act (1991) and the Telecommunications Act (1993) were being drafted, the Internet had not yet registered on the policy radar screen. Nearly a decade later, perhaps it is time to redraft these statutes to bring them into the digital Information Age.

The propensity of bureaucracies for self-perpetuation should never be underestimated. In the current climate of transnational technologies and commercial globalization, however, it is easy to imagine a serious threat to the very existence of regulators. Jealousies between anti-trust officials and regulators already exist, and it appears that anti-trust actions are becoming more prevalent in the new climate of open market competition. In Canada, the Competition Bureau is emerging from relative obscurity to examine major sectoral transactions — notably in banking — while regulators struggle to assert their authority effectively.

Some have advocated the prompt dismantling of regulators altogether and the adoption of a common-law approach to communications. Such an approach to the major issues of cyberspace would mark a significant departure from the statute-and-agency approach that has prevailed in Canada and the United States to date. The major issues would include freedom of speech, privacy, and copyright. The leading advocate of the common-law solution is Peter Huber, an American whose recent book sums up his views succinctly in the title: *Law and Disorder in Cyberspace: Abolish the FCC and Let Common Law Rule the Telecosm*. Huber argues that the "telecosm" — his word for the new communications landscape — should be liberated from the meddling rule-making of rigid bureaucracies whose sole purpose is their own survival. A common-law approach, argues Huber, would be sufficient for communications in the Information Age. For Huber, the choice is between top-down regulators that represent "law by edict and national commission" and bottom-up common law built by adjudication in the courts. The latter would be guided by bills of rights, notably freedom-of-speech and anti-trust laws.

"In the telecosm, as elsewhere, commission law leads society down the road to serfdom," says Huber:

> However good the original intentions, central planning always ends up maintaining the privilege and power of the planners themselves. From markets and the common law, by contrast, there emerges spontaneous order that is rational, efficient, and intelligent. Though never planned, never even fully articulated, common-law rules adapt and evolve by common consent, like the rules of grammar. Society organized by commission is inherently limited by what the minds of the planners can grasp. Common law, in the aggregate, is far wiser. [13]

The common-law approach will not find much favour in the bureaucratic corridors of broadcasting regulators. But it likely will be embraced by the mass of people — whether couch potatoes or cybersurfers — who have been neglected for too long in the closed world of regulatory complicity between state bureaucracies and their favoured corporate clients.

The Web, for better or for worse, signals the end of an era — and the dawning of a new Information Age. The 500-channel universe and the Information Superhighway are finally on the digital horizon. There can be no looking back.

Conclusion

THIS BOOK BEGAN, IT WILL BE RECALLED, WITH THE DEFINITIONS OF three paradoxes: the Confidence-Crisis Paradox, the Competition-Consolidation Paradox, and the Citizen-Consumer Paradox. These three central themes have resonated throughout the preceding chapters. Revisiting them more explicitly here in the conclusion may provide — besides the elegance of analytical symmetry — some insights into how we got to where we are today and, more importantly, what the future may hold.

The Confidence-Crisis Paradox requires little further demonstration. The underlying cause of the Digital Revolution's frustrated arrival was, as has been amply recounted, a carefully orchestrated confusion between industry confidence and crisis that was meant to conceal a profound anxiety about the potentially paralyzing effects of technological change. In the end, neither the Cable Guys nor the Bell Heads were, as they so loudly proclaimed, the visionary architects of the 500-channel universe or the Information Superhighway. Today, technological "convergence" is being driven largely by the World Wide Web. And the cable barons and telephone executives are frantically trying to harness the commercial energies of a technological paradigm shift that, in truth, both groups deeply feared and actively resisted until they no longer had any choice.

The Competition-Consolidation Paradox is, in many respects, a convulsive symptom of the acute tension between industry confidence and crisis throughout the 1990s. If confidence and crisis can be described as attitudes or states of mind, competition and consolidation were the outward forms of behaviour that proceeded directly from each — competition from confidence, and consolidation from crisis. Competition was confidently promised, but it failed to materialize. Today, the media and entertainment industries have consolidated into bigger and bigger corporate colossi that, instead of competing, are actually collaborating on a global scale like a *keiretsu*-style cartel. If this trend continues, the media will soon be dominated by a powerful global oligopoly. A thousand flowers may bloom, but there will likely be very few gardeners. According to the logic of digital capitalism, there may be room for everyone in the marketplace — but big is definitely beautiful.

Industry consolidation will not occur, of course, without a brutal shake-out producing winners and losers. The losers are easier to identify than the winners. While cable barons like Ted Rogers and J.R. Shaw may wax sentimental about the dedication of their families to the business, the cruel reality is that few major family-run cable empires will endure long after the death of their founders. This unsettling prognosis is difficult to admit for those most directly concerned, but the law of genetic atrophy is immutable. An instructive precedent has been furnished by the telephone industry, once a patchwork of family fiefdoms, which followed an inexorable process of rational consolidation into the hands of corporate managers. The cable industry is doomed to succumb to the same inglorious fate. The buyouts of family-run cable groups by corporate titans Time Warner, AT&T, and Microsoft are only the first signs of a larger, longer-term process that will see the North American cable industry consolidated under non-family ownership. Cable barons like John Malone and Ted Rogers are colourful and legendary figures, but have no place in the Information Age of the twenty-first century.

The Citizen-Consumer Paradox is infinitely more complex and far-reaching in its consequences than the previous two paradoxes. Lost in the media coverage of flamboyant personalities, corporate greed, and government fumbling, its paradox is difficult to reconcile because one of its components — the *citizen* — has been conspicuously absent in the hoopla surrounding the Digital Revolution. The 500-channel universe and the Information Superhighway were visions fabricated with hollow promises designed chiefly to appeal to *consumers*. New technologies, new commercial forces, and new government policies were supposed to empower the so-called "new consumer." The needs of citizens, however, were almost an afterthought. Or they were evoked without fanfare as costly good deeds — hooking up schools, libraries, and hospitals to the Internet — that private interests contemplated with decidedly less enthusiasm.

The absence of the citizen in most public debates about the 500-channel universe and the Information Superhighway reveals a profound malaise that runs much deeper than corporate greed or bureaucratic muddle. The Digital Revolution has produced a serious crisis of legitimacy for governments, which frankly have failed to assert themselves meaningfully in a technological and commercial explosion which has been essentially market-driven and transnational. It should not be surprising that the growing impotence of states, faced with the challenge of transborder technologies and commercial globalization, has produced troubling consequences for the status of the citizen. While markets seek the approval of consumers, states cannot hope to survive without the recognition of citizens.

In the past, states often asserted their authority through the efficiency of infrastructure systems. The Roman empire had its roads and aqueducts; the Industrial Revolution had its canals and railways. No communications technology has ever appeared without states immediately seeking to control, tax, and harness its potential to achieve goals established by the states themselves — first among them, to reinforce their own power and legitimacy. In Canada, the nineteenth-century railway was the newly created country's "national dream"; a century later the Canadian broadcasting system was described as the young nation's "central nervous system." But what happens to states, and to their citizens, when communications media — such as satellite TV and the Internet — are effectively transnational and essentially non-territorial?

This book has described the defensive convulsions that afflict states — and in particular regulators — when they are confronted with powerful new communications technologies whose reach extends beyond national borders. In some cases, as we have seen, the bureaucratic instinct for self-perpetuation is capable of alarming hypocrisies, such as the pious evocation of cultural values to conceal a cynical complicity with private commercial interests. This reflex is easily exposed as folly. In the final analysis, the business strategies of national commercial actors will inevitably expand beyond borders and, once operating internationally, will abandon any attachment to territorial-based laws and regulations. Is Nortel, the global telecom giant, really a "Canadian" company? In Hollywood, Universal Studios is owned by Canada's Bronfman family, Columbia is controlled by Japanese interests, and 20th Century Fox is part of Australian-born Rupert Murdoch's News Corp. empire. Are these companies "Canadian," "Japanese," and "Australian"? Or are they "American"? What do these words ultimately mean? Or, as Bill Clinton's former labour secretary Robert Reich aptly asked: "Who is U.S.?" Against this backdrop, the precise status of the *citizen* is increasingly elusive.

In many cases, states are recognizing their own impotence by attaching their legitimacy to the success of designated corporations — or so-called "national champions." Today, presidents and prime ministers lead trade missions to bolster exports — like the many "Team Canada" junkets — and thus create a confusion between the status normally assigned to a statesman and that of the vice-president of marketing for any multinational corporation. Private firms, for their part, will reliably call on states to organize at the international level when it is in their interest to do so — for example, to establish intellectual protection regimes. Most of the time, however, transnational media corporations seek to bypass state authority. The NASDAQ market, for example, isn't located anywhere. Like cyberspace, it's everywhere and nowhere, a giant computerized market with no physical location.

So what, therefore, is the fate of nations — and their citizens — in the Information Age? In the immediate fallout of the Web explosion, the geographic organization of politics does not seem to make sense. If the "death of distance" means that people can work for any corporation in cyberspace from virtually any location on the planet, why should the organization of political life be territorially defined? National communities have been geographically proximate, but the construction of new technology-mediated communities no longer needs to depend on the constraints of space and time. If we are indeed witnessing the emergence of "netizens" claiming allegiance to a "digital nation," what kind of political rights and constraints will they be governed by? Depending on the preferred scenario, nations as we know them will either vanish — becoming components of larger cultural spheres and submitting to an emerging global culture — or they will adapt and reassert themselves.

It has become fashionable to predict the coming of a "new feudalism" that will destroy bureaucratic hierarchies and topple existing elites. According to this neo-medieval vision, new communications technologies will produce a chaotic world — also described as "electronic feudalism" — in which there is no obvious centre of power. Individuals will no longer be citizens, but will have multiple, multi-layered identities that are not necessarily defined by territory. The emergence of the Internet is compatible with this vision, for the Web creates non-contiguous, technology-mediated "communities of interest" whose loyalties are flexible and shifting. Cyberspace is thus conceived as a sort of virtual Holy Roman Empire: It exists in name, but commands no immediate sense of loyalty.

Another vision of the future predicts a "clash of civilizations," pitting powerful, value-driven cultural spheres against one another — notably the West against Islam and the Third World. This opposition between industrial democracy and religious authoritarianism has been expressed in us-and-them terms as "McWorld" against "Jihad" culture. It seems simplistic, but there can be no doubt that hostile sentiments are passionately felt, and easily mobilized, on the Jihad side of the cultural divide. Western television signals beamed into countries like Morocco, Iran, Malaysia, and Singapore have provoked the authoritarian rulers of these countries to fulminate against the pernicious values propagated by the pulsing music videos of MTV. In Canada, the hostile reaction to DirecTV was motivated by a threatened local business elite seeking to preserve its monopoly protections. The death stars saga was, all things considered, a minor spat within McWorld over the distribution of financial benefits. In the Jihad culture, however, the values of religion are much more powerful motivators.

Those who reject the clash-of-civilizations theory often assert that, in fact, the world is being rapidly Americanized by a single cultural super-power. The combined power of Hollywood and Silicon Valley will indeed give the United States an enormous soft-power advantage over other nations in the Information Age. Besides the overwhelming global presence of Hollywood movies, the United States exports more than 75 percent of the world's pre-packaged software, controls more than 60 percent of the worldwide market for pre-recorded music, and captures roughly 35 percent of the global book market. Some welcome America's cultural dominance as good for the spread of democracy. Others rail against U.S. "cultural imperialism" and warn that, as McWorld imposes its norms and values on the planet, we may all be reduced to mere consumers of homogenized American cultural products. Whether the world needs any more Disneyland theme parks is a subject that undoubtedly merits debate. Still, as traditional nation-state "realpolitik" is superseded by "cyberpolitik" in the Information Age, the United States almost certainly will be in a position to reinforce its already awesome hard military power with a tremendous cultural arsenal of soft power.

Some optimists prefer to envisage a New World Order governed by supranational institutions that are not directly controlled by any single nation. The advocates of a supranational world — many are implicitly disparaging of nations and citizenship loyalties — often point to emerging political spheres like the European Union as a model to follow. They also tend to support free-market transnational bodies like the OECD, the World Trade Organization, the World Bank, and the International Monetary Fund. They may sometimes argue that these institutions need urgent reforms, but they nonetheless approve of their existence.

The emergence of supranational bureaucracies has been accompanied by the rise of powerful transnational elites — including the media — whose privileged members meet in places like Davos, Switzerland, to confer about the future course of mankind. They travel first-class from airport to airport carrying laptops, palmtops, and cellular phones. They are plugged into the Web and communicate through e-mail. The populations they govern, however, are often isolated, technologically unequipped, and focused on strictly local problems. As this trend continues, the schism between global elites and local populations risks becoming a contentious chasm between global "haves" and local "have nots" — between the jet-setting Davos clique and the unwashed masses of McWorld.

Perhaps we should celebrate the death of the nation-state and thank new technologies like the Web for abetting its timely demise. Nation-states, after all, have been responsible for the tribalistic sentiments that, over the past century, have provoked two world wars, horrendous acts of genocide, torture, and other atrocities. Maybe media mogul Rupert Murdoch was right when he said that satellite TV represented an "unambiguous threat" to the world's dictators. Today the Web, for its part, is fostering the creation of virtual communities based not on artificial borders, national sentiments, and tribal attachments, but on rational choices based on common interests and associations. The fragmentation of television has also created outlets for linguistically based global television channels such as TV5, which links the world's French-speaking citizens in a common experience not necessarily dictated by geography.

Maybe the CRTC got it all wrong. Perhaps we are not witnessing the emergence of a "new consumer," but rather that of a "new citizen." In the Information Age, individuals may be shedding their old citizenship loyalties and reconstituting their identities based not on territory or tribe, but on rational associations. A Canadian, for example, might feel attached to the country called Canada, but that particular reference point could well be one of many identities — a sort of "nationalism without walls," to employ the term coined by journalist Richard Gwyn. The individual of the future will no longer be the consumption-driven homo economicus, but a socially oriented creature who, thanks to technology, is free to choose his associations.

These are fundamental issues worthy of informed discussion. In the meantime, however, the nation-state isn't likely to disappear. Nation-states remain the privileged units of international affairs — indeed, the word "international" contains the word "nation." Even supranational organizations like the European Union remain largely controlled by the national governments that created them. States may have transferred certain functions to non-territorial and supranational institutions, but national governments either finance or control these organizations. Without states, they would not even exist. And in times of global conflict, supranational institutions are invariably paralyzed, while states consistently show firmer resolve to act.

Media conglomerates may sometimes seek to bypass regulations and constraints imposed by national regulations, but when push comes to shove they submit to state authority. Rupert Murdoch doubtless believed sincerely that satellite TV would challenge the world's dictators, but it was the same Rupert Murdoch who withdrew BBC World News from his Star TV satellite service in order to placate the undemocratic regime in Beijing and, by so doing, gain access to the Chinese market. In democratic countries like the United States and Canada, the same people who denounce governments for excessively meddling in the lives of individuals nonetheless call on governments to police pornography on the Web. Others are opposed to taxation on the Internet, yet insist that privacy and intellectual property rights be protected on the Web. Whatever one's ideological persuasion, the fact is that the deregulatory impetus that facilitated the Web's development has led to a need for some form of re-regulation. Who will impose these rules? The convictions of libertarians notwithstanding, the only structures capable of imposing them are states.

So long as public goods are produced in society, states will be called upon to regulate access to them. In times of crisis, whether social or economic, it is doubtful that we will be able to count on McDonald's, Coca-Cola, Disney, or Microsoft to mobilize their resources to remedy society's ills. Populations still turn to states to perform certain basic functions, and to intervene in times of crisis. New communications technologies will not likely affect these basic realities — at least not in the foreseeable future.

It should not be presumed, however, that states will emerge from the Digital Revolution unaffected. They doubtless will play a more limited role as instruments of social and economic organization. The transfer of state functions to local authorities and supranational institutions is a sign of the recognition by national governments of their own limitations. States now face the challenge of shrinking down in order to assume the appropriate size corresponding to their new functional role. In the communications sphere, the fate of public broadcasters is a part of that process — and the commercial convulsions of public TV networks show how state-owned institutions are attempting to appropriate the values of the market to seek a new kind of justification for their existence. Broadcasting and telecom regulators, too, are undergoing a similar soul-searching exercise. Their challenge is to put institutional realism above bureaucratic self-preservation. This will not be easy.

In Canada, the time-honoured linkage between technology and nationalism can no longer be maintained, if only because it was a dubious marriage to begin with. Canada's technological nationalism has succeeded chiefly in serving powerful Canadian business interests — mainly the major clients of regulators and government ministries — for whom cultural nationalism has been a convenient discourse exploited to justify monopoly protections. In the future, cultural nationalism can no longer be a mere front for commercial opportunism. Canadian cultural policy must focus on cultural production — on software, not hardware; on content, not carriage.

In sum, the fate of Canada and other nations in the Information Age is not as precarious as many might believe. In many respects, states face the same challenges as many of the private corporations whose activities they regulate: they have lost their monopoly power and now face increasing competition. Nations will likely persist and states will almost certainly continue to govern them. But the pretensions of nations and the ambitions of states will be much more modest in the twenty-first century. The fabrication of a "new citizen" — unmoved by tribal passions, liberated from monopoly power, empowered by technology — will be a noble project in the Information Age.

Notes

Chapter 1

1 For an account of John Malone's meeting with Bob Magness and his early career, see L. J. Davis's book, *The Billionaire Shell Game: How Cable Baron John Malone and Assorted Corporate Titans Invented a Future Nobody Wanted* (New York: Doubleday, 1998).

2 Ken Auletta, "The Cowboy: John Malone's Cable Kingdom," *The New Yorker*, 7 February 1994.

3 Interview with John Malone, "John Malone explains it all," *Broadcasting & Cable*, 13 July 1998.

4 Davis, *Billionaire Shell Game*, p. 35.

5 George Gilder, *Life after Television* (New York: W.W. Norton, 1994), p. 191.

6 J. Roberts, "How giant TCI uses self-dealing, hardball to dominate market," *Wall Street Journal*, 27 January 1992, p. A1.

7 See Dan Steinbock, *Triumph and Erosion in the American Media and Entertainment Industries* (Westport: Quorum Books, 1995), p. 81.

8 See Edward A. Comor, *Communication, Commerce, and Power: The Political Economy of America and the Direct Broadcast Satellite, 1960–2000* (London: Macmillan, 1998), ch. 7.

9 Mark Robichaux, "Need more TV? TCI may offer 500 channels," *Wall Street Journal*, 3 December 1992, p. B1.

10 See Auletta, "The Cowboy," also published in Auletta's *The Highwaymen: Warriors of the Information Superhighway* (New York: Random House, 1997), pp. 50–51.

11 See Lawrence Surtees, *Wire Wars: The Canadian Fight for Competition in Telecommunications* (Scarborough: Prentice-Hall, 1994), p. 363.

12 Ronald Grover, "John Malone and the Cable Tangle," *Business Week*, 28 September 1998, p. 19.

Chapter 2

[1] Allan E. Gotlieb, interview by author, Toronto, 2 June 1998.

[2] Robert E. Babe, *Telecommunications in Canada* (Toronto: University of Toronto Press, 1990), p. 223.

[3] André Bureau, CEO of Astral Communications, interview by author, Toronto, 7 July 1998.

[4] Hershel Hardin, *Closed Circuits: The Sellout of Canadian Television* (Vancouver: Douglas & McIntyre, 1985), p. 322.

[5] Peter S. Grant, "CRTC jurisdiction over the activities of Skypix, Aladdin, and their agents or associates in Canada" (Toronto: McCarthy Tétrault, 4 October 1991). See also Andrew Roman, "Comments on Paper by C. Christopher Johnstone Re: CRTC Regulation of Foreign Direct-to-Home Programming Services" (paper presented at the conference New Developments in Canadian Communications Law and Policy: A National Symposium, Toronto, April 1992).

[6] Joel Bell, president of MaxLink Communications, interview by author, Toronto, 30 March 1998.

[7] Michael Neuman, CEO of ExpressVu, interview by author, Toronto, 19 March 1998.

Chapter 3

[1] See the collection of articles in "Technology and International Policy: Essays on the Information Age," *Journal of International Affairs* (spring 1998).

[2] Information Canada, *Instant World: A Report on Telecommunications in Canada* (Ottawa, 1971).

[3] Bernard Ostry, *The Electronic Connection: An Essential Key to Canadians' Survival*, report to the Department of Industry, Ottawa, 1993.

[4] CRTC Public Announcement, The Improvement and Development of Canadian Broadcasting and the Extension of U.S. Television Coverage in Canada by CATV, Ottawa, 3 December 1969.

[5] Phil Lind, interview by author, Toronto, 22 June 1998. Lind suffered a stroke several days after this interview, and left his top executive post at Rogers to undergo rehabilitation therapy.

[6] Robert Brehl, "Rating a megadeal," *Toronto Star*, 8 March 1997, p. E1.

[7] Government of Canada, *Building the Information Society: Moving Canada into the Twenty-first Century*, Ottawa, 23 May 1996. On 9 September 1997, the IHAC issued another report, *Preparing Canada for a Digital World*. The report attracted scant notice.

[8] Mark Robichaux, "Malone says TCI push into phones, Internet isn't working for now," *Wall Street Journal*, 2 January 1997, p. A1.

[9] Richard Siklos, "Rogers defends his strategy to New York investors," *Financial Post*, 14 February 1997, p. 4.

[10] See Anne Kingston, "Ted Rogers Unplugged," *Report on Business Magazine* (March 1997).

[11] Robert Brehl, "Ted Rogers' troubled neighbourhood," *Globe and Mail*, 10 January 1998, p. B1.

[12] Jean-Benoit Nadeau, "The Networker: Teleglobe Inc.'s Charles Sirois Has His Sights Set on a Wireless World That Knows No Bounds," *Financial Post Magazine*, September 1998.

[13] Frances Caincross, *The Death of Distance: How the Communications Revolution Will Change Our Lives* (Cambridge: Harvard Business School Press, 1997), p. 155.

[14] John M. Higgins, "Are cable stocks too high," *Broadcasting & Cable*, 16 March 1998. See also Kent Gibbons, "Media Mergers Set for 98 Surge: Report," *Multichannel News*, 13 July 1998, p. 54.

[15] Peter Elstrom, "Big Mergers, Bad Service: Phone Customers Don't Seem to Gain Much from Consolidation," *Business Week*, 10 August 1998, p. 26.

[16] "Cable Cowboy: John Malone Rides Again," *Fortune*, 16 February 1998; and "Cable's Comeback Kid," *Business Week*, 11 May 1998.

[17] "AT&T–TCI: Telecom Unbound," *Business Week*, 6 July 1998.

[18] "The Accidental Superhighway: A Survey of the Internet," *The Economist*, 1 July 1995.

Chapter 4

[1] See "Silicon Valley: How It Really Works — A Special Report," *Business Week*, 25 August 1997.

[2] Simon Avery, "Rushing to Silicon Valley," *Financial Post*, 11 July 1998, p. 11.

[3] The author made two professional trips to Silicon Valley, the first in March 1997 and the second in February 1998.

[4] George Gilder, *Life after Television* (New York: W.W. Norton & Co., 1990), updated 1994.

[5] See the *Forbes* cover story, "Masters of the New Universe," 27 July 1998. See also "No Slacking in Silicon Valley," *Business Week*, 31 August 1998.

[6] Jason Zengerle, "Silicon Smoothies," *The New Republic*, 8 June 1998.

[7] On Al Gore's links with Silicon Valley interests, see Sara Miles, "A Man, a Plan, a Challenge," *Wired*, 30 January 1998.

[8] Federal Communications Commission, Office of Plans and Policy, *Digital Tornado: The Internet and Telecommunications Policy*, by Kevin Werbach, Working Paper Series 29, Washington, March 1997.

[9] Interview with Ira C. Magaziner, senior adviser to the President of the United States for policy development, in *Journal of International Affairs* 51, no. 2 (spring 1998).

[10] Steve Ham, "The Education of Marc Andreessen," *Business Week*, 13 April 1998, p. 84. See also Joshua Quittner and Michelle Slatalla, *Speeding the Net: The Inside Story of Netscape and How It Challenged Microsoft* (New York: Atlantic Monthly Press, 1998).

[11] See Kara Swisher, *aol.com: How Steve Case Beat Bill Gates, Nailed the Netheads, and Made Millions in the War for the Web* (New York: Time Business, 1998). On Microsoft's business tactics, see Randall Stross, *The Microsoft Way: The Real Story of How the Company Outsmarts Its Competition* (New York: Perseus Press, 1996).

[12] On the relations between Silicon Valley and Hollywood, see Rex Weiner, "Purging the Urge to Converge: Has Hollywood been Sili-conned by the techies?" *Variety*, 2–8 December 1996, p. 1.

[13] Geoffrey Rowan, "Rogers proclaims cable-computer alliance," *Globe and Mail*, 12 June 1997, p. B1.

[14] See Kara Swisher and Leslie Cauley, "With $2.8 billion acquisition, Allen bets his cards on cable," *Wall Street Journal* (interactive edition), 7 April 1998.

[15] See Andrew Kupfer, "How Hot Is Cable, Really?" *Fortune*, 16 February 1998.

Chapter 5

[1] Doug Saunders, "Why Canadian TV will soon be more Canadian," *Globe and Mail*, 25 July 1998, p. A1.

[2] Hershel Hardin, *Closed Circuits: The Sellout of Canadian Television* (Vancouver: Douglas & McIntyre, 1985).

[3] See Peter Mansbridge, "Verbatim — The CBC news anchor defends the national public broadcaster and aims broadsides at Canada's private networks," *Globe and Mail*, 8 April 1996. See also Michael McCabe, "Memo to Mr. Mansbridge: Don't sell private broadcasters short," *Globe and Mail*, 12 April 1996.

[4] Ivan Fecan, CEO of CTV Network, interview by author, Toronto, 5 June 1998.

[5] Brenda Dalglish, "Znaimer extols 'liberation' of TV's dwindling crowds," *Financial Post*, 19 June 1998, p. 6.

[6] Figures are from Paul Kagan Associates. See James Sterngold, "How Cable Captured the Mini-Series — and the High Ground," *New York Times Magazine*, 20 September 1998, pp. 86–87.

[7] Steve McClellan, "Can the Big 4 still make big bucks?" *Broadcasting & Cable*, 8 June 1998.

[8] Michael Stroud, "Broadcast nets offer olive branch," *Broadcasting & Cable*, 30 March 1998, p. 12.

[9] Kyle Pope and Leslie Cauley, "Broadcast, cable duel threatens to delay the debut of digital TV," *Wall Street Journal*, 20 April 1998.

[10] The disallowance of network financial interest went into effect on 1 August 1972, and the ban on network syndication went into effect on 1 June 1973. See Harold L. Vogel, *Entertainment Industry Economics: A Guide for Financial Analysis*, 4th ed. (Cambridge: Cambridge University Press, 1998), ch. 4.

[11] Doug Saunders, "Spending report fuels CTV-Global rivalry," *Globe and Mail*, 6 August 1998, p. 9.

[12] Terence Corcoran, "Black out the broadcasters," *Globe and Mail*, 1 February 1997, p. B2.

[13] Allison Vale, "Global Alberta Revolt," *Playback*, 18 November 1996, p. 1.

[14] Doug Saunders, "Global fights for Manitoba airwaves," *Globe and Mail*, 9 January 1997, p. C1.

[15] John Haslett Cuff, "Baton Broadcasting: Get with the Cancon programming," *Globe and Mail*, 27 February 1997. For Fecan's response, see "Baton Broadcasting: Mr. Fecan replies," *Globe and Mail*, 1 March 1997.

[16] Peter Waal, "Your Move, Ivan," *Canadian Business*, 11 September 1998.

[17] John Allemang, "CTV's pitch: This land is their land," *Globe and Mail*, 14 October 1998, p. D2.

[18] Michael Tracey, *The Decline and Fall of Public Service Broadcasting* (Oxford: Oxford University Press, 1998), p. 33.

[19] Jérôme Bourdon, *Haute fidelité: Pouvoir et télévision 1935–1994* (Paris: Seuil, 1994), p. 59.

[20] Barbara Amiel, "Let me declare my conflict of interest," *Maclean's*, 19 October 1998, p. 13.

[21] Richard Collins, "Reinventing the CBC," *Policy Options* (October 1996).

Chapter 6

[1] Moses Znaimer, executive producer of CHUM-Citytv, interview by author, Toronto, 9 June 1998.

[2] Hershel Hardin, *Closed Circuits: The Sellout of Canadian Television* (Vancouver: Douglas & McIntyre, 1985), p. 293.

[3] David Ellis, *Split Screens: Home Entertainment and New Technologies* (Toronto: Friends of Canadian Broadcasting, 1992), p. 170.

[4] Terence Corcoran, "Banana republic broadcasting," *Globe and Mail*, 26 July 1997, p. B2.

[5] For the dissent of Colville, Oda, and Gordon, see Canadian Radio-Television and Telecommunications Commission, Structural Public Hearing, Public Notice CRTC 1993-74, Ottawa, 3 June 1993.

[6] Harvey Enchin, "Big sales push for new channels: Cable subscribers must pay or lose popular services," *Globe and Mail*, 7 December 1994, p. A1.

[7] For Andrée Wylie's dissent, see Canadian Radio-Television and Telecommunications Commission, Public Notice CRTC 1996-120, Ottawa, 4 September 1996.

[8] See Trevor Cole's magazine article on the Shaw cable empire, "The President's Show," in the *Globe and Mail's Report on Business Magazine* (November 1998).

[9] Juris Silkans, president of Atlantis Broadcasting, interview by author, Toronto, 10 August 1998.

Chapter 7

[1] Christopher Harris, "Lights! Camera! Action!" *Globe and Mail*, 30 October 1997, p. C1. See also Mark Evans, "Hollywood North comes of age," *Financial Post*, 12 September 1996, p. 14.

[2] The FCC's syndication and financial rules also included prime time access rules. See Harold L. Vogel, *Entertainment Industry Economics: A Guide for Financial Analysis*, 4th ed. (Cambridge: Cambridge University Press, 1998), ch. 4.

[3] Michael MacMillan, CEO of Alliance Atlantis, interview by author, 2 September 1998.

[4] Anthony Keller, "Have Can-con, will travel," *Globe and Mail*, 13 September 1997, p. C4.

[5] John Haslett Cuff, "Few English-Language Dramas Living Up to Our Potential: Cuff," *Playback*, 24 August 1998.

[6] Ivan Fecan, CEO of CTV Network, interview by author, Toronto, 5 June 1998.

[7] See Ted Magder, *Canada's Hollywood: The Canadian State and Feature Films* (Toronto: University of Toronto Press, 1993), ch. 2.

[8] James Cowan, "The battle for Canadian film control," *Maclean's*, 15 October 1930, p. 48.

[9] For an account of the tensions between Hollywood and the British government, see David Puttnam, *Movies and Money* (New York: Alfred A. Knopf, 1998).

[10] Ibid., p. 214.

[11] Martin Knelman, "Shooting Games," *Saturday Night* (March 1981).

[12] Janet Wasko, *Hollywood in the Information Age* (Austin: University of Texas Press, 1994), p. 229.

[13] Alice Rawsthorn, "Hollywood turns focus to Europe," *Financial Times*, 16 February 1998, p. 19. See also Martin Dale, *The Movie Game: The Film Business in Britain, Europe, and America* (London: Cassell, 1997), p. 242.

[14] Cliff Rothman, "Harris hobnobs with film moguls," *Globe and Mail*, 13 March 1998, p. E4.

[15] Chris Dafoe, "B.C. gives tax credits," *Globe and Mail*, 3 June 1998. See also Ann Gibbon, "Hollywood North does boffo biz," *Globe and Mail*, 29 January 1997.

[16] Robert Lantos, chair and CEO, Alliance Communications Corporation, speech to a joint meeting of the Canadian and Empire Clubs, 16 February 1998.

Chapter 8

[1] "The Information Appliance," *Business Week*, 24 June 1996. On the origins of the "smart home" see "Home, Sweet Electronic Home," *Reader's Digest* (August 1967). See also "Automated buildings industry poised for new surge of smarter, connected homes," *The Globe and Mail*, 11 July 1997, in "The Smart Home" (special supplement).

[2] "Gates Sees Overhaul of Industry Due to Rapid Growth of Internet," Dow Jones Newswires, 8 September 1998. See also "Whose Web Will It Be?" *Time*, 16 September 1996.

[3] Stentor Resource Centre, *The Impact of Technological Change on Canada's Cultural Industries*, Ottawa, October 1997.

[4] George Gilder, *Life after Television* (New York: W.W. Norton, 1994), p. 216.

[5] "Print faring better than TV in Net era, Time executive says," *Globe and Mail*, 17 October 1998, p. C19.

[6] Randall E. Stross, "How Yahoo! Won the Search Wars," *Fortune*, 2 March 1998. See also "The Info Tech 100: The World's Best-Performing Information Technology Companies," *Business Week*, 2 November 1998.

[7] Nick Wingfield, "Portal pandemonium takes hold as web sites clamor for eyeballs," *Wall Street Journal* (interactive edition), 12 May 1998.

[8] Esther Dyson, "Portal Power Plays," *Brill's Content* (November 1998).

[9] Federal Communications Commission, Office of Plans and Policy, *Digital Tornado: The Internet and Telecommunications Policy*, by Kevin Werbach, Working Paper Series 29, Washington, March 1997.

[10] See European Commission, *Green Paper on the Convergence of the Telecommunications, Media, and Information Technology Sectors, and the Implications for Regulation*, COM (97)623, Brussels, 3 December 1997. See also Organization for Economic Co-operation and Development, *Webcasting and Convergence: Policy Implications*, OECD/GD (97)221, Paris, 1997.

[11] Brenda Dalglish, "CRTC eyes Internet regulation," *Financial Post*, 4 September 1998.

[12] See Timothy Denton, "The Distribution of Signals in Cyberspace: An Examination of What the Internet Means for Signal Distribution and Broadcasting," report submitted to the Canadian Radio-Television and Telecommunications Commission, Ottawa, 14 August 1998.

[13] Peter Huber, *Law and Disorder in Cyberspace: Abolish the FCC and Let Common Law Rule the Telecosm* (New York: Oxford University Press, 1997), p. 205.

References

Acheson, Keith, and Christopher Maule. "Canada's Cultural Policies — You Can't Have It Both Ways." *Canadian Foreign Policy Journal* (winter 1997).

———. "Culture on the I-Way." *Policy Options* (October 1996).

Alleyne, Mark D. *International Power and International Communication.* New York: St. Martin's Press, 1995.

American Society, The. *Cultures in Collision: The Interaction of Canadian and U.S. Television Broadcast Policies.* New York: Praeger, 1984.

Aspen Institute. *Television for the Twenty-first Century: The Next Wave.* Washington: Aspen Institute, 1993.

Aspen Institute. Institute for Information Studies. *Crossroads on the Information Highway: Convergence and Diversity in Communications Technologies.* Washington: Aspen Institute, 1995.

Aspen Institute. Institute for Information Studies. *The Internet as Paradigm.* Annual Review. Washington: Aspen Institute, 1997.

Auletta, Ken. *The Highwaymen: Warriors of the Information Superhighway.* New York: Random House, 1997.

———. *Three Blind Mice: How the TV Networks Lost Their Way.* New York: Vintage Books, 1991.

Babe, Robert E. *Communication and the Transformation of Economics.* Boulder: Westview, 1995.

———. *Telecommunications in Canada.* Toronto: University of Toronto Press, 1990.

Baker, William, and George Dessart. *Down the Tube: An Inside Account of the Failure of American Television.* New York: BasicBooks, 1998.

Banks, Jack. *Monopoly Television: MTV's Quest to Control the Music.* New York: Westview Press, 1996.

Barber, Benjamin. *Jihad vs. McWorld*. New York: Ballantine Books, 1996.

Barnouw, Erik. *Conglomerates and the Media*. New York: The New Press, 1997.

Barrett, Neil. *The State of the Cybernation*. London: Kogan Page, 1996.

Besen, Stanley M., et al. *Misregulating Television: Network Dominance and the FCC*. Chicago: University of Chicago Press, 1984.

Bourdon, Jérôme. *Haute fidelité: Pouvoir et télévision, 1935–1994*. Paris: Seuil, 1994.

Branscomb, Lewis M., and James H. Keller. *Converging Infrastructures: Intelligent Transportation and the National Information Infrastructure*. Cambridge: MIT Press, 1996.

Brinkley, Joel. *Defining Vision: The Battle for the Future of Television*. New York: Harcourt Brace & Co., 1997.

Brownstein, Ronald. *The Power and the Glitter: The Hollywood–Washington Connection*. New York: Pantheon, 1990.

Burns, Tom. *The BBC: Public Institution and Private World*. London: Macmillan, 1977.

Caincross, Frances. *The Death of Distance: How the Communications Revolution Will Change Our Lives*. Cambridge: Harvard Business School Press, 1997.

Canada, Government of. *Connection, Community, Content: The Challenge of the Information Highway*. Final report of the Information Highway Advisory Council. Ottawa, September 1995.

Canadian Radio-Television and Telecommunications Commission (CRTC). *Competition and Culture on Canada's Information Highway: Managing the Realities of Transition*. Ottawa, May 1995.

Carlson, Randall. *The Information Superhighway: Strategic Alliances in Telecommunications and Multimedia*. New York: St. Martin's Press, 1996.

Carlton, Jim. *Apple: The Inside Story of Intrigue, Egomania, and Business Blunders*. New York: Time Books, 1997.

Castells, Manuel. *The Rise of the Network Society*. Oxford: Blackwell, 1996.

Chernow, Ron. *Titan: The Life of John D. Rockefeller Sr.* New York: Random House, 1998.

Collins, Richard. *Culture, Communications, and National Identity: The Case of Canadian Television*. Toronto: University of Toronto Press, 1990.

———. *Television: Policy and Culture*. London: Unwin Hyman, 1990.

Collins, Richard, and Christina Murroni. *New Media, New Policies*, Cambridge: Polity Press, 1996.

Comor, Edward A. *Communication, Commerce, and Power: The Political Economy of America and the Direct Broadcast Satellite, 1960–2000*. London: Macmillan, 1998.

———. *The Global Economy of Communications*. London: St. Martin's Press, 1996.

Crandall, Robert, and Harold Furchtgott-Roth. *Cable TV: Regulation or Competition?* Washington: Brookings Institution, 1996.

Crandall, Robert, and Leonard Waverman. *Talk Is Cheap: The Promise of Regulatory Reform in North American Telecommunications*. Washington: Brookings Institution, 1995.

Cringely, Robert X. *Accidental Empires: How the Boys of Silicon Valley Make Their Millions, Battle Foreign Competition, and Still Can't Get a Date*. New York: Harper Business, 1996.

Dale, Martin. *The Movie Game: The Film Business in Britain, Europe, and America*. London: Cassell, 1997.

Davis, L. J. *The Billionaire Shell Game*. New York: Doubleday, 1998.

Denton, Timothy. "The Distribution of Signals in Cyberspace: An Examination of What the Internet Means for Signal Distribution and Broadcasting." Report to the Canadian Radio-Television and Telecommunications Commission. Ottawa, 14 August 1998.

Dorland, Michael, ed. *The Cultural Industries in Canada: Problems, Policies, and Prospects*. Toronto: James Lorimer & Company, 1996.

Dyson, Kenneth, and Walter Homolka. *Culture First! Promoting Standards in the New Media Age*. London: Cassell, 1996.

Egan, Bruce. *Information Superhighway Revisited: The Economics of Multimedia*. Boston: Artech House, 1996.

Elkins, David. *Beyond Sovereignty: Territory and Political Economy in the Twenty-first Century*. Toronto: University of Toronto Press, 1995.

Ellis, David. *Split Screens: Home Entertainment and New Technologies*. Toronto: Friends of Canadian Broadcasting, 1992.

European Commission. *Green Paper on the Convergence of the Telecommunications, Media, and Information Technology Sectors, and the Implications for Regulation*. COM (97)623. Brussels, 3 December 1997.

Federal Communications Commission. Office of Plans and Policy. *Digital Tornado: The Internet and Telecommunications Policy*, by Kevin Werbach. Working Paper Series 29. Washington, March 1997.

Fraser, Matthew. "Digital Delivery of Cultural Products on the Electronic Highway." *Policy Options*, June 1998.

———. *Télévision sans frontières: Décryptage d'un "grand projet" européen*. Paris: Institut d'Etudes Politiques de Paris, 1996.

———. "Television without Frontiers: Decoding the European Union's Broadcasting Policy." In *The European Union and National Industrial Policy*, H. Kassim and A. Menon. London: Routledge, 1996.

Gilder, George. *Life after Television*. New York: W.W. Norton, 1994.

Golding, Peter, and Phil Harris. *Beyond Cultural Imperialism: Globalization, Communication, and the New World Order*. London: Sage Publications, 1997.

Gotlieb, Allan. *I'll Be with You in a Minute, Mr. Ambassador*. Toronto: University of Toronto Press, 1991.

Gotlieb, Allan, Charles Dalfen, and Kenneth Katz. "The Transborder Transfer of Information by Communications and Computer Systems: Issues and Approaches to Guiding Principles." *American Journal of International Law* 68, no. 2, April 1974.

Grant, George. *Lament for a Nation*. Toronto: McClelland & Stewart, 1965.

Grant, Peter S., et al. *1998–99 Canadian Broadcasting Regulatory Handbook*. Toronto: McCarthy Tétrault, 1998.

Grove, Andrew. *Only the Paranoid Survive*. New York: Doubleday, 1996.

Gwyn, Richard. *Nationalism without Walls: The Unbearable Lightness of Being Canadian*. Toronto: McClelland & Stewart, 1995.

Hafner, Katie, and Matthew Lyon. *Where Wizards Stay Up Late: The Origins of the Internet*. New York: Simon & Schuster, 1996.

Halberstam, David. *The Reckoning*. New York: Morrow, 1987.

Hardin, Hershel. *Closed Circuits. The Sellout of Canadian Television*. Vancouver: Douglas & McIntyre, 1985.

Herman, Edward, and Robert McChesney. *The Global Media: The New Missionaries of Global Capitalism*. London: Cassell, 1997.

Hoffert, Paul. *The Bagel Effect: A Compass to Navigate Our Wired World*. Toronto: McGraw-Hill Ryerson, 1998.

Houle, Michel. *Statistical Analysis on the Relevancy of the Canadian Cultural Policy regarding Distribution*. Ottawa, October 1996.

Huber, Peter. *Law and Disorder in Cyberspace: Abolish the FCC and Let Common Law Rule the Telecosm*. New York: Oxford University Press, 1997.

Huntington, Samuel. *The Clash of Civilizations and the Remaking of the New World Order*. New York: Simon & Schuster, 1996.

Jackson, Tim. *Inside Intel: Andy Grove and the Rise of the World's Most Powerful Chip Company*. New York: E.P. Dutton, 1997.

Johnson, Leland. *Toward Competition in Cable Television*. Cambridge: MIT Press, 1994.

Kahin, Brian, and Charles Nesson. *Borders in Cyberspace: Information Policy and the Global Information Infrastructure*. Cambridge: MIT Press, 1997.

Kahin, Brian, and Ernest Wilson. *National Infrastructure Initiatives: Vision and Policy Design*. Cambridge: MIT Press, 1997.

Keohane, Robert, and Joseph Nye. "States and the Information Revolution." *Foreign Affairs*, September–October 1998.

Klingler, Richard. *The New Information Industry: Regulatory Changes and the First Amendment*. Washington: Brookings Institution, 1996.

Krasner, Stephen. "Global Communications and National Power." *World Politics*, October 1990.

Kroker, Arthur. *Technology and the Canadian Mind*. Montreal: New World Perspectives, 1984.

MacDonald, J. Fred. *One Nation under Television: The Rise and Decline of Network TV*. Chicago: Nelson-Hall Publishers, 1994.

Magder, Ted. *Canada's Hollywood: The Canadian State and Feature Films*. Toronto: University of Toronto Press, 1993.

Maney, Kevin. *Megamedia Shakeout*. New York: John Wiley & Sons, 1995.

National Association of Broadcasters. *Convergence: Transition to the Electronic Superhighway*. Washington: NAB, 1994.

National Association of Broadcasters. *Digital Television in a Digital Economy: Opportunities for Broadcasters*. Report by A. T. Kearney for the NAB. Washington: NAB, 1998.

National Association of Broadcasters. *Internet Age Broadcaster*. Washington: NAB, 1998.

Nau, Henry R. *The Myth of America's Decline: Leading the World Economy into the 1990s*. New York: Oxford University Press, 1990.

Negroponte, Nicholas. *Being Digital*. New York: Vintage, 1996.

Neuman, Russell, et al. *The Gordian Knot: Political Gridlock on the Information Highway*. Cambridge: MIT Press, 1997.

Noll, Michael. *Highway of Dreams: A Critical View along the Information Superhighway*. Mahway, NJ: Lawrence Erlbaum, 1997.

Ohmae, Kenichi. *The End of the Nation State*. New York: Free Press, 1996.

Organization for Economic Co-operation and Development. *Webcasting and Convergence: Policy Implications*. OECD/GD (97)221. Paris, 1997.

Ostry, Bernard. *The Electronic Connection: An Essential Key to Canadians' Survival*. Report to the Department of Industry. Ottawa, 1993.

Price, Munroe. *Television, the Public Sphere, and National Identity*. Oxford: Clarendon Press, 1995.

Puttnam, David. *Movies and Money*. New York: Alfred A. Knopf, 1998.

Quittner, Joshua, and Michelle Slatalla. *Speeding the Net: The Inside Story of Netscape and How It Challenged Microsoft*. New York: Atlantic Monthly Press, 1998.

Raboy, Marc. *Missed Opportunities: The Story of Canada's Broadcasting Policy*. Montreal: McGill-Queen's University Press, 1990.

Reel, Frank. *The Networks: How They Stole the Show*. New York: Charles Scribner's Sons, 1979.

Reich, Robert. *The Work of Nations: A Blueprint for the Future*. New York: Simon & Schuster, 1991.

Ritchie, Gordon. *Wrestling with the Elephant: The Inside Story of the Canada-U.S. Trade Wars*. Toronto: Macfarlane Walter & Ross, 1997.

Ritchie, Gordon, Robert Rabinovitch, and Roger Tassé. *Direct-to-Home Satellite Broadcasting: Report of the Policy Review Panel*. Report to the Ministers of Industry and Canadian Heritage. Ottawa, April 1995.

Rothkopf, David. "In Praise of Cultural Imperialism?" *Foreign Policy*, summer 1997.

Schiller, Herbert. *Information Inequality*. London: Routledge, 1996.

———. *Mass Communication and American Empire*. Boulder: Westview Press, 1969.

Schlosstein, Steven. *The End of the American Century*. New York: Congdon and Weed, 1990.

Schwanen, Daniel. *A Matter of Choice*. Toronto: C.D. Howe Institute, 1997.

Shawcross, William. *Murdoch: The Making of a Media Empire*. New York: Simon & Schuster, 1997.

Sirois, Charles, and Claude Forget. *The Medium and the Muse: Culture, Telecommunications, and the Information Highway*. Montreal: Institute for Research on Public Policy, 1994.

Stanbury, W. T. *Canadian Content Regulation: The Intrusive State at Work*. Vancouver: Fraser Institute, August 1998.

———, ed. *Perspectives on the New Economics and Regulation of Telecommunications*. Montreal: Institute for Research on Public Policy, 1996.

Steinbock, Dan. *Triumph and Erosion in the American Media and Entertainment Industries*. Westport: Quorum Books, 1995.

Stentor Resource Centre. *The Impact of Technological Change on Canada's Cultural Industries*. Ottawa, October 1997.

Stoll, Clifford. *Silicon Snake Oil: Second Thoughts on the Information Highway*. New York: Anchor Books, 1995.

Stross, Randall. *The Microsoft Way: The Real Story of How the Company Outsmarts Its Competition*. New York: Perseus Press, 1996.

Surtees, Lawrence. *Wire Wars: The Canadian Fight for Competition in Telecommunications*. Scarborough: Prentice-Hall, 1994.

"A Survey of Electronic Commerce." *The Economist*, 10 May 1997.

"A Survey of Silicon Valley." *The Economist*, 29 March 1997.

"A Survey of Technology and Entertainment." *The Economist*, 21 November 1998.

"A Survey of the Internet." *The Economist*, 1 July 1995.

Swisher, Kara. *aol.com: How Steve Case Beat Bill Gates, Nailed the Netheads, and Made Millions in the War for the Web*. New York: Time Business, 1998.

"Technology and International Policy. Essays on the Information Age." *Journal of International Affairs* 51, spring 1998.

Tracey, Michael. *The Decline and Fall of Public Service Broadcasting*. Oxford: Oxford University Press, 1998.

Turow, Joseph. *Breaking Up America: Advertisers and the New Media World.* Chicago: University of Chicago Press, 1997.

Vlahos, Michael. "Culture and Foreign Policy." *Foreign Policy*, spring 1991.

Vogel, Harold L. *Entertainment Industry Economics: A Guide for Financial Analysis.* 4th ed. Cambridge: Cambridge University Press, 1998.

Wall Communications. *The Canadian Independent Film and Video Industry: Economic Features and Foreign Investment Related to the Distribution Sector.* Ottawa: Wall Communications, November 1996.

Wallace, James. *Overdrive: Bill Gates and the Race to Control Cyberspace.* New York: John Wiley & Sons, 1997.

Wasko, Janet. *Hollywood in the Information Age.* Austin: University of Texas Press, 1994.

Waterman, David, and Andrew Weiss. *Vertical Integration in Cable Television.* Cambridge: MIT Press, 1997.

Waters, Malcolm. *Globalization.* London: Routledge, 1995.

Watson, William. *Globalization and the Meaning of Canadian Life.* Toronto: University of Toronto Press, 1998.

Wolton, Dominique. *Penser la communication.* Paris: Flammarion, 1997.

Index